DEVELOPMENT COOPERATION IN

TIMES OF CRISIS

INITIATIVE FOR POLICY DIALOGUE AT COLUMBIA UNIVERSITY

THE INITIATIVE FOR POLICY
DIALOGUE AT COLUMBIA

JOSÉ ANTONIO OCAMPO AND JOSEPH E. STIGLITZ,
SERIES EDITORS

Escaping the Resource Curse, Macartan Humphreys,
Jeffrey D. Sachs, and Joseph E. Stiglitz, eds.

The Right to Know, Ann Florini, ed.

Privatization: Successes and Failures, Gérard Roland, ed.

Growth and Policy in Developing Countries: A Structuralist Approach,
José Antonio Ocampo, Codrina Rada, and Lance Taylor, eds.

Taxation in Developing Countries, Roger Gordon, ed.

Reforming the International Financial System for Development,
Jomo Kwame Sundaram, ed.

DEVELOPMENT COOPERATION

in

TIMES OF CRISIS

EDITED BY

José Antonio Alonso
and José Antonio Ocampo

COLUMBIA UNIVERSITY PRESS

NEW YORK

Columbia University Press
Publishers Since 1893
New York   Chichester, West Sussex
cup.columbia.edu

Library of Congress Cataloging-in-Publication Data

Development cooperation in times of crisis / edited by
José Antonio Alonso and José Antonio Ocampo.
p. cm. — (The Initiative for Policy Dialogue at Columbia)
Includes bibliographical references and index.
ISBN 978-0-231-15966-1 (cloth : alk. paper) —
ISBN 978-0-231-50439-3 (ebook)
1. Economic assistance—International cooperation.   2. Economic
development—International cooperation.   3. Sustainable
development—International cooperation.   4. Economic
assistance—Developing countries.   5. Economic development—
Developing countries.   I. Alonso, José Antonio.
II. Ocampo, José Antonio.
HC60.D4744 2012
338.9109172′4—dc23   2012000781

Columbia University Press books are printed
on permanent and durable acid-free paper.
This book is printed on paper with
recycled content.

Printed in the United States of America
c 10 9 8 7 6 5 4 3 2 1

THE INITIATIVE FOR POLICY DIALOGUE AT COLUMBIA

JOSÉ ANTONIO OCAMPO AND JOSEPH E. STIGLITZ, SERIES EDITORS

The Initiative for Policy Dialogue (IPD) at Columbia University brings together academics, policy makers, and practitioners from developed and developing countries to address the most pressing issues in economic policy today. IPD is an important part of Columbia's broad program on development and globalization. The Initiative for Policy Dialogue at Columbia: Challenges in Development and Globalization presents the latest academic thinking on a wide range of development topics and lays out alternative policy options and trade-offs. Written in a language accessible to policy makers and students alike, this series is unique in that it both shapes the academic research agenda and furthers the economic policy debate, facilitating a more democratic discussion of development policies.

Development Cooperation in Times of Crisis is an important addition to this series. Given its scope and magnitude, the current economic and financial crisis is having a serious impact on the international economy and on the living conditions of many people throughout the world. It has reached, albeit unevenly, developing countries, with the ensuing threat of promoting a backward step in the social achievements of recent years and delaying, even more, the attainment of the United Nations Millennium Development Goals (MDGs). It has also affected, and rather centrally, developed countries, limiting fiscal room to support generous international aid policies and fueling the temptation to resort to protectionist responses. Moreover, this crisis has occurred in the midst of a thorough review of the role, structure, and ways of managing the international development cooperation system. For all these reasons, it is necessary to conduct a profound reflection, considering the implications of all these processes on the development agenda. So far, there is no published document that deeply, strictly, and with a sense of opportunity covers this panorama.

Development Cooperation in Times of Crisis aims to fill this gap in the international editorial scene. More specifically, this book analyzes: (1) the effects of the crisis on the global economy and especially on developing countries; (2) the role that development cooperation had in managing the effects of the crisis on developing countries; (3) how to expand the mechanisms for financing development in the context of a new financial architecture; (4) the reform of the cooperation system and of its forms of governance, to include the new actors that have arisen on the international scene; (5) how to make international aid more effective; and (6) the best ways to advance toward the achievement of the MDGs in 2015 in a context of severe economic crisis.

This volume will appeal to a multidisciplinary audience of social science scholars, as well as a broader, educated—but non-specialized—community of civil society and general readers concerned with issues of development cooperation and financing, financial crises and reform of the financial architecture, and achievement of the MDGs through development.

For more information about IPD and its upcoming books, visit www .policydialogue.org.

CONTENTS

DEVELOPMENT COOPERATION IN

TIMES OF CRISIS

CHAPTER 1

Introduction

José Antonio Alonso and José Antonio Ocampo

Although the first signs of the current crisis appeared in mid-2007, it was not until September 2008 that the international community became fully aware of the scale and severity of the threat to the global economy. The dramatic bankruptcy of Lehman Brothers that month left the U.S. financial system on the brink of collapse, endangering international economic stability. The rapid reaction of authorities on both sides of the Atlantic saved the financial system from bankruptcy, but it could not prevent economies around the world from slumping simultaneously into a sharp recession that is still affecting growth and overall well-being. Although the crisis originated in the most developed and sophisticated market in the world— the U.S. financial market—the risks to the whole international system were very quickly perceived, including its effects on developing countries. The means through which the crisis spread were not the same in every case, but the recession has been felt to varying degrees across the entire planet and amounts to the first global crisis of the twenty-first century. The abrupt fall in production and trade, the increase in unemployment, the weakening of national financial systems, and record levels of fiscal imbalances, particularly in developed countries, are some of the most visible effects of the crisis.

To tackle this crisis, governments resorted to truly exceptional measures, first to sustain the financial system, then to stimulate demand to head off a new recession, and finally to rebalance budgets to fight the sovereign debt crises. Countries' individual solutions were supplemented by the use of international coordination in policy responses to the crisis, as well as in proposals to reform the financial system. The chosen framework for this was the G-20, which seems to have become, not without reservations, the preferred leading body for global economic governance. However, successive summits over the past three years (in Washington, D.C., London,

Pittsburgh, Toronto, and Seoul) show that reform initiatives have attained uneven progress. As the most pressing emergencies of the crisis have been overcome, reforms seem to have been diluted, both in the degree of consensus that leaders have displayed at summits and in the importance of the agreements reached.

The truth is that more than three years after the start of the crisis, and despite spending an extraordinary volume of public resources, normality does not seem to have returned. Some have expressed fear that the situation could even be worsening. In 2010, economic activity partially recovered in the industrialized world, many developed countries surpassed their pre-crisis levels, and international trade began to grow again, although without fully recovering lost ground. Nevertheless, symptoms of weakness in the financial systems of many countries remain. Additionally, some of the distortions that were at the root of the present crisis are still in place, such as the global imbalances referred to previously, as well as the absence of an international monetary system that encourages global stability and growth.

In any case, the problems caused by the crisis differ depending on the group of countries under consideration. In developed countries, the challenges have to do with achieving sustainable economic recovery (which is still fragile), with consolidating weakened financial systems (which were very badly hit by the crisis), and with heading off problems associated with high levels of public debt acquired during the last few years. It is not, however, an easy task to find the right balance between supporting economic recovery and correcting existing levels of unemployment, on the one hand, and the demands of fiscal consolidation and the correction of public debt levels, on the other. In terms of the countries most in need of international financing, such as some of the European periphery, that balance seems to have tipped in favor of the latter, leading to severe adjustment programs that are redefining the boundaries of the welfare state as such and fueling growing social discontent.

A second group of countries, which includes many so-called emerging markets, have been the least affected by the crisis, and these countries have returned to growth most quickly and vigorously. Their spectacular rates of GDP growth in 2010 set them apart from the more sluggish performance of the main industrialized economies and have transformed them into the principal focus of dynamism in the international economy. Some of them have benefited from the boom in commodity prices, maintaining comfortable trade surpluses in several cases. For this group of countries, the problem now revolves around making growth compatible with stability, while avoiding the pro-cyclical effect of capital inflows and the induced appreciation of their currencies.

Lastly, there is a third group of developing countries that has suffered the consequences not only from the economic crisis but also from the rise in oil prices and raw materials, including food. This group includes some of the sub-Saharan African countries with the highest levels of poverty, the weakest social protection networks, and the highest dependency on international aid. In these cases, the crisis may be at the root of significant setbacks on the path toward the Millennium Development Goals. These problems have been exacerbated as a result of the expected freezing of international aid, due to the budgetary restrictions of the main donor countries.

Aside from its immediate effects, there is a consensus that the current economic turmoil represents a turning point for the international economy. An increasing number of people feel that the world that will emerge from the crisis will likely be different in many respects from the one we have known. First, the crisis has shown the need for wide-ranging reforms to reduce levels of systemic risks in the international financial system and to equip the world economy with governance mechanisms that are appropriate for today's conditions. These conditions are very different from those that existed when many of our current international institutions were created. Second, the crisis has shaken orthodox economic assumptions about the functioning of markets: in particular, confidence in the efficiency of financial markets has been seriously questioned. Third, the crisis has caused governments to intervene in the economy beyond the limits demanded by the orthodox canon. These factors substantiate the need for the revision of some of the economic assumptions that formed part of what John Kenneth Galbraith called "the conventional wisdom."

The crisis has also proved beyond a doubt the growing importance in the world economy of Asia, as well as new centers of international economic power that have resulted from the consolidated success of emerging economies, many of which have a clear international vocation (China, India, Brazil, etc.). This points to a move toward a multipolar economic system—one with a financial system that is subject to more stringent regulation and obliged to correct so-called global imbalances—in which the U.S. and E.U. economies' degree of dominance will continue to erode.

Furthermore, the crisis has forced a revision of the structure and mechanisms of the development aid system itself. First, historical experience reveals that, beyond rhetorical declarations, the elasticity of growth of international aid is low, even during economic booms. This brings us to the realization that the development aid system needs (1) to explore new sources of development funding and (2) that beyond aid, greater attention must be paid to sharing development opportunities associated with international regulatory frameworks in the fields of trade, investment, and finance.

Second, in a context of budgetary limits, such as the one created by the crisis, more attention needs to be paid to levels of aid effectiveness in order to maximize the impact of resources on recipient countries. The Paris Agenda and the Accra Agenda for Action define some relevant criteria in this area, but their degree of implementation has so far been limited. Beyond this agenda, other problems—such as aid dependence—should also be considered.

Third, in an increasingly global world, alongside traditional aid tasks related to the fight against poverty, other equally relevant tasks related to the adequate provision of international public goods—some of which are key to promoting development in the poorest countries—will need to be added. This obliges us not only to reconsider the agenda but also the resources and institutions involved. Of all such public goods, those related to preventing climate change are the most demanding.

Finally, the changes to the international system make it less and less appropriate to base the aid system on a neat division between recipients and donors, the latter represented by a select group of Organization for Economic Cooperation and Development (OECD) countries. An increasing number of developing countries, particularly middle-income countries, have joined in active aid policies by giving their resources and experience to other developing countries through South-South cooperation. The international aid system should respond to this more complex framework of relationships by translating it to governance mechanisms for development aid.

This book will analyze these factors, the effects of the crisis on developing countries, the responses of the international economic system, and changes to the aid system. The book collects the studies developed for an International Conference, held in Madrid on June 9 and 10, 2010, during the term of Spanish presidency of the European Union (E.U.). Supported by the Spanish Ministry of Foreign Affairs and Cooperation, this event benefited from a broad lineup of specialists—researchers in the field of development and international aid, administrators of aid, and representatives of E.U. member governments and social groups—who came together to debate the international economic situation and the future of the international aid system. After some revision, the central presentations of this seminar have become the chapters of this book. Hereafter, we accompany our introductions of each of these chapters with thoughts on the implications that arise from analysis of their content.

THE CRISIS AND ITS EFFECTS

This book begins with a chapter by Ocampo, Griffith-Jones, Noman, Ortiz, Vallejo, and Tyson in which the authors analyze the crisis and its effects on the developing world. This crisis was a result of diverse factors that combined in an explosive mix. Causes of the present crisis include: global payments imbalances; excessive prolongation of a loose monetary policy by the U.S. Federal Reserve; authorities' excessive trust in the self-regulation of markets; limited use of public instruments to regulate and supervise the financial system; absence of adequate incentives for the managers of financial institutions; intensive search for growing leverage in the financial system to sustaining profitability; desire to stimulate the ability of certain poor sections of society to buy through credit; and the behavior of certain financial administrators, sometimes bordering on the criminal.

Aside from its roots, two traits stand out among those that define the present crisis compared with those that marked the crises of the previous two decades. The first is the global impact of the crisis, which has affected—although to varying degrees—the whole international system, with scarcely any economies remaining free from contagion. This has called into question hypotheses concerning the decoupling of certain emerging markets that emphasized the independence of their cyclical performance. The truth is that all economies, including those, such as China's, that recovered most quickly, were initially affected by the crisis. We are therefore dealing with a crisis that is clearly global, both in terms of size and impact—perhaps the first global crisis in history, considering that entire continents (Asia and Africa) remained unaffected by the 1929 crisis.

The second characteristic of the crisis was its epicenter, which for the first time was far from those economies—the emerging markets—that had featured so prominently in the previous episodes of financial instability.

On this occasion, the crisis originated in a segment of the financial sector in the United States, the most developed and sophisticated market in the world. For the first time, an episode of instability had nothing to do with the behavior of developing countries. In fact, it is due to the recovery capacity of a group of developing countries that the dynamism of the international economy did not fall further.

While its impact was global, the means through which the crisis spread differed, depending on context. In some countries, the financial arena was the most significant channel through which the effects of the crisis spread, with the initial drying up of credit giving way to a subsequent contraction in economic activity. In other countries, however—and this is the case for much of the developing world—the most significant channel through which the crisis spread were found in the real economy, through the effect that the severe fall in trade of goods and services, including tourism, had on their productive activity in 2009. Added to this factor, and depending on the country, there was a contraction in other sources of international financing, especially remittances from emigrants, who suffered the effects of increasing unemployment in industrialized countries, as well as other private financial flows.

Seen as a whole, three factors seem to have been decisive in exacerbating the effects of the crisis in individual countries: first, the degree of contagion of toxic assets acquired by national financial systems and the capacity of those systems to clean up the balance sheets of the affected institutions; second, the degree to which the economic dynamic prior to the crisis had been based on the real estate bubble as the main driver of growth; and third, the degree to which each country depended on international financing to correct previous imbalances. In countries such as Iceland—where all three factors combined—the situation was a perfect storm.

The relative absence of these three factors also explains why the crisis did not affect many developing countries in a severe way. Of course they all suffered from the fall in trade and the contraction of international financial flows, but these countries' financial systems had not been involved in the expansion of toxic assets; their economies had not been driven by the real estate bubble; and they were not generally dependent on international financing, as had previously been the case. The efforts made during prior years to stabilize these economies, to restore basic balance, and to regulate their financial systems, combined with a balance-of-payment surplus from exports due to high commodity prices, allowed some of these countries to pay down their external current liabilities and reduce their international financing needs. All of these factors were key to providing these economies with greater room to maneuver.

In fact, many of the world's developing regions had positive growth rates in 2010—including, in some cases, rates that were frankly high. The rapid recovery of the Asian economies was particularly remarkable. This was so significant in some cases that the problem became focused on tackling the difficulties associated with the management of stability in a context of emerging inflationary pressures and currency appreciation trends, which could affect the sustainability of growth.

The recovery was also accompanied by rising oil and raw material prices, including food prices. This factor is affecting some poorly developed countries, mainly in Africa, that are net importers of food. The combination of the effects of the recession and the effects of the food crisis threatens to cause worrisome social setbacks in these countries, affecting their progress toward the Millennium Development Goals. This trend is all the more worrisome if we bear in mind the limited social protection networks in place and the high proportion of these populations living below the poverty line. This underlines the need for donors to maintain their commitments to international aid.

THE NEEDED SOLUTIONS

The third chapter, by Griffith-Jones and Ocampo, is devoted to the authors' evaluation of the response of the international community to the crisis, which has called into question some of the ideas upon which economic management has been based through previous decades. Specifically, the crisis confirmed that excessive trust that was afforded by economic authorities in major industrial countries in the efficiency of financial markets in terms of their ability to self-regulate and adequately measure risk. This excessive trust fueled the loose regulatory stance evident in some of the most affected markets. In contrast with that stance, the crisis has showed that stability must be maintained through adequate regulation and cautious supervision of such markets, where powerful externalities operate amid imperfect and asymmetric information.

Beyond calling into question economic beliefs, the crisis is proving to be an enormous challenge for national governments, as well as for coordinated international action among them. This challenge derives first from the intensity of the crisis, which required exceptional measures both in the rescue and support of financial systems and in the need to stimulate demand. But the shifting nature of the crisis has posed challenges of its own, requiring changes in response as the crisis evolved. Born as a financial crisis, its problematic effects quickly reached the real economy, turning the situation toward a deep recession, with severe repercussions on economic activity, trade, and employment. Following the episodic appearance of some signs of possible recovery (the "green shoots"), the crisis next entered a new phase, resulting from the tensions that high public deficits provoked in financial markets and leading to the risk of a sovereign debt crisis that is currently affecting mainly European countries.

In any case, the crisis suggested the need to base regulation of the international financial system on new assumptions. In order to avoid new problems in the future, this regulatory response must be based on two central elements. First, regulation should be sufficiently comprehensive to avoid the persistence of grey or opaque areas beyond the oversight of authorities. This would reduce regulatory arbitrage and uncover risks that lead to irresponsible behavior. Second, the regulation should be countercyclical in nature, in order to allow regulatory frameworks to correct (or at least not to exacerbate) the pro-cyclical behavior of markets. This is especially important for developing countries that have less policy space to maintain a countercyclical domestic stance and that are therefore more vulnerable to international markets.

In addition to such regulation, it is necessary to revise the international financial structure to avoid the repetition of destructive episodes such as the current one. The crisis represents a window of opportunity for putting still-unresolved themes on the agenda, including (1) strengthening development financing, with an active role for multilateral financial institutions, and the use of new forms of international financing in the form of taxation (such as a tax on financial transactions); (2) establishment of fast and capable emergency financing, which can be used for countries with liquidity problems without imposing an excessive conditionality; (3) creation of an international monetary system that avoids the recessionary risks and instability generated by dollar dependency; (4) improvement in levels of international macroeconomic coordination through formal institutions that facilitate the early and concerted correction of imbalances; (5) adequate international debt resolution mechanisms that avoid opportunism and treat different sovereign debtors, as well as their creditors, equally; and (6) a deepening of reforms to the structures of governance of international financial institutions to guarantee that their systems properly represent the structure of the current international economy.

What has been proposed so far at the G-20 summits falls far short of what has been suggested here. In fact, although we should not underestimate agreements thus far reached, there is some disappointment over reform efforts achieved by the G-20.

Apart from this verdict, from the analysis of the crisis and the financial structure in this chapter and in Chapter 2, we draw the following general conclusions that may inform economic policy in the immediate future:

- The need for countries—and particularly those that lack reserve currency—to be given enough room to design and implement counter-cyclical policies. Those countries with options (both monetary and fiscal) to implement this type of policy have better resisted the negative effects of the crisis.
- The importance of attaining a better balance between the contribution of domestic and foreign demand to growth. After the crisis, we will probably see a world in which aggressive trade surplus strategies are more difficult to sustain.
- The crucial need to develop financial systems that are solid and properly regulated.
- The importance, revealed by the crisis, of public-sector development banks, both internationally (Multilateral Development Banks) as well as nationally.
- The need for the international system to design an adequate financial safety net to both prevent and manage financial crises. In the absence of such mechanisms, countries will use suboptimal mechanisms to self-insure themselves through the accumulation of international reserves—at a cost to the countries affected and to the stability of the international system.

THE CRISIS AND INTERNATIONAL AID

In the fourth chapter, by Mold and Prizzon, the authors analyze the effect the crisis may have on development funding and on flows of international aid. Studying prior episodes of crisis has not enabled us to anticipate what the permanent effect of the current crisis will be on official development assistance. The results of previous crises have been varied, indicating that the effect on aid is highly dependent on the severity of a given crisis and on the political will of governments and the priorities that they establish.

Examples of other periods of instability reveal that if a fall in resources occurs, it tends to happen some time after the start of the crisis (one year to two years later). This helps explain the relative stability of aid flows during the first phases of the current crisis and suggests that the effects of the recession on aid may yet be felt during later budgetary cycles. It is, therefore, essential to emphasize the need for countries to maintain their international aid commitments.

In periods of crisis, such as the current one, it is likely that budgetary restrictions will limit the resources made available for international aid, and the need becomes clearer for improvements in the quality and effectiveness of international aid. Here the dynamic opened by the Paris Agenda on aid effectiveness constitutes a good foundation for future work. Many of the principles agreed upon in that Agenda (and in the subsequent Accra Agenda for Action) were drawn from the conclusions of studies on aid effectiveness carried out in previous decades and from the assessments that donors and recipients have distilled regarding the best practices. That said, compared to those principles, the following two critical observations should be made:

• Follow-up studies reveal that progress by donors has been very slow and unsatisfactory. In some cases, interruptions in progress toward the proposed goals came as a result of not having foreseen the difficulties that these new forms of development aid management would involve or because of donors' perceptions of an exaggerated risk. As a consequence, much progress remains to be made in terms of higher predictability of aid, the reduction of conditionalities, the improvement of coordination between donors, and the better alignment of donors with partner countries and their administrative practices and public management.

• Some of the difficulties observed have resulted from an excessively bureaucratic (and rather naïve) interpretation of the relationships between donor and recipient countries. Particularly, it would be necessary a richer and more complex vision of the central principle of ownership and, therefore, the need for aid agenda focused on country-specific conditions and needs.

In relation to this last aspect, it is worth revising donor practices of conditionality. Aside from the rhetoric, analysis shows that there is still excessive conditionality attached to aid—sometimes formulated less explicitly than in the past, but producing equally bad results. In some cases, these new conditions appear to be associated with the use of programmed aid and the forms of financing—budgetary support—that accompany such aid.

In the fifth chapter, by Alonso, Garcimartín, and Martín, the authors analyze the insufficient progress that has been made in aid effectiveness. Apart from other critical considerations, it seems that the Paris Agenda does not take into account the true extent of the problem that aid dependency generates in recipient countries. The studies reveal that aid dependency is a serious problem that reduces the capacity for resources to have an impact, and also reduces the development possibilities of the affected countries. Moreover, this is a problem that could become worse in the future, as aid tends increasingly to be focused around a reduced number of low-income countries. The means by which the negative effect of aid dependency manifests itself are diverse, negatively affecting the conditions for competitiveness in the economy of the recipient country, along with its capacity to efficiently absorb the resources received and the quality and capacity for accountability of its institutions.

Chapter 5 offers an estimate on this last aspect that is revealing. Since it is known the effect of institutional quality on growth, the authors seek to determine whether aid affects the institutional quality of the recipient countries. Previous investigations pointed to an effect that was mostly negative, but here a positive relationship is detected, although subject to diminishing returns. While aid does improve the institutional quality of the recipient countries, beyond a determined threshold that effect becomes negative, a result that points to the problem of aid dependency previously highlighted.

The authors also explore whether aid reduces the incentives to consolidate a solid fiscal system in recipient countries. The previous literature on this aspect was rather ambiguous, but in this case, the result confirms that aid has a positive effect—however weak—on the fiscal effort of the countries that receive it, even if that effect is conditioned by the institutional quality of the recipients. In a context of low institutional quality, the effect of the aid can be zero or even negative.

Both results corroborate the damaging effect that high levels of dependence on development aid can have. However, correcting this problem does not necessarily mean reducing aid: doing so would only exacerbate the difficulties of some of the countries most affected by the crisis. Instead, more caution must be taken in certain cases with plans to expand aid, establishing processes to gradually change the amount of aid where the problem is worst, and to pay greater attention to more actively mobilizing the resources of the developing countries themselves, both by strengthening their fiscal systems and by combating phenomena such as tax evasion, capital flight, and illicit financial flows. At the same time, more work should be done on the financing of international public goods, including global regulatory frameworks that condition the distribution of development opportunities internationally. An adequate provision of such goods could conceivably produce better results than aid itself, without affecting previous levels of aid dependency.

In relation to the mobilization of local resources in developing countries, it seems necessary that donors and recipients pay greater attention to strengthening their fiscal systems as a basic component of a development strategy based on national foundations. Studies of fiscal systems reveal that although reforms have been made during the past two decades, much can still be done to improve the effectiveness, efficiency, and fairness of existing systems. To achieve this, progress must be made in various fields related to the design of taxation structures, the efficiency of tax administration, the prosecution of fraud, and the creation of a civic culture upon which tax collection can be based. These are all areas where donors can adopt more active policies to support and assist developing countries.

In international terms, donors can further play an important role in tax cooperation matters, contributing to the fight against fraud by preventing tax evasion and by controlling other illicit financial flows that drain resources from developing countries. Such cooperative action would not only help establish better governance of the international financial system, it would also give developing countries greater opportunities to finance their own development processes.

CHANGES IN THE INTERNATIONAL AID SYSTEM

In the past few years, the international development aid system has seen the arrival of new aid modalities and instruments that have led to the presence of new participants, including some from the private sector (firms, individuals, and foundations). This series of changes is addressed in the sixth chapter by Sagasti and Prada. The authors analyze the financial needs of developing countries, including the capacities of each to mobilize local resources and to access international financing. They offer criteria to adequately classify countries in terms of those two vectors, helping to appropriately adapt development aid solutions for each case.

In terms of international financing, it should be recognized that the range of types of financing has also increased in recent years, with the current focus on strategies employing public-private association, both national and international, along with numerous initiatives in the sphere of corporate social responsibility that have further bearing on the field of international development aid. In any case, this is a trend that needs to be promoted because it increases available resources, encourages innovative initiatives, as well as enlarges social support to development aid policy.

Apart from those elements, it is necessary to bear in mind the important changes taking place in the world economy that affect the configuration of the international aid system in a significant way. One of the most relevant of these changes is the increasing diversity of the developing world. It is increasingly difficult to remedy the situations of developing countries with a single diagnosis or therapy. When analyzed with perspective, a double divergence between countries can be observed (1) in the tendency toward a widening gap between the richest and poorest countries of the world and (2) divergence among developing countries themselves.

This fact poses an initial challenge to the field and agenda of development aid. Two very different responses are possible: either aid is increasingly transformed into an instrument specialized for the fight against extreme poverty, with activity increasingly focused on countries with the most extreme deficiencies, or, alternatively, the aid system becomes integrated to support the development efforts of all countries, regardless of their income level, until achievements become irreversible. Although there are arguments to justify the first option—reasons of prioritizing and limiting available resources—only the second option would allow the creation of a development system with defined incentives that are compatible with global development. It should not be forgotten that, currently, about 70 percent of the world's poorest populations live in middle-income countries. Thus, progress in tackling international poverty would seem inconceivable without a clear development policy for this group of countries. This implies a wider vision for development aid policy, which involves varied instruments and differentiated agendas according to the development needs of each group of countries, including lower-middle-income countries.

Another change associated with growing diversity in the developing world is the progressive emergence of a number of countries as globally important economic and political centers. Many of these countries have initiated an active international development policy; some specialize in aid to neighboring regions, while others take a more global vision. The result of these efforts is the increasingly vigorous South-South cooperation, which looks set to become ever more important within the international development aid system. Sagasti and Prada also analyze in their chapter this mode of development aid.

Promoting South-South cooperation has three benefits: (1) it increases the resources available to correct international inequalities; (2) it favors double-dividend practices in which both participants in the relationship— both developing countries—gain from the development aid; and (3) it allows for governance of the international system to be based on a principle of shared responsibility, meaning that all countries contribute—to the extent that they can—to a fairer and richer international order. For these reasons, South-South cooperation is a promising dynamic that should be supported by donors through help to regional cooperation initiatives among developing countries or through the implementation of triangular cooperation mechanisms.

Some changes to the development agenda and its participants pose a challenge for the governance of the development system. This issue is discussed in the seventh chapter by Barder, Gavas, Maxwell, and Johnson. The authors set out to define some general criteria for proper international governance. Applying those criteria to the current institutions of the aid system, they find notable weaknesses and shortcomings: none of the existing institutions fulfills all the identified criteria to a satisfactory degree. This points to the need to reform governance of the aid system.

Such reform should first consider the emergence of new donors that have not been incorporated into the definition of the international consensuses on development aid policy and are not members of those organizations— such as the OECD's Development Assistance Committee—where the said consensuses are formed. Again, there are two possible options for donors: they can either hold their previous commitments and institutions intact, inviting new donors to join those organizations, or they can rethink development policy to meet a broader framework, including the efforts, resources, and visions of those new donors. Although there are reasons to adopt the first option, only the second is capable of turning the development system into a global system—and not just the policy of a few donors—thereby favoring a sense of ownership of the system by all developing countries. One way to achieve this last objective would be to actively use the Development Cooperation Forum of the United Nations Economic and Social Council—

which was created in 2007 and which calls together old and new donors as well as aid-receiving countries—and to develop new mechanisms for nongovernmental agents to participate.

At the same time, it is necessary to revise the governance of the system in order to avoid costs deriving from a proliferation of participants in a context of poor international coordination. The truth is that this problem has increased in recent years, with the incorporation of new players (mainly private participants) into the aid system and the multiplication of institutional mechanisms (through so-called global partnership funds), but without many improvements in coordination. This has led to inefficiencies and transaction costs in the system that should be corrected.

FINAL CONSIDERATION

This overview is not an exhaustive restatement of the themes tackled in the various chapters. Rather, it presents elements of analysis that readers will find in each of them, as well as proposals for reform, to address the crisis and to strengthen development cooperation policy. At this moment of change in the economy and in international relations, such a space for reflection and analysis is welcome in order to develop proposals to assist in redesigning the world that will emerge from the current crisis.

The succession of phases of instability over these last two decades highlights the need to correct two imbalances on which the globalization process, now under way, has been founded. First is the imbalance between the existence of high levels of sophistication and interdependence of markets and the limited ability of the international system to generate coordination mechanisms capable of governing those interdependencies. Second is the imbalance between the distribution of the benefits of globalization and the assumption of responsibilities in relation to its costs. The first imbalance shows that globalization has been accompanied by a process of increased risk, both as a result of an increased probability of episodes of crisis and the widespread impacts that such crises can have, due to the heightened likelihood of contagion. The second imbalance means that parts of the world's population feel excluded from the benefits of globalization, and that the current institutions and coordinating organizations are seen as lacking legitimacy—a perception that affects the governance of the international system.

Overcoming these problems requires more international cooperation, on the one hand, and greater development opportunities for low-income countries, on the other. The concern that inspires this book is based on these two pillars: the need to strengthen the international development system, and to allow developing countries to make fuller and more efficient use of their possibilities for progress.

CHAPTER 2

The Great Recession and the Developing World

**José Antonio Ocampo, Stephany Griffith-Jones, Akbar Noman,
Ariane Ortiz, Juliana Vallejo, and Judith Tyson**

The developing world experienced a pattern of rapid and broad-based economic growth, at a rate of more than 7 percent per year during the period 2003–2007—much faster than the industrial world, which grew at a rate of 2.7 percent. Such phases of "catching up" (or convergence) with the industrial world have been rare through history, which has been characterized by a divergence in the growth of the developing versus the industrial world, a pattern that was typical in many parts of the developing world during the "lost decade" of the 1980s, as well as through the 1990s and the early years of the twentieth century. The worst situation was, of course, that of sub-Saharan Africa, which experienced not so much a lost decade as a lost quarter century. Latin America also lost a quarter century in terms of poverty reduction; according to the estimates of the United Nations (UN) Economic Commission for Latin America and the Caribbean (ECLAC, 2009), income poverty only returned to the levels of 1980 in 2004. Of course the experience of the 1980s and 1990s was very positive for several developing countries, particularly in Asia, and even more specifically for its two giants, China and India, thus configuring what Ocampo and Parra (2007) termed a "dual divergence"—both between the industrial and the developing worlds and among developing countries.

In light of past experience, there was a widespread expectation in the early part of the century that the UN Millennium Development Goals (MDGs) would *not* be achieved in many parts of the developing world. By the end of the boom, perceptions had changed, and it seemed that it was indeed possible for many developing countries and regions to achieve them. The recovery of official development assistance (ODA) after the UN Conference on Financing for Development held at Monterrey in 2002 was a source of additional hope.

The 2003–2007 boom was fueled by an exceptional mix of circumstances benefiting the developing world: exceptional external financing, in terms of both cost and quantities; booming international trade, including high commodity prices; and, for a significant number of developing countries, also large flows of remittances. The combination of good financial conditions and high commodity prices was last experienced in the 1970s, but the mix of these two factors with large and growing remittances had never been experienced before. The rise of an alternative Asian engine, with China at the center, was an additional element, one that has had a strong influence on world trade and commodity prices, and, in sub-Saharan Africa, on development financing and foreign investment.

After mid-2007, these favorable conditions were replaced by the effects of the subprime financial crisis that erupted in August 2007 in the United States, soon affecting Western Europe. However, for a year after the crisis erupted, commodity prices continued to boom. This factor, together with high foreign exchange reserves, helped attract capital to emerging markets, even at a time of growing world financial uncertainty. In mid-2008, commodity prices started to fall and external financing started to dry out. The real blow came, however, with the U.S. financial meltdown of mid-September 2008, which precipitated the worst world financial crisis since the Great Depression. It has been one of the worst (if not *the* worst) collapses of international trade in history and the worst world recession since the 1930s—now widely branded as the "Great Recession." Developing countries now joined the downturn. The view espoused by the International Monetary Fund (IMF) and some other analysts in 2007 that the developing world would "decouple" from weak economic conditions in industrial countries turned out to be much exaggerated.

The strong countercyclical policies that were put into place in the industrial world and several developing countries, notably China, helped avoid another Great Depression. Recovery began in the second quarter of 2009, though following a pattern that the IMF (2010b) has termed "a policy-driven, multispeed recovery." Financial flows to developing countries and commodity prices also recovered, and quickly relative to past experiences; however, the recovery of world trade has been slow, and the flow of remittances from migrants living in the United States, Western Europe, and Russia remained below pre-crisis levels, though they remained resilient in the Middle East. Overall, the experience of the developing countries was diverse and even novel in some cases, due to the strengths they built during the boom and the rapid return of the Chinese engine of world growth.

In this chapter, we analyze the effects of the crisis in the developing world, which, in the definition we use, includes what in the literature are called "emerging economies" (a concept that lacks a clear definition[1]), as well as the so-called "transition economies" of Central and Eastern Europe (including those that are now members of the European Union [EU]), as well as Central Asia. The chapter is divided into five parts. In the first we briefly look at the nature and phases of the crisis from a global perspective; in the second we analyze all the channels of transmission to the developing world; in the third we consider the performance of developing countries; in the fourth we examine the policy responses by the international community; and in the fifth we draw some policy conclusions. It must be emphasized, however, that although in the chapter we make some comments on the post-crisis recovery, we focus on the effects on the developing world of the Great Recession itself.

It must also be pointed out that throughout this chapter we use a combination of data from the UN and the IMF (and sometimes also the World Bank). This presents some problems, as these institutions use different regional breakdowns. Although UN regional classifications are better for analyzing trends in the developing world, financial data are only available from the IMF (and, again, the World Bank) with a different breakdown. In turn, private data, such as that from the Institute of International Finance (IIF), are only available for the emerging economies. To make things more complicated, the International Labor Organization (ILO) uses still another regional breakdown in its analysis of employment trends, so in our analysis we mix different sources. For aggregate GDP statistics we prefer, for technical reasons, UN data.[2]

A GLOBAL PERSPECTIVE

The peculiarity of the current crisis is, of course, that it originated at the center of the world economy. This is in striking contrast to the experiences of both industrial and developing countries during the preceding postwar decades. After a long period of sustained growth following the Second World War and the stagflation that set in after the first oil shock of the 1970s, the former experienced a "Great Moderation"—that is, an unusual period of smooth business cycles and low and stable inflation since the mid-1980s—a term that the now chairman of the U.S. Federal

Reserve Board (Bernanke, 2004) helped popularize. In contrast, the developing world experienced during the same period what can be called a "Great Volatility," characterized by massive financial crises, which included the debt crisis of the 1980s in large parts of the developing world, the shorter crisis of 1994–1995 (the so-called Tequila Crisis), and the worst and broadest-based crisis, that which emanated from East Asia in mid-1997 and spread to Russia, Turkey, and Latin America, engulfing most of the developing world. Other crises occurred in individual countries (such as Brazil and Argentina). The assorted crises of the developing world typically had causes that were not only similar to each other but also to the current crisis of the developed countries: excessive risk-taking and exuberance in financial markets (Stiglitz, 2010).

The collapse of the market for asset-backed securities in the United States in August 2007, in particular the market for subprime mortgages, marked the start of the world financial crisis. The European financial system was, from the beginning, also at the center of the turmoil, and, in fact, the first major bankruptcies took place there at the end of 2007 (Northern Rock in the United Kingdom and IKB in Germany). This reflected the significant portfolio of U.S. "toxic" securities held by European financial institutions, the end of their own housing bubbles, and, soon after, serious financial turmoil in the European periphery (Iceland and several Central and Eastern European countries).

It is now broadly recognized that the major root of the crisis was the excessive confidence in the capacity of financial markets to self-regulate and self-correct in the face of major disturbances. This was reinforced by the regulatory deficit in finance, especially in industrial countries, which steadily deregulated their financial systems, while many developing economies took steps to strengthen regulation following their own financial crises. Equally important was the incapacity or unwillingness of authorities, through adequate supervision, to effectively enforce even those regulations that were in place.

The expansionary monetary policies of the first half of the 2000s are also widely accepted as a major contributor to the crisis, though the interpretations differ among analysts and are not necessarily incompatible. Some see it simply as a policy mistake that, through attempts by financial institutions to increase their returns in a low interest rate environment (the so-called search for yield), led to risky investments. Others see it as a reflection of the need to compensate, particularly through expansionary monetary and credit policies, for the weak aggregate demand generated by adverse trends in income distribution throughout the world.[3]

Global payments imbalances also figure prominently in the debate on the origins of the crisis, again with contrasting views, which are not necessarily compatible in this case. According to one interpretation, Asian and, particularly, Chinese "mercantilism" generated massive surpluses that increased the demand for U.S. financial assets and kept interest rates—including long-term rates—low. The alternative interpretation emphasizes the fact that the crisis that started in Asia and other emerging economies in 1997 made it clear that the world lacks an efficient mechanism to manage financial crises in developing countries, due to limited and highly conditional IMF lending and the lack of an international debt workout mechanism. According to this view, the rational response of developing countries to this institutional deficit was to "self-insure" against crises by accumulating large amounts of foreign exchange reserves during the 2003–2007 boom. This policy included large savings out of the windfall generated by high commodity prices, as well as the decision to accumulate as additional foreign exchange reserves became a large part (or even all) of the additional pro-cyclical capital flows that came as a veritable flood during some phases of the boom. On top of that, its role as a "consumer of last resort" during the Asian crisis had dramatically increased U.S. current-account deficits. The persistence of high U.S. deficits in later years made it increasingly clear that the international monetary system does not impose any discipline on the country issuing the dominant reserve currency, a problem widely known as the Triffin dilemma.[4]

Viewed in particular from the perspective of the center of the financial turmoil and industrial countries' policy responses, the crisis has had five distinct phases. The first started with the collapse of the subprime market and, more generally, asset-backed securities in August 2007. The response of the authorities in industrial countries was to activate the role of central banks as "lenders of last resort" by making emergency financing to banks more readily available at lower interest rates. The United States added an early, though limited and temporary, fiscal stimulus. The second phase started with the collapse and rescue of a major U.S. investment bank, Bear Stearns, in March 2008. Confidence among financial institutions in the quality of each other's balance sheets decreased markedly after that event, resulting in reduced interbank lending and a much greater use of available central bank credit lines.

The collapse of another major U.S. investment bank, Lehman Brothers, during the weekend of September 13–14, 2008, and the decision of the U.S. government not to rescue it, marked the beginning of the third and, in regard to financial markets, the most dramatic phase of the crisis. During the week that followed, financial markets experienced total paralysis (a "credit freeze"), including of interbank lending and the market for commercial paper, thus seriously disturbing normal payment flows. Many other major financial institutions went bankrupt in the United States, Europe, and some other countries and were now generally rescued, in a major correction of what was very soon perceived as a major policy mistake (to let a systemically important institution, such as Lehman, go bankrupt). Authorities in industrial countries responded with even more massive central bank financial activism that, with variants across the industrial world, included many new credit lines, some of which facilitated access to central banks by certain financial institutions that had traditionally lacked such access; additional purchase of government debt and central bank interventions in several markets (commercial paper and mortgage-backed securities); strengthening deposit insurance; designing different schemes to capitalize financial institutions with public-sector funds; and, to a lesser extent, buying toxic assets.

The critical phase was over by late October 2008, as reflected by renewed interbank lending and the reduction of interest rates in many segments of the market. This may be denoted as the beginning of a fourth phase, in which the worst of the financial panic had been overcome, but financial institutions continued to be seriously undercapitalized, or were outright bankrupt, but continued to operate under the implicit promise that, in the end, they would be bailed out. Since the second quarter of 2009, we can talk of a fifth and, from our point of view in this chapter, final phase of the crisis, which came to be known as "green shoots"—the prelude to the "multispeed recovery." This phase was characterized by a significant reduction in risk premia and a recovery of stock prices and of bond markets; but there was no significant revival or even continued contraction of bank lending in industrial countries. In terms of new policy actions, the most remarkable development during the fourth and fifth phases was the shift by major central banks toward "quantitative easing"—that is, the outright increase in the money supply once central bank interest rates were brought down to zero (or near zero) and therefore ceased to be a useful instrument for further monetary expansion.

During the green shoots phase there was also a vigorous renewal of capital flows to developing countries, particularly to some of the emerging economies, reflecting both the return of risk-taking and massive carry trade facilitated by low interest rates in industrial countries.[5] In the latter case, it is hard to talk of a new financial bubble, as credit remained subdued and some asset prices (particularly real estate) remained depressed. In contrast, in several of the so-called emerging countries, signs of a new bubble in the making were already noticeable by late 2009, as reflected by variable mixes of strong exchange rates, booming stock markets, and, at least in a few countries (China being the most important), booming domestic credit and real estate prices. Worldwide, however, financial conditions remained quite unsettled, as reflected in periodic panics, associated with conditions in some countries (Dubai in late 2009 and peripheral Europe, starting with Greece, in early 2010) or in some markets (commercial property in the United States). The major characteristic of this multispeed recovery is, therefore, the great imbalances between both financial developments and economic activity in emerging and industrial economies (with some differences within both groups). It may perhaps be properly characterized as the return of global imbalances.

An economic slowdown was visible but not dramatic during the first two phases of the crisis. In Europe (with the major exception of the United Kingdom), there was, however, a tendency in political circles to underestimate it, a fact that was reflected in the much more conservative attitude of the European Central Bank and the weaker fiscal stimulus adopted by Continental European countries. Responses in the United States and Japan were more aggressive on both fronts. The dramatic recession in the industrial world that followed the financial meltdown of mid-September 2008 surpassed the most pessimistic expectations. The GDP of industrial countries fell in the last quarter of 2008 and the first quarter of 2009 at an annual rate of 7 to 8 percent, similar to rates during the early phases of the Great Depression, and industrial production dived (see Figure 2.1.A).[6] This was followed by a break in the contraction of economic activity during the fifth, green shoots phase. In the industrial world, recovery was led in the second quarter of 2009 by France, Germany, and Japan, but it spread to the United States and most other countries in the third quarter.

Although developing countries were somewhat hit during the first two phases of the crisis, partly by reduced availability and higher costs of borrowing, most of them continued to grow relatively fast during the first

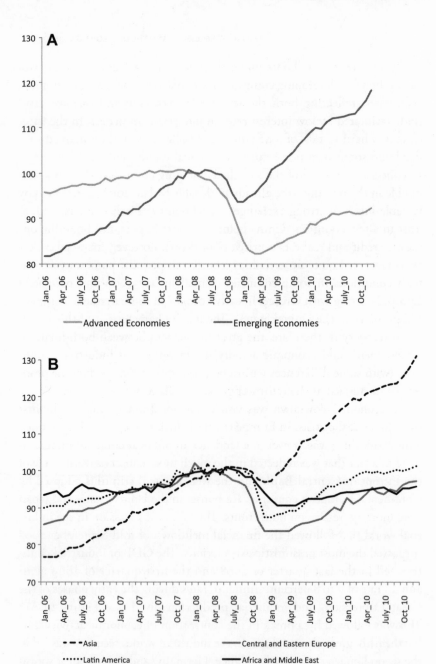

Figure 2.1 Industrial Production, 2006–2010 (First Semester of 2008 = 100)
A. Advanced vs. Emerging Economies
B. Emerging Economies

Source: CPB Netherlands. OECD excludes Turkey, Mexico, Korea, and Central European countries in Advanced Economies.

semester of 2008, due, as we will see, to booming commodity markets and the perception that risks of lending to them were low. The fall of commodity prices beginning in mid-2008 may be seen, therefore, as a more relevant turning point for many developing countries. In any case, the September 2008 financial meltdown was a far more important shock and led to a contraction of industrial production and exports (see Figure 2.1, as well as Figure 2.4 later in the chapter). The resulting reduction of emerging countries' GDP reached an annual rate of over 6 percent in the last quarter of the year and around 4 percent in the first quarter of 2009. This average is an amalgam of two contrasting trends: the limited slow-down in the two Asian giants, China and India, during the worst of the crisis, while other emerging country regions and several East Asian econo-mies experienced a much sharper slowdown or even recessions, in some cases matching the industrial countries' average pace of contraction (see Figure 2.1.B in relation to industrial production).

The early return to the rapid expansion of emerging economies in the second quarter was largely Asia-based; other regions lagged, with some major exceptions (Brazil in Latin America is a notable one), but the recovery became widespread in the third quarter of 2009. By late 2009, the picture was one of very uneven performance in the developing world. Looking at industrial production in emerging markets, Asia had surged above pre-crisis levels, while all other regions remained below those levels, particularly Central and Eastern Europe (again, see Figure 2.1.B). Latin America was the second region to reach pre-crisis industrial production in early 2010.

The fact that a Great Depression, such as that of the 1930s, was avoided marked a considerable policy success, though there are still significant risks ahead, stemming from a long period of relatively slow growth in industrial countries, the risks and fragility in the financial sectors and the fiscal accounts of several of these countries, and the return of global im-balances. Success can be attributed to two major factors. The first is mas-sive policy interventions in the industrial world but also, as we will show, by several developing countries, notably China. This was reflected in the most massive Keynesian macroeconomic package in history. To this we should add the rescue of financial institutions, albeit with the major error of allowing Lehman to fail.[7] The second and crucial factor was the exis-tence of a parallel engine of recovery: China. (India also performed well, but its links to other countries are much more limited than China's.) In-deed, one of the significant differences between the current crisis and the Great Depression is that there was no "China" in the 1930s: a substantial economy without a financial sector in crisis and with the foreign exchange and fiscal room to pursue aggressive Keynesian policies.

CHANNELS OF TRANSMISSION OF THE CRISIS

The crisis was transmitted to the developing world through the sharp reversal of the positive shocks it had experienced during the 2003–2007 boom. In quantitative terms, the two most important channels were the collapse of international trade (including commodity prices) and the paralysis of private capital markets. While the financial channel tended to loosen during the fifth (green shoots) and sixth (return of global imbalances) phases, trade remained below pre-crisis levels in value terms through 2010, and only returned to pre-crisis levels in volume terms by the end of that year. Whereas the financial shock was more severe for middle-income countries, the trade shock affected all economies, and its strength depended more on the commodity composition of exports and trade openness than on the level of development. A third transmission channel, the fall of migrant workers' remittances, was also significant for a subset of developing countries, mostly small economies. We review these three channels in detail, analyzing also the diverse effects they had throughout the developing world. The variations in the shocks as well as in the policy responses by developing countries (and the policy space they enjoyed) explain the diversity of outcomes, which will be analyzed in the third part of this chapter.

REMITTANCES

Although hard quantitative evidence is lacking, new migration flows seem to have fallen sharply as a result of the global financial crisis; however, immigrants who were already settled were generally unwilling to return to their countries of origin, presumably, at least in part, because of fears that they would not be able to reenter once they left because of tighter immigration controls. Nonetheless, initial World Bank expectations that remittances would be relatively resilient due to the latter factor (see, for example, Ratha et al., 2008) did not materialize. Overall, remittances fell 5.5 percent in 2009, but this represented a relatively small shock for the developing countries as a whole (0.1 percent of GDP).

However, regional and national patterns diverged significantly from this average pattern (Ratha et al., 2009). Three regions, and some countries within them, stand out in terms of the significance of the shock experienced because of the reduction of remittance flows: Latin America and the Caribbean, Eastern Europe and Central Asia, and some countries in North Africa. The common characteristic among these regions was their dependence on remittances from migrants living in the United States, Western Europe, and Russia. In contrast, those dependent on remittances from migrants to the Gulf Cooperation Council countries performed relatively well. Also, small countries within the regions most affected were the worst hit, given their heavier dependence on remittance flows.

The Latin America and the Caribbean region was the first to be affected. Remittances grew very slowly both in 2007 and 2008, falling as a proportion of GDP in both years, in sharp contrast to the rapid growth earlier in the decade (see Table 2.1). This was a reflection of the importance of the employment of migrant workers in the U.S. construction sector, which began to experience a severe contraction in 2007 (JPMorgan, 2008). The strength of the crisis in Spain, the major destination of Latin Americans in Europe, added to the decreased opportunities experienced by migrants to the United States Remittances started to fall in the third quarter of 2008. The more comprehensive information by the Inter-American Development Bank (IADB) (2010) indicates that they fell by 15 percent in 2009, with the strongest contraction experienced in the second and third quarters of that year, when they fell by 17 percent. More recent information

Table 2.1   Remittances by Region (Percentage Change)

Region	2005	2006	2007	2008	2009	2010	Impact of Crisis % GDP
Middle East and North Africa	8.4	4.6	21.5	11.8	−6.3	5.3	−0.3
Europe and Central Asia	43.6	24.1	38.5	16.5	−22.7	3.7	−0.5
Latin America and the Caribbean	15.7	18.1	6.9	2.2	−12.0	2.0	−0.3
South Asia	18.2	25.3	27.1	32.5	4.5	10.3	0.3
Sub-Saharan Africa	16.9	34.7	46.7	14.9	−3.7	4.4	−0.1
East Asia and the Pacific	25.1	14.1	23.7	20.2	0.3	6.4	0.0
All Developing Countries	**21.0**	**18.3**	**22.8**	**16.7**	**−5.5**	**6.0**	**−0.1**

Note: Impact of Crisis is calculated as the proportion of remittances in GDP in 2008 times the growth rate of remittances in 2009.

Source: World Bank, Migration and Remittances Team, Development Prospects Group.

indicates that remittances to Latin America and the Caribbean only bottomed out in the first quarter of 2010, before beginning a weak and incomplete recovery.

Although with some lag in comparison to Latin America and the Caribbean, Eastern Europe and Central Asia experienced a stronger negative shock in 2009, with an overall reduction of close to 23 percent, equivalent to 0.5 percent of GDP. As we show later, some former Soviet republics in Eastern Europe and Central Asia, heavily dependent on remittances from migrants living in Russia, were hit the hardest in relative terms. Among the new European Union (EU) members, Poland and Romania, whose immigrants commonly chose the United Kingdom as their destination, also suffered an important decline in remittance income during 2009.

Although remittances to North Africa and the Middle East fell less, the large average share of remittances in the income of these economies meant that this region was also affected. Morocco and Egypt, the principal recipients in the region, which depend on migration to Europe, mainly to France and Spain, experienced the sharpest contraction. Migrants to the Gulf countries (e.g., from Lebanon) fared much better.

Table 2.2 lists the ten countries hardest hit in the developing world, where the remittance shock exceeded 1 percent of GDP. The strongest affected were four former Soviet republics. Five small Latin American and Caribbean countries were also badly hit. In other regions, only Tonga in the South Pacific experienced a strong shock. Of the countries shown in Table 2.2, only one, Guatemala, exceeds a population of ten million.

In contrast, remittance flows to South Asia, a region with heavy dependence on this source of income, grew strongly up until 2008 and experienced

Table 2.2   Countries Hit Hardest by Fall in Remittances

Country	Change of Remittance Flow, 2009 (%)	Remittances as a Share of GDP, 2008 (%)	Impact % GDP
Tajikistan	−31.3	49.6	−15.5
Moldova	−36.2	31.4	−11.4
Kyrgyz Republic	−28.5	27.9	−7.9
Tonga	−7.8	37.7	−2.9
Armenia	−27.6	8.9	−2.5
Honduras	−11.0	20.1	−2.2
Guyana	−9.1	24.0	−2.2
Jamaica	−11.8	14.5	−1.7
El Salvador	−7.2	17.2	−1.2
Guatemala	−9.7	11.4	−1.1

Source: World Bank, *Migration and Remittances Factbook 2011.*

only a modest slowdown in 2009, despite the global economic crisis. The prevalence of migration to the Gulf countries was the stabilizing factor in this case. In some of the major countries in the region, remittances actually increased in 2009, especially as construction activities in the Gulf remained robust. This is the case for Pakistan, Bangladesh, and Nepal. This is also true for the Philippines, the major recipient of migrant income in East Asia after China. Similarly, transfers to sub-Saharan Africa, which come in large measure from other countries in Africa and the Middle East, proved relatively resilient.

Changes in exchange rates played a critical role in the divergent performances during the crisis. One of the main explanations for the sharp fall in remittances from Russia was the depreciation of the ruble. Ecuador, a dollarized economy with heavy migration to Spain, experienced first an adverse and then a positive effect of the variations of the euro/dollar exchange rate. Polish and Romanian migrants to the United Kingdom were negatively affected by the depreciation of the British pound. Several recipient countries experienced a depreciation of their own currencies, compensating and even initially overcompensating for the reduction of remittances in dollar terms. For example, in Mexico and Colombia, the two largest recipients of remittances in Latin America in absolute terms, domestic recipients actually saw an increase in the domestic purchasing power of remittance flows due to the initial depreciation of their pesos.

FINANCIAL FLOWS

The financial channel had been at the center of the two major crises in the developing world in previous decades: the debt crisis of the 1980s and the Asian crisis of the late 1990s. Following a long history of boom-bust cycles (see, for example, Reinhart and Rogoff, 2009), the essential feature in both cases was the sharp change from booming financial conditions to a sudden interruption in lending from international capital markets (to either sovereign or corporations), together with outflows of the most volatile capital (short-term lending and some portfolio flows) and the rapid increase in spreads—the phenomenon that has come to be broadly referred to as a "sudden stop" but generally involves a reversal of flows.

Imitating this pattern, the recent global financial crisis also hit hard private capital flows to the developing world, as reflected by a strong interruption of new lending, massive outflows of volatile capital, and a rapid increase in spreads. Although some financial indicators (stock exchange prices and bond spreads) had been hit by both the subprime crisis in August 2007 and the fall in commodity prices in mid-2008, the strongest shock came with the world financial meltdown of September 2008. However, it turned out to be much less intense than in previous crises. There are two main explanations for this: the strengthening of developing countries' external balance sheets during the boom and the strong countercyclical policy reaction in industrial countries, particularly by their central banks. We return to the first of these issues in the third section, whereas the second was already mentioned. It must be said that this strong countercyclical action was largely absent during the major developing country crises of the last two decades of the twentieth century, where it was limited to additional and highly conditional IMF lending and, with significant lags, initiatives to reduce the debt burden (the 1989 Brady Plan, the failed discussion of a Sovereign Debt Restructuring Mechanism in 2001–2003, and the initiatives to reduce the debt of highly indebted poor countries).[8] Indeed, the only major exception was the rapid bailout of Mexico, with strong U.S. support, after the December 1994 crisis, which made the global effects of that crisis mild (although certainly not in Mexico and some other economies, particularly Argentina).

Regarding the volume of flows, private financial flows peaked from mid-2006 to mid-2007. After a short weakening during the third quarter of 2007 due to the subprime crisis, they recovered and boomed again during the second quarter of 2008 but dropped sharply in the third quarter of 2008 and remained subdued during the last quarter of 2008 and the first quarter of 2009. This was the result of a steep and simultaneous falloff in the issuance of debt securities and equity flows, together with outflows from mutual funds (see Figure 2.2). Emerging countries' equity markets and liquidity in bond markets sharply worsened, as the whole global financial system seemed to crumble after the Lehman collapse. There was virtually no sovereign or corporate bond or equity issuance from emerging economies in international markets between mid-September and mid-December 2008. Local stock markets, meanwhile, experienced the worst yearly decline in recent history, as the MSCI Emerging Market Index dropped 55 percent during 2008, erasing some US$17 trillion in market valuation (World Bank, 2009a, overview). Thus, as in previous crises, contagion moved across categories of flows and was experienced by all developing country regions.

In 2008 the outflows after the Lehman collapse outweighed the positive flows during the first semester, generating net private financial *out*flows

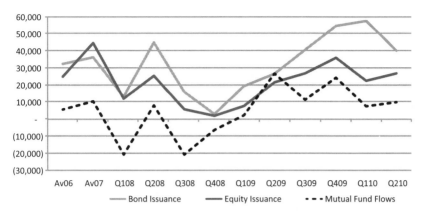

Figure 2.2   Emerging Markets External Financing (US$ Millions)
Source: IMF (2009b).

(i.e., private flows excluding foreign direct investment [FDI]) of US$255 billion for the year as a whole versus net *in*flows of US$279 billion in 2007. Large net financial outflows continued through the first semester of 2009 but were reversed in the latter part so that these *net* outflows were only slightly negative for the year as a whole (see Table 2.3). The sharpest drop was in international bank lending, with a substantial net inflow that turned into a large outflow in 2008 and 2009 (this is reflected in the category "Other private financial flows" in Table 2.3). Data from the Institute of International Finance (IIF) and other sources confirm that this rapid fall in bank lending resulted in negative *net* lending. Only foreign direct investment (FDI), which tends to be more resilient in a crisis given the longer-term horizon of investors (though perhaps less than much of the literature suggested), and the longer gestation periods of the projects being financed remained positive but decreased from US$439 billion in 2008 to US$241 billion in 2009.

Two caveats should be made about these trends. First, the falls in net private flows, though deep, were smaller than the forecasts at the depth of the crisis. This can be seen by comparing IIF October 2008 and January 2009 forecasts (IIF, 2009) versus more recent estimates (IIF, 2010), but this reflects a general pattern. Generally, the forecasts about Latin America and emerging Asia turned out to be excessively pessimistic but too optimistic about emerging Europe. Second, in sharp contrast to previous crises, the collapse of private flows to emerging economies was much shorter in duration. We return to this issue later.

Table 2.3 Developing and Transition Economies Capital Flows, US$ Billion

Region	2006	2007	2008	2009	2010
Emerging and Developing Economies					
Private financial flows, net	253.13	696.49	184.36	234.77	339.64
Direct investment, net	258.27	417.17	438.97	240.84	296.30
Private portfolio flows, net	−36.88	86.85	−82.54	91.52	32.81
Other private financial flows, net	31.74	192.47	−172.07	−97.58	10.54
Official flows, net	−187.56	−103.15	−94.80	84.59	40.21
Total net flows	65.57	593.35	89.56	319.36	379.85
Sub-Saharan Africa					
Private financial flows, net	13.21	29.71	26.78	25.92	36.60
Direct investment, net	9.53	23.21	33.27	27.84	25.44
Private portfolio flows, net	17.51	10.02	−18.54	10.20	11.22
Other private financial flows, net	−13.83	−3.52	12.04	−12.12	−0.07
Official flows, net	−32.19	−7.53	−2.39	6.64	8.64
Total net flows	−18.98	22.17	24.39	32.56	45.24
Central and Eastern Europe					
Private financial flows, net	121.16	187.19	153.10	25.54	66.57
Direct investment, net	65.04	77.23	68.06	32.27	27.87
Private portfolio flows, net	−0.40	−3.15	−9.51	7.56	22.31
Other private financial flows, net	56.52	113.11	94.55	−14.29	16.40
Official flows, net	4.53	−6.72	22.32	46.69	32.72
Total net flows	125.69	180.47	175.42	72.24	99.29
Commonwealth of Independent States					
Private financial flows, net	51.57	129.18	−96.28	−62.20	−1.18
Direct investment, net	21.34	28.28	52.26	15.73	22.65
Private portfolio flows, net	4.86	19.47	−31.44	−9.46	−1.19
Other private financial flows, net	25.38	81.43	−117.10	−68.46	−22.65
Official flows, net	−25.44	−6.03	−19.04	41.94	7.67
Total net flows	26.14	123.15	−115.32	−20.25	6.49
Developing Asia					
Private financial flows, net	51.69	190.00	38.43	161.77	135.36
Direct investment, net	85.64	153.27	134.18	64.60	73.16
Private portfolio flows, net	−45.08	67.31	−3.10	35.83	24.03
Other private financial flows, net	11.13	−30.58	−92.65	61.34	38.17
Official flows, net	−3.53	−1.08	7.05	10.31	7.46
Total net flows	48.16	188.92	45.48	172.08	142.82
Middle East and North Africa					
Private financial flows, net	−23.69	53.16	2.47	58.65	11.08
Direct investment, net	44.90	46.71	57.24	36.58	67.78
Private portfolio flows, net	−29.86	−43.18	−2.17	16.25	−30.28
Other private financial flows, net	−38.72	49.63	−52.60	5.82	−26.43
Official flows, net	−76.59	−75.75	−103.72	−65.77	−42.63
Total net flows	−100.28	−22.59	−101.25	−7.12	−31.55
Latin America and the Caribbean					
Private financial flows, net	39.18	107.27	59.87	25.09	91.22
Direct investment, net	31.83	88.47	93.96	63.82	79.39
Private portfolio flows, net	16.09	36.39	−17.79	31.14	6.71
Other private financial flows, net	−8.73	−17.59	−16.31	−69.87	5.12
Official flows, net	−54.35	−6.03	0.98	44.77	26.35
Total net flows	−15.16	101.23	60.85	69.86	117.56

Source: IMF, World Economic Outlook database.

The financial impact of the global crisis was more severe for emerging markets than for low-income countries, which are less integrated into international private capital markets. Indeed, capital flows to low-income Africa have been the most stable, as well as relatively limited (see Table 2.3). However, detailed surveys conducted by Bhinda and Martin (2009) indicate that private flows to low-income countries are both higher and more volatile than either IMF or national statistics show. One important reason such survey data report higher flows to sub-Saharan Africa is that they measure better South-South private flows. Regarding volatility, Bhinda and Martin (2009) underscore that all categories of flows to low-income countries are volatile, and debt flows particularly so. Furthermore, they stress that capital flows, and especially FDI, can be huge in relation to the size of the countries' economies, which are often less diversified than middle-income countries. This makes low-income countries particularly vulnerable to the negative effects of volatility of capital flows, especially FDI, on employment, income, and poverty.

The economies in transition, including the former Soviet Bloc countries of Central and Eastern Europe that are now members of the EU, experienced the most dramatic reversal: having been heavily dependent on bank financing and rising levels of external debt, they felt strongly the consequence of worldwide deleveraging. Countries with large current-account deficits (compounded in many cases by currency mismatches in the private sector's balance sheets), and therefore most dependent on foreign capital, were hardest hit by the substantial tightening of credit conditions. This is the reason Central and Eastern Europe were so strongly affected, recalling the patterns of the Latin American economies during the earlier crises of the last two decades of the twentieth century. However, even middle-income countries with current-account surpluses were substantially affected by the global financial crisis. Many of them experienced a sell-off in assets that triggered fairly substantial exchange-rates depreciations. Thus there was a large reversal of portfolio flows in East Asia and South Asia (even surprising in several cases). In Latin America, Brazil and Mexico were hit by losses in derivative markets and, in the former, by the unwinding of the carry trade. South Africa was also severely hit.

Furthermore, *net* financial resources continued to flow from poor to rich countries. According to UN estimates (UN, 2010a), developing countries as a group continued to provide net financial transfers (defined as net capital flows less investment income payments) to developed countries in 2009 at a level of US$545 billion after peaking at US$881 billion in 2007.

As indicated, from the point of view of emerging countries' access to financial markets, the worst of the financial collapse was rather short by previous historical records. By far the worst moment was the last quarter of 2008. As Figure 2.2 indicates, bond issuance began to recover in the first quarter of 2009 and was actually booming by the end of the year. It was followed by mutual funds flows and, more weakly, by equity issuance. This was accompanied by a rebound in stock markets in both developed and emerging markets.

The basic explanations for this rapid revival were the sharply expansionary macroeconomic policies in industrial countries, as well as policy measures to recapitalize financial institutions. Particularly important were the massive monetary expansion and lowering of interest rates in developed countries, which led to high international liquidity and the search for better yields than those that could be obtained in developed countries (the well-known push factor). This combined with an increase in risk appetite but also reflected a growing (correct) perception that many developing countries have better growth prospects than developed ones, and possibly fewer fragilities.

One of the reflections of the initial collapse and early revival of capital flows is the evolution of JPMorgan's Emerging-Market Bond Index (EMBI). As Figure 2.3 indicates, emerging market spreads had begun to increase moderately at the start of the financial crisis, in August 2007, but that increase was largely compensated by the decline in the long-term U.S. interest rates that serve as a benchmark, thus keeping ten-year bond yields fairly stable at around 6.5 percent, with only moderate upward trends during the third quarter of 2007 (the subprime crisis) and the third quarter of 2008 (the end of the commodity price boom). Spreads increased sharply after the Lehman collapse, bringing yields also sharply up despite the reduction in benchmark interest rates. However, after peaking in late October 2008 (a yield of 12 percent), they started to moderate, and sharply so, from March 2009. By October 2009, yields were essentially back to the pre-Lehman levels, reflecting a higher spread (of around 100 basis points), compensated for by a reduction in the benchmark interest rate. Viewed in terms of the long sequence of high spreads and yields that characterized the developing world after the Asian and, particularly, the Russian crises, after which it took five years to return to pre-crisis levels, the recent one-year cycle was surprisingly short (see Figure 2.3). Indeed, spreads did not even reach the levels of the previous major disturbance—the one generated in 2002 by the presidential elections in Brazil.

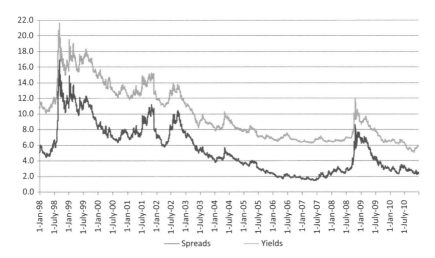

Figure 2.3   Emerging Markets' Spreads and Yields, 1998–2010 (Percentage Points)

Source: JPMorgan.

Financial investors have thus rediscovered an appetite for risk in high-yielding currencies and emerging market equities. The IIF began its January 2010 report by characterizing recent trends in capital flows to emerging economies as "Famine to Feast," as the outlook in terms of growth and tighter fiscal stance actually looks better in many emerging economies than in developed ones. The IMF referred to this development in its *Global Financial Stability Report* (IMF, 2010a), warning that the decline in sovereign debt spreads was driven almost entirely by an improved global appetite for risk and core market liquidity, despite underlying economic fundamentals continuing to deteriorate in some countries.

This has generated a concern that speculative motives associated with returning portfolio flows could become a source of another global financial bubble in the making; this time in major emerging economies, as asset markets and exchange rates get overvalued. The bursting of this bubble could again be very costly for the developing world. At least it could lead to increased volatility in exchange rates and assets prices and, hence, renewed macroeconomic instability, should the appetite for risk in developing countries by foreign investors and lenders fall or the perception of emerging and developing country risks deteriorate. One of the major reasons is the renewed importance of carry trade, which may remain an essential feature of the world economy, given the need of industrial countries to keep interest rates low for a long period of time, a pressure that is certainly absent in developing countries. This means that the carry trade has become a central source of external vulnerability for developing countries, which must require attention from both national and international regulators.

TRADE

In recent decades, world trade has shown two important features. First, it has tended to expand more rapidly than world production, a process that has been accompanied by a rapid diversification of trade structure. Thus, according to UN data, during the recent trade boom, in the period 2003–2006, world trade volumes grew at an annual rate of 9.3 percent, more than twice the rate of growth of world output (3.8 percent) (UN, 2009a, table I.1). Second, these rates of growth have been highly elastic to world output through the business cycle and have, therefore, been more volatile than world production. A major implication of this characteristic is that trade enhances both the upswings and downswings of world business cycles. The effects of the pro-cyclical pattern of capital flows to developing countries are reinforced by the pro-cyclical performance of trade volumes and the more traditional one of commodity prices, thus generating a succession of strong positive and negative shocks that the more open contemporary developing countries face through the business cycle.

Following this pattern, the growth of trade volume experienced a strong slowdown in mid-2007 and turned negative in September 2008. However, the collapse that followed (a fall of −32 percent in value terms between the third quarter of 2008 and the first quarter of 2009) had few historical precedents, being even more severe than that during the comparable phase of the Great Depression (O'Rourke, 2009). The collapse in trade was triggered by the severe decline in global aggregate demand and associated inventory adjustments, compounded by a considerable strain in global financial markets, resulting in a shortage of trade credits. Economies most open to trade received a dramatic shock, which explains the initial rapid reduction of GDP in the most trade-dependent economies, from Asia (Japan and the Asian Tigers: South Korea, Taiwan, Hong Kong, and Singapore) to Germany, Mexico, and Turkey.

Although the trough was reached during the first quarter of 2009, and a substantial recovery followed in the second semester, by the end of the year world trade volumes remained significantly below the peak reached during the first semester of 2008 (which serves as a reference point in Figure 2.4).

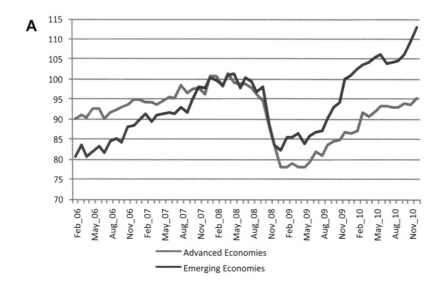

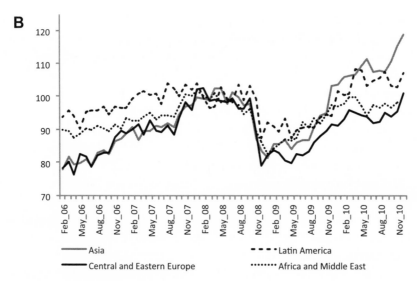

Figure 2.4 **Trade Export Volumes, 2006–2010 (First Semester of 2008 = 100)**
A. Advanced vs. Emerging Economies
B. Emerging Economies

Source: CPB Netherlands (2010). OECD excludes Turkey, Mexico, Korea, and Central European countries in Advanced Economies.

As a consequence, yearly averages of world trade volumes grew only 2.7 percent in 2008 and decreased by 12.6 percent in 2009, compared to the annual rate of growth of 9.3 percent in the period 2003–2006.

No region or, indeed, country was spared the adverse demand shock, reflected in the fall of volume of exports. In the developed world, the EU and Japan experienced the hardest shocks, greater than 4 percent of their GDP (UN, 2010a). Regarding developing countries and economies in transition, those in Central and Eastern Europe and Asia experienced the sharpest drop in volume, but the recovery of Asia came early in 2009, while at the other end of the spectrum, Central and Eastern Europe lagged behind (Figure 2.4.B). Latin America was the region least affected through the export volume channel and the second behind Asia in terms of the export recovery.

Manufacturing trade volumes faced the strongest contraction, reflecting a higher income elasticity than trade in commodities (UN, 2010a). Furthermore, given their high dependence on manufacturing exports, the transition economies of Central and Eastern Europe and the East Asian and Southeast Asian countries were the most affected, as were Mexico and Turkey. China was not spared from this shock but was able to offset it through massively expansionary domestic demand policies. As manufacturing export prices also experienced a reduction, several of these economies saw the value of manufacturing exports decline by 30 percent or more over a year during the first quarter of 2009. China again was also hit, as its export revenues in the first quarter of 2009 were 20 percent below the level of the same quarter one year earlier and continued below pre-crisis levels despite the recovery that began in the third quarter of 2009.

In developing countries more dependent on commodity exports, the price channel was more important and implied the sharp reversal of the positive terms of trade shock they had experienced during the boom years. Indeed, from 2004 to mid-2008, the world economy had experienced the most spectacular commodity boom in over a century in terms of its duration (five years), intensity, and product coverage (UNCTAD, 2009, chap. 3; World Bank, 2009b, chap. 2). However, as Table 2.4 indicates, the boom was stronger for energy and mining products (metals) than for agricultural goods. This is reflected by the fact that, whereas at their peak, during the first semester of 2008, real metal prices were nearly double their average levels of the 1970s (which were just below real averages for the period 1945–1980 for non-oil commodities), real agricultural prices just returned, and briefly so, to those earlier levels. In other words, agricultural prices had just reversed during the recent boom the significant deterioration they had

Table 2.4   Real Commodity Prices (1971–1980 = 100)

	Total Non-Oil	Total Agriculture	Tropical Agriculture	Other Agriculture	Metals	Oil
Annual						
2003	66.2	63.9	50.7	77.3	76.9	123.8
2004	73.5	67.9	58.8	77.2	99.1	151.3
2005	79.5	71.9	64.8	79.2	114.7	213.8
2006	97.2	79.1	68.7	89.7	181.0	253.5
2007	106.1	87.8	76.4	99.3	190.7	265.9
2008	110.3	97.4	91.0	103.8	169.8	342.4
2009	94.6	85.8	79.9	91.9	135.0	234.2
Quarterly						
2008-I	121.2	105.8	100.3	111.4	192.4	339.8
2008-II	119.8	104.0	102.8	105.3	192.8	413.5
2008-III	111.5	97.4	92.1	102.9	176.2	396.6
2008-IV	87.1	81.2	67.5	95.1	114.3	208.8
2009-I	84.4	80.8	69.4	92.4	101.1	170.0
2009-II	94.4	87.7	79.8	95.7	125.3	228.8
2009-III	97.0	86.0	82.2	89.8	148.0	257.8
2009-IV	102.2	88.8	87.7	89.9	164.1	278.0

Sources: Based on the methodology of Ocampo and Parra (2003). Nominal prices deflated by World Bank's MUV up to 2008; quarterly evolution of manufacturing prices in the period 2008–2009, according to CPB Netherlands (2010).

experienced during the 1980s and the Asian crisis. Oil did even better, as it quadrupled in real terms from the already high historical average of the 1970s.

The difference in performance between energy and minerals, on the one hand, and agricultural goods, on the other, indicates that the determinants of the two commodity groups have been very different. In energy and minerals, low prices led to low investment levels from the mid-1980s to the early 2000s. Low production capacity then met in recent years the high demand generated by rapid world economic growth and, in metals, the unprecedented Chinese demand. Investment responded to high prices, but there is a significant lag between investment decisions and increased supplies, leading to a long and strong price boom. In agriculture, and despite the alarms raised by the food crisis during the first semester of 2008, supply-demand imbalances were more moderate and were more rapidly corrected. An important channel of transmission of high energy prices to agricultural markets was, of course, the increasing demand for biofuels (von Braun, 2007). The sharply increased financialization of commodity futures trading since 2005 also helped speed up the price boom—and the subsequent collapse (UNCTAD, 2009, chap. 3). Dollar depreciation during the second semester of 2007 and the first semester of 2008 also fueled the boom in dollar terms.

Commodity prices started to fall from mid-2008. The price turnaround clearly preceded the September financial meltdown but was transformed into a veritable price collapse after this event. By December, real agricultural prices were back to levels only slightly above those experienced during the Asian crisis. Prices for energy and metals fell more strongly, but in real terms the level reached in the first quarter of 2009 was still historically high in the first case and much better than previous troughs in the second. In turn, the contraction in agriculture was stronger for tropical products than for temperate-zone products. Recovery also started in the second quarter and was again stronger for energy and minerals than for tropical agricultural goods (Table 2.4). All of them remained, however, below levels reached during the previous boom and, in agriculture, some 10 percent below the level of the 1970s. As noted earlier, the financialization of commodity markets reinforced the price collapse after September 2008 and the recovery since the second quarter of 2009. The recovery continued through 2010, reaching real levels similar to the previous boom for several non-oil prices, though not for oil.

Services trade was more resilient than merchandise trade. However, tourism represented an exception, since it is a luxury and therefore highly income elastic. Developing countries with important trade service sectors, such as Brazil, Indonesia, Mexico, and South Korea, were also hit by this channel, as their service export revenues fell. Mexico, with an important tourism sector, experienced a fall of more than 16 percent in the first quarter of 2009 (UN, 2010a). Regionally, Central and Eastern Europe recorded the largest fall in tourism (11 percent), while Africa registered a modest increase in tourist arrivals, though a small decline in tourism receipts (World Bank, 2010).

A major implication of the aforementioned patterns is that trade shocks were very unevenly distributed throughout the developing world. This is well illustrated in UN estimates of trade shocks as a proportion of GDP, which captures both changes in the demand for exports, in volume terms, as well as terms of trade changes. Figure 2.5 reproduces the UN (2010b) estimates. As panel A in this figure indicates, energy exporters experienced the strongest positive shock during the previous boom, followed by mineral and manufacturing exporters (though the mineral price boom came to an end earlier). The magnitude of the negative shock in 2009 came exactly in the same ranking. In contrast, agricultural exporters received a weak

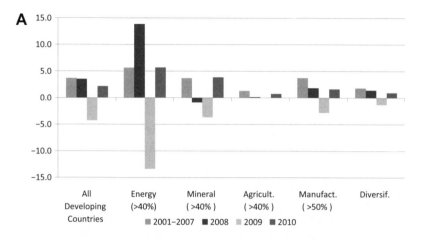

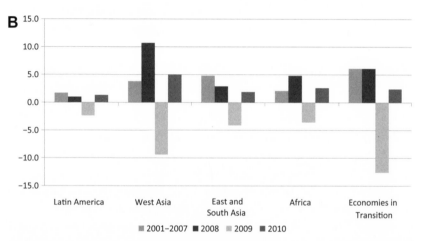

Figure 2.5   Trade Shocks of Developing and Transition Economies (% GDP)
A. Developing Countries by Pattern of Specialization
B. By Region

Sources: UN (2010b). Data for panel A provided to the authors by UN/DESA.

positive shock and a neutral one during the crisis. This reflects the fact that many agricultural exporters in the developing world are also energy import-ers, so that what they won they lost through variations in the prices of the commodities. Regionally, panel B indicates that West Asia and the econo-mies in transition received the strongest positive and negative shocks, whereas Latin America received the weakest.

The contraction of international trade was the most important channel of transmission of the world financial crisis to the developing world. As we have seen, with some exceptions, the remittance channel was overall small and the financial channel intense but short. In contrast, through trade, the developing world went from experiencing a positive shock equivalent to 3.5 percent of GDP up to 2008 to a negative one of 4.3 percent—an astonishing change equivalent to 8 percentage points of GDP! Furthermore, this is a negative shock that developing countries had limited capacity to counteract, given the restructuring that has been taking place for three decades toward more open economies, and the collapse of world trade, which gave them limited scope to export themselves out of the crisis—the strategy that most of them followed during previous, developing-country-centered crises. Not least important, though, the recovery of trade continued in 2010, with the most recent estimates by the IMF (2011) indicating that trade volumes just recovered the 2009 losses but, according to Ocampo (2011), remain close to 10 percent below pre-crisis trends in the relationship between international trade and world GDP since the mid-1980s. This poses serious questions regarding development strategies in the developing world, an issue to which we return in the concluding section of this chapter.

POLICY RESPONSES AND OUTCOMES

POLICY SPACE AND COUNTERCYCLICAL POLICIES

Given the worldwide trend toward the external opening of both trade and financial accounts over the past decades, the recent crisis had severe effects throughout the developing world. As indicated in the previous section, the space for developing countries to export themselves out of the crisis was simply not available this time. Therefore, the space for and effectiveness of countercyclical domestic demand policies played the crucial role in the capacity of individual developing countries to mitigate the strong external shock.

In this area, there was a significant change in relation to past developing-country-centered crises: there was broad-based support for developing countries' countercyclical macroeconomic policies. Indeed, this term, which was tending to disappear from the jargon of orthodox economists and economic authorities, as well as from the IMF, now made a victorious return. Support for countercyclical policies came from the G-20 and the IMF, with some caveats in the latter case on whether developing countries could afford them and, particularly, whether governments that came to the IMF for financing should adopt them. But this shift was not always reflected in practice.

Due to the pro-cyclical pattern of external financing that developing countries face, the room of maneuver for expansionary domestic demand policies during crises has invariably been limited by balance-of-payments constraints. For that reason, the crucial difference this time was the much stronger external balance sheets that developing countries had been building up. This was, first of all, the result of the "self-insurance" against balance-of-payments crises that they had practiced on a broad basis and, in some regions, on a massive scale during the boom and was reflected in the accumulation of large foreign exchange reserves (Ocampo, 2010). This was combined with fairly broad-based reductions in external public-sector debts due to the development of domestic bond markets in several developing countries after the Asian crisis, the debt relief initiatives that had been in place, particularly for low-income countries (the Highly Indebted Poor Countries, or HIPC Initiative, its successor, the Multilateral Debt Relief Initiative), and some individual debt restructuring processes either in the context of the Paris Club (e.g., Iraq and Nigeria) or through unilateral action (e.g., Argentina). To compensate pro-cyclical private financing, broader multilateral financial support was also made available (see the fourth section) but, as we will show, this operated as a secondary factor.

In the case of fiscal policy, the room of maneuver for countercyclical policies was also limited by the magnitude of inherited public-sector debts and the rhythm of fiscal expansion during the previous boom. It also depended on the effects that volatile fiscal revenues (particularly those from natural resources) had in the public-sector finances of individual countries, and on the capacity of domestic bond markets to finance current fiscal imbalances in non-inflationary ways. The situation of developing countries was quite mixed in this area.

Aside from these external balance sheet and fiscal considerations, a third set of circumstances affected the space for countercyclical policies: the health of the financial sectors, as well as the presence or absence of major currency mismatches in portfolios of private-sector agents, particularly, but not only, of domestic financial institutions—the phenomenon known as "liability dollarization" but that in the European periphery meant liabilities in euros or Swiss francs. The trend in most of the developing world was positive in both regards, as many of these countries had strengthened their prudential regulatory and supervisory frameworks after their own financial crises and developed their domestic bond markets, which had also helped reduce currency mismatches. But there were important exceptions. Beyond vulnerability to domestic financial crises associated with these factors, and again reflecting the pro-cyclical patterns of external financing, the dependence of domestic financing on external funding was crucial to avoiding a domestic credit crunch.

There were major improvements in all these areas during the 2003–2007 boom. Developing countries' external balance sheets had indeed improved on a fairly broad basis. Table 2.5 summarizes the evolution of three major external variables during the recent boom—the current-account balance, external debt, and foreign exchange reserves—in ninety developing and transition economies,[9] each with a population of more than five million as of 2007. The table shows the simple averages of ratios of these variables to GDP for each region, as well as the proportion of countries showing improvement in the indicator over the boom.

The dominant pattern over this period was an increasing number of countries with current-account (and, in some cases, large) deficits. In contrast, there were broad-based and generally large improvements in debt ratios, as well as significant foreign exchange reserve accumulation. The latter underestimates the magnitude of the improvement in external balance sheets, as it does not include fiscal funds held abroad by either sovereign wealth or stabilization funds.

In regional terms, the Middle East and Asia show the best performance in the three dimensions and of all but debt in the countries of the Commonwealth of Independent States (CIS). Africa shows large current-account deficits but significant improvements in the other two dimensions. The Latin America and the Caribbean region stands out for its historically unprecedented avoidance of current-account deficits as well as significant improvements in debt ratios. The Central and Eastern Europe region shows by far the weakest stance: large current-account deficits with limited or no improvements in debt and foreign exchange reserves.

Table 2.6 confirms this picture, showing the evolution of these three sets of indicators for major regions, using IMF regional classifications. Current-account surpluses, reserve accumulation, and falling external debt ratios were the rule during the boom years in most regions, with some exceptions. The major one was Central and Eastern Europe, which showed large current-account deficits, increasing external debts, and limited reserve accumulation. The Middle East also experienced a growing debt ratio despite massive reserve accumulation and current-account surpluses. Current-account surpluses and reserve accumulation were rather moderate in Latin

Table 2.5 External Indicators of Developing and Transition Economies with Populations over Five Million

	Number of Countries	Current Account Balance				External Debt			Foreign Exchange Reserves, exc. gold		
		% of GDP 2003	% of GDP 2007	% with Deficit 2007	% with Improvement	% of GDP 2003	% of GDP 2006	% with Improvement	% of GDP 2003	% of GDP 2007	% with Improvement
Africa	31	−5.6	−4.2	87	45	89.7	43.0	97	12.8	18.1	78
Central and Eastern Europe	8	−5.4	−9.1	100	38	56.4	57.3	57	21.0	23.2	63
CIS	8	−1.0	3.1	63	25	56.1	44.5	88	12.9	21.3	100
Asia, inc. NICs	20	2.2	3.0	30	45	52.6	36.9	100	27.2	32.7	69
Middle East, inc. Egypt	7	7.2	6.5	43	43	54.0	28.6	100	41.1	50.1	40
Latin America and the Caribbean	16	−0.7	−0.9	50	38	63.7	37.6	100	11.7	14.8	69
Total	**90**			**63%**	**41%**			**94%**			**72%**

Source: Author estimates based on IMF International Financial Statistics.

Table 2.6 Debt Ratios, Current Account, and Reserve Accumulation by Region, 2002–2010

	2002	2003	2004	2005	2006	2007	2008	2009	2010
External Debt **% GDP**									
Emerging and Developing Economies	**36.60**	**35.14**	**32.33**	**28.91**	**27.39**	**27.70**	**24.49**	**27.30**	**24.68**
Africa: Sub-Sahara	62.01	52.13	44.63	34.17	25.85	24.60	22.00	24.96	21.86
Central and Eastern Europe	50.66	51.06	49.84	45.65	52.63	56.50	54.38	69.18	65.59
Commonwealth of Independent States	45.83	44.19	38.46	35.96	35.80	39.88	33.41	45.02	38.92
Developing Asia	25.66	23.72	22.31	20.67	19.29	17.29	14.94	15.30	14.53
ASEAN-5									
Middle East and North Africa	33.05	31.24	29.28	33.29	31.92	36.24	30.83	36.23	30.56
Latin America and the Caribbean	42.25	41.99	36.79	27.99	23.85	22.75	20.18	22.72	21.30
Current Account **% GDP**									
Emerging and Developing Economies	**1.21**	**1.97**	**2.47**	**4.19**	**5.18**	**4.17**	**3.70**	**1.89**	**1.50**
Africa: Sub-Sahara	-3.87	-3.02	-1.61	-0.44	4.32	1.19	-0.16	-1.71	-1.10
Central and Eastern Europe	-2.99	-4.03	-5.40	-4.97	-6.63	-8.04	-7.87	-2.48	-3.75
Commonwealth of Independent States	6.53	6.23	8.20	8.72	7.40	4.20	4.93	2.59	3.83
Developing Asia	2.52	2.81	2.65	4.16	6.01	6.91	5.86	4.09	2.99
ASEAN-5	3.67	4.03	2.88	1.96	4.87	5.18	2.65	5.10	3.22
Middle East and North Africa	4.06	7.31	10.35	17.23	18.62	15.16	15.32	2.65	4.35
Latin America and the Caribbean	-0.89	0.49	0.98	1.38	1.60	0.41	-0.68	-0.55	-1.20
Reserve Accumulation **% GDP**									
Emerging and Developing Economies	**2.30**	**4.26**	**4.54**	**5.40**	**5.91**	**7.69**	**3.89**	**2.77**	**3.26**
Africa: Sub-Sahara	0.37	0.31	3.57	3.63	4.33	3.54	1.87	-0.86	0.37
Central and Eastern Europe	1.22	1.30	1.27	3.85	2.95	1.85	0.32	1.42	1.87
Commonwealth of Independent States	3.26	5.72	7.09	7.68	9.82	9.84	-1.24	0.49	3.68
Developing Asia	4.18	6.21	6.90	6.83	7.36	10.17	6.79	5.71	4.68
ASEAN-5									
Middle East and North Africa	2.51	6.51	5.67	10.00	10.05	12.90	8.30	-1.34	3.00
Latin America and the Caribbean	-0.08	1.78	1.02	1.25	1.62	3.63	1.18	1.29	1.60

Source: IMF, World Economic Outlook database.

America relative to most other regions but, as we have already pointed out, they were a break with the region's own past.

Unfortunately, no equivalent picture can be drawn for fiscal indicators. However, for those countries for which data are available, large fiscal deficits were generally infrequent at the onset of the crisis. Again, Central and Eastern Europe and, in this case, major South Asian countries stand out as having the weakest stances, and elsewhere there were individual countries with large central government deficits generally mixed with high levels of public-sector debt, such as in Egypt and Jordan in the Middle East.

Thanks to these factors, domestic demand policies were more broadly available in the developing world than during previous crises, but the policy space to use them was unevenly distributed and, in any case, their potential effect is limited in open economies. As a result, such policies were more powerful in the less open economies, most of which are large ones. For this reason, Brazil, China, and India resonate in all discussions as the most successful cases of policies of this kind during the recent crises. Some countries were more reluctant to adopt strong countercyclical policies due to the perception that they could risk downgrades in credit ratings and thus future access to financial markets, or because they would mean a reversal of what countries perceived as being hard-won achievements, particularly in the fiscal area. Among large developing economies, Mexico and Turkey are examples of relatively mild and lagged countercyclical responses associated with concerns of this type (see text that follows).

Due to improved external balance sheets, the room for monetary policies to compensate for the sudden stop in external financing, using the large foreign exchange reserves in the hands of developing countries, was broadly available. Monetary policy in most countries did indeed follow the lead of industrial countries in reducing interest rates, though this generally came with a lag of a few months, and the magnitude of the reduction was in several cases smaller than those of industrial countries. Central bank credit lines to domestic financial institutions were sometimes made available, but a more common expansionary policy was the reduction in reserve requirements (on bank deposits), an instrument that has been largely discontinued in industrial economies but that is still relevant in developing countries. More novel in terms of central bank financing was the use of foreign exchange reserves to compensate for the reduction in external financing by making credit lines in foreign currency available to exporters and to other private firms with a demand for foreign exchange, including to cover losses in derivative contracts. Central banks also used their accumulated foreign exchange reserves to help stabilize strong depreciation pressures on their currencies, but this was generally mixed with exchange rate flexibility in countries that had been practicing floating—which is generally dirty and, in some cases, quite dirty. Brazil was a remarkable case of all these types of central bank interventions (Barbosa, 2010). A strong external balance sheet was the crucial factor making such interventions possible.

These expansionary measures had, in any case, limited effects on domestic demand in the more open economies and were in some cases counteracted by the worldwide credit crunch in private financing, which was transmitted with considerable intensity to domestic banking sectors in several developing countries. This generated a similar situation to that of industrial countries, in which expansionary monetary policies were unable to counteract the private-sector credit crunch. Bank financing is, of course, more important in developing economies than it is in industrial ones, but even in the latter the recovery in bond financing was not matched by a similar trend in bank financing.

In developing countries, those whose domestic banks depended on external funding were the most affected. The credit crunches of Central and Eastern Europe as well as the Middle East are a result of this type of dependence (Calvo, 2010). In Latin America, Chile and, to a much lesser extent, Peru are similar cases (ECLAC, 2009). Indeed, Chile is a remarkable case of strong countercyclical fiscal and monetary policies that were relatively powerless in the face of both a domestic credit crunch and high trade openness. In contrast to this pattern, and in a paradoxical twist of history, countries that had maintained large public financial sectors were at an advantage to undertake expansionary credit policies and compensate the private-sector credit crunch. Brazil, China, and India were able to use their public-sector banks to support their recovery, and in a particularly aggressive way in China (which started to reverse this policy in early 2010).

Due to the high dependence of their banking sectors on external financing, Russia and several Gulf countries are extraordinary examples of a very peculiar macroeconomic pattern: central banks largely and correctly absorbed the excess supply of foreign exchange generated by private external financing during the boom; in turn, during the crisis, as capital flights and the domestic credit crunch ensued, central banks came to the rescue to supply foreign exchange.

Domestic financial crises were infrequent during the recent turmoil in developing, including emerging, economies. Russia and Nigeria are probably the most important exceptions. In Central and Eastern European countries, where banks are largely foreign-owned, the crisis was in a sense "exported" to the home countries of the banks and became part of the broader picture of financial crises in Western Europe. Among these countries, those with flexible exchange rates were also the major cases of currency mismatches in domestic portfolios that generated massive losses when crisis struck and currencies depreciated (as we will show, those with fixed rates faced other problems). Elsewhere, although this pattern was less frequent than in the past, private sectors in some countries accumulated growing foreign exchange risk during the boom through borrowing abroad or, in a more recent fashion, derivative operations. In this case, counteracting the sudden stop in external financing depended heavily on the capacity of central banks to compensate these trends, which was essentially dependent, again, on the availability of foreign exchange reserves.

The worst cases, where monetary policy turned overtly pro-cyclical, were associated with defense-of-currency boards, a pattern present in some countries of the European periphery (the Baltic countries and Bulgaria). Attempts by central banks to smooth depreciation pressures by raising interest rates were much less frequent than during past crises, but not entirely absent.

In the area of fiscal policy, responses were very diverse. Perhaps the most important fact to emphasize is that East Asia was by far the most active region. The UN's *World Economic Situation and Prospects 2010* provides summary estimates of fiscal stimulus packages for fifty-five economies around the world (UN, 2010a, table I.4). An interesting conclusion is that the largest cluster of highly expansionary fiscal policies was concentrated in East Asia: 7 out of the 13 developing economies' packages amounting to more than 5 percent of GDP (China, Thailand, Hong Kong, South Korea, Malaysia, Singapore, and Vietnam);[10] even countries in this region with not particularly strong fiscal positions (such as Cambodia and Laos) joined in this trend. Most South Asian countries also ran strongly expansionary fiscal policies, despite their initial high deficit and debt levels. But otherwise there are significant differences. In sub-Saharan Africa, for example, Kasekende et al. (2010) indicate that some countries (Kenya, Mauritius, South Africa, Tanzania, and Uganda) ran very active countercyclical fiscal policies, while others did not (e.g., Botswana). In Latin America, Chile ran the clearest countercyclical fiscal policy, and other countries (Argentina, Costa Rica, Paraguay, and Uruguay) also had expansions in public-sector spending of over 2 percent of GDP, but others reduced such spending (Bolivia, the Dominican Republic, Ecuador, and Venezuela) (ECLAC, 2009, chap. 2). Obviously, the stimulus measures taken in 2009 mean that the space for further countercyclical policies has shrunk. This is particularly true in countries with initial high public-sector debt ratios, with South Asian countries perhaps being the most important example.

The Latin American case actually reflects the quite different performance of economies that are highly dependent on fiscal revenues from natural resources: Chile, on the one hand, which saved a significant amount of the windfall fiscal revenues during the boom, versus three economies that largely spent such windfall revenues (Bolivia, Ecuador, and Venezuela). In other parts of the world, savings of such revenues during the boom allowed for large countercyclical spending during the crisis. Two important cases are Kazakhstan and Saudi Arabia, the two countries that competed with China as having the largest fiscal packages during the crisis, according to the aforementioned UN report. It should be noted, though, that as most developing countries were expanding public-sector spending at rapid rates during the boom, the expansionary effect of fiscal measures may have actually *declined* relative to the boom years even if fiscal spending continued to increase during the crisis. This is the average performance of Latin America, where fiscal policy had generally been expansionary during the boom (Ocampo, 2009) and government consumption actually generated a stronger expansionary effect up to the third quarter of 2008 than thereafter (see ECLAC, 2009, figure I.11).

The picture that emerges is, therefore, one in which developing countries *did* have larger room for maneuver to adopt countercyclical policies than in the past, due particularly to their improved external balance sheets. The major regional exception was Central and Eastern Europe, where the traditional mix of weak external and fiscal indicators and domestic financing that was highly dependent on external funding still prevailed. This is the familiar combination that, as in the past, generated significant vulnerabilities in the face of the dramatic shock experienced during the global financial crisis. More generally, however, and again with some exceptions, even those developing countries that had more limited space to adopt countercyclical policies or were unwilling to use the space they had at least could *avoid the traditional pro-cyclical macroeconomic policies* that were typical of past crises. Avoidance of high domestic interest rates was, in turn, one factor contributing to the relative absence of banking crises this time.

PERFORMANCE: A GENERAL LOOK

Despite the strength and the greater frequency of countercyclical poli-cies, the shock was severe nearly everywhere. One striking way to summa-rize the available information is in noting that 73 out of the 125 developing and transition economies for which the UN provides data, experienced a reduction in per capita GDP in 2009 versus only 11 in 2007. In turn, only 13 had per capita GDP growth of more than 3 percent in 2009, the thresh-old identified by the UN as vital to achieve large reductions in poverty, versus 86 economies in 2007 (UN, 2010a, table I.2).

Table 2.7 summarizes the performance of developing and transition economies versus industrial countries in 2009 as well as the magnitude of the slowdown vis-à-vis the boom years from 2003 to 2007, according to UN estimates and regional breakdown. Several issues are worth empha-sizing. The first is that the worst performance by far was that of the transi-tion economies and of the CIS in particular, both in terms of contraction of GDP in 2009 and the slowdown from the boom years: a striking 14 percentage points! The transition economies that are members of the EU (all new members excluding Malta and Cyprus) show the second stron-gest slowdowns, though the contraction in 2009 is not as bad, due to the growth of Poland, the largest among them.

The developing countries as a whole experienced moderate growth and a weaker slowdown than the industrial world, but this aggregate figure is biased by the good performance of the two Asian giants, China and India. Another, and perhaps the most positive, outcome from the point of view of meeting the MDGs was that the least-developed countries experi-enced a better performance than the average for the developing world (3.9 percent), with the performance of the largest of them (Bangladesh) being particularly positive. This is consistent with the fact that the two regions with the highest incidence of extreme poverty, sub-Saharan Africa and South Asia, also had a better-than-average performance, with South Asia being the best-performing region in the world. Among the regions with a large share of middle-income countries, North Africa did the best, while East Asia, excluding China, Western Asia (largely due to the strong Turk-ish recession), and Latin America (largely affected, in turn, by the very poor performance of Mexico) experienced stagnation or recession. Indeed, the worst-performing economies belong to the last two developing re-gions (Turkey and Mexico) or are transition economies (the three Baltic countries, Russia, and Ukraine), though a few belong to others (e.g.,

Table 2.7   Growth of Developing and Emerging Economies

	Average 2003–2007	2008	2009	2010	2009 vs. 2003–2007
Developed Economies	**2.7**	**0.4**	**-3.5**	**2.3**	**-6.2**
Developing Countries*	**7.2**	**5.3**	**2.4**	**7.1**	**-4.8**
Africa	5.9	5.0	2.3	4.7	-3.6
North Africa	5.1	4.9	2.8	4.6	-2.3
Sub-Saharan Africa (excluding Nigeria and South Africa)	7.0	6.2	3.1	5.3	-3.9
East and South Asia	8.3	6.2	5.0	8.4	-3.3
East Asia	8.4	6.1	4.9	8.8	-3.5
China	11.3	9.0	9.1	10.1	-2.2
East Asia (excluding China)	5.6	3.0	0.0	7.2	-5.6
South Asia	8.0	6.5	5.5	6.9	-2.5
India	9.0	7.3	6.7	8.4	-2.3
South Asia (excluding India)	5.9	4.8	3.0	3.7	-2.9
Western Asia	6.6	4.3	-1.1	5.4	-7.7
Western Asia (excluding Israel and Turkey)	6.4	6.6	0.8	4.4	-5.5
Latin America and the Caribbean	5.4	4.0	-2.1	5.6	-7.5
South America	6.1	5.3	-0.3	6.3	-6.3
Mexico and Central America	4.1	1.7	-5.9	4.8	-10.0
Caribbean	7.1	3.8	1.3	2.9	-5.8
Economies in Transition	**7.6**	**5.4**	**-6.7**	**3.8**	**-14.3**
Southeastern Europe	5.4	4.3	-3.7	0.1	-9.1
Commonwealth of Independent States	7.8	5.5	-7.0	4.1	-14.8
New EU Member States	**5.7**	**3.9**	**-3.6**	**1.9**	**-9.3**
Memorandum items:					
Least developed countries	8.0	7.1	3.9	5.1	-4.0

Notes: Country groups are calculated as a weighted average of individual country growth rates of GDP, where weights are based on GDP in 2005 prices and exchange rates.
*Covering countries that account for 98 percent of the population of all developing countries.

Source: UN/DESA, based on data of UN Statistics Division and IMF, *International Financial Statistics.*

mineral-exporting Botswana). Some East Asian economies also experienced a strong initial contraction but were able to largely compensate with growth in the second semester of 2009.

The worst-performing countries and regions had two entirely different features. In the transition economies, the dominant feature was the presence of the traditional macroeconomic and financial vulnerabilities emphasized previously. Among the developing countries, it was a high dependence on manufacturing exports. In this regard, it is interesting to see the average performance of different developing countries according to dominant specialization patterns (according to measures of revealed comparative advantage). As emphasized by Ocampo et al. (2009, chap. 4), among others, there has been a superior, long-term growth performance of economies with export patterns dominated by high and medium technological content. Consistent with the latter observation, and despite booming commodity prices, growth was somewhat slower in natural-resource dependent economies than in low-, medium-, and high-technology exporters during the 2003–2007 boom (see Table 2.8). Interestingly, however, high- and mid-tech exporters suffered more heavily from the collapse of international trade during the Great Recession, while exporters of commodities and natural resource-intensive manufactures, on average, performed much better.

The crisis was obviously reflected in employment conditions and poverty. However, the dramatic effects of the crisis that were initially feared never materialized. There were, of course, major job losses in manufacturing export sectors throughout the developing world. There were also rises in unemployment, as well as in informality—vulnerable employment in current ILO terminology—a much more important problem in developing countries. Large increases in unemployment in the developing and emerging economies were concentrated in Central and Eastern Europe and in some Latin American countries but tended to normalize fast in the latter region (ILO, 2010, 2011; UN, 2010a). Similarly, the crisis halted the fairly rapid improvement in poverty levels that had been taking place during the boom years, but there was no major increase in poverty levels, as was initially feared. According to ILO's estimates of the working poor (ILO, 2011), there was a slight increase in poverty levels in 2009 in Latin America and in the transition economies but not in other regions; actually,

Table 2.8 Average Growth Rate according to Specialization Patterns (Unweighted Averages)

	2003–2007 (%)	2008 (%)	2009 (%)	2010 (%)	2009 vs. 2003–2007 (%)
High-Tech Manufactures	6.08	3.92	−0.38	5.62	−6.46
Mid-Tech Manufactures	6.00	4.52	0.61	4.97	−5.39
Low-Tech Manufactures	5.95	5.42	0.94	3.22	−5.01
Natural Resource-Intensive Manufactures	4.63	5.59	1.82	4.64	−2.82
Primary Products	4.45	5.73	1.57	4.45	−2.88

Sources: Growth rates according to UN database (see Table 2.7), unweighted averages of countries in each category. Specialization patterns according to Ocampo et al. (2009), chap. 4.

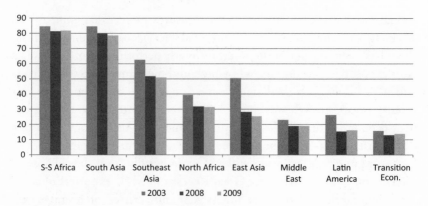

Figure 2.6   Working Poor (Proportion of Workers under US$2 a Day)

Sources: ILO (2011); Cuadro A14.b.

due to the rapid renewal of growth in China, poverty levels in East Asia continued to decline, though at a slower pace than during the boom (see Figure 2.6).

The UN and World Bank estimates of increases in extreme poverty are of small enough magnitudes as to not significantly change expectations for reaching the MDGs' objective of reducing extreme poverty levels by half between 1990 and 2015. According to current projections (Table 2.9), this objective would be reached for the world as a whole and most regions, but it would not be met for sub-Saharan Africa. In any case, according to these projections, the pace of reduction of the proportion of people below US$2 a day is slower, particularly in the two poorest regions of the world. The risk of reduced ODA (see text that follows) indicates that other MDG targets may be affected.

REGIONAL PERFORMANCE

The Asian financial crisis of the late 1990s and the response to that crisis by international capital markets and official agencies, notably the U.S. Treasury and the IMF, continued to reverberate during the boom years that followed and during the global financial crisis itself. The heavy price that many East Asian economies paid for the pro-cyclicality of finance and of the policy conditions on which international assistance was provided arguably contributed to massive "self-insurance" in that region during the boom years, a factor contributing to the buildup of

Table 2.9 Poverty in Developing Countries by Region

Regions or Countries	1990	2005	2015
Percentage of the Population Living on Less Than US$1.25/Day			
East Asia and the Pacific	54.7	16.8	5.9
China	60.2	15.9	5.1
Europe and Central Asia	2.0	3.7	1.7
Latin America and the Caribbean	11.3	8.2	5.0
Middle East and North Africa	4.3	3.6	1.8
South Asia	51.7	40.3	22.8
India	51.3	41.6	20.3
Sub-Saharan Africa	57.6	50.9	38.0
Total	**41.7**	**25.2**	**15.0**
Percentage of the Population Living on Less Than US$2/Day			
East Asia and the Pacific	79.8	38.7	19.4
China	84.6	36.3	16.0
Europe and Central Asia	6.9	8.9	5.0
Latin America and the Caribbean	19.7	16.6	11.1
Middle East and North Africa	19.7	16.9	8.3
South Asia	82.7	73.9	57.0
India	82.6	75.6	58.3
Sub-Saharan Africa	76.2	73.0	59.6
Total	**63.2**	**47.0**	**33.7**

Source: World Bank (2010).

global imbalances. However, it also prevented the recession from turning into another Great Depression—as massive reserve accumulation provided ample space for active and large countercyclical macroeconomic policies in East Asia.

While there is universal agreement that East Asia, led by China, is leading the recovery of the world economy, there is a particularly pronounced and often confusing difference in the array of estimates of growth trends in what is called "East Asia" in documents of various international organizations: 5.0 percent growth in 2009, according to the UN regional breakdown shown in Table 2.7, versus 7.4 percent according to the World Bank.[11] The difference results from the exclusion by the World Bank of the high-income Asian economies of Hong Kong, Singapore, South Korea, and Taiwan, all of which went into a recession in 2009.

Given the high level of integration of the region into the global economy, East Asia was affected early and substantially by the recession, particularly through sharp falls in trade and industrial production between September 2008 and March 2009; China shared the trade recession but was able to avoid a contraction of industrial production. Strong countercyclical fiscal, monetary, and credit policies helped turn this region into the major engine of world economic recovery from the second quarter of 2009, propelling also an impressive rebound of financial markets (stock exchanges, bond issuance, and initial public offerings, though not syndicated loans). Given its large domestic market and smaller ratio of trade to GDP, these policies were more effective in China, but aggressive expansionary fiscal and monetary policies in the rest of the region also contributed to the recovery. This led to some large fiscal deficits in some economies, with the biggest in Vietnam (around 9 percent of GDP) and Malaysia (nearly 8 percent federal and 6 percent consolidated budget deficits), but the largest fiscal turnaround in the region was in Singapore, where a fiscal surplus of 9.7 percent of GDP in 2007 shrank to 5.3 percent in 2008 and turned into a deficit of 0.8 percent in 2009. Growing regional trade integration in recent years also helped the recovery to spread quickly from one country to another. For the year as a whole, most countries experienced a recession. In addition to China, Indonesia and Vietnam proved particularly resilient.

Chinese policies included a massive fiscal package for 2009 and 2010 that was announced early on, in November 2008, equivalent to some 14 percent of GDP. This implied a 22.1 percent increase in total government expenditures (central plus local) in 2009, though only a modest fiscal deficit of a little over 3 percent of GDP. Given excess capacity in the industrial sector, much of the stimulus package was directed at investment in infrastructure. It was accompanied by massive credit expansion and a highly expansionary monetary policy, essentially a sharp stop in the issuance of central bank bills that had been used in previous years to sterilize the massive accumulation of foreign exchange reserves (Yu, 2010). Fears that this aggressive policy would lead to asset price bubbles, especially in housing, led authorities to adopt policies to limit the growth of domestic lending in early 2010.

As noted previously, South Asia was the best-performing region in the world. India served as the second locomotive after China for containing the global recession. Excluding India, South Asia's average growth rate in 2009 was 3.0 percent, according to UN data, which include Iran, and 6.2 percent, according to World Bank data, which do not. Aside from India, Bangladesh, the largest least-developed country, was also resilient and continued to grow relatively fast, at 5.7 percent; Nepal, another least-developed country in the region, also grew, though at a lower rate. By and large, countries in this region have been very measured in both their trade and financial liberalization and hence with their integration into the world economy. Capital accounts and financial sectors have been deregulated with caution and with wariness about exposing them to the procyclicality of financial markets. Though inflation has been modest, fiscal positions have tended to be weak, financed for the most part with domestic non-bank borrowing (especially India) and concessional or long-term external financing (especially in Bangladesh). This is also the region most dependent on remittances from the Gulf countries, which were fairly resilient during the crisis.

For all these factors, this was the region most likely to resist the exogenous shocks that the global financial crisis generated. Nonetheless, growth did slow sharply and active countercyclical macroeconomic policies had to be employed to prevent a greater collapse. This is particularly true of India, but also of Bangladesh and Sri Lanka. It took the form of a steep reduction in interest rates as well as expansionary fiscal policies. India's stubbornly high fiscal deficits, in the vicinity of 9–10 percent of GDP for much of the 1990s and early 2000s, had begun to decline to closer to 6 percent before the crisis hit. The countercyclical measures adopted led to a reversal of this trend, and the deficit was back to more than 9 percent. It began to withdraw this fiscal stimulus in early 2010.

Pakistan is a notable exception to these trends, as its macroeconomic balances had deteriorated seriously in the couple of years preceding the global crisis, leaving no room for countercyclical policies when the crisis hit and requiring support from the IMF. But even this country maintained a positive, though modest rate of growth. Sri Lanka, the most open economy in the region, and, as in Pakistan, having a domestic conflict and an IMF program, also slowed significantly.

As a region, Africa came third after East Asia and South Asia in terms of growth. This average includes the fair performance of both North Africa and sub-Saharan Africa, though in the latter case with an average decline in per capita incomes, given rapid population growth. North Africa's fair performance reflected in part bumper harvests in Algeria and Morocco, as well as fiscal stimuli in Egypt, Morocco, and Tunisia that focused mainly on public investment in infrastructure. The stimulus package in Morocco also included state guarantees for credit to leading export industries and in Egypt a significant easing of monetary policy. Morocco and Egypt were also hit by falling remittances and Tunisia, Morocco, and Egypt by decline in tourism. All these cases reflect the transmission of the European crisis.

For the first time in about a decade, per capita incomes in sub-Saharan Africa dropped and brought an end to the recovery from the most prolonged economic decline that any developing region has experienced since records have been kept—a period we referred to as a "lost quarter century."[12] The rapid growth had reflected booming commodity prices and debt write-offs, above all, with some support from growing official development assistance, rising remittances, FDI in extractive industries, and, to a much smaller extent, private financial flows. The degree to which policy reforms also contributed, and in what particular way, remains a matter of controversy.[13] Go and Page (2008:2–3) address the issue of the extent to which the growth spurt commencing in the late 1990s can be attributed to positive exogenous shocks and to policy reforms. They argue that while booming export prices helped, "growth acceleration . . . is due not only to favorable terms of trade, but also better policy. . . . Nonetheless, the sustainability of that growth is fragile because economic fundamentals such as savings, investment, productivity, and export diversification remain stagnant."

Improved macroeconomic management and exchange rate policies meant, in particular, that both the fiscal and the foreign exchange positions of most countries in sub-Saharan Africa were much better than during previous global crises. This provided the space for several countries to pursue countercyclical monetary and fiscal policies, with significant exceptions (IMF, 2009; Kasekende et al., 2010). IMF advice and conditionality also exhibited a welcome turnaround from their previous pro-cyclical bias. As a result of all these factors, the effects of the Great Recession on Africa were less pronounced than during past crises. Nonetheless, out of the forty-four sub-Saharan African countries that the UN monitors, seventeen experienced a decline in per capita GDP (UN, 2011, table I.2).

Like other developing regions, the intensity and relative importance of the trade, finance, and remittance shocks varied across different countries according to their individual circumstances, in particular, the degree and pattern of integration into the world economy. In the trade area, terms of trade shocks were more important than falling volumes, with agricultural exporters facing a weaker shock than oil and mineral exporters. The decline in exports not only affected the current account of the balance of payments but also dampened budgetary revenues and widened fiscal deficits. The worst affected were the middle-income economies because of their greater global integration, especially in financial markets. Sub-Saharan Africa's biggest economy, South Africa, suffered a recession, notwithstanding the adoption of an important fiscal stimulus package, leading the subregion of Southern Africa to experience the worst performance. West Africa's GDP growth slowed sharply but outpaced population growth. In Nigeria, the region's second-largest economy, agriculture more than offset the decline in industrial and oil production. East Africa's growth was the fastest among sub-Saharan Africa's subregions, reflecting, above all, the continuing dynamism of Ethiopia (at 9.9 percent it was the fastest-growing economy in sub-Saharan Africa in 2009; it had been the second in the preceding three years, after Angola, where growth was oil-led).

The remaining regions in the developing world experienced a contraction of GDP. In Western Asia, this reflects, above all, the steep Turkish recession. Indeed, excluding this country and Israel (which is included in this group by the UN and experienced a moderate recession), the region posted small positive growth. In Turkey, dependence on foreign capital flows, combined with a high initial current-account deficit, proved devastating in an environment characterized by the world financial crisis and a collapse of world trade, in this case imports in Western Europe. In this context, countercyclical policies were undertaken, though with a lag that reflected the initial fears of inflation and reversing the hard-won fiscal gains made earlier in the decade (Özatay, 2010; Uygur, 2010). In the Gulf countries, the dominant factor was the credit crunch generated by a high dependence of the banking system on external funding (Calvo, 2010). This factor, together with cuts in OPEC oil quotas, had negative effects on the Gulf countries, but they were compensated by very expansionary fiscal policies, which operated as the main engine of demand expansion. In turn, the resilience of migration flows from the Gulf countries helped non-oil countries in the region weather the storm (as in South Asia).

Latin America was, no doubt, better prepared than in the past to face the financial shock, due to improved external balance sheets and fiscal accounts. However, macroeconomic policies during the boom, and particularly fiscal spending, had been pro-cyclical in most countries; and although current accounts were in positive territory until 2007, this hides the fact that countries were spending the windfall generated by high commodity prices and the underlying current accounts were deteriorating (Inter-American Development Bank, 2008; Ocampo, 2009). In some cases, particularly of economies that had been running very expansionary fiscal policies and are dependent on natural resources for their fiscal revenues, fiscal policy turned contractionary in 2009 (Bolivia, Ecuador, and

Venezuela). On average, however, countries kept the public spending machine running, or even speeded it up based on discretionary decisions or following explicit countercyclical fiscal rules, particularly in the case of Chile (Ffrench-Davis, 2010).

Monetary policies also became expansionary, and in some cases highly so, based on reduction of central bank interest rates and reserve requirements, but generally with a lag, given the fears that had been generated early in 2008 by rising inflation due to the food price shock. So, in general, monetary policies became expansionary only after January 2009 (Colombia was the first to take important steps in December 2008). As indicated earlier, in Chile and in some other countries, expansionary monetary policies were unable to compensate for the credit crunch generated by dependence of domestic credit on external funding.

Dependence on exports of manufactured goods and some services (tourism), especially to the United States, as well as remittances, amplified the impact of the crisis in the northern part of the region, whereas in South America the collapse of commodity prices had stronger initial effects, but their rapid turnaround also helped a strong recovery. In a sense, as Ocampo (2009) has argued, due to its better financial strength, this was for Latin America more of a trade crisis than a financial one. The most interesting contrast in this region is between the patterns of the two largest economies: Brazil and Mexico. The first adopted an East Asia-type aggressive expansionary package, which included aggressive monetary and credit policies, including large injections of credit in foreign currency through the central bank and of domestic credit through the public-sector banks, and a moderate fiscal package (Barbosa, 2010). In contrast, fears of credit rating downgrades in Mexico caused backtracking during 2009 on the initially moderately expansionary fiscal policy, and although monetary policy followed with a lag like that of the U.S. Fed, it lacked the very aggressive expansionary credit policies of Brazil.

The last two regional groups, which comprise the transition economies of Central and Eastern Europe, and Central Asia were the most vulnerable to the financial crisis; one might even call them "models of vulnerability," reminiscent of Latin American patterns in the past. These were the countries characterized by domestic financial sectors heavily dependent on foreign capital flows, high levels of debt (especially external debt), substantial currency mismatches in both corporate and household balance sheets, and, in some cases, limited or no exchange rate flexibility.

The prime examples are the three Baltic countries, which collectively experienced a catastrophic collapse in GDP (an average of −15 percent).

Among the transition economies that are members of the EU, only Poland experienced moderate growth, due to lower dependence of its banking sector on external funding, relatively lower dependence on exports, and the resilience of its agriculture and services sectors. The heavy reliance of the banking sector (comprised mainly of foreign banks) in several of these countries on foreign capital flows paralyzed domestic financing as the flows were reversed and non-performing loans shot up. They were, to some extent, victims but also, given their heavy dependence on Western European banks operating in their countries, significant protagonists of the banking crisis of Western Europe. Many of these countries were also severely constrained in their ability to pursue countercyclical policies by their desire to join the euro zone (and thus the fiscal and exchange-rate targets that that entails) or the currency boards anchored in the euro. Also, some countries (e.g., Hungary and Latvia) were subjected to procyclical conditionality for financial assistance from the EU and the IMF (a pattern followed in the programs for the economies of Greece, Ireland, and Portugal in 2010 and 2011).

The remaining transition economies, and particularly the CIS countries, experienced the worst performance of any region in the developing world, dominated by steep contractions in the two largest economies, Russia and Ukraine. Many of these countries also shared the vulnerabilities of the new EU member states, emanating from the nexus of a very high reliance on private foreign capital inflows, large current-account deficits, and external debt, as well as currency mismatches. Several, such as Russia, Kazakhstan, and Ukraine, were also hit by sharp declines in the prices of oil and metals. The deep crisis of Russia was also transmitted to several CIS countries through trade and remittances from migrants residing in that country.

The combination of pro-cyclicality of foreign capital flows and falling oil prices overwhelmed the effects of the stimulus provided in Russia, which was reflected in a sharp change in the fiscal balance from a surplus of 4.3 percent of GDP in 2008 to a deficit of 7 percent in 2009, as well as repeated cuts in central bank interest rates, which were brought down to effectively zero in real terms. Ukraine, along with Armenia and the Baltic countries, experienced the worst economic collapse in the world. In Ukraine, political tensions and the related halting implementation of an

IMF program, and the consequent postponement of the release of a large tranche, contributed to this outcome. Some of the small, lower-income economies fared somewhat better, due in some cases to less integration into the global economy or through countercyclical policies supported by the IMF. As in the case of several of the transition economies, for members of the EU, an explicit or implicit peg to the euro became a constraint on monetary easing in most of Southeastern Europe, with Serbia as the major exception.

OFFICIAL FINANCING

The crisis generated a strong response in terms of increased official financing for developing and transition economies. Nonetheless, this response, which was led by the G-20, had a significant bias toward IMF funding, on the one hand, and toward middle-income countries, on the other, with many manifestations. It was reflected, first, in the allocation of IMF Special Drawing Rights, the single-largest response to the crisis, in which low-income countries received only about one-fifth of that given to developing countries, which represented slightly less than 40 percent of the overall allocation (US$250 billion). Similarly, IMF lending supported primarily middle- and high-income economies. Second, only a fairly modest amount of increased lending by multilateral development banks (MDBs) benefited these countries. Third, and crucially, ODA has only increased in a modest way, essentially as a result of the contraction in the gross national income (GNI) of the EU countries, the major source of aid at the global level. The low-income countries were, therefore, the Cinderellas of the G-20 response to the crisis!

From the point of view of broader development objectives, it was important to increase support to middle-income countries, given their weight in the world economy as well as the large number of poor people who live in them.[14] However, it was even more important to increase support to low-income countries, which face significantly more challenges in achieving the MDGs. The fact that the G-20 has taken far less significant initiatives for low-income countries may relate to their lack of representation in the G-20 itself—one of the several problems that this ad hoc mechanism of representation faces.

Another major problem was that increased lending by International Finance Institutions (IFIs) was dwarfed by the massive fall in private flows noted earlier. Therefore, the countercyclical role of IFIs, though valuable, was insufficient. In fact, if we return to Table 2.3, it can be seen that net official financing in 2009 was only US$85 billion, about one-third of the net private financial outflows in that and the previous year (an outflow of US$261 billion). In the critical months following the Lehman collapse, the problems were, of course, even worse. As that table indicates, net official flows were relatively more important in the most affected regions: the two regions dominated by transition economies, as well as to Latin America and the Caribbean and Africa.

IMF financing is analyzed in the parallel chapter in this volume by Griffith-Jones and Ocampo (2012), so we concentrate here on development financing. One of the most positive trends before the crisis had been the trends in ODA, a step not only in accord with old commitments by industrialized countries but also critical in meeting the MDGs. The UN Conference on Financing for Development, held in Monterrey, Mexico, in 2002, was the crucial turning point. ODA by members of the Development Assistance Committee (DAC) of the OECD, which had declined in the 1990s from around 0.33 percent to 0.22 percent of GNI and stagnated since 1997 at that level, started to increase in a more or less systematic way, excluding debt relief. The 2005 commitments made in the Gleneagles G-8 and in the UN Millennium +5 Summits further reinforced this trend. By 2008, ODA had increased to 0.31 percent of the GNI of DAC members. Efforts have also been made to improve the quality of aid in the context of the 2005 Paris Declaration on Aid Effectiveness and the 2008 Accra Accord.

The trend was also important in terms of the structure of the assistance provided. Whereas the initial increase up to 2005 concentrated on debt relief, which is, strictly speaking, not new aid and largely benefited two countries (Iraq and Nigeria), later increases represented new funds. Furthermore, technical cooperation, which is largely spent on personnel from donor countries, has also remained stagnant. Excluding these two components, bilateral aid tripled in dollar terms in the period 2003–2008, as contributions to multilateral institutions increased by almost 80 percent. Aid to Africa also increased sharply. Nonetheless, significant problems remain, including the fact that ODA has continued to fall short, not only of the commitment made since the 1960s in the UN (0.7 percent of the GNI of industrial countries) but even of the Gleneagles commitments made just six years ago. This is particularly true of aid to Africa, which, in 2008, was about US$20 billion below those more recent commitments. Aid has tended to concentrate in a few countries (Iraq and Afghanistan being among the largest recipients, which together account for about one-sixth of total aid) and has shown significant volatility at a country level.[15]

In this light, the recent trends are not entirely encouraging, as Table 2.10 indicates. ODA in 2010 stood only slightly above 2008 levels, despite the fact that it continued to modestly increase as a proportion of the GNI of DAC countries, to 0.33 percent. So the major reason for the slow growth in ODA is the reduction in the GNI of the EU. Indeed, most countries continued to increase the proportion of the GNI destined to ODA. There are, in fact, only three exceptions to this trend—Austria, Ireland, and Italy. Trends may worsen in the future as a result of the fiscal austerity packages being adopted by all industrial economies, although it is encouraging that European countries have continued to reiterate their commitment to reach the aid target, and in one major case (the United Kingdom), ODA was excluded from fiscal austerity measures.

Table 2.10 Official Development Assistance

	Total ODA (millions of dollars)			ODA (% of GNI)		
	2008	2010	2010 vs. 2008	2008	Current Projection 2010	2010 vs. 2008
Total DAC Countries	**121,954**	**128,728**	**6,774**	**0.31**	**0.33**	**0.02**
Total EU	**70,974**	**70,150**	**−824**	**0.43**	**0.49**	**0.06**
Austria	1,714	1,199	−515	0.43	0.37	−0.06
Belgium	2,386	3,000	615	0.47	0.70	0.23
Denmark	2,803	2,867	63	0.82	0.83	0.01
Finland	1,166	1,335	170	0.44	0.55	0.11
France[a]	10,908	12,916	2,008	0.39	0.46	0.07
Germany	13,981	12,723	−1,258	0.38	0.40	0.02
Greece	703	500	−203	0.20	0.21	0.01
Ireland	1,328	895	−433	0.58	0.52	−0.06
Italy	4,861	3,111	−1,750	0.22	0.20	−0.02
Luxembourg	415	399	−16	0.93	1.00	0.07
Netherlands	6,993	6,351	−642	0.80	0.80	0.00
Portugal	620	648	28	0.27	0.34	0.07
Spain	6,867	5,917	−950	0.44	0.51	0.07
Sweden	4,732	4,527	−205	0.98	1.03	0.05
United Kingdom	11,500	13,763	2,263	0.43	0.56	0.13
Australia	2,954	3,849	895	0.32	0.35	0.03
Canada	4,795	5,132	337	0.32	0.33	0.01
Japan	9,601	11,045	1,445	0.18	0.20	0.02
New Zealand	348	353	5	0.30	0.34	0.04
Norway	4,006	4,582	576	0.89	1.00	0.11
Switzerland	2,038	2,295	258	0.41	0.47	0.05
United States	26,437	30,154	3,718	0.18	0.20	0.01

Source: OECD/DAC. http://www.oecd.org/dac/stats/idsonline.

Regarding MDBs, the crisis demonstrated the crucial countercyclical role that they can play when private financial markets dry up. While the international community had emphasized the role that MDBs play in poverty reduction and the provision of global public goods, their counter-cyclical role had not been explicitly recognized. This lack of recognition caused many lessons from past experience to be missed, which indicated that, aside from provision of liquidity during crises, it is equally impor-tant to provide official long-term finance when private finance dries up during and after crises, particularly to maintain the dynamics of public-sector investment projects.

As Figure 2.7 and Table 2.11 indicate, the MDBs as a group signifi-cantly increased their lending commitments to developing and emerg-ing economies—by 71 percent in 2009 compared to 2008. Their dis-bursements also grew by 45 percent in the same year. This was an important countercyclical response, which moderated (though did not fully com-pensate for) the impact of the sharp decline of private flows to develop-ing countries. This helped soften the effect of the crisis on developing countries.

The response of the MDB system was partly constrained by the limita-tion of its capital (te Velde and Massa, 2009). In April 2009 the G-20 agreed to support the recapitalization of MDBs to enable increased lend-ing. Also in April 2009 the capital of the Asian Development Bank (ADB) increased by 200 percent to US$165 billion from US$55 billion.

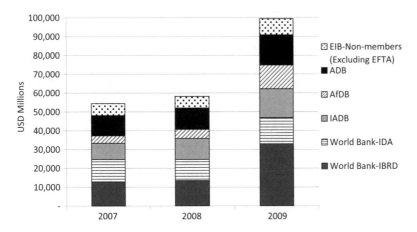

Figure 2.7   MDBs Commitments, 2007–2009, for All Countries

Source: Annual reports of the respective banks.

Table 2.11   MDBs Commitments and Disbursements, 2007–2010

ALL COUNTRIES (USD Millions)	2007	2008	2009	2010	Change 2008–2009
Commitments					
World Bank-IBRD	12,829	13,468	32,911	44,197	144%
World Bank-IDA	11,867	11,235	13,995	14,550	25%
IADB	8,577	11,085	15,278	n/a	38%
AfDB	4,004	4,928	12,636	n/a	156%
ADB	10,770	11,329	16,078	n/a	42%
EIB-Non-member States (Excluding EFTA)	6,390	6,145	8,597	n/a	40%
Total	**54,436**	**58,189**	**99,495**	**n/a**	**71%**
Disbursements					
World Bank-IBRD	11,055	10,490	18,564	28,855	77%
World Bank-IDA	8,579	9,160	9,219	11,460	1%
IADB	6,725	7,149	11,424	n/a	60%
AfDB	2,464	2,926	6,398	n/a	119%
ADB	7,858	9,724	12,946	n/a	33%
EIB-Non-member States (Excluding EFTA)	4,571	4,429	5,121	n/a	16%
Total	**41,252**	**43,878**	**63,672**	**n/a**	**45%**

Source: Annual reports of the respective banks.

The capital of the African Development Bank (AfDB) also increased, by 200 percent in 2009, and, despite the fact that expectations were not entirely fulfilled, that of the IADB increased by US$70 billion in its March 2010 annual meetings. In April 2010 the World Bank received a capital increase of US$86.2 billion, comprising a general capital increase of US$58.4 billion and a selective capital increase of US$27.8 billion; the latter was part of a broader reform aimed at increasing the share of the development countries in the capital and voice of the World Bank.

An interesting feature of the MDB response was that a number of large regional initiatives were launched, which mainly entailed working jointly with other institutions, notably the World Bank working with regional development banks (RDBs). Examples are the joint plans in the regions of Africa, Latin America and the Caribbean, and Central and Eastern Europe (see te Velde and Massa, 2009, for more details). In normal times the World Bank and the RDBs often compete among one another. The massive needs caused by the crisis pushed these institutions to collaborate instead. It would be valuable if this modus operandi could be maintained during normal times, especially for large projects, such as regional infrastructure.

The World Bank responded strongly to the crisis by almost doubling lending commitments, from US$25 billion in fiscal year 2008 (ending in

June) to US$47 billion in 2009, including the International Development Association (IDA). Two of the areas of increased attention were human development and social protection, though financial and private-sector development continued to represent a large share of new commitments. While the World Bank's statements also stressed infrastructure and support for small-and-medium enterprises (SMEs) as priority areas, it is less clear that this occurred on a sufficient scale.

A major issue was the World Bank's insufficient response to the needs of low-income countries. Indeed, whereas lending by the International Bank for Reconstruction and Development (IBRD) to middle-income countries increased in 2009 by US$19.4 billion, or 144 percent, IDA lending to low-income countries rose by US$2.8 billion, or 25 percent (Table 2.11). The proposal, presented at the end of 2009, to create a US$1.3 billion IDA Crisis Response Facility, to disburse IDA funds for protecting core spending on health, education, safety nets, and infrastructure was a step forward, but it started only as a small pilot, and resources will not be additional to existing IDA monies.

The problem of limited attention to low-income countries was also present in other MDBs. Indeed, if we look at MDBs as a group (see Table 2.12), the share of lending commitments to low-income countries, as proportion of the total, fell from 32 percent in 2007 to 28 percent in 2008 and declined further to 22 percent in 2009. For the European Investment Bank (EIB), such lending actually fell. The relative neglect in the response of MDBs is a weakness in an otherwise impressive countercyclical performance.

The dynamics of commitments were not reflected, however, in disbursements. In the case of the World Bank, the increase in IBRD disbursements

Table 2.12   MDBs Commitments for Low-income Countries, 2007–2009

	2007	2008	2009	Change 2008–2009
World Bank-IBRD	-	-	-	
World Bank-IDA	11,867	11,235	13,995	25%
IADB	220	245	278	13%
AfDB	1,577	2,401	2,781	16%
ADB	3,166	1,765	4,066	130%
EIB-Non-member States	701	406	539	33%
Total	**17,531**	**16,052**	**21,659**	**35%**
As % of "All Country" Commitments	**32%**	**28%**	**22%**	

Source: Annual reports of the respective banks.

was impressive (77 percent), though much slower than commitments, whereas the growth of IDA disbursements was insignificant (1 percent). The slower pace of disbursements relative to commitments is even true of policy lending, which should be quicker to disburse, and took place despite a number of measures that were reportedly taken to accelerate disbursements, such as frontloading and fast tracking loans. The story would be worse if we focused on net disbursements (i.e., net of payments by countries to the MDBs). This means in practice that the contribution of the World Bank to the recovery was moderate at best, and certainly so in the case of low-income countries. This needs both urgent review and change for future crises, so as to fully mainstream the countercyclical function.

Some of the RDBs also responded with strong increases in lending during the crisis. The IADB did so with many policies running parallel to World Bank initiatives, including loosening policy criteria and creating a rapid disbursing emergency fund of US$6 billion to allow faster disbursements of funds and increasing callable capital by US$4 billion. The IADB increased its commitments by 38 percent in 2009, having also increased disbursements significantly in 2008, and disbursed 60 percent more in 2009 than in 2008.

The European Bank for Reconstruction and Development (EBRD) increased lending in 2009 by over 50 percent to €7.0 billion, with about one-fourth directed to supporting the financial sector and medium- and small-sized enterprises and transport as additional priorities.

The EIB followed the pattern of other multilateral development banks by substantially increasing lending in response to the crisis, both to EU members, its main beneficiaries, and to developing countries. Lending to developing and emerging countries in 2009 increased by 40 percent, though disbursements by a mere 16 percent. This slow increase in disbursements may be partly explained by the fact that the EIB lends only for projects, which are not disbursed as quickly as sectoral or program lending. It is interesting that in certain regions, such as Asia and Latin America, there was a high demand for EIB lending, but the limit imposed by the existing predetermined envelope of lending to those regions was a constraint.

The African Development Bank (AfDB) also developed a number of changes in programs and policy to respond to the crisis. Its lending commitment increased by an impressive 137 percent between 2008 and 2009, with disbursements growing by 125 percent. This was the largest increase of disbursements in 2009 of any MDBs. However, the scale and targeting to the most vulnerable countries again remained somewhat inadequate. For the Asian Development Bank (ADB), commitments in 2009 grew by 42 percent and disbursements by 33 percent (see Table 2.11).

The main lesson learned is that MDBs need to permanently place their countercyclical function at the center of their priorities and develop the instruments to do so, allowing them to respond rapidly and significantly in times of crisis. MDB disbursements grew far more slowly during the crisis than did commitments, which means that there is a need to create ex ante mechanisms for fast disbursements during crises. Critical in this area is social protection, where speed in delivery is the essence of effectiveness. An important question is whether lower conditionality in lending could have helped. Subregional banks—CAF, Corporación Andina de Fomento—lend more quickly than most MDBs and have less conditionality. A recent example of such fast disbursement is increased lending through intermediaries (global loans) for SMEs by the EIB.

Given that lending was initially constrained by insufficient capital in several MDBs, a crucial policy question is whether greater automaticity in replenishing the capital of these valuable institutions should be introduced. Replenishing the capital is of additional importance given the task assigned to MDBs of helping to meet urgent global public goods, such as mitigation and adaptation resulting from climate change. If capital is not replenished, then the residual capacity to lend for development will fall, as will their ability to lend countercyclically during crises. To accelerate the response to low-income countries, a significant increase in IDA resources is required, as well as grants to finance concessional loans in RDBs.

An alternative to replenishment is increasing the capacity of MDBs to lend in the future via higher leverage. This is especially attractive to developed country governments facing severe budget and debt constraints. There are a number of ways in which an MDB can create more leverage with its capital. The most traditional is the use of guarantees as opposed to loans; but there are less traditional methods of leverage, including the provision of equity or mezzanine financing. It is interesting that IDA has recently recommended that its pilot partial risk guarantee mechanism be mainstreamed and become a regular product.

MDBs can also be more active in providing concessional lending, most notably obtained by blending loans and grants, particularly, but not only, for low-income countries. Sufficient levels and good allocation of grant subsidies is an important factor in enabling this and should be a top priority for policy makers.

One of the areas where the MDBs, including the World Bank Group, were effective in responding to the crisis was in the rapid provision of trade credit facilities. The expansion of trade credit by MDBs overall provided US$9.1 billion in addition to the US$3.2 billion that they had been providing. The short maturity of most trade financing allows funds to be rolled over multiple times, providing more than US$80 billion in trade financing between 2009 and 2011. A majority of banks surveyed by the International Chamber of Commerce (55 percent) were utilizing trade facilitation programs implemented by MDBs by the summer of 2009 (ICC, 2009).

Another set of policy proposals for the future relates to the MDBs introducing lending instruments that make developing countries less vulnerable during crises, either because they reduce currency mismatches by lending in local currency or because they adjust repayments of loans in a countercyclical manner, so that net lending can increase more in bad times.

An instrument that several MDBs have developed successfully in certain countries is, indeed, lending in local currencies. It seems highly desirable that MDBs extend local currency lending to other countries, given that local currency debt implies no currency mismatches for the debtor and therefore reduces the risk of debt crises, as well as risk of bankruptcies of individual companies. Where feasible, this should be funded by issuing debt of the MDB in the same currency. This both eliminates foreign exchange risk for the MDB and helps the development of local capital markets. The MDBs could take a step further and create a diversified portfolio of local currency debt of a variety of developing countries. Such a diversified portfolio could be securitized and sold (see proposals by Dodd and Spiegel, 2005, and by Ocampo and Griffith-Jones, 2008).

The MDBs could also take one step further and innovate by pioneering other new instruments as they did previously with local currency paper. There seems to be a strong case for GDP-linked bonds for developing countries. Such instruments would help stabilize government spending through the cycle, helping to smooth growth and diminish the likelihood of costly debt crises. There seems to be a typical "first mover" problem. Individual governments, though seeing the insurance advantages that have become far more evident in the recent crisis, seem shy about being the first to issue GDP-linked bonds. Therefore, they express a strong preference for MDBs to act as "market makers." The MDBs could do this by making loans linked to the growth of GDP; such loans could then be grouped, securitized, and sold to financial markets.

Another area where the crisis can offer valuable lessons for future action is the need for closer collaboration among different MDBs in order to, for example, build regional infrastructure; the crisis seems to have encouraged different MDBs to work more closely. The institutional mechanisms created for this task should be maintained in normal times.

CONCLUSIONS AND GLOBAL POLICY IMPLICATIONS

The Great Recession had strong, though quite diverse, effects on developing and transition economies. One channel of transmission was through falling remittances, which impacted several, mostly small, countries heavily dependent on remittances of migrants in the United States, Western Europe, and Russia; in contrast, remittances from the Gulf countries to South Asia and the Middle East did not experience a similar downward trend. The financial shock was severe, mainly for middle-income "emerging" economies, but it was short, due to the largest Keynesian stimulus policies ever adopted in history—including those put into place by several major developing countries—and to the massive bailouts of financial institutions in industrial countries. The trade shock was also severe, longer lasting (its effects had not been fully overcome by 2010), and affected all countries. In the developing world, high- and mid-tech manufacturing exporters were hardest hit by the collapse of export volumes. In turn, energy and metal exporters were initially more affected by the collapse of commodity prices than agricultural producers, and all commodity prices recovered soon. Dependence of many low-income countries on agricultural exports thus turned out to be a relative blessing under the circumstances. In a longer-term perspective, however, real agricultural prices came back to levels below those of the 1970s, in sharp contrast to the relatively high real oil and metal prices that have prevailed again since the end of 2009.

Countries and regions hardest hit in terms of GDP contraction are clustered in two groups. The first is made up of those countries with weak external balance sheets (large external debts relative to foreign exchange reserves) or traditional domestic financial vulnerabilities (a previous boom of foreign private-sector borrowing followed by a credit squeeze and, even worse, the devastating effects of currency mismatches in domestic portfolios). This is the situation faced by many transition economies in Central and Eastern Europe, as well as by several that are now members of the EU (with Poland as a major exception). The second group comprises manufacturing exporters heavily dependent on U.S. and European markets. The high-income and highly open East Asian economies of South Korea, Taiwan, Hong Kong, and Singapore, along with Mexico and Turkey, were the main cases in point. China's exports were also strongly affected, but this country came out from the slowdown generated by the Great Recession very soon, thanks to the most expansionary fiscal and credit package in the world. Indeed, in a significant way, aside from the massive Keynesian policies and bailouts, the other major difference between the Great Recession and the Great Depression of the 1930s was that this time the world had, in China, a substantial economy with strong trade linkages and without a financial sector in crisis and, therefore, with the policy space and willingness to pursue aggressive Keynesian policies.

Aside from China, many other developing countries adopted variable mixes of expansionary fiscal, monetary, and credit policies. Most East Asian and South Asian countries (with the major exception of Pakistan), together with Brazil, stand out in this regard; and in South Asia, this was true of fiscal policies, despite their initial weak fiscal stances. There were similar cases of expansionary policies elsewhere, including in sub-Saharan Africa. The existence of state financial institutions (as in Brazil, China, and India) turned out to be a blessing for supporting expansionary policies, whereas the credit squeeze in countries with heavy dependence of banks on external funds defeated otherwise expansionary macroeconomic policies (with Chile and several Gulf countries being major examples of this pattern). There were few domestic financial crises, thanks to stronger regulations in place, as a response to the developing countries' own past crises.

Overall, China and South Asia (notably India, but also the largest least-developed country, Bangladesh) had the best performance, and North Africa and sub-Saharan Africa a fair one (though, on average, per capita income fell in sub-Saharan Africa). The performance of South Asia and much of sub-Saharan Africa, the two regions with the highest incidence of extreme poverty, implied that the effects of the Great Recession on world poverty were relatively muted. Most other economies in East Asia, as well as Brazil and most Latin American countries, experienced a strong recovery after the initial recession. Overall, however, Latin America did not do well initially, despite stronger external, financial, and fiscal stances than in the past. This is particularly true of Mexico, which, along with Turkey, was among the economies that experienced strong contractions. The worst hit by the Great Recession were the transition economies, particularly the CIS countries, but also some that are now EU members.

Multilateral response was strong (and certainly stronger than during past crises), as reflected in the largest emission of Special Drawing Rights (SDRs) in history, a number of IMF programs, and rapid increase in lending by the MDBs. However, that response exhibited two major weaknesses. First, it was more moderate than the shock warranted, given the strong contraction in private financial flows, and it came with a lag. For the MDBs, large expansions in commitments were not matched by an equally dynamic pace of disbursements, so that their contribution to the recovery was moderate. Second, it was biased toward middle-income countries. This was reflected both in the responses from the IMF and the multilateral development banks, as well as the slow growth of ODA.

Going forward, there are major uncertainties that surround the world economy and associated global policy issues. Those that have received greatest attention relate to the early withdrawal of stimulus and the implications of rising public-sector debts in industrial countries. We will leave these issues aside, as well as the important long-term questions pertaining to the relationship between future world economic growth and climate change. We will concentrate, rather, on five issues that we see as particularly important in terms of global economic policy and the developing world.

The first relates to the large asymmetries between the expected growth of industrial and developing countries. The world had never experienced before a situation in which major developing countries are, in a sense, the only available engines of world economic growth. Continuing expansion of these countries is crucial for the world, but so is the capacity of these economies to transmit their growth dynamics to the rest of the world. The most important is, of course, China, which has a much larger share of global trade than other large developing countries. For China the capacity to induce growth in the rest of the world inevitably implies turning its large trade surplus into a balance, or even a trade deficit. This problem is absent in other large developing countries, such as Brazil and India, which have the tendency to run current-account deficits anyway.

For China the transition from export-led to domestic-led growth raises myriad questions, including the capacity to shift domestic demand dynamics from investment to consumption and, therefore, the reversal of the dramatic reduction of consumption and wage shares, as well as the significant overcapacity generated by the highest investment rate ever recorded in history (Akyüz, 2010; Yu, 2010). Also, given that large parts of its trade linkages are associated with the demand for inputs for its export sector, the shift from export-led to domestic demand-led growth may actually reduce Chinese import demand (Akyüz, 2010).

Under any scenario, it is essential that the world does not throw the baby out with the bathwater, to use a classic American saying. In particular, although some real appreciation of the renminbi should be part of this process, a strong and disorderly appreciation may have the effect of seriously affecting Chinese economic growth. This is a likely interpretation of how Japanese growth came to a halt and its costly financial crisis was incubated. In any case, it is the one that Chinese authorities seem to have in mind to avoid repeating the story. The only desirable scenario is, therefore, a Chinese economy that transmits its stimulus to the rest of the world through rising imports generated more by the income (rapid economic growth) than the substitution (real exchange rate appreciation) effects. Opening space for Chinese investment abroad should also be an essential part of this strategy.

A second and interrelated issue is the implication of current trends on global imbalances. One of the major paradoxes of the Great Recession is that building stronger external balance sheets in the developing world through self-insurance during the boom years contributed to global imbalances. They indeed dampened global demand, which then became increasingly dependent on the United States as "the consumer of last resort." But the resulting strong external balance sheets also contributed to the resilience of many developing economies during the Great Recession, which was a major factor behind the recent recovery. Going forward, the worst global scenario is thus one in which *all* or most countries, including now industrial nations, aim at improving their current accounts, since this is nothing but a scenario of weak global demand and even a new recession. A desirable global scenario is thus one in which most developing countries (and not only China) run current-account *deficits*. However, this requires major reforms in the global financial system to reduce the vulnerabilities that this pattern generated in the past and that were reflected in major financial crises in the developing world. Recent IMF reforms are just a small step in that direction, as explored in this volume by Griffith-Jones and Ocampo (2012).

Furthermore, generating these current-account deficits the way they are now being pushed by financial markets, through massive capital flows toward emerging markets, runs the risk of generating future busts, following well-known patterns. So a more orderly way of inducing such current-account deficits without risking the disruption in world economic growth should be on the agenda. In our view, this inevitably requires a serious discussion of capital account regulations in the world, an issue that has been raised by several analysts (see, for example, Subramanian, 2009; Ocampo, 2010) but is surprisingly missing from current discussions of global financial reform.

A third set of questions relates to the weakest link in the current recovery: international trade. There are two scenarios here: a continuation of the rapid recovery of trade that started in mid-2009 and that will generate a return to the situation that prevailed in recent decades, of a world trade that is more dynamic than world GDP; or, alternatively, a situation in which this will not happen, and we are going to see a world in which trade is less dynamic than in the past, and not necessarily because protectionism is back. We are inclined to think that the second outcome is quite likely and, furthermore, that even a successful Doha trade round (a very unlikely scenario) would not make much of a difference for the outcome. If this is so, the best world scenario is, curiously, the return of *inward*-looking strategies, not necessarily protectionist but with a focus on the dynamism of domestic markets. After all, the Keynesian policies that have been the essential ingredient of the current recovery are nothing else than inward-looking policies.

What this implies is that the desirable situation is more like that of the late nineteenth and early twentieth centuries, according to some economic historians (notably Bairoch, 1993), in which economic growth of different nations (in a generally protectionist world) was the engine of world trade, and not the opposite. In recent decades the "trade as an engine of growth" view has curiously, though in different ways, been both the orthodox dogma (preached among others by the IFIs) and the heterodox practice (in several East Asian countries).

A transition toward more inward-looking strategies has, of course, a major implication: it biases growth toward countries with large domestic markets and therefore against small economies. One major implication is that regional economic integration processes may have to play a more important role in the future, as sort of "expanded domestic markets," particularly in those regions where such processes are weakest, in sub-Saharan Africa and South Asia. This is an equally challenging issue for Latin America and Western Asia. A related implication is that developing countries should not forgo such opportunities that exist for benefiting from trade—indeed, by becoming scarcer, such opportunities will be, in a sense, all the more valuable.

This leads to a fourth set of issues that relates to how growth is going to be distributed *among* developing countries. In a sense, if we project current trends, East Asia and India (not South Asia as whole) are likely to be part of the dynamic poles of the new world economy. But this may leave many developing countries behind, particularly those with weak links to these dynamic poles and those that compete with them in global markets, or with patterns of growth that are only partly desirable (e.g., booming Chinese-cum-commodity-led growth in sub-Saharan Africa and South America). The bias in recent international cooperation toward middle-income countries is also part of the problem. So a major issue going forward is to guarantee that we are not in the face of another major divergence in development, not between industrial and developing countries but *among* developing countries. Indeed, this has already been one part of the patterns of global development in recent decades, which Ocampo and Parra (2007) have characterized as a "dual divergence." This implies, in particular, serious thinking about the specific mechanism through which the most dynamic poles of the developing world are going to disseminate their growth to the developing world at large.

What all this implies, fifth and finally, is that the world we are looking forward at is going to be, in economic terms, much more dependent on the developing world than any we have observed in history. Never before has the call of the 2002 Monterrey Consensus (UN, 2002) to increase the participation of developing countries in global economic decision making been more important. Managing this world requires a major reform of global economic governance away from the industrial-countries-centered institutions designed after the Second World War. The G-20 has been a step forward in this regard, but its representation is inadequate (in particular, medium- and small-sized countries are entirely unrepresented, and there are major problems of representation of sub-Saharan Africa, among others); it is still dominated in its specific dynamics by industrial countries; and, particularly, it lacks the legitimacy of a body that is elected as part of a process of global consensus-building. So, in this area, as in the specific mechanisms to manage such a world economy, there is a long road ahead.

NOTES

1. One definition, which is implicit in the recent book by Reinhart and Rogoff (2009), is the countries that have access to private capital markets, which would generally be middle-income countries.

2. This is due to the peculiar methodology used by the IMF, which adds GDPs estimated using purchasing power (PPP) rather than market prices and exchange rates; this makes the regional and, particularly, global data clearly imprecise. The most important bias introduced by IMF methodology is that global GDP growth is consistently overestimated, due to the excessive weight given to the Chinese economy, which is much larger in PPP than in market price estimates. It also makes IMF GDP growth rates not comparable to other data; most notably, trends in real trade variables cannot be compared with PPP GDP estimates. When using financial ratios, the IMF, as do all analysts, uses GDPs at market prices.

3. See, for example, an interpretation along the latter lines in UN (2009c). See also Akyüz (2010).

4. See, on these issues, Ocampo (2010) and the parallel chapter in this volume by Griffith-Jones and Ocampo (2012).

5. We can add that this is so much so that Roubini (2009) has referred to this phenomenon as "the mother of all carry trade."

6. Quarterly GDP growth estimates here and in the following paragraph follow estimates by JPMorgan (2009–2010).

7. The terms of the rescues contained many flaws, but this is beyond the scope of this chapter.

8. See, again, the parallel chapter in this volume by Griffith-Jones and Ocampo (2012).

9. Comparable information is available for the ninety countries in the case of the current account, for eighty in the case of external debt, and for seventy-eight for foreign exchange reserves.

10. We exclude Honduras, which, according to the table, had a large package but did not increase spending as a proportion of GDP, according to ECLAC (2009). This case also makes it clear that the definition of the fiscal package may not be uniform, and may reflect policy announcements with political content rather than effective policies.

11. IMF estimates are in turn biased by the use of PPP estimates (see note 2).

12. Over the decade and a half ending in the mid-1990s, incomes fell to such an extent that despite reasonably robust growth, approaching 5 percent a year on average in the latter part of the 1990s, sub-Saharan Africa's per capita income by 2000 was roughly at the same level it was in 1970. It was not all gloom, as sub-Saharan Africa also included the fastest-growing country in the world during the period 1960–2000: Botswana.

13. See, for example, the contributions in Noman et al. (2011).

14. Middle-income countries as a group are sixteen times larger than low-income countries, according to World Bank definitions (twelve times if we exclude China from the former group).

15. On these and other issues, see UN (2009b).

REFERENCES

Akyüz, Y. 2010. "Global Economic Prospects: The Recession May Be over but What Next?" *Research Paper No. 26* (March). Geneva: South Centre.

Bairoch, P. 1993. *Economics and World History: Myths and Paradoxes.* Chicago: University of Chicago Press.

Barbosa, N. 2010. "Counter-Cyclical Policies in Brazil: 2008–09." *Journal of Globalization and Development* 1 (1): Article 13.

Bernanke, B. S. 2004. (February 20). "The Great Moderation." Remarks at the Meeting of the Eastern Economic Association. http://www.federalreserve.gov/Boarddocs/Speeches/2004/20040220/default.htm.

Bhinda, B., and M. Martin. 2009. *Private Capital Flows to Low Income Countries: Dealing with Boom Bust.* London: Debt Relief International.

Calvo, G. 2010. (February 23). "Policy in Times of Crisis: A View from the South." Presentation for the MENA Region Retreat. Washington, D.C.: World Bank.

Dodd, R., and S. Spiegel. 2005. "Up from Sin: A Portfolio Approach to Financial Salvation." In *The IMF and the World Bank at Sixty*, edited by A. Buira, pp. 85–116. London: Anthem Press.

ECLAC (UN Economic Commission for Latin America and the Caribbean). 2009. *Preliminary Balance of the Economies of Latin America and the Caribbean 2009.* Santiago: ECLAC.

Ffrench-Davis, R. 2010. "Latin America: The Structural Fiscal Balance Policy in Chile: A Move toward Counter-Cyclical Macroeconomics." *Journal of Globalization and Development* 1 (1): Article 14.

Go, D., and J. Page, eds. 2008. *Africa at a Turning Point?* Washington, D.C.: World Bank.

Griffith-Jones, S., and J. A. Ocampo. 2003. *What Progress on International Financial Reform? Why So Limited?* Stockholm: Expert Group on Development Issues (EGDI) Swedish Ministry for Foreign Affairs, Almqvist & Wiksell International.

———. 2008. "Compensatory Financing for Shocks: What Changes Are Needed?" Paper Prepared for the United Nations Committee on Development Policy (April).

———. 2012. "The International Financial Architecture Seen through the Lens of the Crisis: Some Achievements and Numerous Challenges."In this volume.

ICC (International Chamber of Commerce) Banking Commission. 2009. (September 4). "ICC Trade Finance Survey: An Interim Report—Summer 2009." Document No 470-1124 TS/WJ.

IIF (Institute of International Finance). 2009. (January 27). *Capital Flows to Emerging Market Economies.* Washington, D.C.: IIF. www.iif.com/download.php?id=+130eNm7tXk=.

———. 2010. (January 26). *Capital Flows to Emerging Market Economies.* Washington, D.C.: IIF. www.iif.com.

ILO (International Labor Organization). 2009. *World of Work Report 2009: The Global Jobs Crisis and Beyond.* Geneva: International Institute for Labor Studies.

———. 2010. *Global Employment Trends.* Geneva: ILO. http://www.ilo.org.

———. 2011. *Global Employment Trends.* Geneva: ILO. http://www.ilo.org.

IMF (International Monetary Fund). 2009. (October). *Regional Economic Outlook: Sub-Saharan Africa: Weathering the Storm.* Washington, D.C.: IMF.

———. 2010a. (January 26). *Global Financial Stability Report Market Update.* Washington, D.C.: IMF. http://www.imf.org.

————. 2010b. (January 26). *World Economic Outlook Update.* Washington D.C: IMF. http://www.imf.org.

————. 2011. (April). *World Economic Outlook.* Washington, D.C.: IMF. http://www.imf.org.

Inter-American Development Bank. 2008. (April). *All That Glitters May Not Be Gold: Assessing Latin America's Recent Macroeconomic Performance.* Washington, D.C.: Inter-American Development Bank.

————. Multilateral Investment Fund. 2010. *Remittances to Latin America and the Caribbean during 2009: The Effects of the Global Financial Crisis.* Washington, D.C.: Inter-American Development Bank. http://idbdocs.iadb.org/wsdocs/get document.aspx?docnum=35101526.

JPMorgan. 2008. (October 17). "Determinants of Mexico's Remittances from the U.S." *Global Data Watch.* New York: JPMorgan.

————. 2009–2010. *Global Data Watch.* Various issues. New York: JPMorgan.

Kasekende, L., Z. Brixova, and L. Ndikumana. 2010. "Africa: Africa's Counter-Cyclical Policy Responses to the Crisis." *Journal of Globalization and Development* 1 (1): Article 16.

Noman, A., K. Botchwey, H. Stein, and J. E. Stiglitz, eds. 2011. *Good Growth and Governance in Africa: Rethinking Development Strategies.* New York: Oxford University Press.

Ocampo, J. A. 2009. "Latin America and the Global Financial Crisis." *Cambridge Journal of Economics* 33 (4) (July): 703–24.

————. 2010. "Reforming the Global Reserve System." In *Time for a Visible Hand: Lessons from the 2008 World Financial Crisis,* edited by S. Griffith-Jones, J. A. Ocampo, and J. E. Stiglitz, pp. 314–44. New York: Oxford University Press.

————. 2011. "Global Economic Prospects and the Developing World." *Global Policy* 1 (2) (January): 10–19.

Ocampo, J. A., and S. Griffith-Jones. 2008. "A Counter-cyclical Framework for a Development-Friendly International Financial Architecture." In *Macroeconomic Volatility, Institutions and Financial Architecture: The Developing World Experience,* edited by J. M. Fanelli, pp. 25–44. Houndmills, Hampshire: Palgrave Macmillan.

Ocampo, J. A., and M. Parra. 2003. "The Terms of Trade for Commodities in the Twentieth Century." *CEPAL Review* (April): 79.

————. 2007. "The Dual Divergence: Growth Successes and Collapses in the Developing World since 1980." In *Economic Growth with Equity: Challenges for Latin America,* edited by R. Ffrench-Davis and J. L. Machinea, pp. 61–92. Houndmills, Hampshire: Palgrave Macmillan and ECLAC.

Ocampo, J. A., C. Rada, and L. Taylor. 2009. *Growth and Policy in Developing Countries: A Structuralist Approach.* New York: Columbia University Press.

O'Rourke, K. H. 2009. (November 27). "Government Policies and the Collapse in Trade during the Great Depression." London: Centre for Economic Policy Research. http://www.voxeu.org/index.php?q=node/4267.

Özatay, F. 2010. "Europe: Counter-cyclical Policies in Light of the Global Financial Crisis: Case of Turkey." *Journal of Globalization and Development,* 1 (1): Article 18.

Ratha, D., S. Mohapatra, and Z. Xu. 2008. "Outlook for Remittance Flows 2008–2010: Growth Expected to Moderate Significantly, but Flows to Remain Resilient." *Migration and Development Brief No. 8* (November 11). Washington, D.C.: World Bank, Development Prospects Group, Migration and Remittances Team.

Ratha, D., S. Mohapatra, Z. Xu, and A. Silwali. 2009. "Migration and Remittance Trends: A Better-Than-Expected Outcome so Far, but Significant Risks Ahead." *Migration and Development Brief No. 11* (November 3). Washington, D.C.: World Bank, Development Prospects Group, Migration and Remittances Team.

Reinhart, C. M., and K. Rogoff. 2009. *This Time Is Different: Eight Centuries of Financial Folly*. Princeton, N.J.: Princeton University Press.

Roubini, N. 2009. "The Mother of All Carry Trades Faces an Inevitable Bust." *Financial Times*, November 2.

Stiglitz, J. 2002. *Globalization and Its Discontents*. New York: W. W. Norton.

———. 2010. *Free Fall: America, Free Markets, and the Sinking of the World Economy*. New York and London: W. W. Norton.

Subramanian, A. 2009. "Coordinated Capital Controls: A Further Elaboration." *The Baseline Scenario*. http://baselinescenario.com/2009/11/29/coordinated-capital -controls-a-further-elaboration/.

te Velde, D., and I. Massa. 2009. "Donor Responses to Global Financial Crisis: A Stock Take." *ODI Working Paper No. 11* (December). London: Global Financial Crisis Discussion Series. http://www.odi.org.uk/resources/details.asp?id=4630 &title=global-financial-crisis-donor-responses-stock-take.

UN (United Nations). 2002. (March). *The Monterrey Consensus*. Monterrey, Mexico: International Conference on Financing for Development. http://www.un.org/esa /ffd/.

———. 2009a. (January). *World Economic Situation and Prospects 2009*. New York: United Nations.

———. 2009b. (July). *MDG Gap Task Force Report 2009: Strengthening the Global Partnership for Development in a Time of Crisis*. New York: United Nations.

———. 2009c. (September). *Report of the Commission of Experts of the UN General Assembly on Reforms of the International Monetary and Financial System* [Stiglitz Commission]. New York: United Nations. http://www.un.org/ga/president /63/commission/financial_commission.shtml.

———. 2010a. (January). *World Economic Situation and Prospects 2010*. New York: United Nations.

———. 2010b. (February). *World Economic Vulnerability Monitor No.3*. New York: United Nations.

———. 2011. (January). *World Economic Situation and Prospects 2011*. New York: United Nations.

UNCTAD (United Nations Conference on Trade and Development). 2009. *The Global Economic Crisis: Systemic Failures and Multilateral Remedies*. Geneva: United Nations.

Uygur, E. 2010. "The Global Crisis and the Turkish Economy." *TWN Global Economic Series No. 21*. Penang: Third World Network.

von Braun, J. 2007. "The World Food Situation: New Driving Forces and Required Actions." *Food Policy Report* (December). Washington, D.C.: International Food Policy Research Institute.

World Bank. 2009a. *Global Development Finance: Charting a Global Recovery.* Washington, D.C.: World Bank.

————. 2009b. *Global Economic Prospects 2009: Commodities at the Crossroads.* Washington, D.C.: World Bank.

————. 2010. *Global Economic Prospects: Crisis, Finance and Growth.* Washington, D.C.: World Bank.

Yu, Y. 2010. "Asia: China's Policy Response to the Global Financial Crisis." *Journal of Globalization and Development* 1 (1): Article 12.

CHAPTER 3

The International Financial Architecture Seen through the Lens of the Crisis

Some Achievements and Numerous Challenges

Stephany Griffith-Jones and José Antonio Ocampo

This chapter looks at the process of international financial and monetary reform from the Asian crisis until the end of 2010, in terms of the basic objectives that should be met by the international financial architecture. There are essentially five objectives: (1) to regulate the financial and capital markets in all countries, as well as cross-border transactions, in order to avoid the excessive accumulation of risk, which has caused frequent and costly crises in both developing and developed countries; (2) to offer emergency financing during crises, especially to ensure liquidity, complementing the functions of the central banks as lenders of last resort at a national level; (3) to provide adequate mechanisms at an international level to manage problems of over-indebtedness; (4) to guarantee the consistency of national economic policies with the stability of the world economy system, and to avoid the macroeconomic policies of some countries having adverse effects on others; and (5) to guarantee an international monetary system that contributes to the stability of the international economy and is seen as fair by all parties. The Monterrey Consensus, approved by the United Nations International Conference on Financing for Development, which took place in 2002, comes closest to the definition of those goals, although it does not explicitly include some of them (especially the last one).

While some of these objectives focus on crisis prevention, others relate to the management of crises once they have been unleashed. Nevertheless, such a division is not a straightforward one, since some instruments that are good for handling crises also have preventive effects, as the history of central banks throughout the world indicates. Nor is the distinction between microeconomic and macroeconomic matters clear-cut, since, as we show, financial regulation should include an important element of macro-prudential regulation.

This chapter is divided into four parts. Given the importance of the debate under way on financial regulation as a central mechanism for crisis prevention—that is, the first objective of international financial cooperation—the first part tackles this theme as well as corresponding institutional reform issues. The last section of that part analyzes a question that is partially related to these issues that has emerged strongly in recent debates: the potential role of an international tax on some financial transactions. The second part considers some of the main problems concerned with the prevention and management of crises in the developing world. That part concentrates, therefore, on the second and third objectives of cooperation and the way in which developing countries have responded to the flaws in international financial architecture; this section will also look at a closely related question regarding the increasing demand by developing countries for more equitable participation in international financial institutions. The third part analyzes the fourth and fifth objectives mentioned, which, as we show, are interrelated. After briefly considering some of the problems associated with how to guarantee the consistency of national macroeconomic policies, we look more closely at the reform of the international monetary system and propose a reform based on a significant expansion by the International Monetary Fund (IMF) of the use of Special Drawing Rights (SDRs). To conclude, the last part presents an overview of the reform of the international financial architecture since the Asian crisis and of changes in global economic governance.

The chapter focuses on monetary and financial architecture and leaves aside recent events on matters of financing for development, which also show a complex panorama, including some positive developments: the clear recovery of the official development aid after the Monterrey Conference on Financing for Development and the aggressive response of multilateral development banks to provide financing during the recent crisis. We discuss these topics in another chapter of this book.

DEFICIT AND GOVERNANCE OF FINANCIAL REGULATION

THE REGULATORY DEFICIT AND REFORMS UNDER WAY

The seriousness of the global financial crisis laid bare the magnitude of the regulatory deficit that the global financial system faced. This problem was particularly acute in developed countries, as many developing countries had responded to the series of financial crises they had faced since the 1980s by strengthening their regulatory and supervisory frameworks. This regulatory deficit has two different dimensions. On the one hand, although the banking system was regulated, the regulation was insufficient in key areas and enforcement was not adequate due to deficiencies in the supervisory systems. On the other hand, there were significant areas of financial activity and some financial agents (the so-called shadow banking system) that lacked any form of regulation.

The main effort made at an international level before the crisis was the negotiation of the Basel Agreement on banking regulation (Basel II). Although this agreement had various positive elements, it also contained a series of important flaws. One of its most worrisome features, highlighted by a few commentators in the early 2000s (Griffith-Jones, Segoviano, and Spratt, 2002; Goodhart, 2002) and clearly recognized after the global crisis, was the fact that it reinforced the naturally pro-cyclical behavior of bank loans. In fact, the main failure of financial markets is that they allow the tendency, both of lenders and borrowers, to assume excessive risks during boom periods. Those risks lead to significant losses in bank portfolios later, when growth slows down, which can in turn set off financial crises. Basel II exacerbated this pro-cyclical behavior by giving increasing weight to the risk evaluation models of the banks themselves in the determination of suitable capital levels.

The need to introduce specific countercyclical mechanisms in banking regulation had been recognized by some analysts since the end of the 1990s, especially by the United Nations and the Bank for International Settlements (Ocampo, 2003; Griffith-Jones and Ocampo, 2010). In this field, one of the most important innovations was the Spanish system of countercyclical provisions for loan losses, initially introduced in 2000. However, neither those analyses nor the Spanish practice received adequate attention and were ignored by Basel II.

Another problem of Basel II was the tendency to overestimate the risk of bank loans made to developing countries and to overlook the benefits, in terms of risk reduction, of diversifying international portfolios. As a result of this flaw, its application can result in excessive capital requirements for loans to developing countries, reducing those loans and increasing their costs. This problem has not been corrected so far.

The areas that lacked regulation included, first of all, off-balance-sheet bank transactions, which were in fact one of the most important sources by which the global crisis in the mortgage- and other asset-backed securities spread to the banks. In a similar way, contingent loans of banks to other agents were equally unregulated. The problems inherent in rating assets by rating agencies have also been subject to a lot of attention in recent debates, particularly the tendency to poorly evaluate the risk of loans that are not going to be kept on a bank's own books but that are to be sold off. Those loans heavily contributed to the crisis.

The derivatives market and the alternative investment funds (generally called *hedge funds*, although their operations go beyond hedging), which are particularly active in derivatives markets, comprised another area of poor regulation before the crisis. Given the multiple flaws that characterize those markets (which are very incomplete and imperfect, particularly during crises), it is crucial to improve regulation in this area.[1] Lastly, the lack of regulation of the ratings agencies has also been the subject of a great deal of debate, as well as the possible conflicts of interest between their rating business and their advising services to agents whose products they rate (Goodhart, 2010).

One of the most important breakthroughs of the international debate during the last two years was the recognition that the international financial crisis was clearly associated with inadequate regulation and insufficient supervision of financial activities. This is precisely the sphere in which the G-20 has played an important role, especially in reaching agreement on certain principles, the implementation of which nevertheless remains the subject of debate. These reforms have been adopted at a slow pace in Europe. In the United States the 2010 Dodd-Frank bill on financial regulation implied significant progress, as we discuss later, but the fact that it was finalized earlier than European reforms shows that progress in different regions has not been sufficiently coordinated internationally. This will result in regulatory systems having important divergences.

The Basel Committee on Banking Supervision (hereafter the Basel Committee) had already started to discuss some practices as a complement to the regulations that Basel II introduced (Basel Committee, 2009a, 2009b). Far more important, even though still insufficient, is the proposal approved in September 2010 as Basel III (Basel Committee, 2010).

The proposals agreed upon in principle by the twenty-seven member countries in September 2010 have a number of positive elements. First, they raise the Tier 1 capital requirement (the core form of loss-absorbing capital) from 2 to 4.5 percent of risk-weighted assets, and define far more strictly the assets that make up this capital, to strengthen the solvency of financial institutions. The proposals also increase the capital for banks' operations in the financial markets (the so-called trading book) and require an additional capital conservation buffer of 2.5 percent. This implies that banks should have 7 percent of common equity. It also implies the introduction of additional buffers of countercyclical capital, in a range of 0 to 2.5 percent of common equity, which would be implemented nationally along lines that we discuss later. Finally, the liquidity requirements are made explicit, which were practically nonexistent in Basel II; they also introduce a maximum leverage ratio, calculated on total assets and not on risk-weighted assets, whose aim is to restrict the total of assets in relation to capital.

Nevertheless, Basel III has several problems (for a more detailed analysis, see Griffith-Jones, Silvers, and Thiemann, 2010). First, many observers consider that the increases of capital requirements are not enough, especially for banks with very risky assets. A second important critique relates to the excessively long time period over which they will be implemented, culminating in 2022. The main reason is that there have been strong pressures by the banks, both to avoid even higher capital increases and for delaying the reforms. This was combined, in the latter case, with the fear by regulators that an early increase in capital requirements would discourage even more the ability and willingness of banks to lend, which is considered key for the recovery.

A more radical critique is that maintaining risk-weighted assets capital requirements may be inadequate and that it would be better to give a larger role to leverage. Furthermore, it seems likely that the leverage indicator has been put at an excessively high level, as it can reach thirty-three. Another set of questions relates to the design of the liquidity buffers, which may end up by discriminating against loans to small and medium enterprises (SMEs), which play a key role in job creation. There is also an important concern about whether stricter regulation of banks will cause financial activity to move even more to the less regulated or unregulated entities.

It should be emphasized, finally, that—as already mentioned—the possible regulatory discrimination against developing countries has not been corrected in the new proposals. Therefore, it would be highly desirable if Basel III would incorporate a factor that takes account of the benefits of diversification toward those types of assets, as has already been done for loans to SMEs in the previous Accord (Griffith-Jones, Segoviano, and Spratt, 2002). In fact, the recent crisis and, above all, the recovery since mid-2009, in which developing countries have in general had higher growth rates than developed ones, have confirmed the need to introduce the benefits of diversification in Basel III.

THE PRINCIPLES OF A BETTER SYSTEM
OF FINANCIAL REGULATION

These national and international proposals have followed two basic principles that are worth analyzing in detail: guaranteeing a comprehensive as well as a countercyclical (or, more broadly, macro-prudential) regulation. But they have also tackled other matters, among them consumer protection, and discussed (though with no significant action) ways of managing the systemic risks posed by excessively large financial institutions.

The first principle mentioned is that regulation should be comprehensive, or that it should at least have a broad scope in terms of instruments, institutions, and markets (D'Arista and Griffith-Jones, 2010), in order to avoid the serious evasion of regulation through non-banking intermediaries (or barely regulated banking intermediaries) that contributed to the crisis. Moreover, the more comprehensive regulation should be accompanied by an increase in the capital base, which should also be of better quality, consistency, and transparency and should cover all the risks that financial institutions face (including those associated with securitization, investment in shares, bonds, and other securities that form part of the "trading book," and the counterparty risk associated with derivative operations and the financing of operations in the capital market), as recognized in the Basel Committee proposals.

For many analysts, an essential element is the obligation for all markets to be open and transparent and, therefore, to limit over-the-counter trades. The new U.S. legislation, which obliges all standard derivatives to pass through clearinghouses, is a positive step toward improving transparency and reducing counterparty risk, and it should be applied to all derivative transactions. So it is unfortunate that the U.S. legislation has maintained a series of exceptions, especially for derivatives used by non-financial firms. A positive aspect of the U.S. legislation is that it imposes margin requirements on all the derivatives that go through clearinghouses, which diminishes their risks, though again there are exceptions for those that do not go through clearinghouses. We can expect European regulation to follow these U.S. reforms on transparency in the derivatives markets, but it is to be feared that they will also allow important exceptions.

For alternative investment funds, especially for hedge funds, it is the European Union (EU) that took the earliest initiatives to improve transparency by requiring their registration, as well as proposing some precautionary regulatory measures; those proposals have now been approved in spite of opposition from financial players and the reservations of some countries. In turn, the U.S. legislation not only took the initiative to improve the transparency of these agents but also opened the possibility that the newly created Systemic Risk Council can declare some of these funds as systemically important when they are large financial players, and thus impose limits on their leverage or other risk-mitigating measures.

The creation of this council, as well as its equivalent in Europe—the European Systemic Risk Board, whose objective is macro-prudential regulation—is an institutional innovation that is potentially very positive. It is also positive that a rather ambitious architecture has been created involving three Pan-European supervisors for key financial sectors: one for banks, another for insurance and pensions, and a third for capital markets.

These steps imply that it has been recognized that financial intermediaries that are systemically important should be subject to particularly rigorous supervision and even to stricter regulatory norms. This issue has received particular attention in the United States, where the Treasury Department announced in 2009 that capital requirements of large financial intermediaries would be proportionally higher. Since 1994 there have been limits on the ratio of total deposits (10 percent) that can be held by one bank; the new rule would also apply to other liabilities.

An important measure announced by President Obama was intended to ban the use of a bank's resources in its own trading (so-called proprietary trading). In fact the U.S. legislation approved has introduced the so-called Volcker Rule, which forbids the use of banks' own resources and that of its depositors for their capital market businesses. However, this rule was diluted during debate in Congress, and banks were allowed to maintain property of alternative investment funds (hedge funds and equity funds) up to 3 percent of their Tier 1 capital.

The Financial Stability Board has welcomed this initiative but has emphasized that this is just one of various options designed to tackle the issue of organizations being too large to fail, as well as to separate traditional banking business from its more speculative and risky activities. Those options include, for instance, capital, leverage, and liquidity requirements based on size and the complexity of the structures of financial conglomerates.

The question of regulating the bonuses of executives and traders at financial companies has similarly ignited heated national and international debates—though, so far, to rather limited effect. The key problem has been not only that the salaries are excessive but also that they are structured in such a way that they generate incentives to undertake highly profitable short-term activities that are, nonetheless, excessively risky in the medium term and therefore generate risks both for the individual financial institution and the financial system as a whole. The bonuses are also asymmetric, since they are high when short-term profits are high, but they are never negative (and even continue to be high) when there are large losses. The Financial Stability Board has stated its intention to raise the capital requirements of institutions that have bonus systems that increase future risk. Several countries have taken partial measures in this area, although they are insufficient.

The second principle highlighted, which represents an important step forward in recent discussions, was the recognition that prudential norms should have a clear countercyclical, as well as a more broadly macroprudential, focus. The creation of the already-mentioned institutions in charge of avoiding accumulation of systemic risks is an element of this process. The crisis generated, also, a large consensus on the need to adopt countercyclical regulations, as reflected both in G-20 statements (Group of Twenty, 2009a, 2009b) and in several international reports on regulatory matters (UN, 2009, and the Warwick Commission, 2009, for instance). As a result of this, the Basel Committee included some suggestions in this area in its December 2009 and September 2010 proposals, which were detailed in December 2010.

According to the agreed-upon rules, a country's regulator may increase capital requirements when it regards this as appropriate for countercyclical prudential reasons. Other countries would be obliged to follow suit by imposing a proportional capital surcharge based on the exposure of their banks to the country decreeing the countercyclical requirement. An alternative to using capital requirements is the Spanish system that has been in place since 2000, which relies on countercyclical loan-loss provisions. Under the original Spanish system, such provisions were made when loans were disbursed, based on expected losses ("latent losses"), estimated on the basis of a full business cycle. Through the use of capital, loan-loss provisions, or non-distributable reserves (a third alternative that has been suggested), a buffer would be accumulated during periods of rapid credit expansion that would help absorb losses incurred during crises. Although the system forces the accumulation of those buffers, based on the Spanish experience, it may not curb the credit boom as such (Saurina, 2009). Permanent or countercyclical capital and provision requirements should also take into account the risks that different forms of financial institutions' funding generate through the business cycle: short term versus long term, as the Warwick Commission (2009) suggested; wholesale versus retail (deposits), as the Spanish authorities recently determined; or external versus domestic, a crucial issue for emerging markets and also for the European periphery during the global financial crisis.

Another equally important element to countercyclical regulation concerns the rules to avoid the heavily pro-cyclical behavior of financial asset and real estate prices that generate multiplied effects during the booms through an artificially high value of credit guarantees. In this regard, authorities could establish maximum loan-to-value ratios, which are made stricter during the periods of asset inflation; make additional compulsory provisions for credits guaranteed with assets that have rapidly increased their value; or increase the capital requirements in those cases. Any system of this type would have avoided or softened the very costly crisis in low-quality mortgages in the United States and also in European countries such as Spain, Great Britain, and Ireland.

In developing countries the problems of currency mismatches are also very important, especially due to the tendency of exchange rates to appreciate during booms and to depreciate during crises. In the absence of appropriate countercyclical norms—or, better still, of restrictions or bans on those exposures—the risks assumed during the booms tend to be reflected in large capital losses later on, as developing countries found during their own past crises, and as various countries in Central and Eastern Europe also learned during the recent crisis.

Among the debates that continue to take place in this field, an important one is related to the decision about whether to opt for rules or to use the authorities' discretion during boom periods. There is a conceptual preference for preestablished rules, which would reduce the risk of regulatory capture by financial interests or of the excessive enthusiasm that characterizes economic authorities during booms. Rules could be made stricter—but never looser—during periods of market exuberance. Appropriate indicators (such as credit growth and asset prices) would need to be chosen in order to ensure that the countercyclical capital or provisions set aside would behave according to the business cycle. However, under the

December 2010 Basel agreement, discretion was accepted as the principle to be followed.

Accounting rules have also been a subject of much debate. They should satisfy the need for both transparency and financial stability. One interesting alternative that has been suggested is that two accounting balances be estimated: one in which current earnings and losses are reported, according to valuations at market prices, and another in which provisions for future losses are deducted from current profits or a non-distributable "business cycle reserve" is established that could only be used to cover future losses.

In order to avoid regulatory arbitrage, it is important for counter-cyclical regulation to be applied to all institutions, instruments, and markets, both nationally as well as internationally. However, since business cycles do not completely coincide, the regulations should be applied by the host countries, although in accordance with internationally agreed-upon principles. This is what seems to be implicit in the decisions of September and December 2010 of the Basel Committee. One fundamental reason for which coordination is essential has to do with contagion. A crisis in an important country (especially if it is an important creditor, debtor, or trade partner) can seriously affect the financial stability or the economy of other countries even if those countries did not accumulate any systemic risk. Therefore, in a globalized economy, all countries have a legitimate interest in avoiding pro-cyclical excess in other countries.

Two matters connected to the comprehensive and countercyclical nature of the regulations are related to the best moment to introduce the new norms and to the effect on credit availability. On the first issue, it is clearly important to agree upon regulation during crises, when the political appetite for regulatory reforms is high and new rules also help restore confidence in financial agents. In particular, increasing the scope of regulation should be immediately applied. However, rules involving more capital, provisions, and liquidity should be gradually introduced and only fully implemented after the economy is on a clear recovery path. However, as pointed out, the slowness in the implementation schedule of Basel III is highly debatable.

In terms of access to credit, it is worth highlighting that stronger regulations should result in higher spreads and may lead to the exclusion from credit markets of those agents that are considered particularly risky. That could generate less financing for small- and medium-sized firms or for poorer households. Therefore, it might be necessary to introduce additional instruments to guarantee access to credit. Higher margins could also mean that companies with direct access to international credit markets could have an incentive to seek loans abroad, increasing the probability of currency exposure in the portfolios of those agents. This is why it is particularly important to introduce rules aimed at handling currency mismatches.

Among the other issues regarding the process of strengthening regulation is that of consumer protection, which has been particularly important in U.S. debates. Due to the quality of toxic mortgages and high-risk investment vehicles, which were being offered in recent years to households that were not financially sophisticated, consumer protection needs to be strengthened. Also, financial instruments should be as simple as possible because complexity leads to information problems and difficulties for the markets in valuing the corresponding instruments. A positive step in the U.S. regulatory reform was the creation of a consumer-protection authority, with universal power over all the firms that provide financial services to them.

It is also probable that the crisis will end up increasing market concentration in the financial industry. This means that restrictions on market power, and even the possibility of dividing up the largest institutions, should also figure in the new regulations. That includes differential treatment to the largest institutions, mentioned earlier. Lastly, it is essential for safeguards to be applied with rigor and for supervision to be carried out according to the highest standards. Some of the most serious errors that led to the current crisis were the result of a lack of supervision and of strict application of existing norms.

THE GOVERNANCE OF INTERNATIONAL FINANCIAL REGULATION

Despite their growing importance, due to the high integration of financial markets, global regulatory institutions have been and continue to be perceived as undemocratic and of limited effectiveness. One central problem here is the representation of developing countries. While the Bank for International Settlements had selectively increased its members,[2] institutions such as the Financial Stability Forum (FSF) and the Basel Committee continued to exclude developing countries prior to the crisis. An exception to this was the International Organization of Securities Commissions (IOSCO), the organization of stock exchange regulators, which had a wide representation from developing countries. However, its Technical Committee—which generates regulatory initiatives—only had Organization for Economic Cooperation and Development (OECD) countries as members.

Given its importance and authority in establishing international banking standards, the Basel Committee has been the target of most criticisms. The exclusion of developing countries from the Committee doubtlessly distorted the policies designed, which proved ineffective in guaranteeing financial stability and were biased against the interests of the developing world (Griffith-Jones and Persaud, 2008). However, despite this criticism, it was not until the global crisis and the subsequent declaration by the G-20 in November 2008 that some significant changes to the governance of the international regulatory institutions were made.

Representation of different members in the governance of an institution translates into decision making. That has been well discussed in the case of the IMF in which voting rights on the Board influence significantly the decisions of that institution (Rustomjee, 2004; Woods and Lombardi, 2006). A similar effect is observed in regulatory organizations whose support of global financial stability proved less effective due to their biased governance structures.

The bias introduced by the system of representation is evident in several areas. Many of the approaches, assumed and promoted by the large banks, such as the use of sophisticated, but flawed, microeconomic risk models, reflected a confidence in the large banks' ability to measure risk parameters themselves. Various developing countries were skeptical about the viability and effectiveness of those approaches, and they were worried about the procyclical dimensions of the regulation developed. Developing countries had experienced a series of financial crises in the immediate past and, being more aware of their costs, gave greater priority to preventing crises. Their lack of participation in the Basel Committee may have biased decisions in favor of the large international banks and against crisis prevention.

In the midst of the global financial crisis and driven, as we have seen, by the decision of the G-20 of November 2008, an important number of those institutions widened their membership, particularly to include the so-called emerging economies. Table 3.1 summarizes the changes to the regulatory organizations. In early 2009 the Technical Committee of the IOSCO, which, apart from Mexico, had not previously included any other developing country, included among its members Brazil, China, and India. In March 2009 the Basel Committee included for the first time

Table 3.1 Composition of Membership of Regulatory Organizations Members per Country in July 2009 (N: New Countries since September 2008; A: Members Prior to September 2008)

	FSB	Basel Committee	IOSCO (Technical Committee)	CPSS
Argentina	N (1)	N		
Australia	A (2)	N	A	N
Belgium		A		A
Brazil	N (3)	N	N	N
Canada	A (3)	A	A (2)	A
China	N (3)	N	N	N
France	A (3)	A	A	A
Germany	A (3)	A	A	A
Hong Kong	A (1)	N	A	A
India	N (3)	N	N	N
Indonesia	N (1)	N		
Italy	A (3)	A	A	A
Japan	A (3)	A	A	A
Luxembourg		A		
Mexico	N (2)	N	A	N
Netherlands	A (2)	A	A	A
Republic of Korea	N (2)	N		N
Russia	N (3)	N		N
Saudi Arabia	N (1)	N		N
Singapore	A (1)	N		A
South Africa	N (1)	N		N
Spain	N (2)	A	A	
Sweden		A		A
Switzerland	A (2)	A	A	A
Turkey	N (1)	N		
United Kingdom	A (3)	A	A	A
United States	A (3)	A	A (2)	A

Note: Number of representatives per country in parentheses.

Source: Helleiner and Pagliari (2009).

various developing countries (Brazil, China, the Republic of Korea, India, and Mexico), as well as Australia and Russia. In June 2009 it widened its membership still further to include all the G-20 countries that were not already members (Argentina, Indonesia, Saudi Arabia, South Africa, and Turkey), as well as Hong Kong and Singapore. Figure 3.1 shows that this closed a large gap in the degree of representation of the Basel Committee, in relation to the countries that supervised the fifty largest banks in the world. At the same time, the Committee on Payment and Settlement Systems (CPSS) invited the following members: Australia, Brazil, China, India, Mexico, Russia, Saudi Arabia, South Africa, and the Republic of

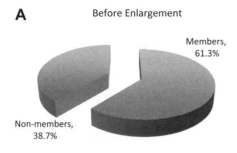

A   Before Enlargement

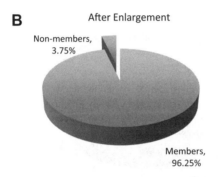

B   After Enlargement

Figure 3.1   Percentage of the Fifty Largest Banks in the World (by Market Capitalization) with Regulators Represented in the Basel Committee, March and April 2009
A. Before Enlargement
B. After Enlargement

Source: Griffith-Jones and Young (2009).

Korea. This is another organization based in Basel that serves as a forum for the central banks to monitor national payment systems as well as cross-border and multiple-currency agreements.

In the second quarter of 2009 the Financial Stability Forum increased its numbers to include all the members of the G-20, including most large developing countries as well as Spain and the European Commission. It was given a new name, the Financial Stability Board (FSB), to reflect its additional powers. This enlargement of the membership was also significant: as Figure 3.2 shows, if measured in terms of world foreign exchange reserves, the FSB has a much better representation than its predecessor.

This increase in the participation of developing countries in the FSB is, of course, a positive step. However, it raises two problems. The first has to do with the number of representatives of different countries. With enlargement, three different categories of countries were created: the BRICs

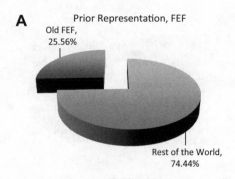

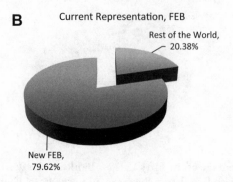

Figure 3.2   Representation in the Financial Stability Forum/Board (FEF/ FEB), Measured by Foreign Exchange Reserves
A. Prior Representation, FEF
B. Current Representation, FEB

Source: Griffith-Jones and Young (2009).

(Brazil, Russia, India, and China) joined the G-7 group of countries, with three representatives each, while Australia, Mexico, the Netherlands, Spain, the Republic of Korea, and Switzerland were assigned two and the rest (Argentina, Hong Kong, Indonesia, Singapore, Saudi Arabia, South Africa, and Turkey) were given one. Even worse, the poorest economies and the small- and medium-sized countries lack any representation.

The second problem is that the FSB is now not only structured around a plenary session but also around a Committee for Initiatives and three additional committees. While this enlargement, and specialization, is welcome, because it strengthens its role, the heads of those five bodies come from developed countries. A greater diversity would be desirable in the future. One interesting example, which could be imitated, is that of the four working groups set up by the G-20 between November 2008 and April 2009. Each working group was headed by one developed country and one developing country.

These critiques are the basis for some of the additional reforms that need to be introduced. We will underline three here. The first is the inclusion of representatives of small- and medium-sized countries in the regulatory bodies. That would ensure that their concerns would be listened to—for instance, the preference for simpler regulation, as well as for small- and medium-sized countries having greater powers to regulate the large international banks active in their countries (see the Warwick Commission, 2009). That could also lead to regulation that reflects much less the interests and preferences of the largest international banks, while being more appropriate for smaller, nationally focused banks. One alternative would be to establish representation by *regions*, rather than individual nations, on regulatory organizations—though counting always with representation from a few major countries. Those representatives could be chosen by the countries of each region according to a system of weighted votes (as occurs in the IMF and the multilateral banks) and with some rules on rotation to guarantee that small- and medium-sized countries are represented. A system of regional representation would also have the advantage that every country would have at least one indirect representative. This fact, as well as the representation of small- and medium-sized countries, would also have the advantage of increasing the legitimacy and efficiency of those organizations. It is urgent that such changes be introduced soon in order to avoid the new structures becoming fossilized.

Second, it is important to include better systems for making regulatory organizations accountable through national parliaments in the case of national regulators. In turn, in the future, international regulatory organizations should be accountable to multilateral representative institutions (UN, 2009).

Finally, the benefits of including developing countries in key international regulatory organizations could be reinforced by the creation of a technical secretariat to support them in their interactions within those organizations. This secretariat could prepare or commission studies, provide a forum for debate between developing countries, and help—when appropriate—define the positions of those countries, especially those that require international action or action by developed countries. One example is the possible international regulation of the "carry trade" that has strong pro-cyclical effects, which is a subject of particular interest to developing countries. In this process the G-24, the major group of developing countries in areas related to the Monetary Fund and the World Bank, could be given a supporting role.

International prudential regulation has developed in a weak and fragmented international context. But finance is globally integrated, and there is therefore an imbalance between the global growth of the financial sector and the international regulatory structure. In the past, regulation and financial supervision have been fundamentally national. The majority of regulatory financial agreements simply acquired the form of "best practices" and "principles" that were not legally binding. Developing countries often found themselves obliged to follow such standards, either because it was a condition for IMF or World Bank borrowing or because the financial markets pressed them indirectly to do so. That is inappropriate.

The need to expand the world's regulatory institutions is in keeping with the principle that, for regulation to be efficient, the regulator's domain should be the same as the market that it is regulating. Important parts of the markets and financial institutions are global; consequently, the regulation should also be global. Moreover, financial activity and risk taking will quickly grow in areas where there are gaps in the regulation or where those gaps give way to regulatory arbitrage.

A global financial regulator would design standards to be applied to all countries and jurisdictions, and it would adopt supervision mechanisms to guarantee their application. This is why it is particularly important for such a global regulator to have real power over those countries whose financial systems have an impact on the global system. Nevertheless, the regulator should allow regulation to be adapted to the different conditions of each country, operating as a *network* of national regulators with strong international coordination. That would follow the principle that global regulation be based on good national regulation (Stiglitz, 2010). For example, the criterion of countercyclical regulation could be internationally agreed upon; nevertheless, as has been highlighted, its implementation would work at a national level in relation with the state of the business cycle in each country. That is one of the reasons, as the United Nations (2009) and Brunnermeier et al. (2009) argue, it is better for international bank subsidiaries to be subject to the regulation of the country where they operate. Additionally, national financial institutions without global connections should continue to be nationally regulated (Reddy, 2010).

Given the difficulty of reaching a consensus for the creation of new international institutions, it would be a good idea to adapt one or more of the existing ones. The best candidate is probably the Bank for International Settlements (BIS), given its interest in the systemic risk in financial markets and the need to regulate them, the high quality of its analysis, and its close ties to central banks and regulatory agencies. Nevertheless, a prerequisite for this institution being transformed into a global financial authority would be a considerable enlargement of the membership to make it a global institution. It would also be essential for the Financial Stability Board, to which the BIS contributes a secretariat, to be a central part of the global regulator.

Additionally, there should be a close process of consultation with the IMF on elements of macroeconomic risks, both at the global and national levels. There is, however, agreement that the IMF is not the appropriate institution to assume the task of global regulator.

For reasons of macroeconomic stability, countries will be allowed to segment their markets with regulations on cross-border capital flows, as the Articles of Agreement of the Fund allow. The regulation of those flows could play a positive role, particularly if financial regulation is seen as insufficient to reduce the volatility of capital flows.

It is important to ensure that the new global regulator is not just effective and efficient but also representative. That is why it is important for developing countries to be adequately represented, in accordance with the criteria outlined earlier.

One reason governments, both in developed as well as developing countries, resist the creation of a global regulator is that they do not wish to relinquish national sovereignty in the field of financial regulation. However, this perception is misguided, since the globalization of private finance means that national authorities no longer have full control over the conditions that determine the financial stability of their countries. That is why, instead of giving up their sovereignty, efforts to coordinate between countries through a global regulator should be understood as an exercise in shared sovereignty, which will allow countries to increase their joint control over the global financial markets.

PROPOSALS FOR A TAX ON FINANCIAL TRANSACTIONS

For some time there have been various proposals to create "innovative sources of financing" that would allow both United Nations official aid targets to be met (0.7 percent of gross national income of industrialized countries) as well as the supply of finance for the provision of global public goods. This matter has been explored in academic terms (see, among others, the essays collected in Atkinson, 2005) and has received repeated support in different United Nations summits since 2000, including the Monterrey Conference on Financing for Development. The greatest advance in international debates was achieved at the World Leaders' Summit on Action against Hunger and Poverty, which took place at the United Nations in 2004 and highlighted the advantages of predictability and potential stability of such innovative flows.

Some of those innovative sources have begun to be adopted by some countries, particularly in the form of special taxes on airline tickets and the issue of bonds backed by expected future contributions from official aid agencies (the so-called international finance facility), which advances the associated resource flows. In both cases, such mechanisms have been used to finance international public health initiatives. Studies already completed show, however, that the greatest flows could come from taxes on carbon emissions and financial transactions, the latter of which we will address here.

The financial crisis has awakened a strong interest in taxes on financial transactions, which have received support not just from civil society but also from the governments of various industrialized countries. This proposal has received the support of the former prime minister and of the head of financial regulation of the United Kingdom, a country with the largest financial center in the world in currency trading. Similarly, the leaders of France and Germany have given important backing to such an idea, which has also won strong support from other European countries, such as Spain, Norway, and Belgium, as well as from Japan and important U.S. parliamentarians.

There are various important reasons for such strong support for a tax on financial transactions. First, even a small tax (of half a basis point, or 0.005 percent) applied exclusively to large currency transactions in the main currencies could generate a significant sum: more than US$30 billion a year (see Schmidt, 2008; Spratt, 2006). Those resources are critical at a moment in which the global crisis has caused a significant rise in deficits and levels of public debt in developed countries, reducing the possibility for attaining the goals on official development assistance. Likewise, the crisis has also increased poverty in several developing countries, making it difficult for them to reach the Millennium Development Goals. Moreover, governments all over the world need additional resources to fund investment in developing countries to fight climate change at a time when the global crisis makes it less likely that the private sector will fund such investments. The fact that a high proportion of large currency trades is carried out by high-earning individuals or specialized financial agents, including alternative investment funds, also makes the imposition of a tax on those transactions attractive.

The second reason the idea of charging taxes on some financial transactions, particularly on currency transactions, is becoming increasingly attractive is that the implementation would be facilitated by the large centralization and automation of clearinghouses. The use of those systems would reduce collection costs and also reduce the risk of significant tax evasion.

Third, political backing for such a tax is greater than before, given the perception that the behavior of the financial sector was one of the main causes of the current crisis. As a small tax, the amounts charged would not affect the functioning of the currency markets nor significantly reduce the volume of their business.

There is also an important tradition of applying taxes to financial transactions at a national level, including in the United Kingdom (the very effective stamp duty on all share sales of 0.5 percent—one hundred times more than the tax proposed for currency trades). Stamp duties on mortgage deals and some other financial deals are also typical in many countries, including the United States. In Latin America, various countries have for several years set taxes on internal financial transactions and sometimes on external ones; Brazil is the one that stands out. Some commentators have, moreover, said that the fact that the currency markets are tax-free despite their high volume is a real anomaly, one that should be corrected (Spratt, 2006). Reserve requirements on capital inflows, applied at different times by Spain, Chile, and Colombia, have similar effects, as in several cases they could be substituted by a payment equivalent to the opportunity cost of such reserves; Malaysia also introduced a tax on capital outflows during the Asian crisis.

The proposal to tax financial deals has a long and distinguished theoretical tradition. The need to correct the difference generated by negative externalities between the marginal public and private profits of a determined economic activity, by taxation, has been recognized at least since Pigou (1920). John Maynard Keynes, in *The General Theory of Employment, Interest and Money*, proposed more specifically a small tax on financial transactions, especially on the stock exchanges, in order to mitigate the volatility generated by the speculative excesses of some market agents (Keynes, 1936). The U.S. Nobel prize-winning economist James Tobin proposed in 1972 a tax of 1 percent on currency transactions. In 1996, however, he said such a tax should be considerably lower, perhaps 0.1 percent. As Tobin (1996) explained, the proposal had two aims: to make the exchange rates reflect fundamental long-term factors to a greater extent, not just short-term expectations and risks, and to make national macroeconomic policies more independent. Seeing that such a tax could generate significant resources, he suggested that the associated revenues be used for international purposes.

The "Tobin tax," as it came to be known, has been widely debated, especially after large financial crises, and has been supported by economists of varying points of view (Jeffrey Frankel, Peter Kenen, Paul Krugman, Joseph Stiglitz, Lawrence Summers, and John Williamson, among others). Recently a new generation of theoretical models has sprung up based on the "microstructure" of markets (see, for example, Shi and Xu, 2009), distinguishing between "fundamentalist" agents, which tend to reduce volatility, and "noise traders" (speculators), which increase volatility. Those models, as well as others, tend to conclude that a tax, as long as it was small, would tend to reduce volatility in currency markets.

In recent years, though, proposals to create a currency transactions tax (CTT) have varied compared to the initial suggestions by Tobin (see, for example, Landau, 2004; Nissanke, 2005; Spratt, 2006). In the search for innovative sources for financing development, a very small international tax (of 0.005 percent) on currency transactions has been suggested. The CTT differs, therefore, from that proposed by Tobin, both in its goal, which now would be to raise additional resources and not to act as a disincentive to speculative flows as such, and in the percentage proposed, which is much smaller, precisely to avoid distorting the currency market. The proposed tax now would be applied not only to spot market transactions but also to foreign exchange derivative trades whose importance has risen significantly in recent decades. Given the high volume of currency transactions, estimated at around US$3 billion a day, it is estimated that a tax of this type could raise more than US$30 billion a year (Schmidt, 2008).

It is important to emphasize that, as a result of the bankruptcy of Herstatt Bank in 1974 and its negative effect on the international settlements system, the regulatory authorities, the central banks, and private banks have undertaken a series of measures to reduce risk in the payment systems. That led to the establishment of the real-time gross settlements system, which aimed to eliminate the systemic risk in currency transactions. That means that all the transactions in foreign currencies are carried out in real time and in a centralized way. Institutions that support these activities and that are centralized and have complete records include SWIFT and the CLS bank. Together with the benefits of recent developments in technology, this makes it easy and inexpensive to charge taxes on currency transactions. Ideally, the tax would be introduced at a multilateral level (or, rather, to the main currencies), but various recent studies have shown that it could be applied to key individual currencies (detailed studies have been done on the euro and pound sterling).

As a result of the global crisis, the authorities in the main financial centers are trying to increase transparency and the centralization of all financial instruments and transactions, including over-the-counter derivatives and credit default swaps, among others. Once such measures are introduced, a small tax on all financial transactions could be considered and used at least in part to finance development. However, that should be seen as a second stage. What could be immediately implemented is a small tax on currency transactions, to gain additional resources to fund development and with some desirable effects, albeit limited ones, on the volatility of financial markets. This seems to be an idea whose time has come.

PREVENTION AND MANAGEMENT OF CRISES IN THE DEVELOPING WORLD

THE MANAGEMENT OF PROBLEMS OF OVERINDEBTEDNESS

Macroeconomic coordination, supervision of macroeconomic policies, and financial regulation all share the fundamental goal of preventing crises. International financial architecture should also have good mechanisms to deal with crises, particularly to avoid those affecting one country or a group of countries from spreading to others—the phenomenon that is now known as "contagion."

One central problem of the current international financial architecture in this field is the absence of a good mechanism to handle debt crises, similar to the bankruptcy regulation that exists in all national legislations. For more than half a century the Paris Club has served as a framework for debt renegotiation with official creditors. The London Club was set up in 1976 to serve as an informal framework for the renegotiation of debts with private banks.

Time and again, however, the main debt renegotiations have taken place outside those frameworks. That was the case with the negotiations between private banks and developing countries during the debt crisis of the 1980s, which were framed by the economic authorities in the United States through the Baker and Brady Plans of the latter part of that decade. The Brady Plan provided a definitive solution, albeit a late one, to the crisis. In the case of low-income countries' public debts, the main renegotiations have used the framework of the Heavily Indebted Poor Countries Initiatives, better known by its acronym HIPC, launched in 1996 and strengthened in 1999, and the subsequent Multilateral Debt Relief Initiative of 2005.

These frameworks have two fundamental deficiencies. The first is that the restructuring initiatives have always arrived late, after debt problems have severely affected countries, and indirectly have also had adverse effects on creditors, given the limited abilities of debtors to pay. The second deficiency is that existing mechanisms do not guarantee equal treatment of different debtors, nor of different creditors. In fact, a repeated criticism of the member countries of the Paris Club is that the private creditors do not accept the restructuring conditions agreed upon by the members of the Club, while benefiting from the reduction of the burden on debtor countries.

There is, on the other hand, no multilateral framework for dealing with crises in international bond markets. There have been numerous proposals since the 1970s to create international bankruptcy courts or forums for mediation or eventual arbitration. These initiatives proliferated after the 1994 Mexican crisis and especially after the 1997 Asian crisis. The corresponding proposals have come from both sectors from the political right, for whom the elimination of "moral hazard" associated with public guarantees to private credits is an essential prerequisite for the good functioning of financial markets, as well as from the left, which sees excess debt levels as a clear obstacle to development.

The most important initiative was the one led by the IMF in the period 2001–2003, under the name Sovereign Debt Restructuring Mechanism (SDRM). This proposal was rejected by both the United States, under clear pressure from its financial sector, and by various developing countries that feared that a mechanism of this nature would end up limiting, or increasing their costs of, access to international capital markets. There was also a clear opposition from some sectors to the IMF leading debt renegotiations, given its clear conflict of interest (since it is also a creditor) and conditionality associated to its financial programs. This is why ad hoc negotiations continued to be the norm, initiated by unilateral indebted countries' defaults, often in open confrontation with their creditors. In the early twenty-first century, the most notorious example was, of course, the Argentine debt renegotiation.

One of the main problems with all these mechanisms is that those parties that do not accept the terms of the agreements can go to the courts in the industrialized countries to defend their rights. An alternative solution to this problem was the spread, since 2003, in the use of collective action clauses for international bonds issued in the United States, a mechanism that was already used in other markets, especially in the English market. This mechanism defines the majorities necessary to restructure a private bond issue. This alternative had been increasingly favored since the Mexican crisis, but it received its final momentum as a result of the U.S. government and financial sector's search for alternatives to the IMF's SDRM initiative. As well as the collective action clauses, some "codes of conduct" were added; that which stands out is the "Principles for stable capital flows and fair debt restructuring in emergency markets," adopted in 2005 by the Institute of International Finance, a private organization composed of large international banks.

Although it may still be too soon to judge if this route—a more decentralized and market-orientated one—is producing the desired effects, the need to count on a multilateral framework for debt resolution, which would be legally enforceable in the main financial markets, remains one of the major gaps in the international financial architecture. An institution of this type would also have the benefit of correcting the two main flaws in the ad hoc structure that has arisen over time: it would lead to restructurings that benefit both creditors and debtors (the essence of a good agreement in this field, in accordance with relevant national bankruptcy legislation), and it would give equal treatment to different debtors and creditors.[3] The recent United Nations Commission of Experts on Reforms of the International Monetary and Financial System has put some alternative proposals on the table in this field (UN, 2009). During the recent crisis, the major debates on this issue have taken place within the EU but have not led, so far, to concrete action.

IMF'S EMERGENCY FINANCING

In contrast to the gap in the existing architecture, since the Second World War, the international community has been able to count on emergency financing from the IMF during balance-of-payment crises.[4] As Figure 3.3 shows, this mechanism provided increasing countercyclical financing until the start of this decade, especially during the debt crisis of the 1980s and the succession of crises that began in 1994: Mexico, East Asia, Russia, South America, and Turkey. One of its overriding characteristics was the tendency to concentrate financing on a few large debtors that have been considered critical since 1994 to avoid the contagion of financial crises and serious problems for developed countries' banks (Mexico, Argentina, and Russia; the Republic of Korea, Indonesia, and Thailand; and then Russia, Brazil, Argentina, and Turkey, in this chronological

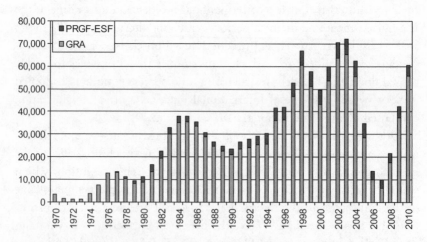

Figure 3.3   IMF Credit Outstanding (Million SDRs)
Notes: PRGF-ESF: Poverty Reduction and Growth Facility and Exogenous Shocks Facility, respectively (credit lines for low-income countries). GRA: General Resource Account.

Source: IMF. http://www.imf.org/external/np/fin/tad/extcred1.aspx.

order). Following this pattern, the IMF increased its loans significantly in 2008, and especially in 2009 and 2010, to countries affected by the global crisis.

After the Mexican crisis, the need to create new credit lines to mitigate balance-of-payment crises caused by sudden stops in external financing or capital outflows began to be recognized. This problem is exacerbated by the fact that the pro-cyclical behavior of capital flows to developing countries reduces the margin for adopting countercyclical macroeconomic policies, and that the conditionality of IMF credits has traditionally tended to reinforce the pro-cyclical nature of those policies. The recent global financial crisis may have represented a turning point in this regard as, in the face of the recessionary risks that the world economy faced, the IMF took an openly countercyclical perspective on the economic policies that industrialized countries and, with greater caution, developing countries, should adopt.

In the context of the financial turmoil that the developing world faced after the Asian crisis, the IMF created two new credit facilities. The first, the Supplemental Reserve Facility, created in 1997, served as a framework for the large loans made during the crises of the late twentieth and early twenty-first centuries. The other, the Contingent Credit Line, had a more preventive aim. The latter was never used because it was perceived as an indicator of vulnerability, and it was suspended in 2003. In 2006 the IMF proposed an alternative line, called the Reserve Augmentation Line, which was under discussion for a long time. Although the proposal was positive in some respects, since it was automatic, doubts were raised about the prequalification process and the scale of the resources.

For the poorest countries, the structural adjustment lines created in the mid-1980s were transformed in 1999 into the Poverty Reduction and Growth Facility, in order to explicitly place the focus on poverty reduction. In January 2006 a credit line was added for those countries that was aimed at facilitating recovery after negative shocks—not just trade ones but also natural disasters—and conflicts in neighboring countries. Curiously, the creation of that line coincided with the weakening of the traditional IMF loan, the Compensatory Finance Facility, which had been designed to cope with negative commercial shocks (especially deterioration in the terms of trade) in low- and middle-income countries. This line had been created in 1963 and comprised about half of IMF loans in the second half of the 1970s. However, it languished due to its excessive conditionality and was not used since 2000.

The global financial crisis led to further reforms in all of these areas. Following the demand for a precautionary credit line, the IMF Board responded in October 2008 with the creation of the short-term liquidity facility (SLF). It provided rapid access to loans for countries with "sound macroeconomic policies" and could be disbursed without the traditional IMF ex-post conditionality. Loans had a three-month maturity and were renewable twice during a twelve-month period; borrowing limits were up to 500 percent of a country's quota. Yet, as the global crisis deepened and spread through the developing world, no country called upon the SLF.

There was active debate at the time on why this facility had not been used. It is probable that the handful of countries that were eligible for the SLF were those that were least in need of loans from the IMF, as they could raise capital through private or bilateral sources. In fact, the same day that the IMF announced the creation of the SLF, the U.S. Federal Reserve finalized reciprocal currency arrangements with Mexico, the Republic of Korea, Singapore, and Brazil—four countries that would have most likely qualified for IMF loans under the SLF. These swap lines were initially given for one year, with limits of US$30 billion, and with maturities ranging from overnight to three months. For these countries, Fed swap lines (and others that arose later on around the world) were clearly superior to IMF loans, both in terms of flexibility and lack of conditionality. An interesting case is that of Mexico, which publicly stated that, though it welcomed its establishment, it had no plans of ever using the SLF but activated the Fed lines in order to help private firms that were facing a scarcity of dollar liquidity after the Lehman collapse. This implies that Mexican officials viewed the SLF as clearly inferior to the Fed swap line.

As a result of strong pressure to take more daring measures, in March 2009 the IMF approved an overhaul to the IMF's lending framework (IMF, 2009c). First, it created the flexible credit line (FCL), which had preventive purposes, for countries with solid fundamentals but that risked problems in their capital accounts. Although three countries rapidly used this credit line (see Table 3.2), the fact that it has not been used by other countries could indicate that it is not sufficiently attractive. For this reason, its terms were improved in August 2010, as the scale of the resources was increased and the period for which it could be used was extended. Reflecting the discussions surrounding similar credit lines in the past, the additional problem of this line is that it artificially divides countries into two groups: those that have "good" policies and those that the IMF does

Table 3.2 IMF Lending by Countries, 2008–2010 (Million SDRs)

Country	Arangement Type	Approval Date	Total Scheduled Amount	Total Withdrawn, December 31, 2010
Low-Income Countries				
LIBERIA	PRGF-EFF	3/15/2008	582	577
TOGO	PRGF	4/22/2008	14	87
MALI	PRGF	5/29/2008	28	24
NIGER	PRGF	5/29/2008	23	13
ZAMBIA	PRGF	6/5/2008	206	202
BURUNDI	PRGF	7/8/2008	46	33
DJIBOUTI	PRGF	9/18/2008	13	5
CONGO, REPUBLIC OF	PRGF	12/9/2008	8	5
KYRGYZ REPUBLIC	ESF	12/11/2008	67	33
SAO TOME AND PRINCIPE	PRGF	3/3/2009	3	1
COTE D'IVOIRE	PRGF	3/28/2009	374	231
TAJIKISTAN	PRGF	4/22/2009	52	65
GHANA	PRGF	7/16/2009	238	149
ETHIOPIA	ESF	8/27/2009	154	154
COMOROS	PRGF	9/22/2009	14	6
CONGO, DEMOCRATIC REPUBLIC OF	PRGF	12/12/2009	346	99
MOLDOVA	ECF-EFF	1/30/2010	370	120
MALAWI	ECF	2/20/2010	52	14
MAURITANIA	ECF	3/16/2010	77	22
GRENADA	ECF	4/3/2010	9	3
GUINEA-BISSAU	ECF	5/8/2010	22	10
LESOTHO	ECF	6/3/2010	42	8
SIERRA LEONE	ECF	6/5/2010	31	9
BENIN	ECF	6/15/2010	74	11
BURKINA FASO	ECF	6/15/2010	46	14
ARMENIA	ECF-EFF	6/29/2010	267	72
HAITI	ECF	7/22/2010	41	8
YEMEN, REPUBLIC OF	ECF	7/31/2010	244	35
Total			**3,443**	**2,009**
Other Countries—Standby Agreements and EFF				
GEORGIA	SBA	9/16/2008	365	577
HUNGARY	SBA	11/7/2008	1,500	7,637
ICELAND	SBA	11/20/2008	420	875
PAKISTAN	SBA	11/25/2008	4,600	4,936
LATVIA	SBA	12/24/2008	629	982
BELARUS	SBA	1/13/2009	1,314	2,270
SERBIA, REPUBLIC OF	SBA	1/17/2009	2,300	1,321
MONGOLIA	SBA	4/2/2009	153	123
COSTA RICA	SBA	4/11/2009	492	0
GUATEMALA	SBA	4/23/2009	126	0

(continued)

Table 3.2 (continued)

Country	Arangement Type	Approval Date	Total Scheduled Amount	Total Withdrawn, December 31, 2010
ROMANIA	SBA	5/5/2009	11,443	9,800
BOSNIA AND HERZEGOVINA	SBA	7/9/2009	494	338
SRI LANKA	SBA	7/25/2009	827	827
UKRAINE	SBA	10/3/2009	8,000	9,250
DOMINICAN REPUBLIC	SBA	11/10/2009	1,095	547
EL SALVADOR	SBA	11/19/2009	1,028	0
ANGOLA	SBA	11/24/2009	859	573
MALDIVES	SBA	12/5/2009	57	10
SEYCHELLES	EFF	12/19/2009	20	5
JAMAICA	SBA	2/5/2010	821	510
IRAQ	SBA	2/25/2010	2,377	772
GREECE	SBA	5/10/2010	26,433	9,131
SOLOMON ISLANDS	SCF	6/3/2010	3	6
ANTIGUA AND BARBUDA	SBA	6/8/2010	81	20
KOSOVO, REPUBLIC OF	SBA	7/22/2010	93	19
HONDURAS	SBA-SCF	10/2/2010	130	0
IRELAND	EFF	12/17/2010	19,466	5,012
Total			**85,123**	**55,542**
Flexible Credit Line				
MEXICO	FCL	3/26/2010	31,528	0
COLOMBIA	FCL	5/8/2010	2,322	0
POLAND	FCL	7/3/2010	13,690	0
Total			**47,540**	**0**

Notes: When more than one credit to a country was approved (Armenia, Seychelles, Malawi, and Honduras), only the most recent one is included.

PRGF: Poverty Reduction and Growth Facility. ECF: Extended Credit Facility. EFF: Extended Fund Facility.

SBA: Standby Arrangement. FCL: Flexible Credit Line.

Source: Monitoring of Fund Arrangements (MONA) database. http://www.imf.org/external/np/pdr/mona/index.aspx.

not classify under this category—which can obviously increase the risks that the market perceives regarding the second group.[5] This classification implicitly transformed the IMF into a credit rating agency.

This is why the other reforms adopted in March 2009 were probably of greater importance. The first was to double the other credit lines and allow a wider use of the ordinary IMF agreements (the stand-by arrangements) for preventive purposes (the so-called high-access precautionary arrangements). In August 2010 an additional step was taken, with the creation of the new precautionary credit line for countries that the IMF has deemed to have good policies but that do not meet the criteria of the FCL. The other significant reform introduced in March 2009 was to eliminate the relationship between IMF disbursements and structural conditionality. These reforms were accompanied by the elimination of several existing credit lines.

In terms of low-income countries, the IMF made new announcements about its concessional credit lines (IMF, 2009d). Apart from doubling the credit limits, in accordance with the March 2009 reforms, it increased the global capacity of the IMF loans to these countries to US$17 billion until 2014. This lending is done through three facilities: (1) the extended credit facility, which replaced the poverty reduction and growth facility (PRGF) and provides help to countries with difficulties in their balance of payments and lasts for various lengths of time; (2) the stand-by arrangements, which can now be used for dealing with external shocks (which used to be addressed through a special credit line) and other balance-of-payments needs; and (3) a rapid credit facility for limited support during emergencies (such as a natural disaster or a temporary external shock), with limited conditionality. The IMF also decided that all low-income countries would receive an exceptional cancellation of all owed interest payments on concessional loans until the end of 2011, as well as lower rates of interest on future loans.

In December 2009 the IMF reformed its concessional credit lines from a single design to a menu of options (IMF, 2009f). The menu aimed to be more flexible to different situations facing low-income countries in relation to their vulnerability to debt and their macroeconomic and public finance management *capacity* (in IMF terminology). Within this framework, each one of the two factors mentioned previously could take two values: "inferior" or "superior." In this way, the framework determines four different concessionary options. Unless the sustainability of the debt is a serious concern (which would be a high value) and the capacity is limited, non-concessionary loans are allowed. On the other hand, countries where the vulnerabilities of the debt are relatively high will always have concessionary loans.

In this framework, low-capacity countries with a high vulnerability to the debt are subject to a minimum concessional threshold of 35 percent, applied to each loan separately. In countries with lower vulnerabilities to the debt, the threshold is set at 35 percent and there is room for non-concessionary loans, based on the sustainability analysis of the debt. For countries with greater capacity and with larger debt vulnerability, the annual limits would be set based on the average debt accumulation in terms of the present value. Lastly, for countries with the best position, those with greater capacity and lower debt vulnerabilities, a minimum concessionary average is set, but that can be completely removed if it is considered appropriate.

Shortly after the creation of the FCL, three countries requested and were granted access to it. Interestingly, on the eve of the April 2, 2009, G-20 meeting in London, Mexico became the first country to use the new facility. As we pointed out earlier, it had explicitly refused to use the SLF and now requested almost three times the amount borrowed during its 1994 crisis. Poland and Colombia soon joined, increasing the demand for the FCL to SDR US$52.2 billion (see Table 3.2). When these initial approvals expired, the three countries again demanded the credit facilities, with a reduction in the sum in the case of Colombia. However, there have been no demands since then on this facility, nor drawings by any of the three countries.

Before the Lehman collapse, demands for IMF resources were very low and came mainly from low-income countries. Only one middle-income country, Honduras, had been approved for a stand-by arrangement by April 2008. Since the Lehman collapse, demand grew rapidly (again, see Table 3.2). A novelty was the fact that, for the first time after a long period, the IMF included among its borrowers high-income countries: Iceland in 2009 and Greece and Ireland in 2010. The credits to the last two countries, together with other large loans (to Romania and Ukraine), represented close to three-fifths of total disbursed loans at the end of 2010. Several middle-income countries also used IMF facilities since the collapse of Lehman, including the preventive facilities, but demand by these countries fell in 2010. In low-income countries, demand has been steadier and preceded the global financial crisis. They absorb only a limited amount of resources.

The history of the last decade indicates that the international system demands that the IMF be more active as a source of emergency financing. The responses it has adopted during the crisis have been an overall improvement, but it needs to continue making progress on designing financing mechanisms with sufficient resources, ones that are automatic and that have a simple prequalification process to deal with the external shocks that developing countries face, especially those coming from the capital account, an issue that is particularly relevant for middle-income countries, and the trade shocks that low-income countries face.

IMF CONDITIONALITY

Debates on IMF conditionality are old but became frontal with the growing scope of the structural conditionality attached to lending in the 1980s and 1990s, particularly after the Asian crisis.[6] Critics underscored the fact that its macroeconomic policy conditions tended to be pro-cyclical—thus enhancing rather than mitigating the effects of external crises—and the fact that the conditions were rigid and not tailored for a country's specific characteristics. Critics also emphasized that IMF programs included structural conditions on economic liberalization that reflected orthodox views on economic reforms, the effects of which were controversial, and were excessively intrusive on domestic decision-making processes in developing countries. They violated the principle of "ownership" of policies by countries that is now widely recognized as a precondition for policies to be effective. Furthermore, many critics also emphasized that those conditions often reflected pressures from influential countries regarding what they wanted specific borrowing countries to do (e.g., opening up their financial sectors to foreign investment, particularly during the Asian crisis).

As a result of these pressures, in the late 1990s the IMF began to reconsider the fiscal and structural conditions attached to its programs. In September 2002 the IMF's board approved a new set of guidelines intended to streamline conditionality. The new guidelines emphasized the need for member countries' ownership of the policies and introduced the requirement that structural conditions be "macro-relevant." Guidelines stipulated that conditions must be "critical to the achievement of program goals," and should thus be "flexible and responsive in discussing alternative policies with countries requesting financial assistance" (IMF, 2002).

Further efforts were made in 2005, 2006, and 2008 along the same lines. In 2005 the IMF's board reviewed the application of the new guidelines and concluded that substantial progress had been made. However, in 2008 the IMF's Independent Evaluation Office (IMF-IEO) completed an assessment of structural conditionality in IMF-supported programs. The report highlighted that conditionality needed to be even more focused and relevant (IMF-IEO, 2008). A new plan approved in May 2008 called for sharpening the application of the 2002 guidelines on conditionality by requiring better justification of criticality, establishing explicit links between goals, strategies, and conditionality, and enhancing program documents.

There were at the time open debates about whether or not conditionality was in fact being streamlined. Whereas Abdildina and Jaramillo-Vallejo

(2005) found evidence that the average number of conditions had declined in recent arrangements, Killick (2005) found no reduction in the number of conditions in programs for low-income countries, and that reliance on conditionality remained high. The IMF-IEO evaluation gave an in-depth numerical analysis of conditionality over time and across sectors. Reviewing the entire lending operations of the IMF between 1995 and 2004, it found that IMF programs, for both middle- and low-income countries, had an average of seventeen structural conditions, and found no statistically significant difference in the number of structural conditions after the IMF approved its new conditionality guidelines in 2002. In PRGF arrangements, the average number of conditions declined from around sixteen to fifteen, while in stand-by arrangements (SBA) they rose from eighteen to nineteen.

The report concluded that conditionality had "shifted out of privatization of state-owned enterprises and trade reform toward tax policy and administration, public expenditure management, and financial sector reform—IMF core areas." The IMF thereafter moved away from controversial areas where it had little impact and that largely fell within the World Bank's areas of expertise (and debates on its own conditionality). The IMF-IEO's conclusion was that the streamlining initiative did not reduce the volume of conditionality, partly because structural conditions continued to be used to monitor other initiatives, such as donors' support programs and the EU accession process. Also, in some cases, members of country economic teams requested specific conditionality to help them leverage their domestic policy goals. Even though the number of conditions did not decline significantly, it was highlighted that the bulk of structural conditions had only limited structural depth: more than 40 percent called for preparing plans or drafting legislation, and about half called for one-off easily reversible changes.

Using the IMF's Monitoring of Fund Arrangements database, which contains information on conditionality in the IMF-supported arrangements and tracks the performance of countries, Table 3.3 shows the IMF's structural conditionality during the current crisis by program. For the SBA program, the average number of structural conditions per country in the period 2008–2010 was 16.5, but this average is biased by a few highly conditional programs, particularly that of Ukraine; in fact, if this program is excluded, the average falls to 14.3. Most of the conditions were structural benchmarks, followed by a large margin by prior action and performance criteria. For low-income country programs, the average number of structural

Table 3.3 Number of Structural Conditions per Country (2008–2010)

A. Programs ECF and PRGF					B. Programs SBA, SCF, and EFF				
Country	PA	SB	PC	Total	Country	PA	SB	PC	Total
CONGO, DEMO. REP.	7	18	0	25	UKRAINE	25	30	11	66
LIBERIA	0	16	9	25	IRAQ	2	25	0	27
BURUNDI	7	9	6	22	ANGOLA	5	20	0	25
GUINEA-BISSAU	0	21	0	21	EL SALVADOR	3	20	0	23
GRENADA	2	17	0	19	GREECE	4	18	0	22
BURKINA FASO	0	18	0	18	SOLOMON ISLANDS	4	16	0	20
MOLDOVA	7	11	0	18	HONDURAS	1	9	8	18
COTE D'IVOIRE	6	11	0	17	JAMAICA	3	15	0	18
SAO TOME	2	14	1	17	ANTIGUA AND BARBUDA	0	16	0	16
TANZANIA	0	17	0	17	PAKISTAN	3	11	2	16
TOGO	2	12	3	17	SERBIA, REP.	6	8	0	14
CONGO, REP.	1	6	9	16	SRI LANKA	6	8	0	14
MAURITANIA	0	16	0	16	BELARUS	7	6	0	13
RWANDA	0	16	0	16	LATVIA	3	9	1	13
MALAWI	4	11	0	15	MONGOLIA	3	10	0	13
ZAMBIA	0	13	2	15	BOSNIA AND HERZEGOVINA	5	7	0	12
ARMENIA	0	14	0	14	IRELAND	1	11	0	12
SENEGAL	2	12	0	14	GEORGIA	0	8	3	11
TAJIKISTAN	5	9	0	14	SEYCHELLES	0	11	0	11
HAITI	3	10	0	13	ICELAND	2	5	2	9
NIGER	0	9	4	13	ROMANIA	0	7	0	7
SIERRA LEONE	0	13	0	13	COSTA RICA	0	6	0	6
BENIN	2	10	0	12	KOSOVO, REP.	4	2	0	6
MALI	1	5	6	12	GUATEMALA	0	3	0	3

(continued)

Table 3.3 (continued)

A. Programs ECF and PRGF						B. Programs SBA, SCF, and EFF			
Country	PA	SB	PC	Total		Country	PA	SB	PC	Total
COMOROS	2	9	0	11						
DJIBOUTI	0	9	2	11						
GHANA	4	6	0	10						
MOZAMBIQUE	0	9	0	9						
CAPE VERDE	0	7	0	7						
UGANDA	0	7	0	7						
LESOTHO	0	6	0	6						
YEMEN	2	3	0	5						

For the nature of the programs, see Table 3.2.

Notes: Types of Conditionality

PA: Prior Action

SB: Structural Benchmarks

PC: Performance Criteria

Source: Monitoring of Fund Arrangements (MONA) database. http://www.imf.org/external/np/pdr/mona/index.aspx.

conditions per country in the period 2008–2010 was 14.5, dominated even more by structural benchmarks. For all IMF programs in the period 2008–2010, the average number of structural conditions totaled slightly more than 15, compared to 17 found in the IMF-IEO report for the period 1995–2004, thus indicating a reduction. For low-income countries, the average number of conditions remained constant, around 15, while in SBA the number of conditions declined significantly from 19 to 14, if we exclude the program for Ukraine.

As per the content of the structural conditions, the same database indicates that, although most conditions were in the IMF's core mandates— public financial management and financial sector soundness—it continued to push conditions in areas beyond such mandates, though less if compared to the period before 2007. These non-core areas include state-owned enterprise reform, social policies, and civil service reform or regulatory reform; this is particularly so for low-income countries.[7] There also remain significant criticisms regarding the character of some of the macroeconomic policies, which many analysts continue to perceive as pro-cyclical.[8] However, the record here has probably improved too, as we have noted, as a reflection of the clearer IMF preference for countercyclical policies during the current crisis. In some cases it may be correct to say that adjustment policies may be required to correct overly expansionary (and thus pro-cyclical) policies during boom years or may be imposed by policy decisions adopted by countries themselves (e.g., decisions to maintain the currency board in Latvia).

THE PREVENTIVE RESPONSES OF THE DEVELOPING WORLD

The two problems noted in IMF financing—excessive conditionality and the lack of appropriate credit lines, and the evidence that the risks implied by the pro-cyclical nature of the capital movements that affect them— explain one of the most generalized approaches that the developing world has adopted in the last few years: a massive accumulation of foreign exchange reserves. In contrast to the debt-crisis resolution mechanisms and emergency IMF financing, this approach is preventive in nature and decisively contributed to the lower vulnerability of these countries during the recent crisis.

The foreign exchange reserves of middle- and low-income countries multiplied by five between 2002 and 2008, reaching US$4.2 trillion (Figure 3.4). By contrast, industrialized countries (OECD) did not face a similar pressure, and the increase reflected in Figure 3.4 is due almost

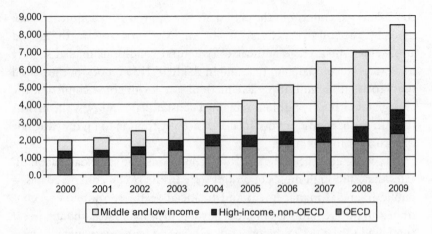

Figure 3.4   Foreign Exchange Reserves (Billion US Dollars)

Source: IMF.

exclusively to Japan's current account surplus. In developing countries, accumulating reserves can be seen as a mechanism of self-insurance against possible financial crises and to avoid excessive IMF conditionality. The international economic conjuncture that characterized the boom that the developing world experienced between 2003 and mid-2008—of abundant, cheap international financing and high commodity prices—facilitated the accumulation of reserves. As Figure 3.3 indicates, one of its effects was the massive reduction in the demand for IMF financing, which was obliged to carry out drastic staff cuts.

Another mechanism with precautionary effects that was extensively used in the developing world after the Asian crisis was the development of domestic bond markets (public but also, increasingly, private), especially in national currencies (Ocampo and Tovar, 2008). The development of these markets has been intended to avoid the currency mismatches generated by external liabilities, which implies that depreciations that take place during crises tended to excessively increase the burden of foreign liabilities. The development of an increasing number of institutional investors in industrialized countries that invest in developing countries and the better ratings of those countries (due to a significant extent to the greater guarantee that growing foreign exchange reserves offer) also contributed to this result; however, they might have generated new mechanisms of pro-cyclical behavior in external financing, to the extent to which those flows respond to the expected evolution of exchange rates in developing countries through the business cycle (appreciation during booms, depreciation during crises).

The accumulation of reserves for self-insurance reasons was, no doubt, a rational response at the level of individual countries to the risks of instability in the international financial system. We should point out, however, that this mechanism has costs—for the countries, as well as of a systemic character. Domestically, it involves the accumulation of assets whose yields are generally lower than that of foreign liabilities. Carrying out policies to "sterilize" the monetary effects of reserve accumulation is also costly when national interest rates exceed the international rates, which is often the case (Rodrik, 2006). Globally, reserve accumulation generates a "fallacy of composition" that contributes to global imbalances. In order to accumulate reserves, developing countries tend to run a surplus in their current accounts, which creates a global recessionary bias unless it is accompanied by deficits in the current account from other countries, especially from the United States. However, such deficits may be unsustainable, and they generate corrections with significant macroeconomic costs. The accumulation of reserves also generates an additional demand for "safe" liquid assets, driving up their prices (and thus reducing their yields), possibly contributing to the generation of asset bubbles. We will return to these issues in the following section.

The East Asian crisis also led to a very important regional project, the Chiang Mai Initiative, adopted in 2000 by the Association of Southeast Asian Nations (ASEAN) countries, China, Japan, and the Republic of Korea (ASEAN + 3). The mechanism was initially conceived as a collection of reciprocal bilateral credits between the central banks of the member countries. Using this mechanism, countries could automatically access up to 20 percent (initially 10 percent) of the maximum of the credit lines agreed upon; over that threshold, they were obliged to adopt an IMF program, which meant that the regional financing was seen as complementary and not as a substitute for IMF support. In 2005 it was further agreed to multilateralize the agreed-upon credit lines. In accordance with this and the later decision adopted in 2007, the system would thus operate as a common reserve fund, but managed by each member country and subject to a single contractual agreement. The corresponding multilateral agreement was signed in December 2009 and included resources totaling US$120 billion.

An institution of this type, set up in the 1960s in Latin America, is the Latin American Reserve Fund. The membership of this institution comprises the Andean countries, Costa Rica, and Uruguay.

The history of the last decade indicates, therefore, that a more active IMF could reduce the domestic costs of the self-insurance policies of developing countries and could contribute to reducing the enormous payments imbalances that characterize the world economy. Regional financing mechanisms could play a complementary role in this task, and in fact the IMF should be seen in the future more as a network of reserve funds than as a mere global fund (Ocampo, 2006). A structure of this type would contribute both to global financial stability and to reducing global imbalances.

REFORMING THE GOVERNANCE OF THE IMF AND THE WORLD BANK

The tendency of developing countries to use unilateral solutions has also been a response to their perception that they are insufficient participators in international financial institutions. This has created a debate, which continues today, about changes to the voice and representation of those countries in the IMF and the World Bank.

In 2006 and 2008 modest agreements were adopted on reforming quotas and votes in the IMF board, which implied a redistribution of the quotas and a tripling of the basic votes to increase the voting rights of developing countries (including the emerging economies) by 2.7 percentage points as a whole. It should be remembered that for a reform to be effective, it needs to be approved by 112 members, representing at least 85 percent of total votes.

During the meetings of the spring of 2010, the ministers in the developing and transitional countries demanded an ambitious additional realignment of the quotas, which would imply an increase of 7 percent in the quotas of developing countries. The specific reforms demanded by developing countries required greater weight being given in the quota allocation to purchasing power parity GDPs and for more precise measures to be adopted to determine the borrowing needs of countries, through an adequate assessment of the macroeconomic volatility that different countries face.

Just before the meeting of the heads of state in Seoul, the ministers of the G-20 approved in October 2010 and the IMF board in November 2010 the principles of the most ambitious reform up to the present of IMF governance, which includes several of the elements mentioned: doubling the quotas, revising the allocation of quotas and voting power of developing countries, while protecting those of the poorest countries, reducing by two the European representatives on the IMF board, and electing all of its members. However, the increase in the quotas (3.9 percentage points in relation to that which prevailed prior to the 2006 reforms) and voting power (5.3 points) of developing and transition economies was less than the expectations of these countries, in such a way that the large gains by some of them (China, Republic of Korea, Brazil, India, Mexico, and Turkey, in that order), totaling 7.3 and 6.7 percentage points in terms of quota and voting power, respectively, came partly at the expense of other developing countries. In Europe, an interesting reform that could be made would be to consolidate all the chairs of the EU into one, which would facilitate Europe speaking with one voice on the board.

An important proposal made on various occasions, which was reiterated by the IMF's Commission for Governance Reform, headed by Trevor Manuel (IMF, 2009b), is for the threshold of votes needed to approve important political changes in the IMF to be reduced from the current 85 percent to, for example, 70–75 percent. That would mean that the United States could no longer exercise a veto on the IMF board on important policy decisions. This commission also proposed accelerating the process to reform the quotas, that all chairs on the board be elected—which has already been agreed upon—and that a Council of Ministers be formed to adopt the most important policy decisions of the institution.

For its part, during the spring of 2010 meetings, the World Bank approved a transfer of 3.13 percentage points of voting power from the developed economies to the developing and transition economies (DTEs), which include Saudi Arabia and the Republic of Korea. The DTEs will now hold 47.19 percent of voting power at the World Bank, and they have received a promise that they will reach parity in the near future. The greatest increase was for China, which gained 1.65 percentage points to become the World Bank's third shareholder. The increases were mainly concentrated in middle-income countries, especially in Asia, which were underrepresented, while low-income countries saw limited change. In the developed countries, the EU and Japan will see their voting power reduced, but not the United States. The developing and transition countries saw this reform as a step in the right direction toward equal voting power at the World Bank, as expressed in the G-24 statement of April 2010.

The change in voting power will be achieved through an ad hoc capital increase. The objective is, however, to develop a formula based on principles for the next revision in 2015; developing countries expressed their clear preference for a more ambitious calendar. That reflects the fact that there was no agreement on a new dynamic formula for participation, one that would capture the changing economic weight of the countries and contributions to the development objectives of the World Bank. Disagreements arose because many shareholders considered those principles, which followed the G-20 commitments at the Pittsburgh meeting in 2009 and the annual IMF/World Bank meeting in Istanbul, as not applying to the World Bank's proposal, which was based almost totally on the economic weight of the countries. The World Bank's development mission is important both for donors and for client countries. For the donors of the International Development Association (IDA), it is important to assign votes in accordance with the size of contributions to the IDA in order to generate incentives to larger contributions to the capital of the Association, which would benefit low-income countries. For medium-income countries, it is also important to bear in mind their character as borrowers.

Finally, it is crucial for the heads of the IMF and the World Bank, as well as the senior management of those organizations, to be elected on the basis of transparent and open processes, based on the merit of the candidates, regardless of nationality. It is encouraging that in the April 2009 G-20 leaders' meeting, those principles were approved, and must now be applied. It would also be useful for the personnel of these institutions to become more diverse, not just in terms of nationality but also in education, professional experience, and gender.

GLOBAL IMBALANCES AND THE REFORM OF THE INTERNATIONAL MONETARY SYSTEM

GLOBAL IMBALANCES

One field in which international financial architecture has monumentally failed is in providing a mechanism for guaranteeing consistent macroeconomic policies among the major economies. These policies continue to be national in almost all countries, including in the economy that issues the main international currency, and a mix of regional and national policies in the euro zone, where monetary policy is now regional (although not for all members), but fiscal policies remain national. That is combined with an international monetary system and, in particular, with the world reserve system, which is still based to a large extent on a national currency, the U.S. dollar.

The reforms that have taken place over time have added some positive elements to this architecture, but they have also suffered significant setbacks and conflicts. The creation of the IMF at Bretton Woods represented the most important attempt to establish a mechanism for macroeconomic policy cooperation based on rules that would allow each country to also adopt policies aimed at guaranteeing full employment (internal balance) and to correct fundamental external deficits (external balance) without causing negative effects on the international economy or on other countries. Countries were allowed to modify their exchange rates while avoiding competitive devaluations, which had contributed to the Great Depression in the 1930s. The IMF's capacity to provide partial multilateral official financing was aimed at avoiding policies aimed at correcting balance-of-payments deficits that would have recessionary effects, again with negative impacts on other countries. The IMF also offered a multilateral mechanism for macroeconomic dialogue and cooperation. These forms of international cooperation were reinforced with the creation in 1969 of a true international reserve currency, the SDRs, issued by the IMF. Of course not all the elements were positive, since the Bretton Woods agreement put the dual dollar-gold standard at the center of the international monetary system, which generated its own instabilities and finally collapsed in the early 1970s.

The collapse of the dollar-gold standard and the system of fixed parities and its substitution by a mechanism of variable parities between the major currencies introduced greater flexibility into the international economic system as well as more independence for national macroeconomic policies, at least for the main countries. It also introduced, however, new potential conflicts if the macroeconomic policies of the major economies were not moving in a consistent direction. In the last decade, for example, one endemic problem has been the contrast between the tendency by the U.S. Federal Reserve to adopt clearly countercyclical policies and the greater caution of the European Central Bank in doing so. Possible tensions in monetary policy mean that the substitution between alternative reserve currencies (the dollar versus the euro, in particular) could exacerbate instead of cushion world financial volatility, to the extent that it is reflected in the instability in the exchange rates between major currencies. In any case the dominant tendency has been toward the use of the dollar as the main international reserve asset (two-thirds over the last decade, according to IMF statistics), which means that the elimination of the dual gold-dollar standard gave way to one fundamentally based on a fiduciary dollar—a "fiduciary dollar standard," as we will call it here.

The macroeconomic coordination mechanisms put into place since the 1970s have also operated outside the IMF and have not been particularly effective. In the 1980s they were ad hoc agreements among the major economies (the Plaza 1985 and the Louvre 1987 Agreements), and subsequently they worked through dialogues within the Group of 7 (the G-7), which clearly left out the main developing countries. The IMF took an interesting step in April 2006 when it created a "multilateral surveillance" mechanism, the aim of which was precisely to deal with the macroeconomic and financial interrelations between members of the IMF. That process involved the euro zone, Saudi Arabia, China, Japan, and the United States, and its objective was to reduce global imbalances without sacrificing economic growth. Although the motivation of the new mechanism was positive, its results were frustrating.

We should also mention that in June 2007 the IMF board adopted a new resolution on surveillance of countries' exchange rate policies, the first in almost thirty years. This resolution put the principle of external stability at the center of the IMF's activities. To the old principles, which already aimed at avoiding exchange rate interventions that negatively affect other member countries, a new criterion was added—avoiding exchange rate policies that generated external instability. From the outset, China expressed strong reservations about this mechanism.

In the direction of increasing the number of agents, one interesting step that took part in the dialogues, and eventually in macroeconomic cooperation, was the G-20 decision in Pittsburgh in 2009 to designate that group "as the premier forum for our international economic cooperation" under the multilateral supervision of the IMF. In this context the Mutual Assessment Process, launched in 2010 to advance the coherence of macroeconomic policies, represents an important advance, though its reach is still subject to clear definitions. In any case, that solution is only a partial step toward the necessary task of placing the IMF again at the center of world macroeconomic policies. The solution also created problems because of the ad hoc nature of the cooperation mechanism adopted.

The need for better macroeconomic coordination mechanisms became clear in light of the large current account imbalances that have characterized the world economy in recent periods, as shown in Figure 3.5. The strong external deficit of the United States and, more recently, that of the EU, contrast with the surplus of Japan, as well as that of China and other developing countries, especially oil producers. The sharp increase in the United States' deficit became acute during the sequence of crises that developing countries experienced since 1997, when the expansion of the U.S. economy served to cushion the contractionary global effects of those

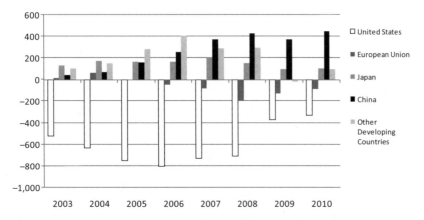

Figure 3.5   Current Account Balances (Billion US Dollars)

Source: IMF (2009e). http://www.imf.org/external/pubs/ft/weo/2009/02/weodata/index.aspx.

crises. That deficit continued to grow until the middle of the past decade and was kept at high levels until the eruption of the recent global financial crisis, despite the dollar's trend toward depreciation, which began in 2003. During the global 2003–2007 boom, the self-insurance policy of the developing countries contributed to the generation of those imbalances. High commodity prices, particularly of oil and metals, also generated surpluses in most commodity exporting countries. The main reflection of this was the rapid increase in the United States' net foreign liabilities, which reached US$2.1 trillion at the end of 2007.

Imbalances were reduced as a result of the global financial crisis and especially as a result of the substantial cut in the United States' deficit and in the surpluses of Japan and developing countries, excluding China (again, see Figure 3.5). The estimates for 2010 included in the figure indicate a moderate increase of such imbalances. Furthermore, IMF (2009e, 2010) and United Nations (2010, 2011) projections show an asymmetry between the adjustment of the United States and other deficit countries (mainly European) and the rising surpluses of China and some other developing countries, mainly oil and mineral exporters. These trends imply that their net effect will be to reduce global aggregate demand—in other words, they will have a recessionary effect—and in practice they will not work out as projected, since the surpluses and deficits will necessarily have to compensate for one another. This reflects the need to maintain expansionary policies at the world level while improving the mechanisms for coordinating national macroeconomic policies to avoid a new global recession.

THE PROBLEMS OF THE WORLD RESERVE SYSTEM

The magnitude of the recent international financial crisis highlighted the problems of the international monetary system and, in particular, the relationship between the world reserve system and global imbalances—and in a wider sense between the monetary system and international economic stability.

The world reserve system shows three fundamental deficiencies (Ocampo, 2010). All are related, in turn, to the fact that there is no mechanism to guarantee that surpluses and deficits of different countries offset one another without negative effects on global economic activity.

The first problem, that emphasized by J. M. Keynes during the debates that led up to the Bretton Woods agreements, is that the present international monetary system—like all systems that preceded it—has a bias against countries running deficits (Keynes, 1942–1943). That tends to generate a global recessionary effect if the corrections that deficit countries need to adopt to balance their external accounts do not find financing in adequate quantities (or if those countries do not think it is appropriate to maintain the deficits and the financing associated with them) and if those adjustments are not offset by expansionary policies in surplus countries. This problem can be called the *anti-Keynesian bias*.

The second deficiency, which has become known as the *Triffin dilemma*, after the pioneering work by Robert Triffin (1961, 1968), has to do with the fact that an *international* reserve system based on one *national* currency (the U.S. dollar)—and, more generally, a limited number of national or regional currencies (the euro currently)—is inherently unstable. The only way the rest of the world can accumulate net assets in dollars is if the United States runs a current account deficit. But such deficits can lead to a loss of confidence in the dollar and, more generally, to strong cycles in the value of the main international currency and the current account of the country that issues it, which strongly affects the rest of the world economy. Deficits also encourage the excessive growth in credit in the United States and price bubbles in financial and property assets, which generate the risk of financial crises.

Being the center of the world monetary system means that, apart from appropriating seigniorage, the United States also benefits from having its deficits financed at low costs by reserve accumulation in the rest of the world. Furthermore, the United States also enjoys the additional privilege of being able to carry out a relatively autonomous monetary policy—and even to impose it on the rest of the world. The basic reason for this is the perception (and subsequent use) of the securities issued by the U.S. Treasury as the "safest assets," which means that the determinants of the U.S. rates of interest are relatively independent of the dollar's exchange rate against other currencies.

For this reason, the United States has not generally considered the real or probable weakening of its currency as a significant problem that needs to be corrected. The absence of constraints on the U.S. monetary policy has meant that, in contrast to Keynes's classic theories on the recessionary bias in the international monetary system, the fiduciary dollar standard on which the world economy has functioned over the last four decades can produce exactly the opposite phenomenon during certain periods: an inflationary bias. The boom that preceded the recent crisis could be considered the most noteworthy example of this type of outcome.

The third deficiency of the current reserve system is its inequitable character. As we have already highlighted, the need to accumulate foreign exchange reserves forces developing countries to transfer resources to those countries that issue reserve currencies. This *inequity bias* has been magnified in the last few decades by financial and capital market liberalization and by the strongly pro-cyclical behavior of the capital flows toward developing countries. This behavior has generated, as we have seen, a massive accumulation of foreign exchange reserves as a form of self-insurance against sudden stops of external financing. This accumulation can also be seen as a rational response to a system that lacks a "collective insurance" in the form of good IMF emergency financing. It also generates the "fallacy of composition" already mentioned, which worsens the distortions in the world balance of payments and can generate, as we have seen, a recessionary bias. We could call this problem the *inequality-instability* link.

The three problems mentioned have been clearly present in the behavior of the world economy. The first and the third have already received attention in previous sections of this chapter. The recessionary biases could present themselves in the next few years if a considerable number of countries try to improve their current account balance (by reducing their deficit or increasing their surplus), as we stated at the end of the previous section. The massive accumulation of reserves by developing countries, and their contribution to global imbalances, is the clearest demonstration of the third, as we showed in the third part of this chapter.

Under the prevailing fiduciary dollar standard, deficits in the United States' balance of payments have been the rule rather than the exception.

During the past three and a half decades, the world has been affected by an ever more intense cycle of growth and contraction in the U.S. current account deficit, which is linked to strong fluctuations in the real exchange rate of the main reserve currency, as shown in Figure 3.6. That implies that the dollar has lacked the main feature that a currency at the center of the system should have: a stable value. Moreover, corrections to the U.S. current account have also taken place in a context of a world economic downturn, as the recent crisis confirmed.

The interaction between the three problems mentioned is particularly clear in the U.S. deficit since the end of the 1990s. As Figure 3.6 indicates, the greatest deterioration in the U.S. current account in history began at the end of that decade. Although it had its equivalent in the deterioration of the domestic deficits of the United States, particularly among households, it should be recognized that the huge size of the current account imbalances was also a result of factors external to the U.S. economy, particularly the recession or slow growth experienced by large parts of the developing world during the succession of crises that started in 1997. The U.S. deficit served to mitigate the anti-Keynesian bias generated by the massive crises experienced by the developing world.

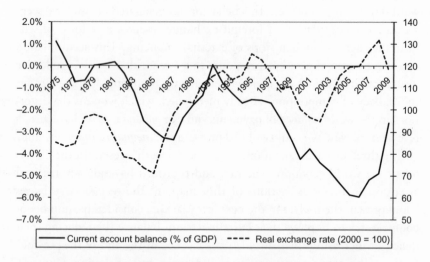

Figure 3.6   U.S. Current Account Balance and Real Exchange Rate

Source: IMF, International Financial Statistics. The real exchange rate is depicted here to show an increase when there is a real depreciation (the opposite convention to that used by the IMF). It is calculated as the inverse of the real exchange rate estimated by the IMF.

On the other hand, although the strong U.S. and global slowdown of 2001 allowed the U.S. deficit to decline, the effect was moderate relative to similar past downturns, and the upward trend in the deficit began again the following year. Although that increase is linked again to internal problems in the U.S. economy, it is also related to developing countries' strong demand for self-insurance, as well as to the surpluses of commodity-exporting countries. This is why the strong but orderly depreciation of the dollar since 2003 was not accompanied, as was the case in the second half of the 1980s, by a significant correction in the United States' current account deficits, which only firmly started in 2008 as a product of the deep U.S. recession—and a world crisis.

REFORMING THE SYSTEM

The first among the alternatives for reforming the international monetary system would be to transform the current system into one based on multiple reserve currencies that compete with each other. That alternative is, in fact, already implicit in the system that has operated since the early 1970s and would be in some sense an inertial solution. However, it is not clear that the system would necessarily evolve in that direction, as the problems that the euro has faced during some phases of the current crisis, especially at the end of 2008 and during several conjunctures in 2010, when that currency experienced strong downward pressures as market agents distrusted the strengths of some members of the monetary union.

Additionally, and more importantly for the issues analyzed in this chapter, a system of this type would not correct the main problems of the current monetary system. It would do nothing to correct the anti-Keynesian bias, and each currency would lack stability, one of the essential characteristics that a reserve currency should have. Furthermore, although this model would offer developing countries the advantage of being able to diversify the composition of their reserves, they would be invested in any case in assets issued by industrial countries, which would maintain the transfer of resources from developing countries to the industrial world. One exception would be if the renminbi were to become a major reserve currency, but that possibility depends on the speed by which China evolves to give full convertibility to its currency and would only benefit one developing country, transformed into a world power.

Curiously, flexibility in exchange rates among major reserve currencies constitutes both the main advantage and the most important disadvantage of the system. The advantage is derived from the fact that a competitive system of reserve currencies would resist attacks on fixed parities that ended up bringing down both the bimetallic (silver-gold) standard in the nineteenth century and the gold-dollar standard in the early 1970s. However, that flexibility adds another additional element of instability compared to a system purely based on the dollar, due to the volatility in the exchange rates among major reserve currencies—a problem that is, in some ways, already present in the current system. Such volatility generates significant profits and losses for central banks in their reserve management and eliminates one of the characteristics that reserve assets should have: to be "safe," or low risk. That is its main disadvantage.

This disadvantage would be exacerbated if central banks responded to fluctuations in exchange rates by changing the composition of their foreign exchange reserves, thereby feeding into exchange rate instability. Under those conditions, a system of multiple reserve currencies could generate growing demand for the adoption of an agreement for fixed exchange rates—in other words, a return to the Bretton Woods scheme, at least for reserve currencies. However, setting exchange rates between the major currencies in a world characterized by massive capital mobility would be a difficult or altogether impossible task. We should add that, given the high demand for foreign exchange reserves, developing countries suffer disproportionately from exchange rate instability among reserve currencies.

All this implies that the main deficiencies can only be resolved by a deeper reform of the global reserve system. Although other alternatives could be designed—such as Keynes's proposal to create an international clearing union and similar solutions[9]—the most viable consists of completing the transition started in the 1960s with the creation of the SDRs. That involves placing a world fiduciary currency at the center of the system, completing a tendency in the evolution of national and international monetary systems since the nineteenth century (Triffin, 1968). Given the pro-cyclical nature of the capital movements that developing countries face, as well as the high demand for foreign exchange reserves that such behavior generates, the adoption of a scheme of this type should be accompanied by other initiatives aimed at guaranteeing that issues of SDRs are used to correct, at least partially, some of the problems that developing countries face under the current system.

The role of the SDRs has changed since the early 1970s with the transformation of the international monetary system toward a fiduciary dollar standard. The questions related to adequate international liquidity, which were the fundamental concern during the early postwar period, and which were still the center of world debate in the 1960s, are no longer important except during extraordinary conjunctures, such as those caused by the severe liquidity crunch that characterized the world financial meltdown of September and October 2008. As we have seen, the fiduciary dollar standard can show an inflationary bias, which reinforces the boom of the world economy, as happened in the period 2003–2007. Nevertheless, other problems that were also the object of attention in the 1960s continue to be fundamental or even more important today, especially those linked to the composition of world reserves, the access of developing countries to liquidity, and questions of equity related to both processes.

After the initial allocations carried out in the periods 1970–1972 and 1979–1981, no further allocations were made for almost three decades. The last of them, approved by the IMF in 1997, for SDR US$21.4 billion, only came into effect in mid-2009 with the approval by the U.S. Congress of the change in the IMF's Articles of Agreement, of which it was part. The current crisis, however, generated renewed interest in this mechanism of international cooperation, as reflected in the G-20 proposal, subsequently approved by the IMF, to allocate SDRs equivalent to an additional US$250 billion, of which little short of 40 percent benefited developing countries under the current system of quotas. That meant that SDR issues reached in 2009 the equivalent of US$283 billion. Although that is an important sum and meant that the SDR increased to somewhat less than 4 percent of world non-gold reserves at the end of 2010, this proportion is still inferior even to that at the time of the first allocations in the period 1970–1972, when it reached 10 percent (Williamson, 2009). The suspension of the SDR issues for more than a quarter of a century had negative effects for developing countries because it coincided with an increase in demand in the foreign exchange reserves by those countries.

Any international monetary reform should involve a considerable increase in the size of the IMF, which has been lagging significantly behind the size of the world economy since the 1998 revision of quotas, and since the 1970s in comparison to the magnitude of world capital flows (IMF, 2009a). The decision adopted by the G-20 in Seoul to double the quota represents an advance, though it still falls short if we compare IMF resources to the size of current global financial flows. Obviously the form by which the IMF obtains its resources is essential. The SDR allocations and the quota increases are much better mechanisms than "arrangements to borrow" in their different forms, the main option chosen by the G-20 in April 2009, as well as in the past, to increase the resources available for the IMF during crises.[10]

The creation of a system based to a greater degree on SDRs would contribute to a large extent to resolving both the Triffin dilemma as well as the distributive effects caused by the use of U.S. currency as the principal reserve asset. In the last few years the proposals to increase SDR issuance have followed two different models. The first consists of issuing SDRs in a countercyclical way, concentrating them basically in periods of crisis and possibly destroying them once financial conditions normalize (UN, 1999; Camdessus, 2000; Ocampo, 2002). That would create a countercyclical element in the management of international liquidity. The second model proposes regular SDR allocations equivalent to the additional demand for reserves at the world level, which is at least US$300 billion a year, a sum similar to that accumulated by low- and middle-income countries, excluding China, in the period 2003–2007. That is also the size of the SDRs that should be issued in the long term for countercyclical purposes. One alternative that combines these two options would be to make regular issues but to keep them inactive and make them effective only under preestablished conditions.

One fundamental problem this reform faces is the distribution of IMF quotas that are also the basis for issuing the SDR and do not reflect the realities of today's world economy. Apart from the subjects that have been discussed in recent debates on IMF quotas, which have led to some improvements, the most important issue is the enormous gap between the demand for reserves from developing economies and industrialized ones, which is at the heart of the inequities in the global reserve system and the inequality-instability link. The problem can only be corrected through a reform or a combination of four types of reforms (since they are not mutually exclusive).

The first would be to include the demand for reserves as a criterion for SDR allocations, which in practice would mean awarding a large part of the issues to developing countries.

The second consists of linking countercyclical SDR issues to IMF financing during crises in order to improve the provision of a "collective insurance" against balance-of-payment crises. One option for doing that would be to consider those SDRs that are not used by countries to be deposits (or loans) to the IMF, which could be employed by the institution to lend to countries requesting emergency financing.[11] Of course, for this task it is essential to improve the IMF's credit lines and their conditionality in order to overcome the stigma associated with its loans. An option that could be considered in this regard is to adopt at least part of Keynes's original plan: to create a drawing line that can be *unconditionally* used by *all* IMF members for a preestablished sum and period. Another possibility, which might be more politically feasible, would be for the IMF to grant unconditional credit to countries suffering shocks that have a clear external origin, whether the shocks affect a country's capital account or its current account. The compensatory credit line, which was scrapped in March 2009, worked when it operated with light conditionality rules.

The third proposal would be to create an explicit "development link" in the SDR allocations (which could be an alternative or a complementary proposal to the first one). One of the proposals along these lines is to use the SDR allocation corresponding to industrialized countries to finance official development assistance and the provision of global public goods (Stiglitz, 2006, chap. 9). This suggestion has many advantages but poses the problem that such transfers would have a fiscal character and therefore might need approval from each national parliament. An alternative to this would be a similar scheme to the one suggested by the Group of Experts gathered by UNCTAD in the 1960s (UNCTAD, 1965): to allow the IMF to buy bonds from multilateral development banks to then finance the long-term demands for the financing of developing countries.

The fourth proposal would be to encourage the creation of funds or other *regional* reserve agreements in developing countries—such as the Latin American Reserve Fund and the Chiang Mai Agreement, mentioned earlier—that would provide a complementary form of collective insurance. One important incentive to such regional agreements would be a provision under which SDRs were proportional not just to the IMF quotas but also to the funds that developing countries have contributed to regional reserve funds (UN, 1999; Ocampo, 2002).

Lastly, there are two complementary reforms that many analysts consider necessary in order to consolidate the role of the SDR in the international monetary system. The first is to allow the use of this currency in some private-sector transactions (see, among others, Kenen, 1983). Of course there are intermediate solutions: allowing the use of the SDRs only for specific purposes, such as those associated with financial institutions' capital or liquidity requirements.

The second would be creating a "substitution account," a suggestion made at the end of the 1970s when the dollar faced adverse pressures. That account would allow countries to exchange their dollar for SDR assets issued by the IMF, thus reducing pressures on the dollar in the market. This would give more stability to the current monetary standard and would be, in any case, a necessary transition mechanism for a global reserve system based on SDRs. The IMF decision of July 2009 to allow the issuing of securities denominated in SDR to draw in resources from some emerging economies can be considered a step in that direction. The fundamental problem, underlined in the debates of the 1970s, is how to distribute the losses that the IMF could incur with a mechanism of this type. That said, those costs are not necessarily very high. Retrospective calculations done by Kenen (2009) indicate that, if the mechanism had been in place in the period 1995–2008, those losses would have been minimal.

The current context could be a good moment to introduce these reforms. First, the inflationary risks associated with SDR issues are low and, on the plus side, such issues could reduce the recessionary risks that the world economy is facing because of the fear of running up deficits, as reflected in the evolution of global imbalances. Second, the United States has embarked on a high fiscal deficit and an aggressive monetary easing. That has potential implications for the stability of the current reserve system, as some countries have pointed out, China especially (Zhou, 2009). In reality, under the current circumstances, the United States could find its central role in the global monetary system rather uncomfortable, since it could be an obstacle to its freedom in economic policy.

In any case, abandoning the dollar as the chief world *reserve* currency is consistent with maintaining its role as the major international means of payment and of financial transactions, unless SDRs were used in a larger set of financial transactions. These uses of the dollar increase demand for the services of the U.S. financial system and have other implications for the country that have been explored by other authors (see Cooper, 1987, chap. 7, for instance). It clearly remains to be seen whether the crisis under way will have permanent effects on the role of the United States as the world's main banker, but these effects have so far been insignificant.

IN CONCLUSION: AN OVERALL LOOK AT THE REFORM
OF INTERNATIONAL FINANCIAL ARCHITECTURE

The Asian crisis of 1997 and its contagion to Russia and Latin America led to great interest in reforming the international financial architecture. A decade later and in the face of what was the prelude to a new financial crisis, which had its epicenter in the largest economy of the world, progress on reform has been disappointing. In fact, global imbalances were probably more pronounced than at any time since the Second World War, the regulatory deficit in the most developed financial markets was massive, and the IMF found itself undergoing its worst crisis in history.

One positive aspect about the period 1997–2007 was the definition of a broad consensus on international financial and development reform, the Monterrey Consensus, adopted in 2002, but its implementation has been frustrating. The main areas of progress during this period were the stronger macroeconomic policies and financial regulation in developing countries and the creation or deepening of domestic bond markets in those countries. In turn, developing countries responded to the absence of a good collective world insurance mechanism against financial and balance-of-payment crises with their own massive self-insurance, through an unprecedented accumulation of foreign exchange reserves. We should add to that East Asia's Chiang Mai Initiative, which created a regional mechanism to support countries during crises. At an international level, IMF credit lines were improved and a failed debate took place on the introduction of a multilateral mechanism to manage sovereign debt crises.

The reform efforts of developing countries were, therefore, the main achievements in international financial reform in the period 1997–2007. The paradox of that was that international reform was based more on the *national* reforms carried out by developing countries than on a true reform of the *international* financial architecture. Those efforts served to cushion the effect of the global crisis of 2007–2008 on developing countries.

As a result of the crisis that hit in September 2008, there have been important advances. The most relevant are the revival of SDRs as a mechanism of international cooperation, the creation of new IMF facilities, and the (incomplete) advances in financial regulation in the main industrialized countries.

One issue emphasized since the Asian crisis has been the need for a world governance structure in which developing countries have adequate "voice and representation" in world economic decision making. The IMF made some timid steps in this direction in 2006 and 2008, which were followed by more ambitious agreements in October and November 2010. The World Bank initiated discussion on the issue with a lag and also adopted a modest reform in 2010. In both organizations the changes that the world economy has experienced demanded that a greater weight be given to Asian developing economies mainly at the expense of European countries. Given the loss of participation of the poorest countries in the world economy, the only way to maintain their voice was to increase the basic votes of countries in the IMF.

The most important change in terms of world economic governance generated by the global financial crisis was the creation of the G-20 at the leaders' level. Since its creation after the Asian crisis, the G-20 had previously operated with limited impact as a forum for finance ministers and central bank governors. One important G-20 decision was to give all its members access to regulatory organizations on financial matters, especially to those assigned to coordinate the tasks of world financial reform, the renamed Financial Stability Board (previously Forum). These reforms increased the representation of developing countries in those organs. Although that represents progress, it also raises serious questions, given the ad hoc way in which the membership of such organizations has been defined, which implies, in particular, the lack of representation of small- and most medium-sized developing as well as industrialized countries. In this sense the creation of the G-20 at the leadership level should be seen as merely a transition to a more representative instrument of global economic governance.

NOTES

We thank Ariane Ortiz for her excellent support in the drafting of this chapter, particularly in the sections on the IMF, of which she is a coauthor. We also thank Carmen Seekatz and Francisca Miranda. This chapter covers events until the end of 2010.

1. See the collected essays on this in the recent book by Griffith-Jones, Ocampo, and Stiglitz (2010).

2. It also included the presidents of the central banks of developing countries (Mexico and China) in its directory.

3. Read the extensive analysis on these topics in the essays collected in the recent book by Herman, Ocampo, and Spiegel (2010).

4. Ariane Ortiz is a coauthor of this and the following section.

5. Just before the creation of the FCL, then UNDP administrator, Kemal Dervis (2008) expressed concern that programs such as the SLF and the Fed's swap facilities effectively created two groups of countries. In this regard, he pointed out that such an "all or nothing categorization will create serious political tensions . . . [and] will

also make it politically difficult for these governments [that are left out] to engage in such negotiations if other countries have immediate access to assistance from the IMF or Central Bank swaps."

6. The best known are those expressed by Stiglitz (2002).

7. This is evident in the review of conditions in the programs that, for reasons of space, is not included here. To properly assess the significance of reductions in numbers, a deeper analysis of the content of the conditionality of specific programs would be required, but this is beyond the scope of this chapter.

8. An important contribution to this debate is the report by the Center for Economic Policy Research in October 2009 (Weisbrot et al., 2009), which indicates that 31 out of 41 countries with IMF agreements have been subject to pro-cyclical fiscal and/or monetary policies, and the IMF has relied on overly optimistic growth forecasts. The latter issue has been emphasized in several evaluations of the IMF throughout the years.

9. See, for example, Stiglitz (2010) and D'Arista (1999), as well as the proposal made in the 1960s to create a commodity-based reserve system, which has particularly interesting countercyclical features (see Hart, Kaldor, and Tinbergen, 1964).

10. See Kenen (2001) on the deficiencies of arrangements to borrow.

11. That would involve eliminating the division between the denominated General Resource and the SDR accounts. See Clark and Polak (2004) and Cooper (1987, chap. 12).

REFERENCES

Abdildina, Z., and J. Jaramillo-Vallejo. 2005. "Streamlining Conditionality in World Bank and International Monetary Fund-Supported Programs." In *Conditionality Revisited,* edited by S. Koeberle, H. Bedoya, P. Silarszky, and G. Verheyen, pp. 85–91. Washington, D.C.: World Bank.

Atkinson, A., ed. 2005. *New Sources of Development Finance.* New York: Oxford University Press.

Basel Committee. 2009a. (July). *Enhancements to the Basel II Framework.* Basel: Basel Committee. www.bis.org.

———. 2009b. (December). *Strengthening the Resilience of the Banking Sector.* Basel: Basel Committee. www.bis.org.

———. 2010. (October). *The Basel Committee Response to the Financial Crisis: Report to the G-20.* Basel: Basel Committee. http://bis.org/publ/bcbs179.pdf.

Brunnermeier, M., A. Crocket, C. Goodhart, A. Persaud, and H. Shin. 2009. (January). *The Fundamental Principles of Financial Regulation.* Geneva: International Center for Monetary and Banking Studies and Centre for Economic Policy Research.

Camdessus, M. 2000. (February). "An Agenda for the IMF at the Start of the 21st Century." Remarks. New York: Council on Foreign Relations.

Clark, P. B., and J. J. Polak. 2004. "International Liquidity and the Role of the SDR in the International Monetary System." *IMF Staff Papers* 51 (1): 49–71.

Cooper, R. 1987. *The International Monetary System: Essays in World Economics.* Cambridge, Mass.: MIT Press.

D'Arista, J. 1999. "Reforming the Privatized International Monetary and Financial Architecture." *Financial Markets and Society* (November): 1–22.

D'Arista, J., and S. Griffith-Jones. 2010. "Agenda and Criteria for Financial Regulatory Reform." In *Time for a Visible Hand: Policy Lessons from the 2007 Crisis*, edited by S. Griffith-Jones, J. Ocampo, and J. Stiglitz, pp. 126–49. New York: Oxford University Press.

Dervis, K. 2008. "Fairness for Emerging Markets." *Washington Post*, November 3.

Goodhart, C. 2002. "Basel and Pro-cyclicality." In *Bumps on the Road to Basel,* edited by A. Hilton, pp. 26–28. London: Centre for the Study of Financial Innovation.

———. 2010. "How If at All Should Credit Rating Agencies Be Regulated?" In *Time for a Visible Hand: Policy Lessons from the 2007 Crisis*, edited by S. Griffith-Jones, J. Ocampo, and J. Stiglitz, pp. 164–184. New York: Oxford University Press.

Griffith-Jones, S., and J. A. Ocampo. 2010. "Building on the Counter-cyclical Consensus: A Policy Agenda." Research Paper prepared for the Intergovernmental Group of 24. http://www.g24.org/Publications/ResearchPaps/researchpapers .html#O. Accessed December 2011.

Griffith-Jones, S., J. A. Ocampo, and J. Stiglitz, eds. 2010. *Time for a Visible Hand: Policy Lessons from the 2007 Crisis*. New York: Oxford University Press.

Griffith-Jones, S., and A. Persaud. 2008. "The Pro-cyclical Impact of Basel II on Emerging Markets and Its Political Economy." In *Capital Market Liberalization and Development*, edited by J. A. Ocampo and J. Stiglitz, pp. 262–87. New York: Oxford University Press.

Griffith-Jones, S., M. Segoviano, and S. Spratt. 2002. (December). "Basel II and Developing Countries: Diversification and Portfolio Effects." Paper prepared for the Capital Market Liberalization Program, Initiative for Policy Dialogue, Columbia University.

Griffith-Jones, S., D. Silvers, and M. Thiemann. 2010. (October). "Turning the Financial Sector from a Bad Master to a Good Servant; The Role of Regulation and Taxation." Paper at the Conference on Global Economic Governance, Washington, D.C. http://www.stephanygj.net/papers.html. Accessed November 2010.

Griffith-Jones, S., and K. Young. 2009. "Reforming Governance of International Financial Regulation." Policy Brief. Initiative for Policy Dialogue, Columbia University. www.policydialogue.org.

Group of Twenty (G-20). 2009a. "Leaders' Statement, the Global Plan for Recovery and Reform, London, 2 April 2009." http://www.g20.org/pub_communiques .aspx.

———. 2009b. "Leaders' Statement, the Pittsburgh Summit, 25 September 2009." http://www.g20.org/pub_communiques.aspx.

Hart, A. G., N. Kaldor, and J. Tinbergen. 1964. "The Case for an International Commodity Reserve Currency." Geneva: UNCTAD. Reproduced in N. Kaldor, ed., *Essays on Economic Policy II*. New York: Holmes and Meier, 1980.

Helleiner, E., and S. Pagliari. 2009. "Crisis and Reform of the Financial Regulatory System." In *Global Finance in Crisis: The Politics of International Regulatory Change*, edited by E. Helleiner, S. Pagliari, and H. Zimmerman, pp. 1–17. London: Routledge.

Herman, B., J. A. Ocampo, and S. Spiegel, eds. 2010. *Overcoming Developing Country Debt Crises.* New York: Oxford University Press.

IMF (International Monetary Fund). 2002. (September 25). "Guidelines on Conditionality." Washington, D.C.: IMF. http://www.imf.org/External/np/pdr/cond /2002/eng/guid/092302.pdf.

———. 2009a. (January). "Review of the Adequacy of and Options for Supplementing Fund Resources." Washington, D.C.: IMF.

———. 2009b. (March). *Committee on IMF Global Governance Reform: Final Report.* Washington, D.C.: IMF.

———. 2009c. (March). "IMF Implements Major Lending Policy Improvements." Washington, D.C.: IMF. http://www.imf.org/external/np/pdr/fac/2009/032409 .htm.

———. 2009d. (July). "IMF Reforms Financial Facilities for Low-Income Countries." Washington, D.C.: IMF. http://www.imf.org/external/np/sec/pn/2009 /pn0994.htm.

———. 2009e. (October). *World Economic Outlook.* Washington, D.C.: IMF.

———. 2009f. (December). "Concessionality and the Design of Debt Limits in IMF-Supported Programs in Low-Income Countries." Washington, D.C.: IMF. http:// www.imf.org/external/np/pdr/concl/.

———. 2010. (October). *World Economic Outlook.* Washington, D.C.: IMF.

IMF-IEO (Independent Evaluation Office). 2008. (January). *An IEO Evaluation of Structural Conditionality in IMF-Supported Programs.* Evaluation Report. Washington, D.C.: IMF. http://www.ieo-imf.org/eval/complete/eval_01032008.html.

Kenen, P. B. 1983. "Use of SDR to Supplement or Substitute for Other Means of Finance." In *International Money and Credit: The Policy Roles,* edited by G. M. von Furstenberg, pp. 327–60. Washington, D.C.: FMI.

———. 2001. (November). *The International Financial Architecture: What's New? What's Missing?* Washington, D.C.: Institute for International Economics.

———. 2009. (November). "Revisiting the Substitution Account." Document presented in the paper "Towards a World Reserve System." Initiative for Policy Dialogue, Columbia University. http://www0.gsb.columbia.edu/ipd/programs/item .cfm?prid=133&iyid=5&itid=1927&list=papers.

Keynes, J. M. 1936. *The General Theory of Employment, Interest and Money.* London: Macmillan.

———. 1942–1943. "The Keynes Plan." Reproduced in *The International Monetary Fund 1945–1965: Twenty Years of International Monetary Cooperation, Vol. III: Documents,* edited by J. K. Horsefield, pp. 3–36. Washington, D.C.: FMI, 1969.

Killick, T. 2005. "Did Conditionality Streamlining Succeed?" In *Conditionality Revisited,* edited by S. Koeberle, H. Bedoya, P. Silarszky, and G. Verheyen, pp. 93–95. Washington, D.C.: World Bank.

Landau, J. P. 2004. *Report to Mr. Chirac, President of the Republic of France.* Paris: Working Group on New International Financial Contributions.

Nissanke, M. 2005. "Revenue Potential of the Currency Transactions Tax for Development Finance." In *New Sources of Development Finance,* edited by A. Atkinson, pp. 58–90. New York: Oxford University Press.

Ocampo, J. A. 2002. "Recasting the International Financial Agenda." In *International Capital Markets: Systems in Transition*, edited by J. Eatwell and L. Taylor, pp. 41–73. New York: Oxford University Press.

———. 2003. "Capital Account and Counter-cyclical Prudential Regulation in Developing Countries." In *From Capital Surges to Drought: Seeking Stability for Emerging Markets*, edited by R. Ffrench-Davis and S. Griffith-Jones, pp. 217–44. London: Palgrave Macmillan.

———. 2006. "Regional Financial Cooperation: Experiences and Challenges." In *Regional Financial Cooperation*, edited by J. A. Ocampo, pp. 1–39. Washington, D.C.: Brookings Institution and CEPAL.

———. 2010. "Reforming the Global Reserve System." In *Time for a Visible Hand: Policy Lessons from the 2007 Crisis*, edited by S. Griffith-Jones, J. Ocampo, and J. Stiglitz, pp. 289–313. New York: Oxford University Press.

Ocampo, J. A., and C. E. Tovar. 2008. (April). "External and Domestic Financing in Latin America: Developments, Sustainability and Financial Stability Implications." Presented at "Debt Finance and Emerging Issues in Financial Integration." UN Workshop, New York.

Pigou, A. C. 1920. *The Economics of Welfare*. London: Macmillan.

Reddy, Y. V. 2010. "Regulation of Financial Sector in Developing Countries: Lessons from the 2008 Financial Crisis." In *Time for a Visible Hand: Policy Lessons from the 2007 Crisis*, edited by S. Griffith-Jones, J. Ocampo, and J. Stiglitz. New York: Oxford University Press.

Rodrik, D. 2006. (September). "The Social Costs of Foreign Exchange Reserves." *International Economic Journal* 20 (3): 253–66.

Rustomjee, C. 2004. (September). "Why Developing Countries Need a Stronger Voice." In *Finance and Development*, International Monetary Fund, Washington, D.C.

Saurina, J. 2009. (July). "Dynamic Provisioning, the Experience of Spain." Crisis Response: Public Policy for the Private Sector, Note Number 7. Washington, D.C.: The World Bank.

Schmidt, R. 2008. *The Currency Transactions Tax: Rate and Revenue Estimates*. Tokyo: United Nations University Press.

Shi, K., and J. Xu. 2009. "Entry Cost, the Tobin Tax, and Noise Trading in the Foreign Exchange Market." *Canadian Journal of Economics* 42 (4): 1501–26.

Spratt, S. 2006. (September). "A Sterling Solution: A Report for Stamp Out Poverty." London: Stamp Out Poverty. www.stampoutpoverty.org.

Stiglitz, J. E. 2002. *Globalization and its Discontents*. New York: W. W. Norton.

———. 2006. *Making Globalization Work*. New York: W. W. Norton.

———. 2010. "Watchdogs Need Not Bark Together." *Financial Times*, February 10.

Tobin, J. 1996. "Prologue." In *The Tobin Tax: Coping with Financial Volatility*, edited by M. ul-Haq, I. Kaul, and I. Grunberg. New York: Oxford University Press.

Triffin, R. 1961. *Gold and the Dollar Crisis*. Rev. ed. New Haven, Conn.: Yale University Press.

———. 1968. *Our International Monetary System: Yesterday, Today and Tomorrow*. New York: Random House.

UN (United Nations). 1999. *Towards a New International Financial Architecture: Report of the Task Force of the Executive Committee on Economic and Social Affairs of the United Nations.* http://www.un.org/esa/coordination/ecesa/ecesa-1.pdf.

———. 2009. (September). *Report of the Commission of Experts of the UN General Assembly on Reforms of the International Monetary and Financial System* [UN Stiglitz Commission]. New York: United Nations.

———. 2010. (January). *World Economic Situation and Prospects.* New York: United Nations.

———. 2011. (January). *World Economic Situation and Prospects.* New York: United Nations.

UNCTAD. 1965. *International Monetary Issues and the Developing Countries: Report of the Group of Experts.* New York: United Nations.

Warwick Commission. 2009. (November). *International Financial Reform.* Report. http://www2.warwick.ac.uk/research/warwickcommission/report.

Weisbrot, M., R. Ray, J. Johnston, J. A. Cordero, and J. A. Montecino. 2009. (October). *IMF-Supported Macroeconomic Policies and the World Recession: A Look at Forty-one Borrowing Countries.* Washington, D.C.: Center for Economic and Policy Research. http://www.cepr.net/index.php/publications/reports/imf-supported -macroeconomic-policies-and-the-world-recession/.

Williamson, J. 2009. (June). "Understanding Special Drawing Rights." Policy Brief. Washington, D.C.: Peterson Institute for International Economics.

Woods, N., and D. Lombardi. 2006. (August). "Uneven Patterns of Governance: How Developing Countries Are Represented in the IMF." *Review of International Political Economy* 13 (3): 480–515.

Zhou, X. 2009. "Reform the International Monetary System." Beijing: People's Bank of China. http://www.pbc.gov.cn/english//detail.asp?col=6500&ID=178.

CHAPTER 4

The Economic Crisis and the International Aid

Andrew Mold and Annalisa Prizzon

For many developing countries the financial and economic crisis that hit the global economy in the period 2007–2008 has been a "good crisis," in the sense that, unlike during previous recessions, the vast majority have sustained economic growth. Indeed, some countries, notably the "Asian giants," China and India, as well as other emerging powers, such as Indonesia, have continued to grow very rapidly. Although lower than pre-crisis peaks, external development finance (through trade, official development assistance [ODA], private investment, and remittances) also withstood the crisis relatively well. Crucially for the prospects of many resource-rich developing countries, despite a sharp drop in the final quarter of 2008, commodity prices rebounded quickly and have subsequently remained strong, helping many raw material exporters to recover. In many senses this has been a very atypical global recession.

Notwithstanding the unexpected resilience of economic growth and many forms of private flows toward the developing world, the poorest developing countries continue to be heavily dependent on aid flows. Africa is most at risk on this score, as aid averages around 9 percent of GDP (see Figure 4.1) (compared, for instance, to South Asia, which has reduced its dependency on aid flows to only 1 percent of GDP).[1]

For these countries, despite the large increases in private financing and the increases in new sources of development cooperation (the growing protagonism of a group of non-Development Assistance Committee [DAC] donors), a lot still hinges on the prospects for ODA from traditional DAC donors over the next five years.

Prior to the crisis, major debate within donor circles had been centered on the scaling up of aid, especially for Africa, in line with the commitments undertaken at the Gleneagles G-8 Summit in July 2005. In reality,

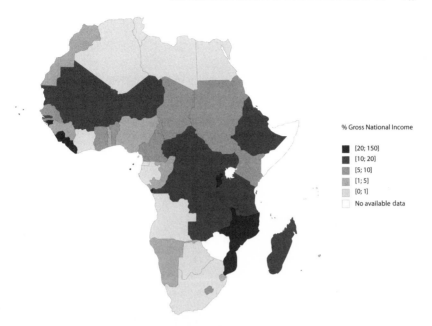

% Gross National Income

■ [20; 150]
■ [10; 20]
▦ [5; 10]
▦ [1; 5]
▦ [0; 1]
☐ No available data

Figure 4.1   Aid Dependency in Africa (2007)

Source: Authors' calculation, based on World Bank Development Indicators.

although total ODA had reached record levels prior to the crisis, progress did not quite live up to expectations: in real terms, aid in 2008 was 30 percent higher than in the 2004 Gleneagles base year, compared to the estimated 60 percent required by 2010 to meet Gleneagles G-8 Summit commitments (OECD, 2008a).

Post-crisis, the prospects of achieving these commitments are in serious doubt. Roodman (2008) has argued that in the aftermath of the financial crisis, even existing aid budgets may be at risk. He points to some particular historical examples (Finland, Japan, Norway, and Sweden) of sharp falls in aid during previous financial crises. For instance, as its economy began to fall into a protracted period of stagnation, Japan's aid fell 44 percent between 1990 and 1996. In Finland, according to Roodman's figures, the fall was even more dramatic; during its banking crisis, between 1991 and 1993, when GDP dropped by nearly 11 percent, development aid fell by 60 percent.

On the basis of national data, historical evidence does indeed seem to show that during sharp economy-wide contractions, aid budgets are vulnerable. In light of these examples, are all hopes of scaling up now dashed?

And are Roodman's (2008) case studies generalizable? What do we know about the impact of economic cycles in the donor countries themselves upon the scale of aid disbursements?

Over the last decade, developing countries as a group have become less dependent on official aid flows as a financing mechanism and are increasingly capable of both mobilizing domestic resources and attracting private capital flows. This trend resulted in a situation prior to the financial crisis in which multilateral institutions like the IMF and the World Bank had seen the demand for their loans and concessional finance dry up—developing countries broadly preferred non-concessional private finance and, increasingly, concessional finance from non-DAC donors.[2] Whether these trends continue post-crisis remains to be seen, but so far the impact of the financial crisis has not been as dire on forms of private financing as many observers were initially forecasting.[3]

Arguably, the time is ripe for a concerted change in the modus operandi of the development finance system. To generate a more effective system of development assistance, we argue that the following four basic complementary changes are necessary:

1. the maintenance of high levels of development assistance, but in conjunction with a much better targeting of assistance toward the countries with greatest needs;
2. an increase in the predictability of all concessional financing flows;
3. a reevaluation of the modalities of aid delivery, with the objective of reducing fragmentation and increasing efficiency in delivery; and
4. a thorough revision of the practice of policy conditionality, which is looking increasingly untenable post-crisis.

We start the chapter with an overview of how aid flows have been affected in previous economic crises. We then elaborate and estimate an econometric model to study the sensitivity of bilateral aid flows to economic growth in the source countries. Finally, we discuss ways in which aid delivery can be improved in light of the financial crisis.

AID FLOWS IN PREVIOUS TIMES OF ECONOMIC CRISIS

Since the Gleneagles G-8 Summit in July 2005, the major debate within donor circles has been about the scaling up of aid, especially to Africa.[4] On that occasion, the G-8 countries and other donors committed themselves to more than doubling ODA disbursed to African countries by 2010, compared to the levels predominant in 2004; that is, by about US$25 billion. Clearly the financial crisis starting in September 2008 poses serious threats to the timely achievement of the ODA target for Africa, as public budgets in many donor countries are under serious stress.

In November 2008 DAC donors made an aid pledge, reaffirming earlier commitments to increase the volume of aid and to maintain aid flows at levels consistent with those commitments (OECD, 2008a). In fact, despite fears, development aid did not fall but grew by a slight 0.7 percent from 2008 to 2009. Yet rigidities and forward planning in public finance mean that budgets are only adjusted after a considerable lag. Political processes for adjusting budgets are time-consuming and complicated. The real question, then, is how sustainable will ODA expenditures be in the coming three or four years, as fiscal tightening proceeds among major DAC donors?

One would expect, other things being equal, that governments with large deficits would be more prone to cut aid. And by undertaking massive interventions to prop up their banking and credit systems, many OECD governments were certainly making huge financial commitments during the period 2008–2009. As Robert Zoellick, president of the World Bank, noted at the time, "At $100 billion a year, the amount spent on overseas aid is a drop in the ocean compared to the trillions of dollars that are now being spent on financial rescues in the developed world" (World Bank, 2008a).

At least US$19 billion must still be added to current forward spending plans if donors are to meet their current 2010 commitments. Africa, in particular, is likely to get only about US$11 billion of the US$25 billion increase envisaged at Gleneagles (OECD, 2011). According to the OECD (2010a) there is a first group of countries—among them Sweden, with the world's highest ODA as a percentage of its gross national income (GNI), at 1.03 percent, Luxembourg (1 percent), Denmark (0.83 percent), the Netherlands (0.8 percent), and Belgium (0.7 percent)—that will meet the ODA target, that is, the ODA flows to a GNI target of 0.7 percent in 2010.[5] A second group of DAC donors—the United Kingdom (UK; 0.56 percent), Finland (0.55 percent), Ireland (0.52 percent), and Spain (0.51 percent)— falls some way behind. Finally, in the rear, a group of countries—France (0.46 percent), Germany (0.40 percent), Austria (0.37 percent), Portugal (0.34 percent), Greece (0.21 percent), and Italy (0.20 percent)—will likely not meet their ODA commitments in 2010.[6]

Judging by precedent, the omens are not good with regard to meeting the targets. Roodman (2008) observes that in the wake of previous financial and banking crises[7] that directly involved DAC countries, those countries sharply curtailed their aid budgets. In Finland, according to Roodman's analysis, during its banking crisis between 1991 and 1993, GDP fell by nearly 11 percent, and its development aid fell dramatically by 60 percent (Figure 4.2.A). Similarly, between 1990 and 1996, Japan's aid fell 44 percent and has never returned to its pre-crisis level[8] (Figure 4.2.B).

Yet evidence such as this must confront the fact that decisions on allocations to the aid budget in other cases do not appear to be strongly affected by the business cycle. Over the period 1960–2007, for instance, there was no statistical relationship between U.S. net ODA and either tax

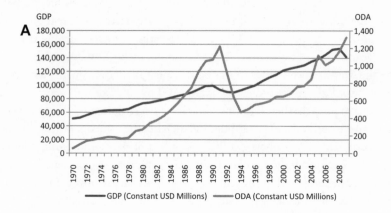

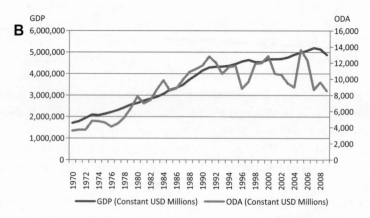

Figure 4.2   Evolution of ODA and GDP Flows in Finland and Japan, 1970–2009
A. Finland
B. Japan

Source: OECD (2010).

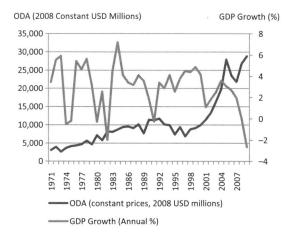

Figure 4.3   U.S. ODA and GDP Growth, 1970–2009

Source: OECD (2010d) and World Bank (2010b).

receipts, deficits, or total government expenditures (Kharas, 2008).[9] And while U.S. aid dropped in 1990 during the recession of 1990–1991, in the 2000–2001 recession, aid was accompanied by a sharp increase (Figure 4.3).

The lack of correlation between the domestic economy's growth performance and aid outflows is borne out in other examples too. As far as Sweden and Norway are concerned, aid flows did not sharply decrease after the eruption of Nordic financial crises in 1991. Even in the aforementioned case of Japan, the country's recession of 1996–1997 did not imply a reduction in aid flows. Finally, during their recessions in 1993, France actually increased its aid disbursement, whereas Germany cut them. But despite the German downturn in the early 2000s, the country expanded its contributions after 2004. Anecdotal evidence therefore does not resolve the question.

AID EFFORT: EVIDENCE FROM PREVIOUS STUDIES

More rigorous econometric studies on "aid effort" or "aid generosity" from donor countries, that is, the determinants of aid supply, are rather more recent and limited in number than the many studies that attempt to measure the allocation of aid from the perspective of recipient countries (the demand side), for example, whether donors allocate aid according to the principle they espouse, in terms of priming poorer recipients or democratic reform. Existing studies from the supply-side perspective include Pallage and Robe (2001); Round and Odedokun (2004); Faini (2006);

Boschini and Olofsgard (2007); Bertoli et al. (2008); and Chong and Gradstein (2008). Widespread concerns about maintaining ODA commitments in the aftermath of the global financial and economic crisis have reawakened interest in research in this specific field (Mendoza et al., 2009; Hallet, 2009; Dang et al., 2010). In a sense, the financial crisis has shifted attention from the recipient to the donor side of the aid relationship.

Pallage and Robe (2001) focus on business cycle characteristics of aid flows both from the recipient's and the donor's sides. Through an analysis of the de-trended business cycle using the well-known Hodrick-Prescott filter (deviations from output trend), they find little evidence that aid is pro-cyclical with respect to the donors' economic performance. In a couple of countries (France and Italy) in their study, aid allocations actually correlate negatively with the business cycle.

Round and Odedokun (2004) investigate the decline in aid flow from 1970 to 2000 looking at the gross disbursement of ODA loans and grants as a proxy for aid *generosity*. The sample is composed of twenty-two DAC countries during the period 1970–1999. Based on a fixed-effects panel data estimation, they assume that *aid generosity* is determined by both non-political and political factors. Among the first group of factors, they include the level of per capita income, the phase of the economic cycle, the fiscal balance, "peer pressure" (ODA loans and grants of all other donors expressed as a fraction of their total GDP), domestic pro-poor spending and the policy stance (the Gini coefficient and income share of the poorest 20th percentile), country size, international strategic and military interests, and temporal factors (e.g., the end of the Cold War). In the second group they take into account the government's political orientation, the constitutional checks and balances, and the degree of polarization within the government itself. They find first that aid is a superior good (i.e., it increases with per capita income). Second, aid shares to GDP decrease with the growth of the donor country population. Third, mixed results are obtained for the time trend (i.e., there is no clear increase in aid budgets over time). Fourth, aid generosity increases with peer pressure, the greater the number of checks and balances, polarization, and fractionalization within the government. Finally, and most importantly from the point of view of this chapter, the fiscal balance as well as the political orientation do not have any significant effect on aid effort.

Faini (2006) analyzes the macroeconomic variables determining the amount of aid for fifteen donor countries over the period 1980–2004. He proxies total aid flows with net official ODA (grants and loans whose grant element is above 25 percent), total official flows, and the net aid transfers measure proposed by Roodman (2006). Covariates are the aggregate fiscal deficit, the stock of gross debt, the output gap, and political orientation. The study finds first that aid flows are a positive function of the donor's fiscal surplus (controlling for government's political orientation, the cyclical position of the donor economy, and its income-per-capita level). Second, the debt stock negatively affects the amount of aid flows. And third, the output gap—to capture output shocks—has no statistically significant effect on aid flows.

Based on a political economy model, Chong and Gradstein (2008) investigate the factors affecting support for foreign aid among voters in donor countries. They consider a sample of twenty-two DAC countries during the period 1973–2002, exploring both fixed-effects panel data techniques and an Arellano-Bond dynamic estimator, including the real GDP per capita, the Gini coefficient, the tax revenues, a proxy for government inefficiencies, and a dummy for left-wing governments. Their main finding is that larger foreign aid flows are positively correlated with public satisfaction of government performance and higher relative incomes.

Bertoli et al. (2008) concentrate on the determinants of aid effort, proxied by aid disbursements, net of debt relief. They consider four sets of factors: structural variables (real income per capita, income inequality, population size, and government receipts and redistribution), historical factors (past colonial history), macroeconomic determinants (fiscal deficit, trade balance over GDP, and the output gap), institutional features (independent aid agency, peer effect, and political orientation), and, finally, alternative sources of foreign finance (remittances). The sample is composed of twenty-two DAC members during the period 1970–2004. They find that the output gap, the trade balance variable, government intervention and redistribution, political orientation, and fiscal deficit all have a positive significant impact on aid effort. Perhaps surprisingly, they find that conservative governments are more likely to be associated with increases in the aid budget than left-wing ones. Negative and significant impacts are found for growing income inequality and population size. These results have been updated in Allen and Giovannetti (2009) and extend the analysis of the twenty-two DAC donors up to 2008. They predicted a fall of total DAC aid by 22 percent from 2008 to 2009.

Hallet (2009) finds only a weak correlation between aid and OECD donors' growth between 1971 and 2008. After a one-year lag, aid cuts were associated with about half of the episodes of all deep or protracted recessions.

Mendoza et al. (2009) focus their analysis on the United States. By use of a misery index (an equally weighted index of inflation and unemployment), they show that a 1 percent increase in the misery index is associated with a decline of ODA of 0.01 point as a percentage of GDP. They conclude from this finding that ODA from the United States could fall from 13 to 30 percent, depending on the depth of the economic recession. Finally, based on a sample of twenty-four donor countries during the period 1977–2007, Dang et al. (2010) find evidence that supports Roodman's earlier contention that aid flows are significantly correlated with episodes of banking crises in donor countries. The authors estimated that aid flows would fall by an average of between 20 to 25 percent, assuming an elasticity of 3 for per capita aid flows to donors' incomes.

How can we explain this lack of evidence of a clear-cut relationship between aid flows, government revenue, and donor performance, respectively? First, previous financial crises and economic recessions might not have been so severe as to provoke large cutbacks and revisions in aid budgets (something that may be different when the recession is deep and global in nature, as is the present one). Second, the optimistic interpretation is that aid is not determined by the economic cycle in donor countries but, rather, by the needs of the developing countries themselves,[10] as well as the willingness to fulfill international commitments. Third, aid may not be determined by either the economic cycle or the needs of the developing countries themselves; rather, it may be principally motivated by the geostrategic objectives of donor countries (Alesina and Dollar, 2000; Maizels and Nissanke, 1984). In this sense it is worth remembering that at the beginning of the 1990s there was much talk of a "peace dividend" following the end of the Cold War. A substantial cut in military budgets was foreseen, and hopes were pinned on a corresponding increase in the amount of financial resources dedicated to enhancing the "soft power" of the major donors through development aid programs. However, far from reaping the hoped-for peace dividend, real net ODA declined over the decade by nearly a third.[11]

ECONOMETRIC ANALYSIS

In this section, we empirically estimate the relation between aid flows and donors' performance considering the following model

$$dlog(x_{it}) = \alpha + \beta dlog(x_{it-1}) + \delta dlog(y_{it}) + \gamma z + \eta_i + \varepsilon_{it}$$

where i indicates the specific country and t ranges from 1960 to 2007. The dependent variable x is aid from each donor. First, aid budgets are determined on the basis of the amount allocated by the donor country in the previous year. Aid flows are measured in terms of net bilateral ODA and are taken from the OECD.Stat databases. GDP figures come from World Bank World Development Indicators. Second, y represents our independent variable of interest, that is, the GDP growth rate of the donor's country, also taken from World Development Indicators. We use *dlog* of these variables to consider their rate of increase. Alternatively, we use the "output gap" to identify the effect of aid on economic cycle. The variable z is a control variable, the fiscal balance to GDP ratio, which is expected to have a positive sign, since countries with a larger fiscal surplus may be in a better situation to dedicate more resources to aid. The fiscal balance is inclusive of grants. The source is OECD.Stat and various national statistics offices. Finally η_i is the country effect and ε_{it} the error term. The panel is unbalanced, but consistency is not compromised by sample selection, since it is due to nonresponse of country units uncorrelated with our regressors (Wooldridge, 2002). In order to eliminate the bias in our time series attributable to inflation and exchange rate movements, where reasonable, amounts have been transformed into 2006 constant prices as well as a constant 2006 USD exchange rate.[12]

We test our dynamic panel data model equation considering the system-GMM estimator (columns 1 and 2 in Table 4.1)[13] because our data present values for beta coefficients close to unity: under these circumstances, Blundell and Bond (1998) show that the instruments used in the Arellano and Bond (1991) first difference GMM estimator become less informative. Our model reasonably satisfies the sequential exogeneity assumption, under which past and present observations need to be uncorrelated with unobserved heterogeneity. We use the second lag of the dependent variable as an instrument, under the assumption that the country-specific effect is correlated with the error term.

According to the econometric results presented in Table 4.1 (columns 1 and 2), the lagged dependent variable—aid to GDP ratio—is not significant, perhaps reflecting the high volatility of aid, in the sense that one year's ODA does not help predict that of the following year. Second, the fiscal balance is not statistically significant, suggesting that fiscal imbalances have no impact on aid budget. Even though over the last three years average fiscal balances have deteriorated considerably (from −1 percent in 2007 to −8.7 percent for high-income countries in 2009) (IMF,

Table 4.1   Econometric Analysis—Dependent Variable: ODA to GDP Ratio

	Blundell-Bond		Fixed Effects	
	(1)	(2)	(3)	(4)
Dependent Variable	Dlog aid	Dlog aid	Dlog aid	Dlog aid
Lagged Dependent Variable	0.001	0.002	0.001	0.002
	0.002	0.002	0.002	0.002
Dlog GDP	0.014***		0.014***	
	0.003		0.003	
Log "Output Gap"		0.120**		0.092*
		0.045		0.047
Fiscal Balance as a Percentage of GDP	0.004	−0.001	0.001	−0.006
	0.020	0.020	0.020	0.020
Number of Obs.	782	685	782	685
F-stat/Wald chi2	28.55	8.92	1.85	1.69
P value	0.00	0.03	0.01	0.03

Notes: Standard errors are reported under parentheses. The levels of significance are as follows: * 90 percent level, ** 95 percent level, *** 99 percent level.

2010) because of the financial commitments undertaken during the crisis, the impact is thus likely to be negligible.

Finally, in accordance with some of the studies reviewed in previous sections, we find a statistically significant positive elasticity between GDP growth and aid in all four estimations. The estimated coefficient suggests that economic growth in donor countries did not play a decisive role in aid allocation in the past. The alternative measure of the economic cycle, the "output gap," gives a significant and notably larger parameter estimate (0.12) using the Blundell-Bond technique. A key issue is of course whether these conclusions are still valid in the context of the 2008–2009 financial crisis, as most of the DAC donors have been experiencing contemporaneously negative GDP growth rates—a unique event in recent history.

SHIFTING PATTERNS OF DEVELOPMENT FINANCE

Regardless of the econometric results, a reduction in aid flows may not be the only consequence of the financial crisis—the composition of ODA may also be radically affected. In particular, in the period 2009–2010, there was a sharp rise in multilateral contributions, as resources were channeled through the IMF and World Bank. Increasingly, we have also seen a rise in the protagonism of regional banks. The African Development Bank, for instance, now has a larger portfolio in Africa than the World Bank. The situation is similar for the Asian Development Bank and the Inter-American Development Bank, which have found their funding generously replenished in the aftermath of the crisis and have correspondingly expanded their financing.[14] Not all these flows are concessional and thus do not count as ODA. But it still reflects a major change in emphasis regarding the balance between bilateral and multilateral financing after a prolonged period of meager multilateral activity.[15] As well as affecting the composition of flows, the crisis is also having an impact on discussions regarding aid efficiency, as will be discussed in the following section.

Even if the OECD's DAC member countries still provide the majority of total official development assistance, the first decade of this century has seen an increasing diversification of sources of development finance, as well as development partners. Most are themselves developing countries that have been able to sustain a positive growth performance, even during the 2008–2009 financial and economic crisis, including emerging market countries, such as Brazil, China, India, Malaysia, the Russian Federation, Thailand, and oil-rich countries, such as Saudi Arabia and Venezuela.

However, as Figure 4.4 shows, the most recent figures of South-South development assistance are still far below the level—in real terms—achieved in the 1970s and early 1980s, mainly ascribed to assistance granted by Arab oil-exporting countries and by regional development banks, such as

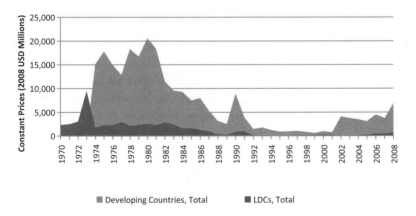

Figure 4.4   Official Development Assistance, Non-DAC Countries, 1970–2009

Source: OECD/DAC Creditor Reporting System 2010.

the Kuwait Fund for Arab Economic Development, the Islamic Development Bank, and the Arab Bank for Economic Development in Africa.

According to OECD/DAC figures, Saudi Arabia is now the largest single non-DAC donor, followed by China, whose development assistance more than doubled from 1998 to 2007 (Qi, 2007). In 2007 the Indian annual budget for development cooperation was around US$1 billion (OECD, 2009). Brazil plays an important role both bilaterally and multilaterally, particularly within the group of Lusophone nations; the Brazilian aid program amounts to nearly US$500 million.

Estimates of assistance delivered by southern countries range from US$9.5 billion to US$12.1 billion in 2006 (UN/ECOSOC, 2008), representing between 7.8 and 9.8 percent of total flows. In particular, both Saudi Arabia and Venezuela provided development assistance of more than 0.7 percent of gross national income. If southern countries meet their pledges, their development assistance could exceed US$15 billion in 2010 (UN/ECO-SOC, 2008), around 12 percent of total ODA expected for 2010 (OECD, 2010e).

TOWARD GREATER AID EFFICIENCY

AID FRAGMENTATION

One of the key recommendations given to DAC donors in recent years, encapsulated in the Accra Agenda for Action, is the importance of increasing aid efficiency. The crisis inevitably puts this goal into sharp relief. Even in the face of the possible stagnation of aid budgets, there might be a payoff if donors react in a way that is pro-poor in terms of aid allocation. Put another way, there is nothing like a hard-budget constraint to concentrate the mind on the efficient use of resources. Significant portions of aid budgets have grown enormously over the last ten to twenty years—particularly technical cooperation—and yet the rationale for supporting such a large expansion of these expenditures, in terms of aid efficiency, is more doubtful.

A consensus exists that the international aid system suffers some serious deficiencies. Chief among them are concerns about the proliferation of actors, lack of coordination, fragmentation of aid effort, and volatility in disbursements (Frot and Santiso, 2008). In the last two decades a sharp rise in the number of donors has occurred, with the predictable consequence that the average size of projects has declined (UNDESA, 2010:34).

Another serious problem that persists is the lack of prioritization in the allocation of financial resources toward the poorest. Despite declarations to the contrary, it is evident that the principal recipients of ODA are not necessarily the countries with the greatest need for additional financial resources (Table 4.2). Some of the major recipients of international aid are in fact countries with their own overseas aid programs—countries such as China, India, and Turkey—giving rise to the strange situation whereby they are simultaneously recipients and donors. Similarly, in a recent paper, Sumner (2010) has argued that the vast majority of the world's poor no longer live in countries that are classified as "poor" but, rather, in middle-income countries that, in theory at least, have the resources available to tackle their own problems of poverty. In this sense there is no "bottom billion," as Collier (2007) famously described—the number of poor living in low-income and vulnerable countries is now perhaps no more than a quarter of the global poor (300 million out of a total of 1.2 billion living on less than US$1.25 a day).

Increasingly, therefore, at a global level the challenge of poverty reduction becomes one in which domestic policies come to the fore, with the need to prioritize at the national level the reduction of inequalities and the empowerment of poor people. From such a perspective, the responsibilities for poverty reduction reside squarely in the hands of the governments of middle-income countries themselves. ODA may have a complementary role in such a scenario, particularly as a facilitator of know-how, but is less valuable for its financial resources.

Table 4.2   The Ten Largest Recipients of Bilateral ODA, 2008

	US$ Million	Share of Total Bilateral	
1. Iraq	9,462	The top 5	22 percent
2. Afghanistan	3,475	The top 10	31 percent
3. China	2,601	The top 20	43 percent
4. Indonesia	2,543		
5. India	2,263		
6. Vietnam	1,745		
7. Sudan	1,743		
8. Tanzania	1,603		
9. Ethiopia	1,551		
10. Cameroon	1,396		

Source: OECD (2010a).

The logical corollary of this is that financial resources of ODA should increasingly be focused only on the poorest, most vulnerable states. Yet as a glimpse at the list of major recipients in Table 4.2 shows, it is evident that geostrategic and security motives still continue to play a major role in the allocation of ODA. Econometric studies confirm this impression—according to a survey of the literature by Mold (2009), contrary to popular rhetoric, the allocation of ODA resources is barely sensitive to indicators such as corruption or the consolidation of democratic government.

The Paris Declaration addresses some of these issues, but unfortunately objective evaluations of the degree of implementation of the declaration have so far been fairly critical of the slow rate of progress (OECD, 2010a). Why is this? The persistence of the problems, despite a widespread recognition and consensus of their importance, suggests that there are some structural problems that perhaps the donor communities themselves are unable to address. The proliferation of actors—bilaterals, multilaterals, nongovernmental organizations, decentralized cooperation, non-DAC donors, global funds, and so on—is one of the key structural problems, making coordination extremely difficult. This has led some authors to go so far as to suggest that the aid system is unreformable in its current configuration, and that the only people in a plausible position to tackle some of these problems are the recipients themselves (Whitfield, 2009). Though it may be overestimating the power of recipient countries to shape and control the framework within which ODA is provided, the idea that aid coordination should be carried out by recipient countries rather than by the donor community is certainly one that is fully compatible with the ideas of the Paris Declaration on ownership, putting developing countries very much in the "driver's seat." Another important issue that has not been tackled sufficiently is the sectoral composition of aid flows. Currently around one-third of aid flows is dedicated to technical cooperation. An extreme documented example of this was Tanzania at the end of the 1990s, when technical cooperation accounted for about 70 percent of all aid received by the country.

There is of course an important role for donors to play in providing technical expertise and knowledge. But such a high share in total ODA is difficult to justify by any measure. Getting the sectoral balance right is clearly a major issue. In particular, there is an urgent need to redress the chronic neglect of the productive sectors. The popularity of Chinese cooperation in Africa highlights the demand among aid recipients for more investment in infrastructure, roads, buildings, and factories. A recent study by UNCTAD (2008) shows that of all the different kinds of aid, support to the productive sectors is one of the most growth-enhancing, and yet they are sectors that have been much neglected over recent decades.

One particularly notable example has been the low and declining share of ODA for agriculture. From the mid-1980s to the mid-2000s the share of aid devoted to agriculture relative to total ODA declined from about 18 percent to less than 4 percent. This led to situations such as that during the famine in Ethiopia in 2003, when the U.S. government spent more than US$500 million on food aid to help the 14 million Ethiopians who were starving but spent less than US$5 million on agricultural development aid to Ethiopian farmers (Thurow, 2010:106).

BUDGET SUPPORT AND CONDITIONALITY

In the nearly three decades prior to the crisis, donor conditionality had expanded in a way that was perhaps inconceivable in the 1960s and 1970s.[16] The expansion of conditions began under programs of structural adjustment in the 1980s, when it was decided that ODA was ineffective in bad policy environments. The policy conditions attached to the loans became frequently onerous and touched upon many spheres of government but broadly evoked a greater economic liberalization, deregulation, and privatization of the economy. As is well acknowledged, for various reasons those policies did not achieve the desired results—economic performance was poor in most parts of the developing world in the 1990s (OECD, 2010e). Only in the 2000s did economic growth resume strongly in the developing world, and it is debatable whether this was due to a (belated) payoff from the economic reforms, as some have argued,[17] or if it was the consequence of a more favorable external environment (high levels of global liquidity, low interest rates, a strong recovery in raw material prices, and a greater dynamism in South-South flows of investment, trade, and aid).

Over the last ten years, after appreciating the extent to which extensive donor conditionalities under Structural Adjustment Programs (SAPs) had not been effective, the donor community has been sensitive toward the arguments in favor of reducing the amount of conditionalities. Both the bilateral and multilateral donors have adopted programs expressly to curtail conditionalities. The verdict is, however, still out on how much has been achieved (Mold, 2009). In some dimensions of aid policy, it is clear that conditionality is still onerous, as witnessed by the extensive conditionality associated with initiatives such as the Millennium Challenge Account (MCA). Donors still place many constraints on host government policy execution and broader political governance, both through the international financial institutions and bilateral conditionalities. To take just one example, in 2007 the IMF's own evaluation department came to the conclusion that "the streamlining initiative did not reduce the volume of conditionality, partly because structural conditions continued to be used to monitor other initiatives such as donors' support programmes and the European Union (EU) accession process. . . . Fund arrangements still included conditions that seem not to have been critical to programme objectives" (IMF, 2007:4).

It should hardly need stressing that the economic and financial crisis of 2008–2009 represents a major challenge to the credibility of much of the advice given to developing countries during the last three decades. It has not gone unnoticed in many developing countries that in the wake of the crisis the industrialized countries themselves have adopted a whole host of policies that would have been prohibited under the old structural adjustment programs (including the massive intervention in the banking sector and strategic support given to the automobile industry). Arguably, in the future it will be much more difficult to convince aid recipients to abide by the kind of comprehensive conditions that became commonplace in the 1980s and 1990s. The growing presence of non-traditional donors, particularly countries such as Brazil, China, and India, that do not impose such onerous conditionality on their loans will make the sustainability of traditional conditionality frameworks all the more difficult.

How can donors limit the difficulties associated with conditionality? Part of the solution involves reexamining the case for different aid modalities. Most donors mix aid modalities depending on local contexts, with no one preferred way of delivering aid (OECD, 2008c:15). Many donors still rely on project aid, whether or not as part of sector or program approaches, to maintain contact with field realities, to work with non-traditional actors such as the private-sector and civil society, to develop innovative approaches, and to compensate for weak national capacity. The proliferation of decentralized cooperation, especially in donor countries, such as Spain, which have expanded their cooperation significantly in recent years, has increased the visibility of project aid.

Yet the prevalence of project aid is precisely one of the causes behind the fragmentation of aid effort observed earlier. The traditional critique of project aid is well summarized by Killick (2008:4):

Traditional assistance can lead to a proliferation of projects which is incoherent, non-transparent and inconsistent with the national government's priorities. Project aid also spawns large numbers of Project Implementation Units (PIUs), often outside the government's structures, tending to weaken efforts to build capacities within the public service. More generally, assistance programmes are often not well aligned with national development strategies, institutions and procedures.

As a consequence, in the last two decades we have witnessed a marked shift toward more ambitious and innovative forms of program aid—that is, any form of contribution made available to a recipient's country for general development purposes, such as balance-of-payments support, general budget support, commodity assistance, or debt relief, and that is not tied to specific projects.

In the last decade, in particular, many hopes have been pinned on budget support in particular as a purportedly innovative model. Budgetary support, in the form of broad financial support to an agreed government program, is very much intended to put the recipient country in the driver's seat, in terms of setting its own priorities and executing them. Donors such as the EU and the UK now channel large shares of their aid through budget support.

Much hope has been pinned on budget support as a way of reducing the problems associated with the aforementioned proliferation of donors and reducing the fragmentation of aid effort. There is a wide range of expectations from general budget support. These include improved coordination and harmonization among donors; alignment with partner country systems and policies; lower transaction costs; higher allocative efficiency of public expenditure; greater predictability of funding; increased effectiveness of the state and public administration; and improved domestic accountability through increased focus on the government's own accountability channels (IDD and Associates, 2006:1).

Yet despite a strong a priori rationale, the empirical evidence for the superiority of budget support over old-fashioned project aid is quite ambiguous. The few impact studies undertaken so far have all had to confront conceptual and methodological problems arising from the difficulty of tracing the effects on poverty and income levels from adding aid to overall budgetary resources (Riddell, 2007:201). Further complications arise because budget support may constitute only a relatively small proportion of total aid resources, and thus its impact is difficult to disentangle from that of aid delivered through other modalities.

One of the most extensive recent evaluations of budget support has been a three-year study commissioned by a consortium of donors in 2003, at the request of the OECD. It involved development of a methodology to evaluate budget support and case studies in seven countries: Burkina Faso, Malawi, Mozambique, Nicaragua, Rwanda, Uganda, and Vietnam. The published report (IDD and Associates, 2006) endorsed budget support but had mixed conclusions on its effectiveness. On the positive side, it found that funding of basic public services in health and education increased during the provision of budget support and found some evidence of reduced transaction costs of multiple meetings, donor visits, and reporting requirements. But it also found an underestimation of the political risks in several countries, with overly optimistic assumptions about the ability of international partners to influence matters deeply rooted in partner countries' political systems. It drew attention as well to some fundamental tensions regarding the desire of donors to establish benchmarks and controls, their temptation to indulge in micromanagement, and recipient countries' wish to enjoy maximum liberty to determine expenditures according to their own priorities.

The risk that budget support could paradoxically end up strengthening donor interference and control over recipient governments was spelled out very clearly by White and Dijkstra (2003:550):

> In most countries there is an enormous scope for improvement in public financial management, in budget reporting procedures and in accountability of budget performance to parliament and to the public at large. If donors succeed in focusing on these issues . . . and if they succeed in harmonising and simplifying their procedures with regard to budget support, these positive systemic effects become a reality. However, if they attempt to micro-manage the use of the funds and if each donor continues to set its specific requirements for that use or for reporting, budget support will become a drag on development.

Killick (2005:95) also makes a similar warning: "It could be that the relationships that have developed on a partnership basis are evolving as a substitute for conditionality, but it could easily result in more old-style policy stipulations. It could go either way."

It is not clear yet whether donors have managed to avoid these problems. In their study of Multi-Donor Budget Support for Ghana, Killick and Lawson (2007:4) note that

> it has not achieved a sufficient critical mass and it has strayed too far from its initial objective of reducing transactions costs. These flaws have prevented it from minimizing the risks of injecting budget support into a still weak fiscal system. While it is seen as having kept reform on the agenda and as having a generally pro-poor influence, it has neither been able to minimize the risks by galvanizing more effective performance finance management systems nor to maximize the payoff in terms of poverty reduction.

A UK Parliamentary Committee (Committee of Public Accounts, 2008:5–7) on the use of budgetary support by the Department for International Development (DFID) arrived at the conclusion that the decision process governing countries that receive budget support is still opaque: "DFID have stated principles which must be met before working with government partners, and have developed useful tools to help appraise prospects for budget support and assess risks. Most budget support proposals, however, do not clearly weigh up the risks and benefits. In addition, the pattern of budget support that has arisen appears arbitrary."

Knoll (2008:12) notes that the donor community, which includes bilateral development agencies, the European Commission (EC), and regional development banks, still views recipient compliance with the terms of the IDA's Poverty Reduction Support Credit (PRSC) and the IMF's poverty reduction and growth facility (PRGF) as a precondition for general budget support disbursal. Among the bilateral agencies, for instance, the Swedish International Development Cooperation Agency (Sweden) directly or indirectly (via the EC) attaches its release decision to recipient compliance with PRGF conditionality and makes decisions on a case-by-case basis. The Belgian budget-support scheme for Burkina Faso is attached to PRSC conditionality, while the DFID (UK) draws its disbursal conditions from the Poverty Reduction Strategy Paper (PRSP) (or from the terms of the PRGF, if those are considered consistent with the British approach). In the United Republic of Tanzania, the Danish International Development Agency (Denmark) partly referred to PRSC prior actions but also took into consideration conditions directly from the PRSP. Linking budget support to International Financial Institutions (IFIs) programs means that, despite the intentions of budget support, conditionality is still pervasive.

A RECONSIDERATION OF AID MODALITIES

It would seem reasonable to conclude that budget support is still far from delivering, in terms of its promise to reduce conditionality and enhance recipient country ownership. Moreover, it appears to be particularly un-suited to fragile states with weak institutional structures. If that is the case, then there is a danger that it ends up legitimizing a new kind of ex ante conditionality, whereby budget support is considered appropriate for some countries but not for others. In addition, because of its all-encompassing nature, budget support, however well designed, almost in-evitably leaves an enormous amount of discretion to donors in terms of deciding whether a country is progressing well or not, and thus is worthy of continued support. It has led to a situation whereby donors demand greater participation in policy discussions and planning in a number of countries and become deeply involved in core policy processes. Donors have also lacked important political economy insights as to the nature of domestic power struggles. Disappointing or politically complicated expe-riences of budget support in recent years with previously designated aid "darlings" (countries such as Ethiopia, Rwanda, and Uganda) have con-vinced some members of the donor community to stay on the sidelines for the time being: they have either set a ceiling to this aid modality (25 per-cent in Denmark) or they make little use of it (Canada, France, Portugal, Spain, and the United States) or, in some cases, they make no use of it at all (Greece and Luxembourg) (OECD, 2008c:15).

Precisely for these reasons, there have been a growing number of voices questioning the wisdom of a greater emphasis on budget support (de Ren-zio, 2006; Deaton et al., 2006; Whitfield and Maipose, 2008; de Renzio and Hanlon, 2009). And, in spite of the impression that budget support is an innovatory modality of aid delivery, it is not by any stretch of the imagi-nation new. The UK provided budget support to a number of former African economies in the wake of independence during the 1960s but gradually phased this out in favor of project aid. In the 1990s there were a number of experiments in budget support in Bangladesh, Cape Verde, Nicaragua, and Tanzania. Again, the experiences were mixed and conditionality quite per-vasive in the implemented programs (White and Dijkstra, 2003). Most Australian aid to Papua New Guinea, from its independence in 1975 until the mid-1990s, also took the form of budget support. The Australian government estimated the total disbursements up to the early 2000s at US$14 billion, so the sums were enormous. Yet an extensive official Australian evaluation carried out in 2003 heavily criticized the results, especially in terms of the accepted primary objective of budget support—increasing the autonomy and capacity of national institutions (AusAID, 2003). The report concluded (2003:xi): "In considering the impact of aid since independence, it is relevant to recognise that there was a clear rationale for budget support in the immediate post-independence period but, in time, it was recognised that budget support had an adverse impact on incentives to develop and implement effective economic development policies."

All these doubts have led some observers to question the emphasis on budget support and to advocate a return to "old-fashioned" project aid. Banerjee (2007:21) puts the arguments in a very forceful way:

> Donors are unclear about what they should be pushing for. Given that, it is easy to lead them to grandiose and unfocused project designs where none of the details are spelled out clearly and diverting money is a cinch. From this point of view, the current fashion of channelling aid into broad budgetary support (rather than specific projects) seems particularly disastrous. We need to go back to financing projects and insist that the results be measured.

However, to dichotomize the whole issue into budget support versus project lending is to risk simplifying a complex question. And there are many intermediate aid modalities; different aid modalities will continue to coexist. The argument here is certainly not against program aid as a concept but simply in favor of a more cautious assessment of the implications of budget support as a "low conditionality" aid modality. There are alternatives. For instance, SWAps (sector-wide approach), where support is given for a particular sector, underpin some of the same objectives as budget support but arguably within the more modest and achievable context of building up local capacity at a sectoral level.

Moreover, none of this implies an automatic endorsement of the current portfolio of projects. Donors have clearly promoted too many small, fragmented projects. The errors of the past need to be avoided—for example, the World Bank's increased lending orientation since the 1990s toward both huge, non-project emergency bailout packages and direct private-sector support in such areas as luxury hotels, the alcoholic beverage industry, banking, and so on, all sectors with small or negligible impacts on poverty reduction. As Rich (2002:26) notes, "both priorities have even less connection to directly helping the poorest of the poor than do more traditional Bank project loans."

At the same time, many projects in the productive sectors remain without funding: the African-instigated New Economic Partnership for African Development, for example, identified many priority infrastructure projects, yet financing has often not been forthcoming. The UK-led Commission for Africa (2005) suggested that Africa required an additional US$20 billion a year in infrastructure investment, in the form of support for African regional, national, urban, and rural priorities, ranging from rural roads and slum upgrading to information and communication technology, and proposed that donors provide half of the additional funding up to 2010.

Regrettably, it has become much easier to mobilize resources for non-project purposes, such as technical assistance, debt relief, food aid, and emergency relief, than for real development projects and programs. In 2005 debt relief accounted for nearly one-quarter (US$25.4 billion) of total official aid, including the Paris Club's extraordinary debt cancellation for Iraq and Nigeria. By providing funds in this fashion, donors bypass the need to have well-designed and well-implemented development projects (Kharas, 2008:12). The rise in technical cooperation, the most dynamic component of spending patterns over the last twenty years, also has stemmed partly from the proliferation of ambitious new aid modalities—particularly budget support—all requiring extensive monitoring and technical capacities. In 2005 the US$29 billion spent on technical cooperation accounted for some 40 percent of total ODA net of debt relief and remains largely tied to expensive northern contractors and donor control. For some recipient countries, the share went much higher. It peaked at 73 percent in Uganda in the late 1990s (Riddell, 2007:202). As much as 70 percent of aid for education is spent on technical assistance (The Reality of Aid, 2008:8). In Zambia more money is received each year in the form of technical assistance than the whole of the government budget for education (Glennie, 2008:69).

In the aftermath of the crisis, Paul Romer's adage that "a crisis is too big an opportunity to waste" has oft been quoted. For all the reasons expounded here, it is certainly an opportune moment to reexamine the modalities of ODA. The financial crisis should act as a stimulus to explore various ways in which to improve aid delivery and to use the financial crisis as an opportunity to rethink the framework for development cooperation—it certainly should not be ignored in favor of returning to "business as usual."

CONCLUSIONS

As the world economy moves out of the economic crisis, there are serious concerns about future prospects for ODA. The size of the budget deficits in many OECD countries suggests that difficult decisions will have to be made over the short to medium term. We have reviewed evidence on aid levels and aid efficiency considering the wider context of the financing needs of developing countries. We have also established econometrically that although there is a relationship between economic growth and ODA levels, the impact is, on average, small, suggesting that the financial crisis may not have the dramatic negative impact on aid volumes that many analysts predicted when the crisis struck (see, e.g., Roodman, 2008). Indeed, in the aftermath of the financial crisis, from 2008 to 2009, total net official development assistance from members of the OECD DAC did not decrease but rose slightly in real terms (+0.7 percent) to US$119.6 billion, and increased by 6.8 percent, if debt relief is excluded from the figures.

This is not to minimize apprehension over falling aid budgets—clearly, this is still a source of concern. While our econometric analysis shows little evidence of a relationship between economic growth in the OECD countries and a significant but negligible effect of the budgetary situation on development aid, it is worth stressing that the depth of the recession in the period 2008–2009 was unparalleled since the 1930s, and at the time of writing (November 2011) appears to have every chance of converting itself into a "double-dip recession."

Against this backdrop, we have discussed various ways in which to improve aid delivery and to use the financial crisis as an opportunity to rethink the framework for development cooperation. Among those, issues related to the fragmentation and lack of coordination of aid should clearly be a priority. A real supply-side problem exists in the sheer number and diversity of new aid players, both public and private.

In this chapter we also propose a serious reevaluation of the modality of aid delivery, including a reduction in technical assistance, an increase in support for productive sectors, and a reconsideration of the relative merits of project aid. Project aid has been much maligned over recent decades, on the grounds that it contributes to the problems of fragmentation and fungibility: Would the funds provided for project aid really translate into increased investment in development, or would they simply allow more leeway for governments to spend more on less socially desirable goals such as military spending? The project modality is also considered to be less amenable to promoting country ownership. But, arguably, these questions have considerable validity for other aid modalities too and may be even more relevant for budget support, where oversight of government expenditures can be far more onerous. While some recipient countries profess their enthusiasm for budget support, what they surely have in mind is large-scale, no-strings-attached program aid—not the kind of intrusive conditionality currently inherent in much budget and program aid.

In a post-crisis world, old frameworks of conditionality will be difficult, if not impossible, to sustain. The newfound dynamism of economic performance in much of the developing world, together with the rise of new actors in development cooperation, means that developing countries themselves are now much more confident and less likely to accept policy advice or strictures from their development partners. Now more than ever, country ownership needs to become a reality rather than simply an aspiration.

NOTES

1. There are, of course, wide variations across countries even within Africa, with some like South Africa receiving only a small amount of aid as a share of GDP, while others are still highly aid dependent (e.g., Mali, 13 percent; Malawi, 20 percent; Sierra Leone and Burundi, more than 30 percent) (Glennie, 2008:22).

2. Only post-crisis have the international financial institutions found a renewed demand for their services, as their funds have been replenished amid widespread concern that developing countries would suffer serious financing shortfalls.

3. In January 2010 the Institute for International Finance (IIF, 2010) revised its figures for private capital flows upward from its initial estimates of US$165 billion to US$435 billion. Although net global capital flows to developing countries fell 20 percent in 2009 to US$598 billion (3.7 percent of gross national income [GNI]); most of the falls were concentrated in the Eastern European and Central Asian region (World Bank, 2010a). Sub-Saharan Africa actually received the highest net capital inflows of any region in 2009 in relation to GNI (5.2 percent). Net capital flows rose 16 percent to US$45 billion, driven by a resurgence of portfolio equity inflows and a doubling of net debt inflows from official creditors.

4. More specifically, in the Gleneagles communiqué, the G-8 agreed to increase aid to Africa by US$25 billion per year by 2010, increase aid to all developing countries by US$50 billion per year by 2010, and cancel 100 percent of debts for eligible Heavily Indebted Poor Countries (HIPCs) to the IMF, the World Bank, and the African Development Fund.

5. See Clemens and Moss (2005) for a discussion on the origins and the motivations of ODA GNI targets.

6. Kharas (2010) suggests that countries that promised to give more, and were more ambitious in setting targets for higher aid, actually were able to deliver more aid even if they fell short of their targets.

7. Roodman (2008) adopts the Laeven and Valencia (2008) classification of systemic banking crisis, that is, in a systemic banking crisis, a country's corporate and financial sectors experience a large number of defaults, and financial institutions and corporations face great difficulties repaying contracts on time.

8. In Norway and Sweden, Roodman (2008) estimates that after the Nordic crisis of 1991, Norway's aid fell 10 percent and Sweden's 17 percent, from peak to trough after adjusting for inflation, considering the measure of net aid transfers that, despite net ODA, is net of interest payments on loans to donor countries as well as debt cancellation on old non-ODA loans.

9. The simple correlation in the U.S. case is just 0.06.

10. See, for example, Bandyopadhyay and Wall (2006) and Nunnenkamp et al. (2004).

11. It is a controversial point, but there is a fair amount of econometric support that political motivations do indeed explain a major part of aid flows. See, for instance, Alesina and Weder (2002) and Easterly (2007).

12. The 2006 GDP deflator has been calculated from the World Bank (2008b) and the 2006 USD exchange rate from the OECD (2008c).

13. A robustness check considers the fixed effects estimation in columns 3 and 4 of Table 4.1.

14. The African Development Bank doubled its lending in four years from US$8.5 billion in 2006 to nearly US$15.6 billion in 2010 (AfDB, 2010). The Asian Development Bank approved sovereign lending of US$12.8 billion in 2009, an increase of 48.6 percent compared to the US$8.6 billion approved in 2008 (ADB, 2010). The IDB approved US$15.5 billion in loans and guarantees in 2009, a 38 percent increase over 2008 approvals. Disbursements also rose from US$7.6 billion in 2008 to US$11.8 billion (IDB, 2010).

15. Buoyed by their much improved financial performance over the last decade, recently there has even been some tentative talk within the Africa Union of establishing an African Monetary Fund (AMF). See "Timmide avancée pour le FMA," *Jeune Afrique* 2607–2608 (December 26–January 8, 2011).

16. This section draws widely on Mold (2009).

17. See, for instance, Edwards (2001).

REFERENCES

ADB (Asian Development Bank). 2010. *ADB Annual Report 2009.* Mandaluyong: ADB. http://www.adb.org/documents/reports/annual_report/2009/adb-ar2009-vi -chap6.pdf.

AfDB (African Development Bank). 2010. "Bank Group Doubles Portfolio to USD 15.6 Billion in 4 Years." http://www.afdb.org/fr/news-events/article/bank-group-doubles -portfolio-to-usd-15-6-billion-in-4-years-6896.

AfDB and OECD Development Centre. 2010. *African Economic Outlook.* Paris: OECD Development Centre.

Alesina, A., and D. Dollar. 2000. "Who Gives Foreign Aid to Whom and Why?" *Journal of Economic Growth* 5 (1) (March): 33–63.

Alesina, A., and B. Weder. 2002. "Do Corrupt Governments Receive Less Foreign Aid?" *American Economic Review* 92 (4): 1126–37.

Allen, F., and G. Giovannetti. 2009. "Fragile Countries and the Current Economic Crisis." Paper prepared for the Conference "Moving Towards the European Report on Development" organized by the European Report on Development, Florence, June 21–23.

Arellano, M., and S. Bond. 1991. "Some Tests of Specification for Panel Data: Monte Carlo Evidence and an Application to Employment Equations." *Review of Economic Studies* 58 (2): 277–97.

AusAID. 2003. (June). "The Contribution of Australian Aid to Papua New Guinea's Development 1975–2000: Provisional Conclusions from a Rapid Assessment." *Evaluation and Review Series* 34. Canberra, Australia: AusAID.

Bandyopadhyay, S., and H. J. Wall. 2006. "The Determinants of Aid in the Post-Cold War Era." *Federal Reserve Banks of St. Louis Review* 89 (6) (November–December): 533–48.

Banerjee, A. V. 2007. *Making Aid Work.* Boston: Boston Review Books/MIT Press.

Bertoli, S., A. G. Cornia, and F. Maranesi. 2008. (September). "Aid Effort and Its Determinants—A Comparison of the Italian Performance with Other OECD Donors." Working Paper No. 11. Dipartimento di Scienze Economiche, Università degli Studi di Firenze.

Blundell, R., and S. Bond. 1998. "Initial Conditions and Moment Restrictions in Dynamic Panel Data Models." *Journal of Econometrics* 87 (1): 115–43.

Boschini, A., and A. Olofsgard. 2007. "Foreign Aid: An Instrument for Fighting Communism?" *Journal of Development Studies* 43 (4): 622–48.

Chong, A., and M. Gradstein. 2008. (August). "What Determines Foreign Aid? The Donors' Perspective." *Journal of Development Economics* 87 (1): 1–13.

Clemens, M., and T. Moss. 2005. "Ghost of 0.7 Percent: Origins and Relevance of the International Aid Target." Working Paper No. 68. Washington, D.C.: Center for Global Development.

Collier, P. 2007. *The Bottom Billion.* New York: Oxford University Press.

Commission for Africa. 2005. *Our Common Interest—An Argument.* London: Penguin Books.

Committee of Public Accounts. 2008. "Providing Budget Support for Developing Countries: Twenty-seventh Report of Session 2007–08." London: House of Commons, Department for International Development. www.publications.parliament.uk/pa/ cm200708/cmselect/cmpubacc/395/395.pdf.

Dang, H.-A., S. Knack, and H. Rogers. 2010. "International Aid and Financial Crises in Donor Countries." Policy Research Working Paper No. WPS 5162. Washington, D.C.: World Bank. http://econ.worldbank.org/external/default/main?pagePK=64165259&theSitePK=469372&piPK=64165421&menuPK=64166093&entityID=000158349_20091229212514.

Deaton, A., A. Banerjee, N. Lustig, and K. Rogoff. 2006. (September). "An Evaluation of World Bank Research 1998–2005." Report. Washington, D.C.: World Bank.

de Renzio, P. 2006. "Aid, Budgets and Accountability: A Survey Article." *Development Policy Review* 24 (6): 627–45.

de Renzio, P., and J. Hanlon. 2009. "Mozambique: Contested Sovereignty? The Dilemmas of Aid Dependence." In *The Politics of Aid—African Strategies for Dealing with Donors*, edited by L. Whitfield, pp. 246–70. New York: Oxford University Press.

Easterly, W. 2007. "Are Aid Agencies Improving?" *Economic Policy* 22 (52) (October): 633–78.

Edwards, M. S. 2001. "Crime and Punishment: Understanding IMF Sanctioning Practices." Mimeo. Rutgers University.

Faini, R. 2006. (June). "Foreign Aid and Fiscal Policy." Discussion Paper No. 5721. London: CEPR.

Frot, E., and J. Santiso. 2008. "Development Aid and Portfolio Funds: Trends, Volatility and Allocation." Working Paper No. 275. Paris: OECD Development Centre.

Glennie, G. 2008. *The Trouble with Aid: Why Less Could Mean More for Africa*. New York: Zed Books.

Hallet, M. 2009. (November). "Economic Cycles and Development Aid: What Is the Evidence from the Past?" Policy Brief No. 5. ECOFIN, the European Council.

IDB (Inter-American Development Bank). 2010. "Increase in Lending." Washington, D.C.: IDB. http://www.iadb.org/en/news/the-idb-and-the-financial-crisis/increase-in-lending,1787.html.

IDD and Associates. 2006. (May). *Evaluation of General Budget Support: Synthesis Report*. School of Public Policy, University of Birmingham. www.oecd.org/datao ecd/25/43/37426676.pdf.

IMF. 2007. (November 27). "An IEO Evaluation of Structural Conditionality in IMF-Supported Programs." Washington, D.C.: Independent Evaluation Office, International Monetary Fund.

———. 2010. (October). *World Economic Outlook*. Washington, D.C.: IMF.

Institute for International Finance (IIF). 2010. (January). "Capital Flows to Emerging Market Economies." IFF Research Note.

Kharas, H. 2008. (December 5). "More Excuses from Donors at Doha." Washington, D.C.: Brookings Institution. http://www.brookings.edu/opinions/2008/1205 _development_kharas.aspx.

———. 2010. (February 19). "The Hidden Aid Story: Ambition Breeds Success." Washington, D.C.: Brookings Institution. http://www.brookings.edu/opinions/2010/0219 _foreign_aid_kharas.aspx.

Killick, T. 2005. "Did Conditionality Streamlining Succeed?" In *Conditionality Revisited: Concepts, Experiences and Lessons*, edited by S. Koeberle, H. Bedoya, P. Silarsky, and G. Verheyen, pp. 93–96. Washington, D.C.: World Bank.

———. 2008. "Taking Control: Aid Management Policies in Least Developed Countries." Background paper for UNCTAD's *The Least Developed Countries Report: Growth, Poverty and Terms of Development Partnership 2008*. Geneva: UNCTAD. www.unctad.org/sections/ldc_dir/docs/ldcr2008_Killick_en.pdf.

Killick, T., and D. Lawson. 2007. (July). "Budget Support to Ghana: A Risk Worth Taking?" ODI Briefing Paper No. 24. London: Overseas Development Institute.

Knoll, M. 2008. "Budget Support: A Reformed Approach or Old Wine in New Skins?" Discussion Paper No. 190. Geneva: UNCTAD.

Laeven, L., and F. Valencia. 2008. (November). "System Banking Crises: A New Database." IMF Working Paper No. 224. Washington, D.C.: IMF.

Maizels, A., and M. K. Nissanke. 1984. "Motivations for Aid to Developing Countries." *World Development* 12 (9) (September): 879–900.

Manning, R. 2006. "Will 'Emerging Donors' Change the Face of International Cooperation?" *Development Policy Review* 24 (4): 371–385.

Mendoza, R., R. Jones, and G. Vergara. 2009. "Will the Global Financial Crisis Lead to Lower Foreign Aid? A First Look at United States ODA." Fordham Economics Discussion Paper Series. Department of Economics, Fordham University.

Mold, A. 2009. "Policy Ownership and Aid Conditionality in the Light of the Financial Crisis: A Critical Review." OECD Development Centre Study. Paris: OECD.

Nunnenkamp, P., G. Canavire, and L. Triveño, L. 2004. "Targeting Aid to the Needy and Deserving: Nothing but Promises?" Kiel Working Papers 1229. Kiel, Germany: Kiel Institute for the World Economy.

OECD. 2008a. *Development Cooperation Report.* Paris: OECD.

———. 2008b. "OECD Calls for Aid Pledge from Donor Countries." Paris: OECD. http://www.oecd.org/document/2/0,3343,en_2649_33721_41601282_1_1_1_1,00.html.

———. 2008c. *OECD.Stat.* Online databases. Paris: OECD. http://stats.oecd.org/WBOS/index.aspx.

———. 2009. *Development Cooperation Report.* Paris: OECD.

———. 2010a. *Development Cooperation Report 2010.* Paris: OECD.

———. 2010b. (February 17). "Donors' Mixed Aid Performance for 2010 Sparks Concern." Paris: Development Assistance Committee. http://www.oecd.org/document/20/0,3746,en_2649_34447_44617556_1_1_1_1,00.html.

———. 2010c. "50 Years of Official Development Assistance." http://www.oecd.org/document/41/0,3746,en_2649_34447_46195625_1_1_1_1,00.html.

———. 2010d. *OECD.Stat.* Online databases. Paris: OECD. http://stats.oecd.org/Index.aspx.

———. 2010e. *Perspectives on Global Development—Shifting Wealth.* Paris: OECD Development Centre.

———. 2011. "Development Aid Reaches an Historic High in 2010. " http://www.oecd.org/document/35/0,3746,en_2649_34447_47515235_1_1_1_1,00.html.

Pallage, S., and M. Robe. 2001. "Foreign Aid and the Business Cycle." *Review of International Economics* 9 (4) (November): 641–72.

Qi, G. 2007. (June 11–12). "China's Foreign Aid: Policies, Structure, Practice and Trend." Paper presented at University of Oxford/Cornell University Conference "New Directions in Development Assistance."

The Reality of Aid. 2008. *Aid Effectiveness: Democratic Ownership and Human Rights.* Quezon City, Philippines: Ibon Books. http://realityofaid.org/downloads/ RoA Reports2008_full.pdf.

Rich, B. 2002. "The World Bank under James Wolfensohn." In *Reinventing the World Bank,* edited by J. Pincus and J. Winters, pp. 26–53. Ithaca, N.Y.: Cornell University Press.

Riddell, R. 2007. *Does Foreign Aid Really Work?* New York: Oxford University Press.

Roodman, D. 2006. "Aid Project Proliferation and Absorptive Capacity." Working Paper No. 75. Washington, D.C.: Center for Global Development.

———. 2008. (October 13). "History Says Financial Crisis Will Suppress Aid, Global Development: Views from the Center." Washington, D.C.: Center for Global Development. http://blogs.cgdev.org/globaldevelopment/2008/10/history _says_financial_crisis.php.

Round, J. I., and M. Odedokun. 2004. "Aid Efforts and Its Determinants." *International Review of Economics and Finance* 13: 293–309.

Sumner, A. 2010. "Global Poverty and the New Bottom Billion: Three-quarters of the World's Poor Live in Middle-income Countries." IDS Working Paper No. 349. Brighton, United Kingdom: IDS.

Thurow, R. 2010. "The Fertile Continent." *Foreign Affairs* 86 (6) (November/ December).

UNCTAD. 2008. *The Least Developed Countries Report: Growth, Poverty and Terms of Development Partnership.* Geneva: UNCTAD.

UNDESA. 2010. *World Economic and Social Survey.* New York: UNDESA.

UN/ECOSOC. 2008. (April). "Trends in South-South and Triangular Development Cooperation." Background Study for the Development Cooperation Forum. New York: UN/ECOSOC.

White, H. N., and A. G. Dijkstra. 2003. "Programme Aid and Development beyond Conditionality." *Routledge Studies in Development Economics No. 29.* London and New York: Routledge.

Whitfield, L. 2009. *The Politics of Aid: African Strategies for Dealing with Donors.* New York: Oxford University Press.

Whitfield, L., and G. Maipose. 2008. "Managing Aid Dependence: How African Governments Lost Ownership and How They Can Regain It." Oxford: Global Economic Governance Programme, University College.

Wooldridge, J. 2002. *Econometric Analysis of Cross Section and Panel Data.* Cambridge, Mass.: MIT Press.

World Bank. 2008a. (November 18). "Statement by World Bank Group President Robert B. Zoellick on the Summit of G20 Leaders." Washington, D.C.: World Bank. http://web.worldbank.org/WBSITE/EXTERNAL/NEWS/0,,contentMDK :21979460~pagePK:64257043~piPK:437376~theSitePK:4607,00.html.

———. 2008b. *World Development Indicators.* Washington, D.C.: World Bank.

———. 2010a. *Global Development Finance 2011.* Washington, D.C.: World Bank.

———. 2010b. *World Development Indicators.* Washington, D.C.: World Bank.

CHAPTER 5

Aid, Institutional Quality, and Taxation
Some Challenges for the International Cooperation System

José Antonio Alonso, Carlos Garcimartín, and Víctor Martín

In the last few years the international community has taken significant steps forward in defining its commitment to tackling poverty in a much more precise way. Through the Millennium Declaration—and the Millennium Development Goals (MDGs)—an agenda committing the whole of the international community has been achieved. Such progress has gone hand in hand with a series of proposals for reform to the methods of managing international aid in order to improve its effectiveness. Specifically, there is now a focus on the need for greater aid ownership by recipient countries and on the requirements for better coordination, harmonization, and alignment of donor policies. The 2005 Paris Agenda and the subsequent Accra Agenda for Action in 2008 are the clearest results of those efforts. Added to these, on the European side, have been the European Consensus on Development and the later European Union (EU) Code of Conduct on Complementarity and the Division of Labor in Development Policy, the goal of which is likewise to improve the operative capacity, effectiveness, and coherence of the aid policy of EU member countries.

These important changes in development aid doctrine were accompanied by devoting a greater focus on targeting resources at the countries with the most acute levels of poverty. Inadequate allocation of resources in the past was considered to have limited aid effectiveness. As a result, low income countries (LICs) and, particularly, sub-Saharan Africa ones have become much more important aid recipients, while middle-income countries have become less important, some even seeing the closure of donor delegations in their countries. There has also been a change in the sectors that aid has targeted, with more resources going to social matters (such as education and health), at the expense of actions more directly related to growth and support of the productive fabric of recipient countries. The opportunity of some of these changes is, nevertheless, debatable.

Despite the changes promoted within the aid system, there is a feeling that development policy is not up to the challenges of today's reality. We could say that although the international aid system has changed, the international reality has changed more profoundly and more rapidly. Some of these important changes in the international arena include the growing heterogeneity in the developing world; the emergence of new regional and global powers coming from the developing world; the presence of new development aid players—many of them linked to the private sector; and, finally, the enlargement of the sphere of international public goods.

These doubts about the aid reform come at a time when there seems to be a renewed skepticism about the effectiveness of international aid. Fueling that skepticism are not only recent and meticulous research papers (Rajan and Subramanian, 2005, for example) but also essays, varying in approach and quality but with high media impact (Moyo, 2009, for example). Some of these essays not only question the effectiveness of development aid but actually declare its impact to be negative.

We aim in this chapter to contribute some reflections and evidence on these matters. The chapter is structured around four sections. In the first section we review the conclusions of the specialized literature on the overall effectiveness of international aid. In accordance with the changing results of the empirical exercises, dominant opinion has alternated between periods of moderate optimism and profound skepticism; in the latest essays on development aid, a rather pessimistic tone seems to prevail. In the second section we present our own assessment of aid effectiveness. In order to do so, we use an indirect strategy: since the positive effect of institutional quality on economic development possibilities is known, as is the impact of tax resources on institutional quality, we look at the effect that aid has on institutional quality and the tax effort. The results of the estimation lead us to deduce that both effects are positive, although conditional upon other characteristics in the given country, such as the degree of dependence on aid and on the level of institutional quality. In the third section we discuss the relationship between the agenda for aid reform and the conclusions of studies on aid effectiveness and donor practices. Although the proposals inspired by the Paris Agenda might be along the right lines, there are elements regarding their implementation that require correction, and other aspects, such as the problems stemming from dependency on aid, that are not even considered. In the fourth section we compare the reforms of the development aid system with the changes experienced in the international system. It is the gap between the two that poses a series of challenges that the international system must address.

AID EFFECTIVENESS

The impact in developmental terms of international aid has long been polemical: for more than four decades, studies have used different approaches, empirical methods, and data, showing weak, if not ambiguous, relationships between the resources received and the development of the recipient country. The best that can be said is that aid can be effective, but not immediately, nor in a robust manner. The best microeconomic support for hypotheses and the use of ever-more sophisticated statistical and econometric methods have allowed the quality of studies to be improved over time but have not eliminated the controversy underlying their results. The studies have fed different viewpoints, in accordance with the distinctive phases in which the work was produced. After a period of profound skepticism at the end of the 1980s and the first half of the 1990s, a rather more optimistic perception of aid opened up: aid could be effective, although that result depended on certain traits in the recipient country. Part of the subsequent debate was focused on establishing the recipient countries' characteristics that were most important. However, after the first half of the decade of the 2000s, new question marks have been placed around aid, due to discouraging results drawn by some research papers. This has been reinforced by other recent publications that have received more media coverage and that not only question the effectiveness of aid but insist on its negative effect on the countries that receive it. Their arguments are not always convincing, but their effect on opinion has been significant, leading to another phase characterized by renewed skepticism. Before offering our own assessment, which distances itself from that skeptical spirit, we review the main conclusions of the specialized literature.

ANTECEDENTS: A BRIEF CHRONICLE

It is possible to separate the studies on aid effectiveness into different phases, in accordance with data availability, dominant specifications, and doctrinal frameworks used.[1] The initial articles used a simple Harrod-Domar model (or a "two-gap" model) to analyze the economic growth dynamic of the countries; these considered international aid as a financial source of domestic investment. Under this approach, aid could affect investment (and perhaps savings) and, through that, the rate of growth. In general, these papers were based on *cross-country* exercises, with aid considered an exogenous variable. Some of them tried to analyze the effect of aid on savings (Griffin, 1970; Griffin and Enos, 1970; Massell et al., 1972; Weisskopf, 1972; Newlyn, 1973; Papanek, 1973); others studied the impact of aid on investment (Haveli, 1976; Levy, 1987, 1988; Khan and Hoshino, 1992); and, finally, others also considered the global effect of aid on economic growth (Levy, 1988; Dowling and Hiemenz, 1982; Mosley et al., 1987).

As time has passed, the availability of data has improved, and it has become possible to use more flexible growth models. A good example of these improvements is Mosley et al. (1987), in which the authors analyze the effectiveness of aid from a fiscal response model, or Boone (1994, 1996), in which the author considers the effect of aid in the framework of a political utility function. Although the results of these kinds of studies are not conclusive, the dominant tone is rather pessimistic, as far as these works obtained a negative (or null) aid effect on economic growth in recipient countries.

Aid effectiveness studies had an important revival as a consequence of the influential work of Burnside and Dollar (2000). Besides its affect on the academic community, this article also gave theoretical support to the World Bank (1998) report *Assessing Aid: What Works, What Doesn't and Why?* Burnside and Dollar believe that aid effectiveness depends crucially on the institutional framework and policies put into place by the recipient. To support that position, they carry out an estimation with a *pool* of data. In their growth equation specification, they include not only a variable on aid but also an interactive term between aid and policies. The estimation produces an aid coefficient that is not significantly different to zero, while that corresponding to the interactive term is positive and significant. The World Bank draws a significant conclusion from the study mentioned: it is important to be more demanding in the selection of countries to receive aid, focusing resources only on those countries that enjoy a proper policy framework. This selectiveness would mean replacing ex-ante conditionality, which characterized the 1980s, with a new ex-post conditionality, reserving development aid for only those countries that can demonstrate a *good policy framework* (even the real meaning of "good policy framework" is debatable).

The publication of the work of Burnside and Dollar (2000) led to a renewal in studies on aid effectiveness. Although carried out in a relatively similar theoretical framework, the new research contributed a number of interesting findings. Perhaps the main variations refer to the control variables used in the convergence equations, to the way of handling the endogenous nature of aid, and to the assumption that the aid effect is not linear. In terms of this last element, in some cases the possible existence of decreasing returns on the aid was admitted, and it was measured through the square of aid; in others, however, it was supposed that the impact of aid was conditioned by other characteristics in the recipient country, either endogenous (institutions and politics, for example) or exogenous (geographical location or external shocks, for example).

Among the studies referred to, in all those where squared of aid was incorporated, the estimation confirms the existence of decreasing marginal returns on aid (Hadjimichael et al., 1995; Durbarry et al., 1998; Hansen and Tarp, 2001; Rajan and Subramanian, 2005, 2008). Although it is debatable where the threshold lies,[2] it seems clear that after a certain level the accumulation of received resources (in terms of GDP) can end up having negative effects on the recipient country. That result can be interpreted in various ways, which are not necessarily incompatible with one another, considering it to be the result of a "Dutch disease" syndrome caused by the excessive importing of foreign funds (Durbarry et al., 1998; Rajan and Subramanian, 2005), the result of a limited capacity of the recipient to absorb resources (Hadjimichael et al., 1995), or the result of institutional harms caused by a high dependency on foreign aid (Lensink and White, 2001).

Many of the studies incorporate the existence of decreasing marginal returns, stating that aid is effective in itself, without needing to condition that result on the presence of correct policies in the recipient country (Hansen and Tarp, 2001; Durbarry et al., 1998; Lensink and White, 2001; Easterly et al., 2004; Dalgaard and Hansen, 2001; Dalgaard et al., 2004), a result that calls into question the conclusions drawn by Burnside and Dollar (2000).

This new generation of studies also opened up some new issues worth considering. Lensink and Morrissey (2000), for instance, sought to relate aid effectiveness not so much to the characteristics of the recipient but more to the donor's way of operating. In particular, they analyzed the effect of uncertainty and the instability of aid flows. The results of their estimation suggest that when a variable expressing the variability of foreign assistance is integrated, that variable is significant and has a negative impact on growth, while the effect on the received aid is revealed as positive and clearly significant. One plausible interpretation of these results suggests that uncertainty of aid flows has a negative impact on growth, but that once that uncertainty is under control, the effect of aid on the dynamic of the economy is positive.

A second line of research tried to follow the approach of Burnside and Dollar (2000), incorporating the odd variable related to the recipient country's circumstances. Burnside and Dollar (2004) here confirmed their own previous conclusions, incorporating new data into their series and improving the indicator on the recipient's institutional quality. Despite this result, both Roodman (2007a) and Easterly et al. (2004) question the degree of robustness of this kind of study where aid effectiveness is conditioned by the recipient country's policies. In fact, when Roodman (2007a) submits three of the most important studies on aid effectiveness (including Burnside and Dollar, 2000) to a sensitivity analysis, the two that seemed most robust (Dalgaard et al., 2004; Hansen and Tarp, 2001) suggest that aid has a positive impact without any conditions being set on applied policies.

Other studies refer, however, to alternative conditioners, such as the presence of an export price shock in the affected countries (Collier and Dehn, 2001), the degree of vulnerability of their economies (Guillaumont and Chauvet, 2001; Chauvet and Guillaumont, 2002), previous conditions of violence in the country (Collier and Hoeffler, 2004), political instability (Chauvet and Guillaumont, 2002), the level of democracy (Svensson, 1999), or the limited size of the government (Economides et al., 2008). In all these studies the effectiveness of aid conditioned by the recipient country's circumstances is confirmed, although the results are highly sensitive to the methodologies used in the respective estimations (Roodman, 2007b).

As a whole, the studies carried out during the first half of the decade of the 2000s seemed to portray a somewhat more optimistic image of aid: although some doubts persist, the dominant effect of aid seems positive, although conditioned on other factors (Herzer and Morrisey, 2009).

MOST RECENT CONTRIBUTIONS

Arndt et al. (2009) suggest that the most recent phase in studies on aid effectiveness, which began in the second half of the decade of the 2000s, amounts to a revitalization of the so-called "micro-macro paradox" (good results in the micro-level evaluations and deceptive results in the macro-level analysis) (Mosley, 1986). Some recent econometric studies have contributed, as we will show, to fueling this perception. Nevertheless, the largest impact came from a group of essays that, using different approaches and varying analytic solidity, started to highlight the potentially negative effects of aid. This group ranges from those clearly against the continuation of development aid (Moyo, 2009; Hubbard and Duggan, 2009) to those who demand deep reforms to its management, including a certain restriction of the resources allocated (Easterly, 2006; Calderisi, 2007; Glennie, 2008, among others). Our attention will concentrate exclusively on those studies based on econometric estimations of the effects of aid. Specifically, we will refer to four such studies and two that could be called "meta-analyses" on aid effectiveness: the contradictory results of those studies are highly illustrative of the state of theory in this area.

Among those studies, the one that stands out is by Clemens et al. (2004) and is based on the assumption that not all aid is identical in type: some categories of aid (such as humanitarian aid) have no relationship at all to the recipient's growth, while others (such as health or education expenditure) only produce effects in the very long term. Therefore, it is necessary to refine aid flow, leaving only those elements that have an effect on growth within a relatively short time scale so that they will be reflected in the estimates, which are carried out through Two-Stages Least Squares (2SLS), with instrumental variables, or Generalized Method of Moments (GMM) techniques. The conclusions point to a positive, robust relation between aid and recipient growth in the short term (in periods less than four years), a relationship that is resistant to multiple specifications and diverse periods. That result is also independent of the quality of applied policies and other control variables. At the same time, the result confirms that aid is subject to decreasing returns, which means it could have a negative effect on countries with a great aid dependency.

Dalgaard et al. (2004) try to find an explanation for the contradictory results that aid effectiveness studies produce, suggesting that aid can work in some places and not in others. They incorporate the percentage of the total land mass occupied by tropics in a given country as one of the explanatory variables. For the estimate, the authors use a complex process of instrumentation of variables, estimating their model through the GMM (in its versions of differentials and of the system). The results suggest that aid is not effective around the tropics, but it has a positive effect on growth in those countries that are far from said geographical area. To explain this, in line with the arguments of Gallup et al. (1998), Dalgaard et al. (2004) refer to the effect that the geographical and climatic conditions in the tropics have on the life conditions and the productivity of the people and the land, conditioning institutional quality and the level of development of those countries. Unfortunately, as Roodman (2007b) highlights, the results of Dalgaard et al. are highly dependent on the behavior of a limited number of countries far away from the tropics (among them Jordan, Syria, Egypt, and Botswana). Excluding these four countries from the sample would mean a serious change to the results.

Among the most skeptical studies, and also among the most influential, are those by Rajan and Subramanian (2005, 2008). These authors take a conventional neoclassical model and assume that aid affects growth mainly through the effect it has on financing capital stock. For their estimation they use a sophisticated instrumentation strategy (similar to that of Frankel and Romer, 1999) based on a model to determine bilateral aid flows, composed from the characteristics of the countries involved (colonial ascendant, the size of the population, and their cross-product).[3] They use 2SLS as instrumental variables as well as dynamic panels (GMM) in their estimation. Despite the careful weighting of the estimation strategy, they cannot find any robust relationship at all between aid and growth, and this despite trying to refine the statistical procedure used through various tests, time periods of varying lengths, and different methods of measuring aid. The explanation, in their view, for the absence of a relationship is chiefly concerned with two potentially negative aid effects: first, the impact that aid has on the political and institutional climate of the recipient country, which reduces the quality of the governance, and, second, the effect that aid has on the recipient country's competitiveness, which refers to the Dutch disease problem of receiving foreign funds. In any case, aid contributes to a productive reallocation in the recipient country in favor of sectors targeting domestic markets, reducing the competitiveness of those sectors most open to international competition (Rajan and Subramanian, 2008). Their summary conclusion is that it is difficult to discern any systematic effect of aid on growth.

Lastly, Herzer and Morrisey (2009) try to discern the long-term relation between aid and GDP levels through a procedure that avoids the problems related to omitted variables, the heterogeneity of countries' behavior, and the endogenous nature of aid. They use a heterogeneous panel with co-integration techniques (DOLS). Their main result is that aid has, on average, a negative effect on GDP. Nevertheless, this average hides a series of different behaviors, with about a third of countries showing a positive effect. To capture the variables explaining these differences between countries, they carry out cross-country regressions using as a dependent variable the effect on estimated output in the previous step. Out of the nineteen variables tested as potentially explaining the differential behavior, the ones that are significant are government size, religious tensions, and the rule of law and order. Although the research procedure is ingenious, it is difficult to admit as intuitive these variables seemingly associated with the best performance of aid.

Besides these four highlighted studies, others have tried to do second-level exercises in order to evaluate the studies carried out. The first of these is really a collection of meta-studies, done by Doucouliagos and Paldam (2005a, b, c), who revise (1) the forty-three previous studies that tried to determine the effect of aid on savings and investment; (2) the sixty-eight works that studied the effect of aid directly on growth; and (3) the thirty-one studies that assumed a conditional type of relationship where the effect on aid depended on a third factor. The procedure used for their analysis is the Meta-Significance Meta-Regression Model (MSTMRA), which is based on descriptive statistics as well as on significance tests of parameters obtained in the studies under evaluation. The results they reach through this exercise are the following: (1) aid has a small negative effect on savings and an equally small, but insignificant, negative effect on investment; (2) the effect of aid on growth is positive, but not significant; and (3) the effects associated with conditional estimates cannot be replicated. The authors admit the pessimistic tone of their conclusions and state that "these results are not what we would have liked to see, and it certainly suggests that aid should be reformed to perform better" (Doucouliagos and Paldam, 2005a:19).

The second study is by Arndt et al. (2009), who carry out an application of the Rubin Causal Model to the most recent publications on the effect of aid. Through that procedure they try to construct a countercase, in terms of potential results, which they take from the evaluation publications. In particular, they apply this procedure to the Rajan and Subramanian (2008) study, submitting it to the following corrections: (1) they change the strategy for the instrumentation of the variables; (2) they use official development assistance (ODA) per capita instead of ODA as a proportion of GDP to avoid spurious correlations with the instruments; (3) they introduce fixed effects per donor; (4) they use Heckman's correction procedure of bias in the selection; and (5) they incorporate an estimator that is twice as robust and that can be used with instrumental variables. Their results suggest that the elasticity of growth in terms of the weight of aid on GDP is somewhere between 0.10 and 0.23 for the longest time periods. That implies that the effect on aid exceeds its supposed contribution to generating capital stock (estimated by Rajan and Subramanian, 2005) and also positively influences the evolution of total productivity. According to the value of the confidence intervals, we cannot rule out the possibility that elasticity falls into the negative zone, but that it is positive wherever the results are the most solid.

A NEW ESTIMATION: AID, INSTITUTIONAL QUALITY, AND TAXES

The overview of the studies on aid effectiveness carried out in the last section is sufficient to confirm that the existing literature on the relationship between aid and growth is far from conclusive. Despite that, if we had to highlight any of the results as being the most plausible, we would select the following: (1) the effect of aid seems easier to detect in the short term than in the long term, perhaps because in more drawn-out periods, positive effects are watered down by negative effects (Clemens et al., 2004); (2) aid seems more effective in contexts where it contributes to relaxing obstacles to a country, such as factors that make it vulnerable, external shocks, or internal conflicts (Collier and Dehn, 2001; Guillaumont and Chauvet, 2001; Collier and Hoeffler, 2004); (3) the relationship between aid and growth seems to be subject to diminishing returns, to the extent that from a certain level of dependency, negative impacts can take place: there is no unanimity, however, on where that threshold lies, nor on which are the precise factors that explain this behavior (Hadjimichael et al., 1995; Durbarry et al., 1998; Hansen and Tarp, 2001; Rajan and Subramanian, 2008); (4) potentially, there are national factors, specific to recipient countries, that condition aid effectiveness, but there is no certainty about what those factors are; and (5) the way in which aid is managed by donors can affect aid effectiveness (Lensink and Morrissey, 2000).

ESTIMATION STRATEGY

As we have seen, despite the efforts made, the analytical capacities used, and the diversity of approaches and procedures, the outcome of this extensive literature is rather meager. To explain why, we need to look at the difficulties surrounding both the theoretical foundations of the work as well as the empirical estimation of the assumed relationship between aid and growth.

In terms of the *theoretical foundation,* the first studies are based on a simple version of the Harrod model, in which aid affects the capacity to finance investment and—through that—to affect the growth dynamic. There is hardly any change to this scheme when, in addition to the savings gap, researchers add another gap related to the financing of the country's import needs (as argued in their time by Chenery and Strout, 1966). This theoretical framework is related to the inflexibility with which the economic dynamic is considered, as a consequence of the assumption of fixed coefficients in the production function.

This is why the most recent studies abandoned that stance to assume instead the approach arising from the Solow model, giving aid a role in the convergence path followed by each country toward its particular steady state (in the way argued by Barro, 1997). Here, however, there are at least two problems to consider. First, it is necessary to define the very conditions of the steady state: in this respect, the tendency of researchers has been to include a wide range of control variables whose justification is, often, more empirical than theoretical. The second problem is related to how to incorporate aid into this approach. In general, there has been a tendency to assume that the main effect of aid is translated into a rise in the economy's capital stock: in other words, it is assumed that aid finances (at least partially) investment. This fact entails an undesirable consequence, since it means that investment has to be left out of the estimation on the convergence function (despite the fact that it is the most relevant economic variable in that process), assuming that aid constitutes an adequate proxy to investment (which is debatable).

From the empirical point of view there are also numerous limitations that need to be addressed. The following three stand out:

• It is necessary to tackle the *potential endogenous nature* of aid by admitting that the relationship with the recipient's GDP per capita might work both ways (aid affects GDP per capita, but GDP-per-capita conditions aid allocation). There is not, however, an accepted procedure to resolve this problem, since the selection of instrumental variables is subject to a certain degree of discretion, and the use of delayed variables might be debatable when there are problems of auto-correlation.

• The relationship between aid and GDP per capita might *not be linear in nature*. There are two ways in which researchers have tried to reflect that non-linearity: (1) through the squared value of the same variable when marginal returns are not constant; and (2) through an interactive term if it is considered that a third variable could condition the impact of the aid. In both cases, however, the solution proposed can generate co-linearity problems between the variable and its transformation. This problem becomes more acute in the case of regressions with instrumental variables.

• The estimation has to tackle the fact that there are *many variables* that influence growth and that, out of all of them, aid has a smaller weighting. It is not simple to translate those relationships into empirical terms since, on the one hand, an extreme simplification can lead to specification problems due to omitted variables, but, on the other hand, an excessively ambitious specification could generate severe co-linearity problems.

These are the theoretical and empirical problems that, along with problems of low data quality in some variables, could be behind the inconclusiveness of results. In accordance with that, the approach to the estimation that we will offer here aims to explore an alternative means of identifying the effects of aid on growth. We work from the assumption that aid, as well as affecting growth through investment, influences the level of institutional quality in recipient countries, although the research, to date, is ambiguous on this effect. We also assume that institutions constitute a relevant factor in promoting long-term development, as a wide range of studies demonstrates. It is conceivable, therefore, that a positive impact of aid on institutional quality could have a positive medium-term impact on countries' potential for development. This effect could be reversed, however, through the negative impact of aid on other variables, which in turn also affect institutional quality. The most important of those variables is, without a doubt, the state's capacity to collect taxes: certain studies suggest that the sign of this effect is negative. We aim, therefore, to check this combination of relationships.

This estimation strategy is carried out in three successive stages: (1) we confirm the effect that institutions have on promoting the long-term growth of economies; (2) we analyze the impact that aid has on the quality of a country's institutions; and (3) we study the effect that aid has on the tax-raising capacity of recipient countries. The estimation procedures combine the use of 2SLS with instrumental variables and dynamic panels

(GMM) where the data allow. The results of this exercise suggest that aid has a clear and robust positive effect on institutional quality, in contrast to the belief of those defending the "curse of aid" hypothesis (Djankov et al., 2008) or the "aid-institutions paradox" (Moss et al., 2008). The effect of aid on taxes is never negative in any case and, under reasonable assumptions, can be expected to be slightly positive, as Gupta (2007), Brun et al. (2007), and Clist and Morrissey (2011) suggest. But the effect of aid on institutions has diminishing returns, and its effect on tax effort is conditioned by institutional quality of the recipient country.

GROWTH AND INSTITUTIONAL QUALITY

Specialists are increasingly convinced about the importance of institutions in promoting a country's economic progress. The institutional structure defines the incentives and penalties that shape social behavior and collective action. In an uncertain world in which independent agents operate, institutions reduce uncertainty, moderate transaction costs, and facilitate social coordination. This is why institutions are a potential factor in explaining long-term development.

Confirming this relationship is, however, no simple task. The estimation has to tackle the deficiencies in the institutional quality indicators and the problems associated with estimating a relationship that is assumed to be endogenous in nature and that seems to be influenced by diverse variables, some of them co-linear. Despite this, in the last few years, a wide collection of empirical studies has tended to support this hypothesis, confirming the relationship that exists between institutional quality and the level of development and, although in a less conclusive way, the relationship between institutional quality and the growth dynamic (Aron, 2000). This is shown in cross-country analyses (such as Hall and Jones, 1999; Acemoglu et al., 2002; Rodrik et al., 2002; Easterly and Levine, 1997; Alonso, 2011), in data panel analyses (Henisz, 2000; Tavares and Wacziarg, 2001; Varsakelis, 2006), and in case studies (for example, Rodrik, 2003).

Although the evidence is sufficiently convincing, it is worth carrying out an additional test integrating the institutional quality variable in a conditioned convergence equation, expressed in the simplest form. Specifically, growth in per capita income in a country during a determined period depends on the per capita income that the country starts from (which is a negative symbol), on the investment effort made (a positive symbol), and on the institutional quality (positive). At the same time, factors influencing the determination of the steady state are considered and, therefore, the level of a population's human capital (approximated through the education rate) and the growth rate of the population are used as control variables. In other words

$$\frac{dy_t}{y_t} = \beta_1 + \beta_2 Y_0 + \beta_3 I + \beta_4 IQ + \beta_5 TS + \beta_6 CP + U \qquad (1)$$

where y is per capita income in PPP; I is investment as a proportion of GDP; IQ is institutional quality; TS is the education rate; and CP is the population growth (an explanation of the variables can be found in the Appendix). There is no indicator of institutional quality without its problems; nevertheless, we have used the World Wide Governance Index (World Bank), which is the most complete and accurate available indicator.

Given the existence of an endogenous relationship between per capita income and institutional quality, in the estimation, we need to use procedures to avoid this problem. As well as through Ordinary Least Squares (OLS), estimates have been done through 2SLS with instrumental variables, using delayed per capita income, ethnic divisions, and dummy variables on the colonial origin of the countries as instruments, all common variables for this type of estimate (Table 5.1).

As was to be expected, investment has a positive influence on the process of economic convergence, activating growth. At the same time, in all the specifications tried, the coefficient associated with institutional quality (measured through the average of the Worldwide Governance Index) is positive and significant. In fact, it is seen both when institutional quality is considered an independent variable (specifications 1 and 3) as well as when the interactive effect between investment and institutional quality is estimated (specifications 2 and 4). Of all the models tried, the one that also includes population growth as well as population skill levels (specification 3) as control variables is the most convincing. In all cases, it is necessary to include a dummy variable related to Eastern Europe, which has its own particularities in terms of institutional quality that should be taken into consideration (Alonso and Garcimartín, 2008).

AID AND INSTITUTIONAL QUALITY: PREVIOUS STUDIES

Having confirmed that institutions affect growth, the next step is to identify the factors that determine institutional quality and to discover

Table 5.1 The Effect of Institutional Quality on Economic Growth

	(1)		(2)		(3)		(4)	
	OLS	IV	OLS	IV	OLS	IV	OLS	IV
Intercept	0.4119 (1.36)	0.8002 (1.58)	0.3450 (1.15)	0.5615 (1.30)	0.4854*** (1.63)	0.8607*** (1.86)	0.4212 (1.43)	0.6243 (1.60)
Initial Income (Y_0)	−0.0692** (−2.15)	−0.1183** (−2.25)	−0.0665* (−2.07)	−0.1083** (−2.16)	−0.0862** (−1.98)	−0.1256** (−2.27)	−0.0853*** (−1.93)	−0.1166** (−2.16)
Growth Population (CP)	−0.3792 (−1.33)	−0.2881 (−0.85)	−0.3790 (−1.32)	−0.2825 (−0.83)	−0.3419 (−1.13)	−0.3308 (−0.97)	−0.3338 (−1.09)	−0.3235 (−0.95)
Education (TS)	—	—	—	—	0.0460 (0.62)	0.0348 (0.44)	0.0482 (0.65)	0.0408 (0.51)
Investment (I)	0.1670* (2.83)	0.1845** (2.69)	0.1806* (3.15)	0.2322* (3.39)	0.1278*** (1.85)	0.1420*** (1.79)	0.1422** (2.13)	0.1833*** (2.35)
Institutional Quality (QI)	0.0835*** (1.84)	0.2682** (2.16)	—	—	0.0930** (2.02)	0.2569** (2.18)	—	—
QI×I	—	—	0.0250*** (1.67)	0.0801** (2.04)	—	—	0.0293*** (1.92)	0.0751** (2.05)

ECA	0.4058*	0.4496*	0.4084*	0.4580*	0.3696*	0.3930*	0.3734*	0.3961*
	(4.29)	(4.05)	(4.29)	(4.04)	(3.95)	(3.61)	(3.97)	(3.63)
N	118	100	118	100	117	99	117	99
F	14.24	12.02	14.09	11.87	11.84	9.94	11.75	10.00
(p-value)	(0.00)	(0.00)	(0.00)	(0.00)	(0.00)	(0.00)	(0.00)	(0.00)
R2	43.31	—	43.16	—	41.54	—	41.52	—
Centered R2	—	38.69	—	39.39	—	38.27	—	39.67
Uncentered R2	—	73.11	—	73.42	—	73.18	—	73.78
UI Test LM	—	11.40	—	11.23	—	12.00	—	11.96
(p-value)		(0.08)		(0.08)		(0.06)		(0.06)
OI Test	—	3.48	—	3.7	—	3.60	—	3.83
(p-value)		(0.62)		(0.59)		(0.61)		(0.57)

Notes: Robust "t" statistic in brackets.

Instruments for CI = latitude, British colony, French colony, ethnic, linguistic, and religious divisions.

*, **, *** = significance of the parameter to 1%, 5%, and 10%, respectively.

whether aid is one of them. Here the available publications are not very conclusive: in fact, as Rodrik (1996) recognizes, foreign resources received by the country can serve both as a stimulus for implementing reforms judged to be necessary and to reduce the costs associated with failing to carry out reforms. It is not surprising, therefore, that positions diverge in this field. In essence, we could group the main opinions around three contrasting stances.

The first is the most traditional opinion (and that held by development aid managers): that aid is a mechanism that can be useful in promoting improvements to the institutions of recipient countries. The understanding here is that resources, experience, and technical skills are transferred from the donor through aid, and they can be put at the service of moves to consolidate and improve the institutional framework of the recipients. In the end, developing countries face to budgetary limitations of their administrations, which prevent them from devoting resources to institutional reform, limit their spending on equipment, and condition the payment of civil servants. Aid can help relax some of those limitations. In accordance with this opinion, a significant sum of aid resources has traditionally been dedicated to improving and strengthening institutions in recipient countries. We should, however, highlight that the successes of donors in this field have been rather limited, as Riddell (2007) recognizes. Still, beyond the errors, there is faith that institutional quality can be positively influenced by aid.

This vision changes as a result of the turnaround that Burnside and Dollar (2000) and the World Bank (1998) gave to aid effectiveness studies. It was accepted that institutional quality influenced aid effectiveness, but it was felt that aid was incapable of influencing the policies and institutions of recipients (in other words, institutional quality is assumed to be independent of aid). This is why they suggested abandoning ex-ante conditionality and substituting it for a type of ex-post conditionality: aid should only be granted to countries that already had good policies and institutions. As a result of this approach, various donors incorporated institutional quality indicators into their criteria for allocating aid. The most significant example of this procedure is that of the Millennium Challenge Account, put into place by the United States at the start of the last decade (Radelet, 2003).

Finally, a third group of authors thinks that institutional quality is a dependent variable that can be influenced by aid, but the authors suggest that the effect is overwhelmingly negative. They believe that this result is most likely when the aid as a proportion of public resources passes a certain threshold. The arguments they use to justify this expectation are diverse, but among them the following seven are worth highlighting:

- First, because of its discretional nature, aid contributes to increasing the sphere of rent-seeking and corruption activities (Svensson, 2000; Alesina and Weder, 2002; Djankov et al., 2008).
- Second, because of its unpredictable nature and its variability, aid can distort the recipient's budgetary planning processes (Heller and Gupta, 2002; McGillivray and Morrissey, 2001b).
- Third, since aid helps relax fiscal limitations, it can contribute to poor spending practices, encouraging unsustainable projects (Bräutigam and Knack, 2004; Killick, 2004).
- Fourth, aid influences the size and composition of spending, tending to increase public spending the greater the aid received (McGillivray and Morrissey, 2001a; Remmer, 2004) and to increase the levels of public consumption related to investments (Khan and Hoshino, 1992).
- Fifth, because of the way in which aid is managed, the operations of the development agencies on the ground have been a source of recruitment of local technical resources (expert personnel), sometimes at the expense of the respective public administrations (Bräutigam, 2000).
- Sixth, when aid starts to play a certain role in the sources of public financing of the recipients, institutional quality deteriorates by weakening the mutual demand between citizens and the state and making the state more concerned about answering to donors than to its citizens (Moore, 1998; Alonso and Garcimartín, 2010).
- Seventh, the continued receiving of aid can be a disincentive for the country to develop a solid fiscal system that gives the state proper resources and contributes to a more demanding relationship between citizens and the state (Heller, 1975; Kimbrough, 1986; Bräutigam and Knack, 2004).

The empirical studies on this subject have contributed to consolidating the negative image of aid. That happens, for instance, when the studies are carried out by specialists drawing on accumulated experience on the ground (among them Bräutigam, 2000; Van de Walle, 2005). However, econometric studies also seem to suggest this inverse symbol relationship, although not always with conclusive evidence.

For example, this conclusion is shared by a collection of more or less related recent studies (Bräutigam, 2000; Knack, 2004; Bräutigam and Knack, 2004). Specifically, Bräutigam (2000) finds a negative relationship between aid and institutional quality, with institutional quality measured through the International Country Risk Guide (ICRG) and aid through the proportion of aid to GDP and public expenditure. The estimation is carried out through OLS as well as through 2SLS with instrumental variables, the negative effect of the aid coefficient being greater in this last case.

The conclusion of Knack (2004) is very similar, using as a dependent variable the rate of variation of the components of quality of bureaucracy, corruption, and the state of law of the ICRG. The cross-country analysis, through both the OLS and 2SLS with instrumental variables, confirms the negative relationship that exists between institutional quality and aid (measuring in terms of GDP as well as in terms of governmental expenditure). The effect is, moreover, important: an increase of 20 percentage points in the proportion of aid to GDP coefficient reduces the ICRG by about 3 points.

The last work in this series, by Bräutigam and Knack (2004), is similar to the previous work and obtains a similar conclusion: aid negatively influences institutional quality. The population is also included in this case as a proxy for economies of scale and institutional quality is defined on variation rates. Only the initial value of institutional quality is significant, and also the value of aid when the estimation is 2SLS with instrumental variables. The result is independent of whether the study period is divided into two phases to reflect the greater attention that donors have paid to institutional quality since the 1990s.

Djankov et al. (2008) believe aid has a similar effect to the abundance of valuable mineral resources, negatively affecting growth by increasing income-seeking activities. The means by which they suggest that this effect is produced is through deterioration in governance conditions in the country. To verify this, they try to relate institutional quality to aid, the proportion of oil income to GDP, and shocks in exchange terms. They approach institutional quality through the checks and balances indicator of the Database of Political Institutions created by Becker et al. (2001) (and, alternatively, the democracy indicator of Polity IV). They carry out the estimation through instrumental variables as well as a GMM system. The results confirm the negative effect of aid on institutional quality, which resists changes to the institutional quality indicators and the use of alternative instruments. The conclusion on the impact of aid would be negative in this case, especially in those countries that are most dependent on these types of financial flows (which happen to be the poorest countries).

Despite the finality of their conclusions, the estimates referred to raise two important elements for criticism. First, in no case is an explanatory equation used on institutional quality but, rather, a simplified function in which aid and another control factor are incorporated (among those, the delayed dependent variable, GDP per capita and population growth rates). This is why there are reasons to suspect a serious problem of omitted variables. In fact, in many of the estimations, the only variable that finally explains the evolution of institutional quality is aid: an unacceptable result that suggests possible specification problems. The second criticism of the studies cited is that they consider the relationship between aid and the quality of the institutions linear. Nevertheless, there are many reasons to think that the relationship has diminishing returns, so that only after a determined threshold of dependency on aid will its effect turn negative (a relationship that will be confirmed later on in our estimate).

In this framework the only study that produces positive results is that by Tavares (2003), although in this case, institutional quality as a whole is not being studied so much as one of its components: corruption. The study uses the corruption component of the ICRG, across five years, making it depend on the per capita GDP at the start of the period, and aid, controlled by variables such as region, the origin of the legal system, or religion, among others. The study carries out the estimation through OLS as well as 2SLS with instrumental variables, obtaining the conclusion that we are dealing with a negative relationship: the more aid, the less corruption.

To sum up, if we want to advance in this debate, it seems obligatory to build a model of institutional quality that is acceptably complete, to which aid can be added afterward, in order to avoid the problems related to specification.

FACTORS DETERMINING INSTITUTIONAL QUALITY

Identifying the factors that determine institutional quality is not a simple task. To justify a persuasive explanation, it is first necessary to look at the functions that institutions fulfill in economic life. Those functions provide answers to the problems posed by social interaction in an uncertain world in which the agents decide independently and with imperfect information. In this context, the institutions constitute a means of reducing the degree of freedom with which agents operate and, through them, limiting opportunistic behavior. Additionally, by shaping social behavior, institutions allow social interaction and collective action with lower coordination costs. Both factors—the reduction of the costs of transaction and improvement in coordination—relate to institutions with potential improvements in social efficiency. But it would be notably simplistic to suppose that this effect is obligatory: institutions are also the mechanism through which diverse social groups implement their interests. As North (1994:360) pointed out, in many cases institutions respond to "the interests of those who have the power to set new rules." That is why countries do not necessarily have the institutions they need, and those that they have are not necessarily the best.

A large part of the specialized publications in this field has given special attention to efficiency criteria as the basis for defining institutional quality, and these criteria are also those that preferably inspire institutional indicators. However, for institutions to work, it is as important to define good norms as to generate the conditions for individuals to meet them. This last element puts institutional credibility (or legitimacy) high on the agenda in determining the quality of the institutional framework. In turn, the credibility of an institution is conditioned by the means with which returns are distributed by that institution. This is why it is difficult for institutions to gain legitimacy in social climates where high levels of inequality have proved chronic over time and are accompanied by low social mobility.

Taking into account these aspects, in Alonso and Garcimartín (2008, 2010), four criteria are suggested for institutional quality: first, *static efficiency*, measured by the capacity of an institution framework to locate the economy on the productive and technological frontier; second, *credibility (or legitimacy)*, measured by the capacity of the institution to design credible inter-temporal contracts; third, *security (or predictability)*, measured by the ability to reduce the uncertainty associated with human interaction; and, fourth, *adaptability (or dynamic efficiency)*, measured by the capacity of institutions to anticipate changes in society.

Translating these considerations into the empirical sphere is difficult, especially because some of the factors considered potentially explanatory of the institution quality are endogenous, and because the relationships only exist in the long term. In an effort to facilitate the estimation, some of the studies sought exogenous variables—such as historical factors or geographical characteristics—to explain the genesis in the institutional framework. Specifically, they looked at variables including those related to a country's location (relation to the tropics), its colonial origin, the judicial tradition of its legal system, its dominant religion, the ethno-linguistic fragmentation of its society, and the endowment of valuable natural resources. It is worth highlighting that the theoretical foundation of some of these relationships is debatable (Alonso, 2007; Alonso and Garcimartín, 2008), and that many of them lose their statistical significance when combined with control variables related to the country's level of development. Along with those factors, it is worth considering other variables that are more directly related to the economic and social characteristics of the country in question. The most frequent have to do with the level of development, the degree of openness of the country, the level of education of its population, and the grade of social inequality. In particular, in Alonso and Garcimartín (2008, 2010) an estimation is carried out on what determines institutional quality, identifying the four explanatory variables cited earlier as criteria for institutional quality.

The equation estimated in that work was

$$IQ = \alpha + \beta_1 y + \beta_2 G + \beta_3 T + \beta_4 Ed + \beta_5 OR + Di \tag{2}$$

where IQ represents the institutional quality of each country; y its level of development; G the degree of inequality; T the tax resources of the state; Ed its educational level; OR its grade of international openness; and Di regional dummies (again, a description of variables is found in the Appendix).

According to the results, institutional quality depends on (see the first column in Table 5.2) the following: (1) the level of development of the country—a greater degree of development provides more resources to generate quality institutions but also creates greater demand for these types of institutions; (2) the level of social equality of the country, measured through the Gini index, perhaps because it requires a certain degree of social cohesion to ensure that institutions are predictable and legitimate; (3) the existence of an adequate taxation system, not only because it increases the resources available to create quality institutions but because it helps establish a more demanding relationship between the state and its citizens; and (4), although in a less robust way, the educational level of the people, because this conditions the capacity for innovation and the adaptation of the institutional framework to the changing reality of the environment.

Of the factors identified by Alonso and Garcimartín (2010), especially noteworthy is the relationship detected between taxation and institutional quality, for at least the following three reasons: (1) it questions the idea, transmitted by some indicators (such as the Index of Economic Freedom), of associating institutional quality with low tax collection by the state; (2) it underscores the nature of institutions as an implicit contract that, in the

Table 5.2 Aid and Institutional Quality

	Aid Variables Excluded	Aid Variables Included			
		ODA	ODA and ODA^2	OAD ppp	ODA ppp and ODA^{2}ppp
GDPpc	0.26 (2.12)	0.36 (2.58)	0.48 (3.08)	0.40 (2.48)	0.49 (2.97)
Gini	−0.75 (−2.40)	−0.58 (−1.98)	−0.59 (−2.07)	−0.60 (−2.09)	−0.64 (−2.26)
T/GDP	0.73 (2.76)	0.67 (2.79)	0.58 (2.50)	0.61 (2.36)	0.55 (2.38)
Education	0.33 (2.03)	0.31 (1.50)	0.27 (1.36)	0.28 (1.38)	0.27 (1.43)
ODA		0.055 (1.20)	0.28 (2.16)	0.13 (1.34)	0.554 (2.05)
ODA^2			−0.04 (−1.79)		−0.14 (−1.96)
EO	−0.69 (−4.81)	−0.42 (−2.68)	−0.35 (−2.20)	−0.40 (−2.48)	−0.36 (−2.22)
Mena	−0.59 (−2.49)	−0.55 (−2.58)	−0.60 (−3.47)	−0.56 (−2.78)	−0.57 (−3.26)
Instruments	gdppc90 (gdppc90)^2 fuel fetn al ao as sa	AOD00 gdppc90 (gdppc90)^2 fuel fetn al ao as sa	AOD00 AOD05^2 gdppc90 (gdppc90)^2 fuel fetn al ao as sa	AODPPA00 gdppc90 (gdppc90)^2 fuel fetn al ao as sa	AODPPA00 AODPPA05^2 gdppc90 (gdppc90)^2 fuel fetn al ao as sa
N	78	79	79	79	79
Centered R^2	0.80	0.79	0.81	0.80	0.81
Underidentification Test (Kleibergen-Paap rk LM Statistic) (P-value)	0.0211	0.0332	0.0390	0.0553	0.0617
Hansen J Statistic (Overidentification) (P-value)	0.0551	0.1255	0.1675	0.1240	0.1756

Notes: First column based on Alonso and Garcimartín (2010); EO: Eastern Europe; Mena: Middle East and North Africa; AL: Latin America; SA: South Asia; AS: Sub-Saharan Africa; fetn: ethnical fragmentation; fuel: percentage of fuels, ores, metals, precious stones, and non-monetary gold on total exports; 90 indicates the year 1990, 00 the year 2000, and 05 the year 2005. T-ratio in parentheses.

state, is expressed through the underlying fiscal agreement; and (3) aid can negatively affect the taxation rate and, through that, the institutional quality, as argued in certain publications (an aspect that we will discuss later).

ESTIMATION

Now that the factors determining institutional quality have been identified, it is time to look at the effect of aid on the institutional framework. To do that, we will use equation (2) and the same sample and data employed by Alonso and Garcimartín (2010), incorporating the potential effect of the aid (measured as a percentage of GDP averaged over the five years) into this explanatory structure.[4] Those components that behave erratically have been removed from the aid (humanitarian aid, food aid, and debt relief operations). In addition, as aid can be endogenous to institutional quality, it is instrumented through the same delayed variable (corresponding to the previous five-year period).[5] Also, to avoid problems with the valuation of the aid, it is measured both in constant dollars as well as in purchasing power parity.[6]

If only ODA is included (in constant dollars or purchasing power parity [PPP]), the coefficient is not significant (although it has a positive sign) (Table 5.2). There are no problems of under- or over-identification. However, as has been highlighted, there are reasons to believe that the effect of aid is subject to diminishing returns, which could be reflected by incorporating the squared variable into the table. When both variables are considered, the two are significant, with aid having a positive sign and squared aid a negative one. In other words, aid has a positive effect on institutional quality, but is subject to diminishing marginal returns, so that from a certain threshold the total impact becomes negative. The turning point is about 3.8 percent; in other words, if ODA is higher (lower) than that ratio to the recipient's GDP, it will have a negative (positive) effect on institutional quality.

An additional problem is that the institutional quality indicator is composed of an indicator that is relative in its nature. In other words, it is conceivable that a country could improve its institutional quality, not so much because it improves its institutions but because everyone else's institutions have worsened or because the sample changes over time. To avoid this problem, all the variables should be measured in relative terms. The estimation has been repeated with this transformation: the results essentially coincide (Table 5.3). Again, aid is non-significant when it is considered

Table 5.3 Aid and Institutional Quality (*with Relative Variables*)

	Aid Variables Included			
	ODA	ODA and ODA²	ODAppp	ODAppp and ODA²ppp
GDPpc	0.36 (2.60)	0.48 (3.10)	0.41 (2.51)	0.49 (3.01)
Gini	−0.58 (−1.97)	−0.60 (−2.08)	−0.60 (−2.08)	−0.64 (−2.25)
T/GDP	0.66 (2.79)	0.58 (2.49)	0.61 (2.36)	0.55 (2.37)
Education	0.31 (1.50)	0.27 (1.40)	0.28 (1.38)	0.28 (1.47)
ODA	0.17 (1.22)	0.862 (2.16)	0.19 (1.37)	0.774 (2.08)
ODA²		−0.277 (−1.79)		−1.409 (−1.99)
EO	−0.42 (−2.68)	−0.35 (−2.20)	−0.40 (−2.48)	−0.36 (−2.21)
Mena	−0.55 (−2.58)	−0.61 (−3.50)	−0.56 (−2.78)	−0.57 (−3.27)
Instruments	AOD00 gdppc90 (gdppc90)² fuel fetn al ao as sa	AOD00 AOD05² gdppc90 (gdppc90)² fuel fetn al ao as sa	AODPPA00 gdppc90 pib-cua90 fuel fetn al ao as sa	AODPPA00 AODPPA05² gdppc90 (gdppc90)² fuel fetn al ao as sa
N	79	79	79	79
Centered R²	0.79	0.81	0.80	0.81
Underidentification Test (Kleibergen-Paap rk LM Statistic (P-value)	0.0331	0.0388	0.0548	0.0623
Hansen J Statistic (Overidentification) (P-value)	0.1261	0.1662	0.1243	0.1768

Notes: EO: Eastern Europe; Mena: Middle East and North Africa; AL: Latin America; SA: South Asia; AS: Sub-Saharan Africa; fetn: ethnical fragmentation; fuel: percentage of fuels, ores, metals, precious stones, and non-monetary gold on total exports;; 90 indicates the year 1990, 00 the year 2000, and 05 the year 2005. T-ratio in parentheses.

alone, although the sign with which it appears is positive. Once the squared variable is incorporated, both variables are significant. Aid has a positive influence, but with diminishing returns, on institutional quality. Therefore, after a certain level of aid dependency, the effect of the aid turns negative.

AID AND TAXES: DOCTRINAL DEBATE

One of the arguments habitually offered to justify the negative effect of aid on institutional quality is the negative impact that foreign flows have on incentives to set up a solid fiscal system in the recipient country. However, obtaining that objective is indispensable to the progress of nations, affecting the economic behavior of individuals and determining the capacity of the state to provide public goods for society and to carry out programs of income redistribution and economic stabilization. In reality, the fiscal system defines the social contract through which taxes are swapped for representation and citizenship, facilitating the holding to account of the public powers upon which democracy is based (Tilly, 1992; Moore, 2009). Additionally, it is an obligatory route for countries to move from aid dependency to self-sufficiency, just as Kaldor (1963) recognized early on. Studying how aid affects taxation is, therefore, a crucial aspect of the argument that is being developed.

To avoid biased assumptions, it is worthwhile—before adding the effect of the aid—to consider the variables determining countries' levels of taxation, on which there is a wide range of reference publications. In particular, the following factors have been highlighted as the most relevant:

- First, *per capita income:* a greater level of development tends to increase the need for public expenditure (Tanzi, 1987) and improves the citizens' ability to pay taxes (Musgrave, 1969). Most of the empirical research confirms this relationship (e.g., Lotz and Morss, 1967; Tanzi, 1992).
- Second, the level of tax collection depends on the *production structure* of the country, particularly in terms of the weighting of agriculture and mining. In the first case, because the agricultural sector is difficult to tax and tends to have an important black economy, we can expect the importance of the sector to have a negative relationship to taxation power, as Chelliah (1971), Chelliah et al. (1975), Tanzi (1992), Leuthold (1991), and Stotsky and WoldeMariam (1997) confirmed. In mining, the relationship is somewhat more ambiguous: on the one hand, it is an easier sector to

tax, but on the other hand, governments can also gain income from the sector through different mechanisms than taxation. This ambiguity is confirmed in the empirical studies: For example, Tanzi (1981) finds a positive relationship between taxes and the importance of mining; Stotsky and WoldeMariam (1997) find the relationship a negative one; and Eltony (2002) finds it negative in the case of oil exporter countries but positive in those that are not.

• Third, *economic openness* also influences taxation power. Again, it is an ambiguous relationship: on the one hand, trade abroad is an activity that is easy to tax, but on the other, a high level of economic openness might be driven by a low level of protection, which could mean low border taxes (Gupta, 2007; Keen and Simone, 2004). The empirical estimates have tended to, nevertheless, confirm a positive relationship, either with trade openness (Lotz and Morss, 1967; Gupta, 2007), with its weight on imports (Tanzi, 1992), or with the weight on exports (Leuthold, 1991; Stotsky and WoldeMariam, 1997).

• Fourth, it is necessary to consider the *inflation effect*. In principle, the relationship is supposed to be negative, which might be true for the following three reasons (Ghura, 1998): (1) the Tanzi-Olivera effect, since in a high inflationary context, real taxes are reduced, because the payment is always delayed compared to the moment when the taxable fact occurs; (2) the loss in value of specific taxes that tend to have fixed rates not duly adjusted to inflation; and (3) the fact that agents buy goods that escape taxation (land, jewelry, foreign capital) in order to compensate for inflation. However, it is also plausible that the opposite might occur in progressive tax systems, since inflation could increase nominal income and, thereby, increase the taxes collected.

• Fifth, more recently, new factors, such as institutional quality, have been considered, for instance, Bird et al. (2004) identify factors such as corruption, the state of law, and market entry regulation as factors explaining tax collection capacity; Ghura (1998) and Gupta et al. (2002) confirm the effect that corruption has on fiscal power; and Gupta (2007) finds that political and economic stability have positive effects, but not corruption or the rule of law. Finally, Tanzi (1992) also considers the importance of external debt as one of the factors determining taxes, since it obliges recipient countries to sustain superior tax collection capabilities.

Although with more limited evidence, there are also works that have studied in a more specific way the effect that aid has on taxes (a good summary of this literature is found in Brun et al., 2007; McGillivray and Morrissey, 2004). This type of work originally led to notably pessimistic results: received aid contributed to reducing the tax level of the recipient (Heller, 1975; Cashel-Cordo and Craig, 1990; Khan and Hoshino, 1992). However, the most recent work has not been so conclusive, and the empirical evidence is ambiguous, with some studies reaffirming the negative relationship, others identifying no links between the two variables, and still others finding a positive relationship.

Bräutigam and Knack (2004) are examples of the first group and try to determine the effect of ODA on the evolution of tax income. They use as independent variables aid as a proportion of GDP and as a proportion of public spending, the growth rates of the population and the GDP per capita, and the initial value of tax income. None of the traditional determinants of the tax ratio—with the exception of GDP per capita—appear in the specification of Bräutigam and Knack (2004). Moreover, as neither the variation of GDP per capita nor the population is significant, the fiscal power of the steady state is exclusively determined by the aid and a variable of political violence. This is not very acceptable and all the less so if we take into account that the coefficient of the taxation income for the initial year is not significantly different to 1, which means the variable instantly adjusts itself to the changes in aid.

Among the studies that are incapable of finding any relationship at all between the variables are those of Ouattara (2006) and Morrisey et al. (2007). The first uses a dynamic panel with data corresponding to forty-six countries, for the period 1980–2000, without any relationship whatsoever being identified between aid and tax income, although a positive effect is found between aid and public investment and public spending on health and education. Neither do Morrisey et al. (2007), with a sample of fifty-five developing countries for the period 1975–2000, find any robust relationship between aid, the composition of the aid, and taxation income. A similar conclusion comes out of the work of Teera and Hudson (2004), which estimates a panel from 122 developing and developed countries for the period 1975–1998. Their conclusions are contradictory, since the effect of tax income is positive with random effects and negative when fixed effects are adopted.

Despite those results, the fullest works on this topic seem to detect a relationship with a positive sign between aid and taxation power. That is the case, for example, with Gupta (2007), who analyzes the determinants for taxes in developing countries, controlling with structural factors. Gupta uses an unbalanced panel, with few data in some of the variables, which include 105 developing countries, over a period of twenty-five years, with the dependent variable being tax income as a proportion of GDP. The independent variables are GDP per capita and ratios of agriculture, imports, debt, and aid as a proportion of GDP. The study also includes institutional variables (corruption, law and order, government stability, political stability, and economic stability) and factors having to do with taxation policy (composition of tax income, maximum income tax rates, and company tax rates and average customs duties). In the estimations of fixed and random effects, Gupta finds a positive, although weak, relationship between aid and tax income. Considering aid as endogenous, and using lagged aid as instruments, does not modify the results substantially. Finally, the study performs estimates using dynamic panels and observes that aid continues to have a significant, positive impact.

An interesting recent work, finally, is by Brun et al. (2007), which follows a complex research strategy. First, the authors estimate the tax ratio from structural variables (such as GDP per capita, imports as a percentage of GDP, the weighting of agriculture on GDP, and the weighting of oil and mineral exports as a proportion of total exports). From this estimate they obtain what they call "fiscal power," defined as what is left over (in other words, the difference between real fiscal power and the theoretical fiscal power derived from the model). They relate this fiscal effort to three types of determinants: (1) the macroeconomic policy, estimated through the delayed primary deficit, the service of debt as a percentage of GDP, the rate of inflation, and the real effective exchange rate; (2) the quality of the institutions, measured through corruption, the quality of the public administration, and democratic responsibility; and (3) the proportion of the aid (considering total aid, donations, loans, and the instability of the aid). One important element of the authors' work is the careful instrumentation of aid, which is based on a gravitation model (with geographical, linguistic, and religious distance) and with the deficit and debt as a proportion of GDP measuring the taxation ability of the donors.

As a result of their estimation, per capita income appears a significant determinant for fiscal power only when random effects are adopted for the whole of the sample (developing countries as well as transition countries). Subsequently, in trying to explain the taxation effort, the aid results are in general positive and significant, the institutional quality is not significant except in two cases (one positive and the other negative), and the interaction between both variables is positive in one case (the quality of bureaucracy) but not in the other two. Moreover, in contrast to Gupta et al. (2002), Brun et al. (2007) do not find differences between loans and donations. Although the strategy of determining the fiscal effort through the random use of what is left over, instead of through the fixed effects of each country, is not clear, their conclusions seem to stand up to a change in the specification.

THE IMPORTANCE OF THE DATA

Many of the studies cited face a serious problem having to do with the tax data used in the estimates. Frequently, they use data corresponding to the central government, taken from IMF information or from the World Bank (*Government Finance Statistics* or *World Development Indicators*, respectively), which are far from representative of the actual taxation of countries with a high degree of decentralization or a high proportion of social contributions.

Some examples can illustrate the errors that this deficiency in the data has produced. When Gupta (2007) estimates the potential tax income, the study reaches the conclusion that countries such as Argentina, Brazil, Peru, Panama, or Costa Rica (in Latin America) or Latvia, Lithuania, or the Slovak Republic (in Eastern Europe) are below their potential for resources. However, this conclusion is the result of only taking into account data from the central government; because, when the tax collection of decentralized institutions or social contributions is considered, the panorama radically changes. So, for example, the average central government taxes for the period 1996–2006 in Brazil are 14.2 percent of GDP, but the fiscal power climbs to 30.4 percent of GDP if regional taxes and social contributions are taken into account; in other words, the taxation is at a level comparable to some developed countries. The same occurs with the tax ratio of other countries that, according to Gupta, have little fiscal power: in Argentina, 10.3 percent for the central government, compared to a total of 22.6 percent; in Colombia, 11.0 percent and 16.2 percent; in Costa Rica, 12.5 percent and 19.5 percent; in Panama, 9.5 percent and 15 percent; in Slovakia, 17.8 percent and 33.1 percent; and in Lithuania, 18.7 percent and 29.7 percent.

Another example of this type of mistake is provided by Teera and Hudson (2004), who find low taxation at 19 percent in Switzerland, despite its high developmental level, while they find the Netherlands, which has clearly inferior income, to have double the taxation, at 43.7 percent. This is the same mistake mentioned earlier: Switzerland is a highly decentralized country (which is not the case for the Netherlands), so the taxation figures of the central government are not representative. The average tax from the central government as well as social contributions for the period 1996–2006 is 37.2 percent in the Netherlands, compared to 17.3 percent in Switzerland. Taking into account all levels of government, the totals are 39 percent and 29.1 percent, respectively; the level of tax increases by 2 percentage points in the Netherlands, and by almost 12 points in Switzerland.

As far as we know, the only work to point out this problem is Gupta et al. (2002), but they dismiss its seriousness, considering that "given most international aid is channeled through the budget of the central government, the lack of availability of data on income collected at a sub-national level should not be a serious difficulty." That argument is debatable, though, since it is only acceptable in cases where both types of income are totally independent. Brun et al. (2007) also identify this problem, leading the authors to compile their own database on the subject, but they do not specify their method of doing so.

To sum up, the first important step for a study like this is to use a database for taxes that reflects as closely as possible the reality of the countries under study, including income from all forms of government (central, regional, and local), as well as from social contributions. Unfortunately, there is no homogeneous database of this type at an international level, so we have had to build our own database from various sources (explained in the Appendix). Although for some countries the only available data are on the central government, in most cases we were able to complete the information, so that the picture given by the data is richer than that used in previous studies.

ESTIMATES

Before incorporating aid into the determination of taxation income, it is a good idea to estimate the most complete structural equation possible. Here we have taken into account the most traditional variables: GDP per capita, hydrocarbons and metals as a proportion of total exports, the proportion of agriculture in the GDP, the percentage of the population that is urban, the level of openness, and the rate of inflation. We have also added another, less common variable that could, nevertheless, be extremely important in tax collection: income distribution. This is based on the understanding that an unequal distribution could increase the black economy, encouraging tax evasion and resistance by elite groups in generating sufficient tax income. Gupta's (2007) work is one of the few that includes this variable, although it is indirectly approximated through the percentage of taxes on goods and services as a total of tax income. In our case, we opted for the Gini index, which is the most direct way of measuring inequality. Unfortunately, there is no database offering enough timely data, so in the estimates, income distribution in each country for the estimation period (1996–2007) has been considered constant. Since we are not dealing with a very extensive period, and because that income distribution is relatively constant, we believe that this does not pose serious problems.

On the other hand, the estimates are carried out through a panel of developed and developing countries, the number of which depends on the available data in each case. The panel was unbalanced with three-year averages of each variable (in other words, four time observations in each one). However, given the limited time availability of Gini indexes, the panel was compared to the results of carrying out a cross-country study on the sample using the institutional quality estimation data.[7] Finally, given that taxation income determines institutional quality (see Table 5.2), and that this in turn influences per capita income (see Table 5.1), we opted to consider this last variable as endogenous.

The results of the cross-sectional analysis (OLS) reveal that only three variables appear as permanently significant: per capita income (positive), the Gini index (negative), and the rate of inflation (positive). The same analysis was carried out removing the population rate due to problems of co-linearity between that variable and the weighting of agriculture, but the results hardly change. If the estimate is carried out with instrumental variables, the conclusions are the same (Table 5.4).

The panel estimation produces the following results. If a pooled type of estimation is used, GDP per capita and the Gini index remain significant; inflation is only significant in instrumental variables and openness in OLS (Table 5.5). In estimating using static panel techniques, in fixed effects no variable is significant, which is probably due to the limited time information (ten years) of the panel used (Table 5.6). However, when random effects are used, the relevance of GDPpc and, to a lesser extent, the Gini index, is confirmed, and the degree of openness also results as significant. In addition, it is worth highlighting that the Hausman test suggests that random effects must be used.

Once the tax equation has been analyzed, the incorporation of aid into the estimation is carried out, with this variable considered endogenous and using instruments such as birth rate and population size: the first as a

Table 5.4 Tax Ratio Determinants (*Cross Section*)

	OLS				IV (GDPpc and Gini) Robust			
	Value	t-Ratio	Value	t-Ratio	Value	t-Ratio	Value	t-Ratio
GDPpc	0.25	3.1	0.24	-3.28	0.27	2.2	0.23	2.49
Gini	-0.32	-2.19	-0.32	-2.25	-0.9	-3.02	-1.01	-3.82
Fuel and Metals	-0.05	-1.56	-0.05	-1.73	0.01	0.61	0.01	0.21
Agriculture	-0.08	-1.10	-0.08	-1.09	-0.02	-0.29	-0.02	-0.29
Urban Population	-0.02	-0.22			-0.09	-0.63		
Openness	0.02	0.21	0.02	0.15	0.12	1.61	0.11	1.4
Inflation	0.01	2.54	0.01	2.54	0.01	2.94	0.01	2.82
Instruments	Gdppc90 $(Gdppc90)^2$ fetn eo				pibpc90 $(pibpc90)^2$ fetn eo			
N	91				88			
Adjusted R^2 (centered in IV)	0.52		0.53		0.51		0.49	
Underidentification test (Kleibergen-Paap rk LM Statistic (P-value))					0.0		0.0	
Hansen J Statistic (Overidentification) (P-value)					0.41		0.30	

Notes: EO: Eastern Europe; fetn: ethnic fragmentation; 90 indicates the year 1990.

Table 5.5 Tax Ratio Determinants (*Panel Pooled*)

	OLS				IV (Gini and GDPpc) Robust			
	Value	t-Ratio	Value	t-Ratio	Value	t-Ratio	Value	t-Ratio
GDPpc	0.223	6.54	0.239	7.89	0.378	2.58	0.367	2.9
Gini	-0.545	-6.75	-0.528	-6.67	-0.789	-3.22	-0.789	-3.21
Fuel and Metals	-0.004	-0.35	-0.001	-0.1	0.004	0.26	0.001	0.09
Agriculture	-0.015	-0.43	-0.019	-0.52	0.120	1.1	0.130	1.03
Urban Population	0.055	1.07			-0.059	-0.46		
Openness	0.104	2.97	0.104	2.98	0.094	1.91	0.021	1.1
Inflation	0.021	1.28	0.024	1.42	0.025	1.46	0.367	2.9
Instruments			fetn eo (*)		fetn eo (*)		fetn eo (*)	
N	427		427		425		423	
Ad. R^2 (centered in IV)	0.59		0.59		0.56		0.56	
Underidentification Test (Kleibergen-Paap rk LM Statistic (P-value))					0.0		0.0	
Hansen J Statistic (Overidentification) (P-value)			Exactly id		Exactly id		Exactly id	

Notes: EO: Eastern Europe; fetn: ethnic fragmentation. (*)GDPpc90 has been eliminated along with its squared as instruments because there are problems of overidentification.

Table 5.6 Tax Ratio Determinants Panel IV (*Gini and GDPpc*)

	Fixed Effects				Random Effects			
	Value	t-Ratio	Value	t-Ratio	Value	t-Ratio	Value	t-Ratio
GDPpc	1.089	0.5	1.592	1.74	0.335	1.81	0.308	2.51
Gini	-0.010	-0.36	-0.014	-0.58	-0.762	-1.42	-0.871	-1.70
Fuel and Metals	0.300	0.43	0.454	1.48	0.011	1.19	0.011	1.22
Agriculture	0.305	0.32			0.085	0.95	0.067	0.76
Urban Population	-0.121	-0.24	-0.229	-0.96	0.028	0.16		
Openness	0.018	0.49	0.025	1.25	0.079	2.09	0.076	1.98
Inflation					0.008	0.83	0.010	0.95
Instruments	Eo fetn nat		Eo fetn nat		Eo fetn nat		Eo fetn nat (*)	
N	425		425		425		425	
N° Groups (Average per Group)	118 (3.6)		118 (3.6)		118 (3.6)		118 (3.6)	
R²Total	0.51		0.50		0.58		0.58	
Hausman Test	0.89		0.79		0.89		0.79	

Notes: EO: Eastern Europe; fetn: ethnic fragmentation; nat: birth rate. (*) The birth rate is included as an instrument because if it was not, the GDPpc coefficient could not be estimated in fixed effects, since the other instruments are constant.

proxy of the needs of the recipient countries and the second of the donors' interests.[8] The main results obtained in the estimation are the following (Table 5.7): First, the aid coefficient is positive in all cases, being significant (to 90 percent) in the cross-sectional estimation and in the pooled panel, but not in the random effect estimation. The results suggest, therefore, that the estimation is not very robust. Second, the per capita income and the Gini index maintain their significance and the adequate sign. Finally, the openness rate is significant in all cases, although in the panel it has a 90 percent probability, while inflation appears in the cross-sectional and pooled estimates, but not in the random effects.

In conclusion, when aid is considered alone, although it presents a positive coefficient, it does not seem to have a robust impact on taxes, once taxes are controlled by their determinants and the entirety of taxes at all levels of government is taken into account.[9] Nevertheless, some authors have stated that the impact of aid can be conditioned by the institutional quality of the recipient country (Azam et al., 1999), although there are scarcely any empirical works that take this fact into account, with the exception of Gupta et al. (2002) and Brun et al. (2007). In the former, estimations are carried out by country groups according to the level of corruption, and the authors observe that the positive impact of loans is reduced as the level of corruption increases. For their part, Brun et al. (2007) include the product of the aid by institutional quality as a dependent variable and find that it is positive in the case of the quality of the bureaucracy, but not in the other two indicators they use.

Proceeding in a similar way to Brun et al. (2007), we incorporated the product of institutional quality by aid into their previous estimation, using the average of the World Bank's governance indicators for institutional quality. In principle we considered that variable to be exogenous, despite its being a transformation of two potentially endogenous variables. The reason for this is that the two components move in opposite directions, which means their result is not necessarily endogenous to the dependent variable.[10] That verdict is confirmed by analyzing the residuals of the estimation, especially in the case of random effects.

The results of the estimation reveal that both the aid coefficients and those of the interactive term (aid by institutional quality) are significant to at least 95 percent, except in the case of the cross-sectional estimation, where the interactive variable is to 90 percent (Table 5.8). This means that aid positively influences tax resources, but its effect depends on the quality of a country's institutions. Given that governance indicators are

Table 5.7 Taxation Determinants with ODA

	IV without a Panel (ODA, Gini, and GDPpc) Robust		IV Pooled Panel (ODA, Gini, and PiBpc) Robust		Panel EA (ODA, Gini, and GDPpc)	
	Value	t-Ratio	Value	t-Ratio	Value	t-Ratio
GDPpc	0.466	2.16	0.367	5.77	0.367	4.56
Gini	−0.835	−3.22	−0.881	−10.03	−0.863	−5.14
Fuel and Metals	0.010	1.15	−0.003	−0.18	0.011	1.12
Agriculture	−0.052	−0.32	0.073	1.21	0.092	1.73
Openness	0.238	2.66	0.072	1.71	0.074	1.93
Inflation	0.009	2.48	0.039	2.06	0.009	0.85
ODA	0.217	1.72	0.039	1.9	0.019	0.92
Instruments	gdppc90, (gdppc90),^{2} fetn, eo, nat, pob, al		fetn, eo, nat, pob, al		fetn, eo, nat, pob, al	
N	87		423		423,117 groups; 3.6 Obs. Media	
Centered R^2	0.35		0.54		0.57 (total)	
Underidentification Test (Kleibergen-Paap rk LM Statistic (P-value)	0.0		0.0			
Hansen J Statistic (Overidentification) (P-value)	0.73		0.59			

Notes: EO: Eastern Europe; fetn: ethnic fragmentation; 90 indicates the year 1990; nat: birth rate; pob: population size; AL: Latin America.

Table 5.8 Tax Determinants with ODA and Institutional Quality

	VI without a Panel (ODA, Gini, and GDPpc) Robust		VI Panel Pooled (ODA, Gini, and GDPpc) Robust		Panel EA (ODA, Gini, and GDPpc)	
	Value	t-Ratio	Value	t-Ratio	Value	t-Ratio
Gdppc	0.64	3.54	0.36	5.38	0.36	5.29
Gini	−0.69	−2.59	−0.92	−10.22	−0.92	−7.53
Fuel and Metals	−0.003	−0.19	−0.004	−0.28	−0.004	−0.36
Agriculture	0.15	1.19	0.07	1.16	0.07	1.22
Openness	0.20	1.89	0.04	1.11	0.04	1.11
Inflation	0.007	1.49	0.04	2.48	0.04	2.25
ODA	0.37	2.26	0.07	2.2	0.07	2.78
Aid* Inst. Qual.	0.32	1.77	0.06	2.06	0.06	3.29
Instruments	gdppc90, (gdppc90)^2, fetn, eo, nat, pob, al		fetn, eo, nat, pob, al		fetn, eo, nat, pob, al	
N	87		423		423, 117 groups, 3.6 Obs. Average	
Centered R^2	0.34		0.55		0.56 (total)	
Underidentification Test (Kleibergen-Paap rk LM Statistic (P-value)	0.08		0.00			
Hansen J Statistic (Overidentification) (P-value)	0.63		0.36			
Aid Correlation * Inst. Qual./leftover (Val. Abs.)	0.14		0.24		0.00	

Notes: EO: Eastern Europe; fetn: ethnic fragmentation; 90 indicates the year 1990; nat: birth rate; pob: population size; AL: Latin America.

between −2.5 and 2.5, the total effect can be negative if institutional quality is fairly low (lower than −1.1). In terms of control variables, GDP per capita, the Gini index, and inflation seem to be confirmed as relevant, with inflation showing a positive sign.

Given that the estimation of ODA in constant dollars might pose problems, the estimation has been repeated using ODA values in purchasing power parity. The results (which we omit here) are not very different: aid is significant, at least in 90 percent of the cases, while the result of the interactive variable (aid by institutional quality) is only significant in the estimation for random effects, although it remains positive and comes close to significance in the other two. Additionally, we repeated the estimation with all the variables in relative terms. In that process part of the sample was lost, since it is obligatory for the panel to be balanced. The results of the estimation (which we also omit here) show that aid and the interactive variable are significant in all cases to at least 95 percent (except the last one in the cross-sectional analysis, which was significant to 90 percent). In terms of the control variables, the GDP per capita and the Gini index are confirmed once again as the other relevant variables, while inflation and the level of openness lose robustness.

Now that we have reviewed the estimations, it is worth giving a balance of the results. First, if we want to study the effect of aid on taxes, it is important to have available reliable data that include all sources of income for the various state levels. Second, it is important to perform a specification that includes all the structural determinants of fiscal power in order to subsequently check the effect of aid. Third, the effect of this variable can be non-linear—something that should be reflected in the specification. Taking these elements as a starting point, the results highlight that (1) GDP per capita and the Gini index turn out to be very robust variables in the explanation of fiscal power; (2) the rate of inflation and the level of openness also seem to affect the ability to collect taxes (something similar could be said about fuel and metal production); (3) agriculture, by contrast, does not seem to affect tax collection capability once it is controlled against GDP per capita; (4) aid in general shows a positive effect; and (5) that effect seems to be conditioned by the institutional quality of the recipient, so that in the countries with the lowest levels of institutional quality, the effect of aid on taxes can be negative. This result gains significance as the estimation is improved by controlling for national peculiarities, and it is not altered when the criterion for measuring aid is changed (expressing it in purchasing power parity) or when the variables are expressed in relative terms. Despite the solidity of the results, we must sound a note of caution given the panel limitations: their time period is limited, it is not balanced, and we have had to consider income redistribution as constant.

AID EFFECTIVENESS: DONOR RESPONSE

The estimates presented in the previous section provide a more optimistic picture than that offered in many prior studies on aid effectiveness. In principle, aid can positively influence institutional quality, and there is nothing to suggest that it has a negative effect on taxes (the impact possibly even proving positive). Through both means, aid can positively influence the growth potential of recipient countries, although it is difficult to reveal that effect in a direct manner. Nevertheless, aid can be subject to diminishing marginal returns, so that from a certain threshold, its effect both on institutional quality and taxation can become negative. That conclusion underlines the attention that should be paid to avoiding the phenomenon of aid dependency in certain countries, and the precautions that should accompany demands for increased resources in some cases.

As in all complex research fields, these conclusions are dependent on the quality of the data, the approach adopted, and the estimation procedures used. Despite our confidence in the results obtained, it is not possible to banish the doubts that some people have about aid effectiveness, nor to reject the possibility that in certain circumstances aid can have zero or negative impact. Even in a case where the effect of aid is positive, that effect seems to be relatively minor, which is enough to back the efforts by the international community to improve its effectiveness. Although those efforts seem to be well directed, there are aspects that require correction and others, of debatable importance, that have not even been addressed.

THE PARIS AGENDA

The widespread doubts about aid effectiveness have motivated donors to start a revision process on aid management practices. The origins of this process can be tracked back to the document *Shaping the 21st Century*, approved by the Development Assistance Committee (DAC) in 1996, but the drive for reform gained a renewed boost at the end of that decade as a result of the revision of the Highly Indebted Poor Countries Initiative, the debates around the Millennium Declaration, and the dynamic that accompanied the Monterrey Conference on Development Financing. This reforming spirit was translated into a series of high-level meetings organized by the DAC to study and improve levels of aid effectiveness. One of the most notable developments in this process was the declaration on Harmonization of Donor Practices, approved in Rome in 2003, the Paris Declaration on Aid Effectiveness, in 2005, the Accra Agenda for Action, in 2008, and the Busan Partnership for Effective Development Cooperation, in 2011, on this same theme. These agreements emphasize the following five principles in relation to aid effectiveness: (1) recipient *ownership* of development interventions; (2) *alignment* of donor strategies and procedures with strategies and management systems of the recipient countries; (3) *harmonization* among donors; (4) *management through results,* both for donors and recipients; and (5) *mutual accountability.* These principles were revised at the summit held in Accra in September 2008. The Action Plan added new elements to the agenda that had not previously been addressed. So, for example: (1) the principle of ownership was associated more precisely with a wider dialogue involving parliaments, local governments, and civil society; (2) there was an insistence that donors align their contributions more closely with the fiscal and budgetary systems of the developing countries, demanding that 50 percent of bilateral ODA should be channeled through these routes; (3) the plan called for greater importance to be given to programmed aid, to 66 percent of bilateral ODA; (4) more precision was given to the demand that aid be predictable, suggesting periodic information on donor forecasts for three to five years; and (5) transparency and mutual accountability of the accounts were insisted upon. At the same time that these components were made more specific, new elements were added to the agenda, although with varying degrees of precision, such as the innovative role of South-South cooperation, the need to maintain the fight against corruption, the treatment of countries with fragile states, and the demand that the Development Cooperation Forum (ECOSOC) be used as the site for international dialogue on matters related to aid.

Without a doubt, this was an agenda that obliged donors to change their traditional means of operating. Moreover, to prevent the Paris agreement from remaining purely rhetorical, a guide of fifty-one commitments and up to twelve indicators was drawn up for countries to evaluate their operations. The Organization for Economic Cooperation and Development's (OECD's) DAC has undertaken to follow the process through three reports (in 2006, 2008 and 2010) that sum up, through replies to an extensive questionnaire, the evaluation by the countries themselves of how the agreements are being applied (OECD, 2008). The picture that emerges from the last report is ambiguous: progress has been made, especially in the use of reliable public management systems and in the coordination of technical assistance, but commitments on the rest of the elements are still far from being met (Table 5.9). *The Evaluation of the Implementation of the Paris Declaration*, a report commissioned by the Danish government, reaches very similar conclusions. It concludes the need for greater political commitment from donors, the strengthening of institutional and technical capacities of the partner countries, more careful attention to the particular context of each country, and the adequate administration of the transition costs of one or another model of aid management.

During this process the EU has made its own recommendations, which were summed up in the 2005 *European Consensus on Development* and in the subsequent 2007 *Code of Conduct on Complementarity and the Division of Labour in Development Policy*. The aim of those initiatives is to put into place a "voluntary, flexible and self-regulated" mechanism to

Table 5.9   Degree to Which the Paris Agenda Is Being Met (2008)

	Baseline 2005 (%)	Present Situation (%)	Goal 2010 (%)	Degree to Which Goal Is Being Met (%)
Operative Development Strategies	17	24	75	12
Reliable National Systems (GFP)	36	50% of the countries are improving	72	—
Aid Flows Registered in Budgets	42	48	85	14
Aligned and Coordinated Technical Assistance	48	60	50	Met
Donors Use the GFP of the Recipient	40	45	80	12
Donors Use Recipients' Supply Systems	39	43	80	10
Donors Avoid Systems of Parallel Contracts	1,817	1,601	611	18
The Aid Is More Predictable	41	46	71	17
The Aid Is Untied	75	88	Progress over time	—
Donors Use Coordination Mechanisms	43	46	66	13
Donors Coordinate Their Missions	18	20	40	9
Donors Coordinate Their Country Studies	42	42	66	0

Source: DAC.

incorporate a certain rationality into the behavior of EU donors, so that countries take advantage of the complementarities between their various aid actions, in a concerted work to promote harmonization and coherence to benefit the partner countries. Underlying this goal is an increasing will to move toward a more united EU cooperation policy. The central theme of this process is the promotion of a greater division of labor between donors, which in principle is envisaged at three levels: sectoral on a global scale, in the framework of the recipient countries, and in the selection of partners on an international scale.[11] The EU has developed some operational mechanisms to facilitate this process, which is still at a very early stage, such as the *EU Toolkit for the Implementation of Complementary and Division of Labour in Development Policy* and the *Fast Track Initiative on Division of Labour*. Through these initiatives, some advances have been made in the mapping of donors, the promotion of delegated cooperation experience, and the analysis of pilot experiences of labor division.

SOME CRITICAL OBSERVATIONS

In principle the dynamic that started with the Paris Declaration has to be judged positively. These proposals tie up with some of the conclusions of the aid effectiveness studies and include the experience of professionals and development agencies in their work on the ground in the previous decades. Their insistence on the ownership of aid intervention by recipient countries, the desire to give greater predictability to aid allocations, the insistence on more ambitious instrumental resources (such as programmed aid), the promotion of coordination between donors, and the use of the recipient's management channels are all conclusions that stem directly from aid-effectiveness studies. In some ways, as Booth (2008:1) highlights, the Paris Declaration constitutes a synthesis "of the lessons of half a century of experience trying to achieve good results and to avoid doing damage with aid."

However, these agreements are also the product of the framework in which they were adopted. Two traits stand out here: first, the decisions were mainly led by the donors, even if recipient countries were invited to the debate and approval (both in Paris and in Accra): there is a problem with the representativeness of the forum (DAC) from which this dynamic was originated and driven; and, second, perhaps again because of the nature of the forum in which these recommendations were adopted, their assumptions are shot through with an excessively technocratic (and rather naïve) vision of social dynamics (Booth, 2008; Whitfield, 2008). Both aspects are limitations that must be overcome in the future.

To be more precise, if we take an overall look at the agreements, we see that the main reform efforts made by the donors seem to have been directed, very centrally, at correcting two important problems that penalize aid effectiveness: the existence of perverse incentives stemming from the information asymmetries within the aid chain, on the one hand, and high transaction costs from the proliferation of donors and fragmented interventions, on the other. Both aspects are important, although they are not the only problems that need to be addressed, as we shall insist later.

The first of the highlighted aspects returns to the problem that aid shares with other spheres of public action: transactions take place in a context where information is incomplete and unevenly distributed between players. In fact, the whole aid chain rests on a system of principal-agent relations that condition the incentive framework in which the players act: the donor (who is the principal) is able to decide the allocation of resources, but with a limited capacity to control the effective management process of those resources, for which the recipient (the agent) is responsible (Gibson et al., 2005; Martens et al., 2002).[12] The fungibility of aid is a manifestation of this problem.

As a consequence, the aid system suffers significantly from problems that affect these types of relations, among others, the problem of moral hazard, which comes from the effect that aid has as a mechanism for relaxing a recipient's efforts and responsibilities; the effect of what Buchanan (1977) called the "Samaritan's Dilemma," which expresses the inability of the donor to sanction a failure by the recipient to carry out what has been agreed; or even the problem of *adverse* selection if by granting aid to the most vulnerable countries irresponsible or indolent behavior ends up being rewarded.

Resolving problems of incentive caused by this system of relationships is not simple. In the past, donors sought a solution through conditionality that aimed to operate as a sort of implicit contract associated with the aid. However, this route has proved rather toothless. In a context of imperfect information, it is not plausible to expect an optimal contract design that would exhaustively define in advance all conceivable states of nature. It is also debatable whether, in such a climate, the donor is in a better position than the recipient to define responses to the development problems that the recipient is facing. Therefore, even if a donor had the capability of enforcing a recipient's respect for an agreement, it is not clear that a framework of conditions imposed by the donor would necessarily lead to an efficient result.

The only possibility for progress on correcting problems with lack of balance in information would be through stricter alignment of the goals of both parties in the transaction, and that is precisely the meaning of the principle of *ownership*. In this case the recipient defines its priorities more clearly and independently, and the donor identifies those recipients' needs to which it wants to contribute aid. Steps toward this goal include drawing up national development strategies (or the poverty reduction strategies) as a foundation for defining the priorities under which aid should be subordinated; the use of programmed aid instruments to support national policies (through the sector-wide approach, for instance); the formulation of medium-term budgetary frameworks that focus the aid commitments (mid-term expenditure frameworks), and the option of direct formulas for financing the budget (budget support).

However, the ways in which this type of response has been handled are open to numerous criticisms. The following four are worth highlighting here:

• First, there has been a certain reduction—which could be called technocratic—in the concept of ownership. The reduction has been such that, frequently, ownership (a process that is eminently political) has tended to be confused with the capacity of a recipient government to define a comprehensive development plan with sets of indicators and solvent statistical systems for monitoring progress. While the comprehensive development plan is purely instrumental, the essential part of the process of ownership is the political dynamic, through which a national will on development policy is created, which is capable of building sufficient social consensus to be viable. Generating such will requires movements in the field of political economy, in the debate between political interests and choices, institutional changes, and incentive—terrain that has been abandoned by donors.

• Second, an excessively naïve perception of social dynamics has supported the national development strategies (whether or not they adopt the form of a Poverty Reduction Strategy [PRS]). The Accra Agenda for Action aims to make more explicit the necessary consensus of parliaments, regional governments, and civil society around which development action is built. This is a desirable goal, but it is difficult to arbitrate. In societies that are fragmented, public action is the result of a confrontation between visions and interest, and of an institutionally channeled political struggle.

In that context the demand for national consensus as a prior condition for public action is simply misguided.

• Third, the alignment of the donor with the goals of the recipient has tended to be understood as a merely functional problem of adapting priorities. It is as if, at the bottom of that process, there were a substantial match between the interests of the two parties involved. The rhetoric of the principle of partnership has been built on that supposed fiction. It is necessary to insist that, within that dialogue, there is also a conflict and divergence of interests (Whitfield, 2008). The agreement, therefore, will be the result of a strategic game in which both parties use independent strategies and mobilize resources to gain their way. Instead of assuming that their interests coincide, it is important to properly analyze the scope for potential conflict, to study the resulting strategies, and to define the framework of the most appropriate incentives for negotiation and agreement.

• Fourth, this type of approach has gone hand in hand with donors using highly intrusive formulas of negotiation and control, which have given rise to demands for monitoring and evaluation systems of aid use (Whitfield, 2009). This type of requirement was softened in the second generation of PRS, but there is still excessive meddling by the donor in the micromanagement of development programs, and in the insistence on highly demanding overall formulas for the partner countries. The efficiency of actions is not, however, linked to these types of demands. As a recent investigation revealed, success can be achieved by much simpler means (World Bank et al., 2007).

The other problem of aid that donors have tried to tackle is connected to high costs of transactions of aid. This problem has been increasing as a result of the proliferation of players in the aid system, as well as from the overlapping nature of their priorities and the growing dispersal of their action (Acharya et al., 2006; IDA, 2007). Donors have tried to address this problem by defining a more active coordination process, and by ensuring a fuller integration of their initiatives into the budgetary procedures of the partner country. The principles of harmonization and alignment are steps toward those goals. The promotion of the division of labor between donors, backed by the EU, also aims to achieve those goals.

Here, too, this is a process that should be judged positively, but that presents some limitations that are worth highlighting. The first has to do with the lack of trust that underlies the behavior of the donors, which makes them enormously resistant to progressing in an effective way on formulas to support budgets, and to placing their resources in the management channels of the recipients. They are also influenced by the perception, perhaps exaggerated, of the risk involved in concentrating their resources in public management channels of the partner country. This is why donors either openly renounce the use of such formulas, or they prefer to use mechanisms (presented as transitional) that preserve their ability to control the management, albeit in a concerted way (such is the case, for example, with the common basket funds). Experience reveals that those intermediary formulas end up providing options for avoiding the national public management systems of the recipient. Although the lack of trust by donors might be justified in some cases, there are few alternative routes to encourage the institutional and technical capabilities of the recipient countries and to integrate the increasingly broad and plural presence of donors.

Second, despite the fact that some conditions have been reduced, conditions associated with policies or agreed-upon reforms still remain, in many cases, including among those donors (such as the European Commission) that have declared themselves in favor of removing them. What is questionable here is not so much that the donors want to debate the policy framework into which they are going to put into place their aid resources but, rather, that the fixing of conditions for payout constitutes a fruitless method of guaranteeing the adequate execution of those policies. Experience shows that this manner of proceeding tends to be counterproductive.

Lastly, limited achievements have been made on complementarity and labor division among the donors. Despite the Accra formula and the agreements reached within the EU, experiences are still very limited. Some donors have advanced toward a more selective definition of geographical priorities, but that process has been carried out on the margin of identifying complementarities with other donors. There has also been some progress in the field of labor division within single countries (national complementarity), but hardly any on international complementarity.

Of course we should recognize that it is still early to judge these types of initiatives. However, following are some difficulties that may condition their application:

• First, the analytical bases to identify, unequivocally, the country and sector advantages of each donor are clearly insufficient. In fact the practice of donors reveals the existence of a wide overlap in their spheres of action. This is clearly shown, first of all, in the low indexes of sector concentration of aid, which suggest that the level of donor specialization is low, and,

Table 5.10   Concentration, Dispersal, and Similarity of the Aid Sector of the Donors

Donors	Concentration by Sector (Herfindahl Index)	Dispersal by Sector (Shannon Index)	Similarity Index by Sector (DAC)
Australia	0.0440	0.6874	53.64
Austria	0.1618	0.5789	46.39
Belgium	0.0305	0.7574	57.41
Canada	0.0222	0.7717	57.48
Denmark	0.0289	0.7335	54.21
Finland	00267	0.7499	53.54
France	0.0859	0.6286	52.38
Germany	0.0436	0.7378	62.67
Greece	0.1177	0.5446	35.55
Ireland	0.0415	0.6845	53.53
Italy	0.0281	0.7516	55.54
Japan	0.0329	0.7337	53.16
Luxembourg	0.0259	0.7310	44.34
Netherlands	0.0411	0.7305	63.48
New Zealand	0.0510	0.6914	58.89
Norway	0.0240	0.7734	64.64
Portugal	0.0767	0.5794	34.25
Spain	0.0185	0.7981	58.71
Sweden	0.0271	0.7510	60.60
Switzerland	0.0554	0.6727	52.75
United Kingdon	0.0477	0.6666	56.46
United States	0.0476	0.6952	61.58
DAC Countries	0.0172	0.8196	
Non-DAC countries	0.0240	0.7644	65.57

Notes: Herfindahl Index Normalized: $HIN = \dfrac{\sum\limits_{i=1}^{i=n}(S_i^j)^2 - \dfrac{1}{n}}{1 - \dfrac{1}{n}}$

Shanon Index: $SI = \dfrac{\sum\limits_{i=1}^{i=n}S_i^j Ln(1/S_i^j)}{Ln(N)}$

Similitude Index: $SimI = \sum\limits_{i=1}^{i=n} \min\left[S_i^j, S_i^{DAC}\right]$

with i sector of aid; j donor country; N number of sectors; and $S_i^j = \dfrac{ODA_i^j}{\sum\limits_{i=1}^{i=n}ODA_i^j}$

Source: DAC.

second, in the high indexes of similarity between them, which reveal that specializations are not contrasted, making the supposed and sought-for complementarities difficult to identify (Table 5.10).

• Second, in terms of geographical priorities, factors come into play in their selection that are difficult to subordinate to an indisputable technical criterion (as donors' political or economic interest). Trying to create a coherent framework of priorities, in which gaps and overlaps between donors are minimized, is a difficult task, and probably only partial achievements can be made.

• Third, the recipients themselves are not certain whether they prefer a world where they address a single donor or one where they can negotiate with various donors, on an alternative basis. A plural presence of donors can allow recipients to take advantage of the varying capabilities, attitudes, and negotiating positions of the donors.

To sum up, it is possible that progress is being made in some spheres of labor division, but more likely that such progress is incomplete and in spheres of secondary interest for the donors. This does not make the task irrelevant, but it makes relative its potential as a response to the problems of aid transaction costs. In addition, even if decided progress is made in this field, doubt will always remain about whether a prior and deliberated division of labor is the best alternative to the growing complexity of the aid system, especially if we take into account the active presence in the aid system of very disparate players, many from the private sector. This suggests that in order to efficiently manage such complexity, which is likely to increase in the future, the required response from the governance system would have to be different from the simple use of a "voluntary, flexible, and self-regulated" division of labor.

AID DEPENDENCY

Perhaps the most relevant criticism engendered by the Paris Declaration is the absence from consideration of one of the chief problems affecting aid effectiveness: the high dependency that aid generates in many developing countries. This is a delicate problem, difficult to explain to the public, but its address is absolutely crucial if the commitment to establishing the foundations of development in the poorest countries is truly serious.

As we have discussed, one of the results that is most regularly obtained in studies on aid effectiveness is the fact that aid presents decreasing mar-

ginal returns. While it is positive, the effect of aid diminishes as its proportion to a recipient's overall public resources (or GDP) increases—until it
reaches a point in the balance where it unequivocally turns negative. Our
own estimation confirms those results: aid has a positive effect on institutional quality, but this effect is corrected once levels of aid (refers to developmental components of aid) are greater than 4 percent of the recipient's
GDP. At the same time, although in a less firm way, aid can have a positive
effect on the recipient's tax collection capability; but, again, that effect is
not linear, depending on the level that the aid reaches and the quality of
the recipient's institutions. These conclusions only confirm the important
role that the degree of aid dependence has on the balance of aid results.

We have already stated that there are various reasons (which are potentially complementary) for this behavior. Intense aid can generate an
adverse effect on the recipient's competitiveness ("Dutch disease"); undue
pressure on the capabilities of the recipient to absorb the resources efficiently; recipient complacency about the need to carry out budget management reforms or to search for its own resources; a drawing away of the
limited capabilities and human and technical resources of the recipient
(particularly from the administrations); and a negative effect on the quality of institutions and their public accountability.

Some of the research that has been critical of international aid is based
on exactly these aspects. Moyo (2009:143) states that "the absolute imperative to make Africa's positive growth trajectory stick is to rid the continent of aid-dependency, which has hindered good governance for so long";
Glennie (2008:101, 105) states that "Africa needs less aid and better aid," and
that "the West gives aid not because it works, but because it is easy";
Calderisi (2007:209) warns "contrary to conventional recommendations,
direct foreign aid to most African countries should be reduced, not increased"; and, finally, Hubbard and Duggan (2009) talk about the need to
get out of the "aid trap." Arguments about the curse of aid (Harford and
Klein, 2005; Djankov et al., 2008) also refer to these aspects, as does the
aid-institutions paradox argument (Moss and Subramanian, 2005; Moss
et al., 2008). One does not need to share the disparate arguments of these
studies to agree that they point to a real and unsettling problem.

In fact if we turn to the data we observe that levels of dependency are
very high in a wide range of countries (Table 5.11). There are about forty
countries in the developing world where the proportion of aid is higher
than 10 percent of GDP. Generally that coefficient is multiplied by a factor of between 3 and 4, to determine the proportion of aid in the public

Table 5.11 Aid Dependency (Proportion of Aid in the Recipient's GDP, 2007)

Region	5% to 10%	10% to 20%	20% to 30%	More Than 30%
Sub-Saharan Africa	Benin	Burkina Faso	Malawi	Burundi
	Botswana	Cape Verde	Mozambique	Guinea Bissau
	Chad	Central R.	Rwanda	Liberia
	Comoros	Africa	São Tomé	
	R. Congo	D. R. Congo	and Ppe.	
	Eritrea	Djibouti	Sierra Leone	
	Ghana	Ethiopia		
	Guinea	Gambia		
	Lesotho	Mali		
	Madagascar	Mauritania		
	Senegal	Niger		
	Sudan	Tanzania		
	Zambia	Togo		
		Uganda		
Latin America	Dominica	Guyana		
	S. Vicente and	Nicaragua		
	Gran.	Haiti		
	Granada	S. Kitts-Nevis		
Middle East				Palestine Territories
Asia	Kyrgyzstan	Timor-Leste		Afghanistan
	Nepal	Laos		
	Tajikistan			
	Bhutan			
	Cambodia			
	Mongolia			
	Georgia			
Europe	Moldavia			
Oceania	Tonga	Kiribati	Palau	Micronesia
	Samoa	Vanuatu	Marshall I.	Salomon I.

Source: DAC.

resources. Doubtlessly, in these cases there is a clear problem of aid dependency: the institutions are being pushed to direct more attention toward their relationship with international donors than toward the demands or requirements of their citizens. This aid dependency problem affects sub-Saharan Africa above all: of the region's fifty countries, aid contributes more than 10 percent of GDP in twenty-three.

Resolving this problem does not necessarily mean an unexpected withdrawal of resources or the freezing of aid. Such a response could have far higher costs than those we are trying to avoid. For some recipients, aid resources are a source of financing social policies that is currently difficult to replace. Aid dependency, however, makes it doubtless necessary to be much more cautious around plans to increase aid, on the understanding that more is not always better; establish plans to gradually downsize aid in those cases where such a decrease is viable, in order to reduce dependency, meanwhile seeking alternatives to sustain and improve achievements in the society concerned; pay greater attention to existing routes for mobilizing domestic resources from developing countries, which would involve strengthening tax systems as well as tackling tax fraud, capital evasion, and illegal finance flows; and, finally, dedicate more resources to provide international public goods related with development goals.

CHANGE IN THE INTERNATIONAL SYSTEM: CHALLENGES FOR AID POLICY

In the previous section we referred to the changes that the aid system has undergone in the last few years; despite their limitations, these are important advances that reflect the energized reform spirit behind them. However, as we emphasized at the start, although the aid system has changed, international realities have likewise transformed in a faster and much more profound way. It is a good idea, therefore, to look at the changes in the international climate and identify the challenges these present for the aid system. Our attention will focus on three large trends that promise to gain in importance in the future. The first is the growing heterogeneity of the developing world, which obliges us to wonder whether aid policy should multiply its concerns in order to reflect that diversity, or whether it should focus its attention on a core of countries with the greatest need—thus becoming a policy specialized to alleviate extreme poverty. The second trend has to do with the progressive multipolarization of the international system, which stems from the emergence of new poles of economic and political power, some from the developing world. Of these countries, some are aid recipients but also active donors, obliging us to rethink the aid system and its mechanisms of governance to reflect this new reality. The third tendency is related to the wider space for international public goods, which will require effective progress in terms of development in order to ensure their adequate provision. It is essential to look at the existing relationship between the international public goods agenda and that of international aid. We will investigate each of these three aspects more closely.

HETEROGENEITY IN THE DEVELOPING WORLD: FOCUSED POLICY VERSUS WIDE-SCOPE POLICY?

International aid was born in the 1950s, confident in its (largely shared) diagnosis of the problems characterizing underdevelopment. Since then, developing countries have experienced very disparate progress dynamics. One group of countries—strikingly, those countries located in Southeast Asia—managed to drive a successful growth process, which put them at similar levels to developed nations. Another group of countries—grouped around the term least developed countries (LDC)—increased their distance from leading countries, suffering a growing gap. A third large group of countries, situated between these extremes, increased their levels of internal heterogeneity as a result of very different growth dynamics.

A simple way of illustrating this is through a double graphic that represents the absolute convergence for each group of countries and, on the other hand, the comparable dynamic of each group compared to the world average: this is what the panel of charts (Figure 5.1) does for the period 1950–2006. In the LDCs, the data reveal that a certain convergence occurred within the group (those countries that started with lower GDP per capita tended to grow more), along with a distancing of the group in terms of the world average. This suggests that the LDCs have behaved like a group of countries caught in a poverty trap (Guillaumont, 2009).

High-income countries (HICs) have also undergone a convergence process, especially if the group of oil producers is eliminated from the relationship. But, in contrast to the LDCs, their dynamism has been above average, with few exceptions. Therefore, they have had to consolidate their leadership in the international economy.

The third group of countries (middle-income countries [MICs] and low-income countries [LICs]), has hardly converged within their group, especially if we exclude particular cases (such as China and Botswana). Moreover, the dynamism of the group has also been very diverse, with one group of countries more dynamic than the average, and the bulk of the countries being below that average. Therefore, there is a clear divergence within the group.

Throughout the period a double divergence (Ocampo and Vos, 2008) has been produced, which has meant that, first, the arc of income distribution at a global level has opened up, reflecting the growing distance between the extremes (LDCs and HICs), and, second, the heterogeneity

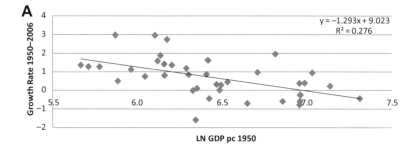

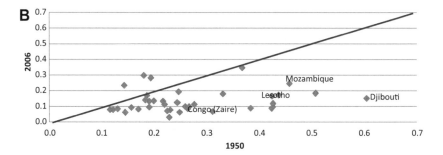

Figure 5.1   Convergence and Growth
i. LDCs (excluding Equatorial Guinea):
A. Growth Rate and GDP per Capita PPP
B. GDPpc PPP in Relation to World Average

Source: Based on Maddison (http://ggdc.net/maddison/Maddison.htm).

among developing countries has increased. As a consequence of this double process, it is increasingly difficult to identify the reality of developing countries under a single title. Divergences grow and, as a result, they require different diagnoses and treatments.

Responding to this growing diversity constitutes a challenge for the aid system, for which there are two extreme options: either maintain an integral perspective, through a differentiated policy in accordance with the many needs of developing countries, or transform aid into a focused policy, aiming to specialize in fighting extreme poverty in the most vulnerable countries.

The Millennium Declaration seems to point to the second option. Although this has not been expressed explicitly, it is confirmed by the fact that the MDGs amount to an agenda adapted to the situation and priorities of the lowest-income countries. Following this stance, the donors

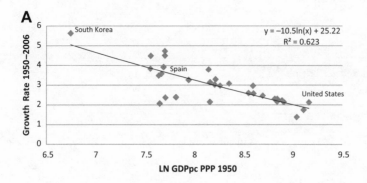

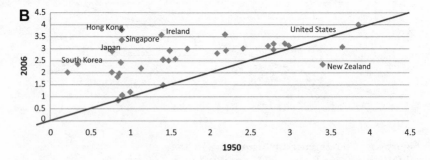

Figure 5.1   Convergence and Growth (continued)
ii. HICs (excluding Qatar, United Arab Emirates, Kuwait, and Oman):
A. Growth Rate and GDP per Capita PPP
B. GDPpc PPP in Relation to World Average

Source: Based on Maddison (http://ggdc.net/maddison/Maddison.htm).

initiated a process to refocus and concentrate aid flows toward the poorest countries, at the expense of those middle-income countries that were among their previous priorities. In some cases—for example, in various countries in Latin America—that process was accompanied by the closing of delegations of donor agencies.

Without a doubt, there are some reasons to back this trend in the aid system; the opening of the arc in world income could be a justification for donors focusing their attention on those countries that have moved farther away in developmental terms from the world average. The aim would be to focus resources on those cases that are witnessing the clearest exclusion from the benefits of globalization, increasing the gap with others apparently in better condition to access, even partially, the beneficial effects of the inter-

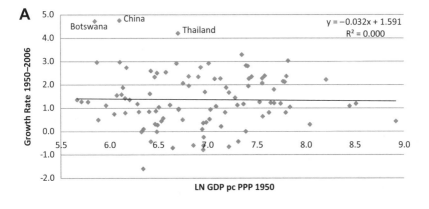

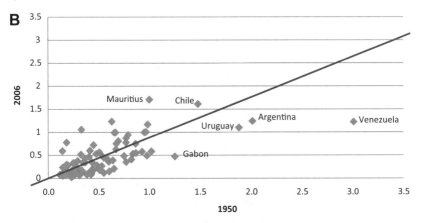

Figure 5.1   Convergence and Growth (continued)
iii. LICs and MICs (excluding Venezuela):
A. Growth Rate and GDPpc PPP
B. GDPpc PPP in Relation to World Average

Source: Based on Maddison (http://ggdc.net/maddison/Maddison.htm).

national market. This would aid the profile of a policy increasingly focused on the fight against extreme poverty in the poorest countries.

Despite the arguments supporting such a strategy, there is another, equally reasonable option that, while recognizing that greater attention should be given to the poorest countries, also considers it necessary to maintain a wider perspective on international development needs. This means support given in a gradual way, in relation to their level of income, to countries as long as their progress is at risk. Such an approach would involve maintaining a omprehensive vision of development policy, transforming it into a differentiated policy in keeping with the needs and developmental level of all needful countries, including those MICs with severe vulnerabilities.

There are important reasons to justify the second option. Among the arguments that can be offered are the following five (Alonso, 2007):

• First, more than 70 percent of the world's poor population—people with less than US$1.25 a day—live in MICs (Summer, 2010): If we want to eradicate poverty, effective achievements in development and social cohesion must be made in MICs.

• Second, MICs are highly vulnerable to circumstances in international markets, often falling victim to frequent regressions in their levels of material well-being as a result of external shocks or internal crisis. International action could help mitigate those risks.

• Third, MICs are key to the provision of international public goods—particularly environmental ones. International aid could stimulate their more active involvement in this agenda, which is closely related to development goals.

• Fourth, some MICs have a crucial demographic or economic weighting in their regional environment: because of this, their success in developmental terms can stimulate progress in surrounding countries, providing stability to the international system.

• Fifth, it is important to support middle-income countries because we need to build an aid system that is incentive-compatible with the aims of development, avoiding perverse incentives that could result from a clear-cut and abrupt border between countries that are the subject of international aid.

It is worth maintaining support for the development efforts of MICs not only to avoid eventual regressions in their social progress but also to support progress in their regions and to allow more stable governance of the international system. Moreover, abandonment of that support, drawing a clear line among potential recipients for aid, would contribute to the perversion of incentives in the development aid system. This would be the case if only deficient results—and not successes—were rewarded with international support.

That said, for a system of this type to be coherent, it is necessary to contemplate a certain involvement by all countries (not just today's donors) in sustaining international aid as nations advance in development. We will refer to this in the following section.

MULTIPOLARITY: AID DONOR EXCLUSIVE
POLICY VERSUS A SHARED SYSTEM?

Development aid was born in a bipolar world, characterized by the presence of two blocs in conflict—a struggle that permeated all international relationships. Development aid was, in many cases, part of that confrontation dynamic, aiming to maintain cohesion in each bloc, beyond the international inequalities that existed. Aid was aimed at avoiding poverty, in a context of growing decolonization, with strong forces encouraging recently independent countries to desert their respective reference blocs. Some of the contradictions of international development aid in the past have to do precisely with the system's subordination to this bipolar dynamic.

Today, that international reality has disappeared. Instead, a more complex and multipolar world is being consolidated. Powers from the developing world have been added to traditional powers, and these new powers are highly dynamic and have a notable capacity to project their influence. A simple look at the international reality reveals the weight that some of these emerging powers have acquired in their regions, even with potentially global projection (Table 5.12). Some of these emerging powers seem likely to play an even greater role in the future.

This change also has important implications for the aid system, since some of these countries—along with other developing countries—have become actively involved in sustaining their own aid-for-development programs as part of their growing international projection. In some cases the sphere of their activity as donors is focused on countries within their region (as is the case with Chile, Colombia, South Africa, and India), but others have developed programs that have transcended those limits (China being the most notable example). The most habitual instrument for this type of activity is technical assistance, but there is no shortage of donors—such as China and Venezuela—that use a wider range of instruments, including concessional credits.

The exact volume of this South-South aid is not known. Deficient registration systems in the countries involved contribute to the lack of information in this area, but there is also a limited precision as to what needs to be measured, since many South-South cooperation practices are far from the common practices registered as ODA. In any case a clearly understated estimation by ECOSOC puts the aid at 8–10 percent of ODA, and DAC gives a similar figure (7 percent) for aid coming from countries that are not members of its organization. That said, neither of these two estimates

Table 5.12   The Weight of Key Countries in the Regional Total

Regions (Only Low- and Middle-Income Countries)	Number of Middle- and Low-Income Countries	Population %	GDP (PPP) %
Latin America			
Brazil		33.9	32.5
Mexico		18.6	25.4
Weighting on the total region	*33*	*52.5*	*58.0*
North Africa			
Egypt		49.8	45.0
Weighting on the total region	*5*	*49.8*	*45.0*
Western Africa			
Nigeria	*23*	45.6	51.8
Weighting on the total region		*45.6*	*51.8*
Eastern Africa			
—			
Southern Africa			
South Africa		31.2	67.3
Weighting on the total region	*14*	*31.2*	*67.3*
Western Asia			
Iran		33.5	31.4
Weighting on the total region	*16*	*33.5*	*31.4*
Eastern Asia			
China		62.5	47.2
Indonesia		10.7	5.2
Weighting on the total region	*14*	*72.3*	*52.4*
Southern Asia			
India		71.0	74.8
Weighting on the total region	*14*	*71.0*	*74.8*
Europe and Central Asia			
Russia		45.8	50.6
Turkey		23.9	20.5
Weighting on the total region	*11*	*69.7*	*71.1*
TOTAL: 11 Countries		53.3	30.5

Source: World Bank (1998).

include all non-OECD donors, suggesting that the total figures must exceed those mentioned.

South-South aid incorporates important new elements into the aid system. On the one hand, because it is more horizontal, it has a greater capacity to invoke a proper feeling of ownership on the part of the recipient, while its activities also generate a clearer "double dividend"—with benefits for the donor and recipient, through the stimulation of technical and institutional capabilities in both. But beyond these factors, most important is that South-South aid contributes to spreading a sense of shared responsibility, and not only from traditional donors, in the task of correcting international inequalities. Even so, this type of aid has problems and deficiencies, many of which (politic conditioning, lack of accountability, absence of evaluation) are similar to those arising with traditional aid.

Apart from its potential, South-South aid poses a challenge to the concept and structure of the governance of the international system. Again, this opens up two different options: (1) try to preserve the concept, content, and consensus on which traditional aid policy has been built, seeking to add new donors to this tradition, or, alternatively, (2) try to open up debate on new aid methods in order to define a new consensus that involves these new players without renouncing accumulated aid experience. In the first case DAC could continue to play its role as a central force in the debate and definition of aid policy; in the second case, however, a more inclusive forum should be sought, in which all involved countries are represented (the Development Cooperation Forum of ECOSOC is the alternative that seems closest to that idea).

Without a doubt, there are reasons to believe that the agreements reached by DAC members should be preserved as the most refined expression of good practices in international development aid. The problem is that if this criterion was followed, with DAC as the main player, an increasingly large portion of international aid could be left at the margins of consensus mechanisms and policy definition. Inviting new donors to take part in debates (as was done at Paris and Accra) cannot get around the fact that the forum where such agreements are promoted is exclusively for developed countries.

Looking at the likely evolution of the international system in the future, it would seem more reasonable to work toward incorporating new South-South aid practices into the framework of a wider and more integrating aid policy. That process will have to work alongside a displacement of governance structures toward more inclusive and representative organizations. To put it another way, just as we argued that an abrupt demarcation of countries fit to receive aid should not be established, neither should a line be drawn establishing those that contribute to the aid system. Rather than an excessively dual system that neatly separates the functions of donor and recipient, the progressive implication of "more developed" developing countries should be promoted in aid work. This would suppose ever more active involvement in aid along the lines of South-South cooperation, which should be supported by other donors through various forms of triangular and regional cooperation.

This response would not only allow the aid system to be democratized, with shared ownership by all involved countries (donors and recipients), but it would also increase the potential for further transformation, incorporating the experiences and capabilities acquired by low- and middle-income countries in their developmental process.

INTERNATIONAL PUBLIC GOODS: AID POLICY VERSUS GLOBAL PUBLIC POLICY

The globalization process under way has tended to accentuate interdependencies of all types between countries, increasing the indirect effects (so-called externalities) of a transnational character. Activities that were formerly the exclusive responsibility of national states—such as national security or the preservation of public health—nowadays have to be tackled in a context of increasing international coordination. At the same time, similar coordination is being demanded for new goods and activities that emerge as global in nature in the current international scenario, such as the fight against climate change. The relationship works both ways: decisions adopted at a local level increasingly generate effects beyond national borders, while the international context influences the national framework in an increasingly powerful way, limiting the room for autonomous decisions by governments and societies.

The transnational interdependencies referred to can be both positive and negative in nature; but, as a whole, they affect crucial aspects of our well-being. The sphere of international public goods arises from these interdependencies. These goods are characterized by a strong externality, which means that, once provided, their benefits are available for everyone in an unlimited way (and the same could be said of public ills). Such public goods are very diverse in nature and related to the international regulatory order, the sustainability of life, and the possibility for societies to advance (Table 5.13).

The characteristics of public goods dictate that, frequently, the market proves incapable of ensuring their efficient provision, and some form of collective action is then required, either through coordination, cooperation, or coercion. In the national sphere such a response is channeled through the available institutional framework, especially the state. In the international

Table 5.13 Spheres of International Public Goods

Main Objective	Area
Configuration of Social Order	International Justice International Norms International Institutions
Preservation of Life	Control of Contagious Diseases Global Common Goods Protection from Crime and Drug Trafficking Peace and Security
Wealth Promotion	Financial Stability Knowledge Diffusion Trade Insertion

sphere, however, there is no institution similar to the state, so the response must be carried out through diverse coordination and voluntary cooperation formulas between the players of the international system. The multilateral system is the most appropriate framework to promote and articulate such cooperative action. However, there is a widely shared view that this multilateral system, in its current form, does not meet the conditions necessary to efficiently promote the public goods that society demands.

Such a goal gains importance at a time like the present, when the international community is trying to put into action a series of shared development goals, the Millennium Development Goals. While these objectives are not necessarily public goods in themselves, it is necessary to invest in international public goods (IPGs) in order to achieve the MDGs. The discovery of malaria inoculation, the development of treatments for HIV/ AIDS, the adequate management of climate change, the preservation of peace, the facilitation of access to knowledge, the promotion of financial stability, and the establishment of a more open and fair commercial order— all these goals are, by nature, international public goods, and they will have a measurably greater effect on poverty than international aid itself. In fact between a quarter and a third of international aid is already targeted at activities that are, by nature, public goods.

The link between IPGs and the development agenda goes beyond the relationships described. In fact to ensure the efficient provision of many IPGs, a correction of international inequalities is necessary, for the following three reasons:

• Many (although not all) IPGs involve a technology of addition, where the global level is determined by the society that has the least (weakest-link technology goods). Therefore, to increase the total level of provision, it is necessary to improve the position of those who have the least.

• It is not enough to create global regulatory frameworks to provide public goods. It is also necessary to support countries in adapting their local activities to those aggregated frameworks. While the former are called central activities, the latter are considered complementary. Both are necessary, however, to manage an international public good. It is necessary to reinforce the means available to those relatively less-developed countries, and the lower the economic and technological capability of a country, the more intensive the support will need to be, again pointing to the need to correct inequalities.

• The correction of inequality is necessary because its most extreme manifestation—poverty—is in itself a global public ill. In an interdependent world, poverty is a source of trouble that affects everyone, rich and poor. International insecurity, recurrent humanitarian crises, uncontrolled migratory pressures, and environmental degradation are fed, although not exclusively, by extreme poverty that ultimately affects a large part of humanity.

International public goods are necessary to promoting security, stability, and world progress, but without certain measures of cooperation and a correction of inequalities, it is difficult to make progress on the provision of those goods. Herein lies a new challenge for a more active aid policy. Again, two options are conceivable: either maintaining both spheres as separate agendas, or merging them in a progressive way within a broader global public policy.[13]

There are reasons to try to preserve the demarcations of current aid policy: in the end, the traditional agenda that originally shaped this field of public action (the eradication of poverty) has yet to be achieved. The work undertaken in defining institutions, instruments, and policies in the field of aid would be another reason to preserve this area in a relatively independent way. However, in an interdependent world, it is difficult to achieve effective results in the fight against poverty if action is not simultaneously taken in the sphere of international public goods. This suggests the need for an increasingly integrated perspective for both agendas.

Such integration does not have to suppose a displacement of aid resources to new tasks of public goods provision but, rather, an effort to identify new sources of income, or new frameworks, to stimulate the capacity to support that new agenda. Integrating both goals and the complementarities from respective sources of resources should also lead to a joint displacement of the foundations on which this policy is built. Development policy would cease to be the field of action of just one ministry, becoming instead the integral work of governments. It would thereby move from being a means of policy cooperation to a global public policy.

FINAL CONSIDERATIONS

Studies on aid efficiency produce a relatively disappointing assessment. Despite the diversity of the research, results have not been able to dispel critical doubts about the impact of aid. As in other areas of the economy (open trade, for example), there are reasons to believe that the weak empirical results have more to do with the difficulties of statistically capturing a complex relationship than with the nonexistence of that relationship. It might prove pertinent to follow the suggestion of Bourguignon and Sundberg (2007) and explore inside the "black box" of aid effectiveness, if we want to advance in this field.

In our case we have sought to capture the effect of aid through an indirect route. Considering the effect that institutional quality has on a country's progress, we have investigated whether aid affects institutional quality in a way that can be statistically checked. Previous publications have pointed to a dominantly negative effect, but our own results contradict that image: aid positively influences institutional quality, even if its effect is subject to diminishing returns. In other works, after a certain threshold of aid dependency, the total effect could be negative in sign: a relevant conclusion, given the tendency toward increasing aid dependency in some countries, especially in sub-Saharan Africa.

Although the effect of aid on institutional quality has been shown to be positive, less clear is whether it slows incentives for governments to consolidate a solvent tax system. Publications have also emerged on this issue, with rather ambiguous results. Our own estimation confirms the positive effect that aid has on taxes. But in an environment of low-quality institutions, the effect of aid on taxation can be zero or negative. The solidity of these results is dependent on the limited quality of the available data on taxation in developing countries.

These results throw new light on efforts by donors to improve aid effectiveness, starting with the Paris Declaration. Although the aim of that reform can be judged as positive, the method of putting it into practice reveals shortfalls in need of correction. Most of these stem from an excessively technocratic (and sometimes naïve) approach to the dynamic of social change and the political economy of donor-recipient relations. But, beyond these limitations, the agenda does not respond to one of the basic problems emerging from aid effectiveness research and confirmed by our estimates: aid dependency. Greater awareness about this problem should lead to a more cautious view on aid programs, and to the search for alternative financing for development that avoids the risks of one party making all the choices around aid.

Finally, all such reforms need to be judged in the wider context of the challenges that development aid faces, as a result of the changes to the international system. Three are particularly relevant: the growing heterogeneity of the developing world; the emergence of new powers, far from the OECD, with the capacity to put active aid policies into place; and the expansion of the sphere of international public goods, many of them connected to the development agenda. These three changes are good reasons to advocate for a revision of aid policy and to target efforts around creating a more complex and integrated system of public developmental policy on a global scale.

APPENDIX: DATA SOURCES AND DESCRIPTION OF VARIABLES

1. INSTITUTIONAL QUALITY

All variables are in logs, except ODA and the World Bank Governance Indicators (since these can be zero or negative).

- Data used are the same employed in Alonso and Garcimartín (2010), with the exception of fuel (a larger sample has been employed) and ODA.
- Institutional quality: 2006 World Bank Governance Indicators average.
- Per capita income: Constant PPP per capita GDP, 2004 and 1990. Source: World Bank.
- Gini index: Latest year available. Source: World Bank.
- Education: Average years of school for the population over twenty-five years of age. Source: Barro and Lee (2000).
- Taxes: For Latin America, Gómez Sabaini (2005) has been employed, except for Venezuela, whose data correspond to the World

Bank; for the OECD countries, OECD. For other countries, two sources have been used—first, the World Bank in countries for which data are available and reliable. The World Bank provides data from income tax, excluding social security, and also provides data for the latter separately. Therefore, these two figures have been added. The University of Michigan World Tax Database (http:// www.bus.umich.edu/OTPR/otpr/) is the second source used, in countries for which the World Bank has no data, or where data are not reliable. The data year is 2000. In some cases, where data were not available for a given year, we selected the closest year available, with a maximum difference of three years. When possible, data cover general government and include social security contributions.

- Ethnic fragmentation: Source: Alesina et al. (2003).
- Fuel: Percentage of fuels, ores, metals, precious stones, and non-monetary gold on total exports. 2004. Source: UNCTAD.
- ODA: Five-year average net ODA less humanitarian aid, food aid, and debt relief. Source: OECD.

2. TAX REVENUE

All variables are in logs, except ODA and the World Bank Governance Indicators (since these can be zero or negative), and computed as a three-year average (except the Gini index and institutional quality).

- Institutional quality: World Bank Governance Indicators average. Before 2002, data are available only for the years 1996, 1998, and 2000. Therefore, for the period 1996–1998, we have computed the two-year average between 1996 and 1998, while for the period 1999–2001, we have used the value for 2000.
- Taxes:
  - OECD countries: OECD.
  - Latin American countries: ECLAC.
  - African countries. African Development Bank (African Statistical Yearbook), except where otherwise indicated.
  - Asian countries: Asian Development Bank, except where otherwise indicated.
  - Bulgaria, Cyprus, Estonia, Latvia, Lithuania, Malta, Romania, and Slovenia: Eurostat.
  - Croatia: Central Bureau of Statistics.

- Russia: A. Ivanova, M. Keen, and A. Klemm. A., "The Russian Flat Tax Reform," IMF Working Paper, WP/05/16 (2005).
- Ukraine: Institute for Economic Research and Policy Consulting.
- South Africa: South African Revenue Service.
- Tanzania: Tanzania Revenue Authority.
- Ethiopia: Ministry of Revenue.
- India: Ministry of Finance.
- China: National Bureau of Statistics of China.
- Nigeria, Senegal, Comoros, Sierra Leone, Armenia, Kazakhstan, Moldova, Syria, Yemen, Brunei, Cambodia, Laos, and Mongolia: IMF Country Reports.
- Rest of countries: World Bank WDI.
- Taxes refer to general government, except for those countries whose data source is AfDB, the World Bank, or ADB (except Bangladesh, Georgia, Kiribati, Kyrgyzstan Republic, Pakistan, Philippines, Sri Lanka, and Tajikistan, whose data refer to general government).
- Taxes include social contributions, except for Algeria, Angola, Benin, Bhutan, Botswana, Burundi, Cameroon, Central African Republic, Congo D. R., Congo R., Djibouti, Egypt, Equatorial Guinea, Fiji, Gambia, Guinea Bissau, Jamaica, Kenya, Kiribati, Kuwait, Kyrgyzstan Republic, Laos, Lebanon, Liberia, Madagascar, Malawi, Malaysia, Maldives, Mali, Micronesia, Myanmar, Niger, Papua New Guinea, Philippines, Rwanda, Singapore, Solomon, Sudan, Swaziland, Thailand, Togo, Tonga, Turkmenistan, Tuvalu, Uganda, Uzbekistan, Vanuatu, Vietnam, and Zimbabwe. No social contributions data are available for these countries.
- Per capita income: Constant PPP per capita GDP. Source: World Bank.
- Gini index: Latest year available. Source: World Bank.
- Fuel: Percentage of fuels, ores, metals, precious stones, and nonmonetary gold on total exports. 2004. Source: UNCTAD.
- Agriculture: Agriculture value added (% of GDP). Source: World Bank.
- Urban: Urban population (% of total). Source: World Bank.
- Openness rate: Exports plus imports as a percentage of GDP. Source: World Bank.
- Inflation: GDP deflator (annual %). Source: World Bank.
- Ethnic fragmentation: Source: Alesina et al. (2003).

- ODA (% of GDP): Net ODA less humanitarian aid, food aid, and debt relief. Source: OECD.
- Population: Source: World Bank.
- Birth rate: Source: World Bank.

NOTES

The authors are affiliated with the Complutense Institute for International Studies at the Universidad Complutense of Madrid.

1. A greater development of this material can be found in, among others, Tsikata (1998), Hansen and Tarp (2000), Roodman (2007b), and Alonso (1999).

2. For example, Hadjimichael et al. (1995) consider the turning point a ratio of official development assistance (ODA) to GDP of 25 percent. That threshold is increased to between 40 and 45 percent in the case of Durbarry et al. (1998) and between 41 and 58 percent in Lensink and White (2001).

3. Despite the criticism that Rajan and Subramanian (2008) make of the previous instrumentation methods used in research on aid impact, and the work they undertake to justify their instruments, their own option is not flawless, as Roodman (2007b) points out.

4. See the Appendix for data definition and sources.

5. The results do not vary if, alternatively, the variable is instrumented using population and birth rate. Note that all independent variables except education were considered endogenous. The instruments used are shown in Table 5.2. On the other hand, there can be a problem of collinearity between taxes and ODA. Yet ODA remained non-significant when taxes were dropped from the estimation.

6. Note that the aid is measured in dollars but that GDP is translated from the local currency of the recipient country, which means that the ratio (ODA/GDP) is subject to variations in exchange rates. To avoid that problem, estimates have also been done with aid (as with GDP) in purchasing power parity.

7. The definition of the variables and the sources of the data are detailed in the Appendix.

8. As a proxy of the needs of the donors, mortality, fertility, and life expectancy rates were used. Given that the results obtained were similar, and the availability of data is superior for birth rates, it was decided to use this as a variable.

9. We also tried eliminating the rest of the variables with the exception of GDP per capita and the Gini index, but the results were similar.

10. Moreover, the correlation between said product and aid is −0.16 and to institutional quality 0.32; in other words, they are sufficiently small and contrary in sign not to consider said product as endogenous a priori.

11. In the first case, the purpose is to identify the comparative advantages of each donor; in the second, the objective is to concentrate aid interventions; and in the third, the intention is to promote higher complementary partner selection by European donors.

12. In the case of aid, this type of relationship appears at the very least between those citizens providing the resources and their government in the donor country, between the donor country and the development agency that manages the resources, and between the agency and the recipient institutions in the partner country.

13. This expression is taken from Severino and Ray (2009).

REFERENCES

Acemoglu, D., S. Johnson, and J. A. Robinson. 2002. "Reversal of Fortunes: Geography and Institutions in the Making of the Modern World Income Distribution." *Quarterly Journal of Economics* 117 (4) (November): 1231–94.

Acharya, A., A. T. Fuzzo De Lima, and M. Moore. 2006. "Proliferation and Fragmentation: Transaction Costs and the Value of Aid." *Journal of Development Studies* 42 (1): 1–21.

Alesina, A., and B. Weder. 2002. "Do Corrupt Governments Receive Less Foreign Aid?" *American Economic Review* 92 (4): 1126–37.

Alesina, A., A. Devleeschauwer, W. Easterly, S. Kultat, and R. Wacziarg (2003): "Fractionalization." *Journal of Economic Growth* 8, 2: 155–94.

Alonso, J. A. 1999. "La eficacia de la ayuda: Crónica de decepciones y esperanzas." In *La eficacia de la cooperación internacional al desarrollo: Evaluación de la ayuda*, edited by J. A. Alonso and P. Mosley. Madrid: Cívitas.

———. 2007. "Inequality, Institutions and Progress: A Debate between History and the Present." *CEPAL Review* 93: 61–80.

———. 2011. "Colonisation, Institutions and Development: New Evidence." *Journal of Development Studies* 47, 7: 937–58.

Alonso, J. A., and C. Garcimartín. 2008. *Acción colectiva y desarrollo. El papel de las instituciones*. Madrid: Editorial Complutense.

———. 2010. "The Determinants of Institutional Quality. More on the Debate." *Journal of International Development*

Arndt, C. H., S. Jones, and F. Tarp. 2009. "Aid and Growth. Have We Come Full Circle?" Discussion Paper 2009/05. UNU-WIDER.

Aron, J. 2000. "Growth and Institutions: A Review of the Evidence." *World Bank Research Observer* 15 (1): 1203–28.

Azam, J. P., S. Devarajan, and S. A. O'Connell. 1999. "Aid Dependence Reconsidered." Policy Research Working Paper No. 2144. Washington, D.C.: World Bank.

Barro, R. J. 1997. *Determinants of Economic Growth: A Cross-Country Empirical Study*. Cambridge Mass.: MIT Press.

Barro, R. J., and J-W. Lee. 2000. "International Data on Educational Attainment: Updates and Implications." NBER Working Paper No. 7911. Washington, D.C.: National Bureau of Economic Research.

Becker, T. H., G. Clarke, A. Groff, P. Keefer, and P. Walsh. 2001. "New Tools in Comparative Political Economy: The Database of Political Institutions." *World Bank Economic Review* 15 (1): 165–76.

Bird, R. M., J. Martinez-Vázquez, and B. Torgler. 2004. "Societal Institutions and Tax Effort in Developing Countries." International Studies Program Working

Paper 04–06. International Studies Program, Andrew Young School of Policy Studies, Georgia State University.

Birdsall, N., W. D. Savedoff, A. Mahgoub, and K. Vyborny. 2010. *Cash on Delivery: A New Approach to Foreign Aid.* Washington, D.C.: Center for Global Development.

Boone, P. 1994. "The Impact of Foreign Aid on Savings and Growth." Mimeo. London School of Economics.

———. 1996. "Politics and the Effectiveness of Foreign Aid." *European Economic Review* 40, 2: 289–329.

Booth, D. 2008. "Aid Effectiveness after Accra: How to Reform the 'Paris Agenda.'" ODI Briefing Paper No. 39. London: Overseas Development Institute.

Bourguignon, F., and M. Sundberg. 2007. "Aid Effectiveness: Opening the Black Box." *American Economic Review* 97 (2): 316–20.

Bräutigam, D. 2000. *Aid Dependence and Governance.* Stockholm: Almqvist & Wiksell.

Bräutigam, D., and S. Knack. 2004. "Foreign Aid, Institutions, and Governance in Sub-Saharan Africa." *Economic Development and Cultural Change* 52 (2): 255–86.

Brun, J.-F., G. Chambas, and S. Guerineau. 2007. "Aide et mobilisation fiscale." Study conducted at the request of AFD, CERDI.

Buchanan, J. M. 1977 [1972]. "The Samaritan's Dilemma." Reprinted in *Freedom in Constitutional Contract*, edited by J. M. Buchanan. College Station: Texas A&M University Press, 1977.

Burnside, C., and D. Dollar. 2000. "Aid, Policies and Growth." *American Economic Review* 90,4 (September): 847–68.

———. 2004. "Aid, Policies, and Growth: Revisiting Evidence." Policy Research Paper 2834. Washington, D.C.: World Bank.

Calderisi, R. 2007. *The Trouble with Africa: Why Foreign Aid Isn't Working.* New Haven Conn.: Yale University Press.

Cashel-Cordo, P., and S. Craig. 1990. "The Public Sector Impact of International Resource Transfers." *Journal of Development Economics* 32, 1: 17–42.

Chauvet, L., and P. Guillaumont. 2002. (June). "Aid and Growth Revisited: Policy, Economic Vulnerability and Political Instability." Paper submitted to the Annual Bank Conference on Development Economics. Washington, D.C.: World Bank.

Chelliah, R. J. 1971. "Trends in Taxation in Developing Countries." *IMF Staff Papers,* 18, 2: 254–331. Washington, D.C.: International Monetary Fund.

Chelliah, R. J., H. J. Baas, and R. Kelly. 1975. "Trends in Taxation in Developing Countries." *IMF Staff Papers* 22: 187–205. Washington, D.C.: International Monetary Fund.

Chenery, H. B., and A. M. Strout. 1966. "Foreign Assistance and Economic Development." *American Economic Review* 56, 4: 149–79.

Clemens, M. A., S. Radelet, and R. Bhavnani. 2004. "Counting Chickens When They Hatch: The Short Term Effect on Aid on Growth." Working Paper No. 44. Washington, D.C.: Center for Global Development.

Clist, P., and O. Morrissey. 2011. "Aid and Tax Revenue: Signs of a Positive Effect since the 1980s." *Journal of International Development* 23 (2): 165–81.

Collier, P., and J. Dehn. 2001. "Aid, Shocks, and Growth." Working Paper No. 2688. Washington, D.C.: World Bank.

Collier, P., and A. Hoeffler. 2004. "Aid, Policy and Growth in Post-Conflict Societies." *European Economic Review* 48: 1125–45.

Council of the European Union. 2005. "The European Consensus on Development." Joint Statement by the Council and the Representatives of the Governments of the Member States Meeting within the Council, the European Parliament and the Commission on European Union Development Policy. Brussels: EU.

———. 2007. "Code of Conduct on Complementarity and the Division of Labour in Development Policy." Communication from the Commission to the Council and the European Parliament of 28 February. Brussels: EU.

Dalgaard, C.-J., and H. Hansen. 2001. "On Aid, Growth, and Good Policies." *Journal of Development Studies*, 37: 17–41.

Dalgaard, C.-J., H. Hansen, and F. Tarp. 2004. "On the Empirics of Foreign Aid and Growth." *Economic Journal* 114 (496): 191–216.

Djankov, S., J. Montalvo, and M. Reynal-Querol. 2008. "The Curse of Aid." *Journal of Economic Growth* 13 (3): 169–94.

Doucouliagos, H., and M. Paldam. 2005a. "Aid Effectiveness on Accumulation: A Meta Study." Working Paper 2005: 12. Department of Economics, Aarhus University.

———. 2005b. "Aid Effectiveness on Growth: A Meta Study." Working Paper 2005: 13. Department of Economics, Aarhus University.

———. 2005c. "Conditional Aid Effectiveness: A Meta Study." Working Paper 2005: 14. Department of Economics, Aarhus University.

Dowling, J. M., and U. Hiemenz. 1982. "Aid Savings and Growth in the Asian Region." Asian Development Bank Economics Office Report Series (International) No. 3. Mandaluyong City: Asian Development Bank.

Durbarry, R., N. Gemmel, and D. Greenaway. 1998. "New Evidence on the Impact of Foreign Aid on Economic Growth." CREDIT Research Paper No. 8, University of Nottingham.

Easterly, W. 2006. *The White Man's Burden*. New York: Penguin.

Easterly, W., and R. Levine. 1997. "Africa's Growth Tragedy: Policies and Ethnic Divisions." *Quarterly Journal of Economics* 112 (4): 1203–50.

Easterly, W., R. Levine, and D. Roodman. 2004. "New Data, New Doubts: A Comment on Burnside and Dollar's Aid, Policies, and Growth." *American Economic Review* 94, 3: 774–80.

Economides, G., S. Kalyvitis, and A. Philppopoulos. 2008. "Does Foreign Aid Distort Incentives and Hurt Growth? Theory and Evidence from 75 Aid-Recipients Countries." *Public Choice* 134, 3–4: 463–88.

Eltony, M. N. 2002. "Measuring Tax Effort in Arab Countries." Paper presented at the Conference Paper, Economic Research Forum, Ninth Annual Conference, American University in Sharja, the United Arab Emirates.

European Commission. 2009. *EU Toolkit for the Implementation of Complementary and Division of Labour in Development Policy*. Brussels: EU.

Frankel, J. A., and D. Romer. 1999. "Does Trade Cause Growth?" *American Economic Review* 89 (3) (June): 379–99.

Gallup, J. L., J. Sachs, and A. Mellinger. 1998. "Geography and Economic Development." NBER Working Paper No. 6849. Cambridge, Mass.: National Bureau of Economic Research.

Ghura, D. 1998. "Tax Revenue in Sub-Saharan Africa: Effects of Economic Policies and Corruption." IMF Working Paper No. 98/135. Washington, D.C.: IMF.

Gibson, C. G., K. Andersson, E. Ostrom, and S. Shivakumas. 2005. *The Samaritan's Dilemma: The Political Economy of Development Aid.* Oxford: Oxford University Press.

Glennie, G. 2008. *The Trouble with Aid: Why Less Could Mean More for Africa.* New York: Zed Books.

Gómez Sabaini, J. C. (2005): "Evolución y situación tributaria actual en América Latina: Una serie de temas para la discusión." Paper presented in CEPAL, Santiago de Chile.

Griffin, K. 1970: "Foreign Aid, Domestic Savings and Economic Development." *Bulletin of the Oxford University Institute of Economics and Statistics* 32: 99–112.

Griffin, K., and J. Enos. 1970: "Foreign Assistance: Objectives and Consequences." *Economic Development and Cultural Change* 18: 313–27.

Guillaumont, P. 2009. *Caught in a Trap: Identifying the Least Developed Countries.* Paris: Economica.

Guillaumont, P., and L. Chauvet. 2001. "Aid Performance: A Reassessment." *Journal of Development Studies* 37 (6): 66–92.

Gupta, A. S. 2007. "Determinants of Tax Revenue Efforts in Developing Countries." IMF Working Paper No. 07/184. Washington, D.C.: IMF.

Gupta, S., H. Davoodi, and R. Alonso-Terme. 2002. "Does Corruption Affect Income Inequality and Poverty?" *Economics of Governance* 3: 23–45.

Hadjimichael, M. T., D. Ghura, M. Mühleisen, R. Nord, and E. M. Uçer. 1995. "Sub-Saharan Africa: Growth, Savings, and Investment, 1986–93." Occasional Paper No. 118. Washington, D.C.: IMF.

Hall, R. E., and C. I. Jones. 1999. "Why Do Some Countries Produce So Much More Output per Worker Than Others?" *Quarterly Journal of Economics* 114, 1 (February): 83–116.

Hansen, H., and F. Tarp. 2000. "Aid Effectiveness Disputed." In *Foreign Aid and Development*, edited by F. Tarp. London: Routledge.

———. 2001. "Aid and Growth Regressions." *Journal of Development Economics* 64, 2: 547–70.

Harford, T., and M. Klein. 2005. "Aid and the Resource Curse." Public Policy for Private Sector Note 291. Washington, D.C.: World Bank.

Haveli, N. 1976. "The Effects on Investment and Consumption of Import Surpluses of Developing Countries." *Economic Journal* 86: 853–58.

Heller, P. S. 1975. "A Model of Public Fiscal Behavior in Developing Countries: Aid, Investment and Taxation." *American Economic Review* 65, 3: 429–445.

Heller, P. S., and S. Gupta, S. 2002. "More Aid—Making It Work for the Poor." *WorldEconomics* 3 (4) (December): 131–46.

Henisz, W. J. 2000. "The Institutional Environment for Economic Growth." *Economics and Politics* 12 (1): 1–31.

Herzer, D., and O. Morrisey. 2009. "The Long-Run Effect of Aid on Domestic Output." CREDIT Research Paper 09/01, University of Nottingham.

Hubbard, R. G., and W. Duggan. 2009. *The Aid Trap: Hard Truths about Ending Poverty.* New York: Columbia Business School Publishing.

IDA. 2007. *Aid Architecture: An Overview of the Main Trends in Official Development Assistance Flows.* Washington, D.C.: World Bank.

Kaldor, N. 1963. "Will Underdeveloped Countries Learn to Tax?" *Foreign Affairs* 41, 2 (January): 410–19.

Keen, M., and A. Simone. 2004. "Tax Policy in Developing Countries: Some Lessons from the 1990s and Some Challenges Ahead." In *Helping Countries Develop: The Role of Fiscal Policy,* edited by S. Gupta, B. Clements, and G. Inchauste. Washington, D.C.: International Monetary Fund.

Khan, H. A., and E. Hoshino. 1992. "Impact of Foreign Aid on the Fiscal Behavior of LDC Governments." *World Development* 20 (10): 1481–88.

Killick, T. 2004. "Politics, Evidence and the New Aid Agenda." *Development Policy Review* 22 (1) (January): 29–53.

Kimbrough, K. P. 1986. "Foreign Aid and Optimal Fiscal Policy." *Canadian Journal of Economics* 19 (1): 35–61.

Knack, S. 2004. "Aid Dependence and the Quality of Governance: A Cross-Country Empirical Analysis." World Bank Policy Research Working Paper No. 2396. Washington, D.C.: World Bank.

Lensink, R., and O. Morrissey. 2000. "Aid Instability as a Measure of Uncertainty and the Positive Impact of Aid on Growth." *Journal of Development Studies* 36: 31–49.

Lensink, R., and H. White. 2001. "Are There Negative Returns to Aid?" *Journal of Development Studies* 37 (6): 42–65.

Leuthold, J. H. 1991. "Tax Shares in Developing Countries: A Panel Study." *Journal of Development Economics* 35, 1: 173–85.

Levy, V. 1987. "Does Concessionary Aid Lead to Higher Investment Rates in Low-Income Countries?" *Review of Economics and Statistics* 69: 152–56.

———. 1988. "Aid and Growth in Sub-Saharan Africa: The Recent Experience." *European Economic Review* 32: 1777–95.

Lotz, J. R., and E. R. Morss. 1967. "Measuring Tax Effort in Developing Countries." *IMF Staff Papers* 14 (3) (November). Washington, D.C.: International Monetary Fund.

Martens, B., V. Mummert, P. Murrell, and P. Seabright. 2002. *The Institutional Economics of Foreign Aid.* Cambridge: Cambridge University Press.

Massell, B. F., S. R. Pearson, and J. B. Fitch. 1972. "Foreign Exchange and Economic Development: An Empirical Study of Selected Latin American Countries." *Review of Economics and Statistics* 54, 2: 208–12.

McGillivray, M., and O. Morrissey. 2000. "Aid Fungibility in Assessing Aid: Red Herring or True Concern?" *Journal of International Development* 12 (3): 413–28.

———. 2001a. "Aid Illusion and Public Sector Fiscal Behavior." *Journal of Development Studies* 37 (6): 118–36.

———. 2001b. "New Evidence of the Fiscal Effects of Aid." CREDIT Research Paper No. 01/13, University of Nottingham.

———. 2004. "Fiscal Effects of Aid." In *Fiscal Policy for Development*, edited by T. Addison and A. Roe. Bassingstoke: Palgrave-WIDER.

Moore, M. 1998. "Death without Taxes: Democracy, State Capacity, and Aid Dependency in the Fourth World." In *Toward a Democratic Developmental State*, edited by G. White and M. Robinson. New York: Oxford University Press.

———. 2009: "How Does Taxation Affect the Quality of Governance?" IDS Working Paper 280, Sussex, United Kingdom.

Morrisey, O., O. Islei, and D. M'Amanja. 2007. "Aid Loans Versus Aid Grants: Are the Effects Different?" CREDIT Research Paper No. 06/07. School of Economics, University of Nottingham.

Mosley, P. 1986. "Aid Effectiveness: The Micro-Macro Paradox." *IDS Bulletin* 17 (2): 22–27.

Mosley, P., J. Hudson, and S. Horrell. 1987. "Aid, the Public Sector and the Market in Less Developed Countries." *Economic Journal* 97: 616–41.

———. 1992. "Aid, the Public Sector and the Market in Less Developed Countries: A Return to the Scene of the Crime." *Journal of International Development* 4 (2): 139–50.

Moss, T., G. Petterson, and N. Van De Walle. 2008. "An Aid-Institutions Paradox? A Review Essay on Aid Dependency and State Building in Sub-Sahara Africa." In *Reinventing Foreign Aid*, edited by W. Easterly. Cambridge, Mass.: MIT Press.

Moss, T., and A. Subramanian. 2005. "After the Big Push? Fiscal and Institutional Implications of Large Aid Increase." Working Paper No. 71. Washington, D.C.: Center for Global Development.

Moyo, D. 2009. *Dead Aid: Why Aid Is Not Working and How There Is a Better Way for Africa*. New York: Farrar, Straus and Giroux.

Musgrave, R. A. 1969. *Fiscal Systems*. New Haven, Conn., and London: Yale University Press.

Newlyn, W. T. 1973. "The Effect of Aid and Other Resource Transfers on Savings and Growth in Less Developed Countries: A Comment." *Economic Journal* 83: 863–69.

North, D. C. 1994. "Economic Performance through Time." *American Economic Review* 84, 8: 359–68.

Ocampo, J. A., and R. Vos. 2008. *Uneven Economic Development*. London: Zed Books.

OECD. 2008. *2008 Survey on Monitoring the Paris Declaration: Making Aid More Effective by 2010*. Paris: OECD.

Ouattara, B. 2006. "Foreign Aid and Government Fiscal Behavior in Developing Countries: Panel Data Evidence." *Economic Modelling* 23 (3) (May): 506–14.

Papanek, G. 1973. "Aid, Foreign Private Investment, Savings and Growth in Less Developed Countries." *Journal of Political Economy* 81, 1: 120–30.

Radelet, S. 2003. *Challenging Foreign Aid: A Policymaker's Guide to the Millennium Challenge Account*. Washington, D.C.: Center for Global Development.

Rajan, R. G., and A. Subramanian. 2005. "What Undermines Aid's Impact on Growth?" IMF Working Paper No. 05/126. Washington, D.C.: IMF.

———. 2008. "Aid and Growth: What Does the Cross-Country Evidence Really Show?" *Review of Economics and Statistics* 90 (4): 643–65.

———. 2009. "Aid, Dutch Disease, and Manufacturing Growth." Working Paper No. 196. Washington, D.C.: Center for Global Development.

Remmer, K. L. 2004. "Does Foreign Aid Promote the Expansion of Government?" *American Journal of Political Science* 48 (1): 77–92.

Riddell, R. 2007. *Does Foreign Aid Really Work?* Oxford: Oxford University Press.

Rodrik, D. 1996. "Understanding Economic Policy Reform." *Journal of Economic Literature* 34, 1: 9–41.

———, ed. 2003. *In Search of Prosperity: Analytic Narratives on Economic Growth.* Princeton: Princeton University Press.

Rodrik, D., A. Subramanian, and F. Trebbi. 2002. "Institutions Rule: The Primacy of Institutions over Geography and Integration in Economic Development." IMF Working Paper No. 02/189. Washington, D.C.: IMF.

Roodman, D. 2007a. "The Anarchy of Numbers: Aid, Development, and Cross-Country Empirics." Working Paper No. 32. Washington, D.C.: Center for Global Development.

———. 2007b. "Macro Aid Effectiveness Research: A Guide for the Perplexed." Working Paper No. 134. Washington, D.C.: Center for Global Development.

Severino, J-M., and O. Ray. 2009: "The End of ODA: Death and Rebirth of a Global Public Policy." CGD Working Paper No. 167. Washington, D.C.: Center for Global Development.

Stotsky, J. G., and A. WoldeMariam. 1997. "Tax Effort in Sub-Saharan Africa." IMF Working Paper No. 97/107. Washington, D.C.: IMF.

Summer, A. 2010. "Global Poverty and the 'New Bottom Billion': What If Three-Quarters of the World's Poor Live in Middle-Income Countries?" IDS Working Paper No. 349. Brighton: IDS.

Svensson, J. 1999. "Aid, Growth and Democracy." *Economics and Politics* 11, 3: 275–97.

———. 2000. "Foreign Aid and Rent-Seeking." *Journal of International Economics* 51, 2: 461–73.

Tanzi, V. 1981. (September). "The Impact of Macroeconomic Policies on the Level of Taxation and the Fiscal Balance in Developing Countries." *IMF Staff Papers* 36. Washington, D.C.: International Monetary Fund.

———. 1987. "Quantitative Characteristics of the Tax Systems of Developing Countries." In *The Theory of Taxation for Developing Countries*, edited by D. Newbery and N. Stem. New York: Oxford University Press.

———. 1992. "Structural Factors and Tax Revenue in Developing Countries: A Decade of Evidence." In *Open Economies: Structural Adjustment and Agriculture*, edited by I. Goldin and L. Alan Winters. Cambridge: Cambridge University Press.

Tavares, J. 2003. "Does Foreign Aid Corrupt?" *Economics Letters* 79 (1) (April): 99–106.

Tavares, J., and R. Wacziarg. 2001. "How Democracy Affects Growth." *European Economic Review* 45 (8): 1341–78.

Teera, J., and J. Hudson. 2004. "Tax Performance: A Comparative Study." *Journal of International Development* 16 (6): 785–802.

Tilly, C. 1992. *Coercion, Capital and European States, AD 990–1992.* Oxford: Blackwell.

Tsikata, T. M. 1998. "Aid Effectiveness: A Survey of the Recent Empirical Literature." IMF Policy Discussion Paper No. 98/1. Washington, D.C.: International Monetary Fund.

Van de Walle, N. 2005. *Overcoming Stagnation in Aid Dependent Countries.* Washington, D.C.: Center for Global Development.

Varsakelis, N. C. 2006. "Education, Political Institutions and Innovative Activity: A Cross-Country Empirical Investigation." *Research Policy* 35, 7: 1083–1090.

Weisskopf, T. E. (1972): "The Impact of Foreign Capital Inflows on Domestic Savings in Underdeveloped Countries." *Journal of International Economics* 2: 25–38.

Whitfield, L., ed. 2008. *The Politics of Aid: African Strategies for Dealing with Donors.* Oxford: Oxford University Press.

———. 2009. "Reframing the Aid Debate: Why Aid Isn't Working and How It Should Be Changed." DIIS Working Paper No. 2009:34. Copenhagen: Danish Institute for International Studies.

World Bank. 1998. *Assessing Aid: What Works, What Doesn't and Why?* Washington, D.C.: World Bank.

World Bank, BMZ, and GTZ. 2007. *Minding the Gaps: Integrating Poverty Reduction Strategies and Budgets for Domestic Accountability.* Washington, D.C.: World Bank.

CHAPTER 6

The New Face of Development Cooperation

The Role of South-South Cooperation and Corporate Social Responsibility

Francisco Sagasti and Fernando Prada
(with the collaboration of Mario Bazán, Jorge Chávez Granadino, and Gonzalo Alcalde)

This chapter is an overview of international development finance and its future prospects and emphasizes two aspects that have emerged during the last decade. With this aim, the authors examine here the motivations of donors and providers of grants and other forms of financing, the capacity of recipient countries to mobilize domestic and external resources, and the financial instruments that connect donors and providers with recipients of financial resources. These elements provide a context in which to examine (1) South-South cooperation (SSC), which has acquired a new dimension as a number of developing countries have improved their living standards and strengthened their links with relatively less developed nations; and (2) the role of the new actors in international cooperation, in particular, that of the private sector through corporate social responsibility (CSR) initiatives and various types of associations with multilateral and bilateral actors.

In the coming years the evolution of the system of international cooperation and the role of new actors will depend on the interaction of three factors. The first factor is the *balance between the domestic stimulus programs and international cooperation programs* in developed countries, particularly because a reduction in aid flows appears probable, despite the fact that presidents and prime ministers of the donor countries of the Organization for Economic Cooperation and Development (OECD) have committed themselves to maintaining aid levels to ease the impact of the crisis on developing countries. The question is whether these resources will be available in the near future, as pressure persists in developed countries to strengthen domestic financial systems, and as national assistance programs begin to stress government budgets. Also to be taken into account is the effect of the probable increase in interest rates, which remain close to zero, as part of the programs to strengthen internal capital markets. In this context, as the relative weight of conventional official development assistance (ODA) continues to decline as a percentage of financial flows to developing countries, new opportunities emerge to explore other forms of financing and cooperation, in which new actors become more prominent and could, at least partially, replace official aid flows in specific areas of development financing.

The second factor refers to *the capacity for innovation in the financial sector and the capital markets* that are geared toward financing development. Various emerging and developing countries have been capable of mobilizing resources using instruments to reduce private investment risk, particularly in infrastructure and the development of capital markets (public-private partnerships, guarantees, derivatives, and instruments for strengthening the domestic capital markets, among others). Following the financial crisis, both bilateral and multilateral donors have made available contingency lines of credit, liquidity, and countercyclical funds, as well as instruments to ensure that emerging countries have access to the international capital markets. However, the financial crisis requires a review of the real potential and limits of international financial markets as a source of development financing, as well as a more careful appreciation of the capacity of different types of developing countries, to mobilize internal and external resources.

The third factor is the growing interest regarding *institutional reforms in the architecture of development finance.* The financial crisis has encouraged initiatives to reform development finance institutions, but so far the main efforts have been aimed at increasing the capital base of multilateral institutions. Less progress has been made on issues of governance and development effectiveness, although modest steps have been taken to include emerging countries in the decision-making process on global issues and international agreements. Initiatives to reform the international architecture for development and to design adequate governance systems should take into account the roles that new actors are now playing, as well as the increasing diversity of options to mobilize and utilize financial resources that are available to developing countries.

Finally, it is important to note that what may be called the "international development finance system" was experiencing limitations in its ability to channel resources effectively, even before the 2007–2009 crisis. The financial crisis and global recession have deepened these limitations, but at the same time they have generated responses from various actors and have opened up opportunities for establishing innovative and effective cooperation schemes. These initiatives could help the process of designing and implementing the institutional reforms needed to improve the performance of the international system of development finance. In addition, the presence of new actors offers an opportunity to innovate in the modalities of cooperation and in the capacity to mobilize resources for development. However, these actors are still not completely integrated into the international system of development finance and have not developed their full potential as sources of finance and generators of ideas to complement those of the traditional actors. The concluding section of this chapter suggests some options for advancing in this direction.

CHANGES IN THE INTERNATIONAL DEVELOPMENT FINANCE SYSTEM

MAIN TRENDS IN INTERNATIONAL COOPERATION FLOWS IN THE CONTEXT OF THE FINANCIAL CRISIS

The financial crisis and economic recession have reversed some of the trends in financing flows to developing countries that had gained ground in the last three decades (Sagasti et al., 2005). These trends can be summed up as growth in net private flows, particularly in the form of foreign and portfolio equity investment, and, to a lesser extent, as debt, mainly in the corporate sector; steady growth in workers' remittances; and a reduction of net official debt flows, which became negative in the first decade of the 2000s due to prepayments to multilateral institutions and debt relief operations of bilateral and multilateral creditors—despite the fact that official grants grew over the decade. The data up to 2008 clearly show the reversal of these trends (Table 6.1).

The most evident trend has been the reversal of private flows in a greater magnitude than in previous crises, such as during the "lost decade" of the 1980s and the Asian crisis at the end of the 1990s. Developing countries received US$752.3 billion in net private flows in 2008, US$470 billion less than the US$1,200 billion in 2007, a fall of around 3.3 percent of global

Table 6.1   Net Capital Flows to Developing Countries, 1980–2008 (*Annual Average, US$ Billion*)

	1980–1989	1990–1999	2000–2006	2007	2008
1. Net Private Flows[a]	**41.56**	**145.96**	**373.78**	**1,223.6**	**752.3**
2. Net Official Flows[b]	**35.74**	**51.14**	**24.96**	**74.1**	**114.3**
3. Net FDI and Portfolio Equity Inflows	**13.45**	**113.99**	**296.85**	**663.8**	**536.5**
4. Net Debt Flows	**50.60**	**54.30**	**40.42**	**557.8**	**243.8**
4.1 Official Creditors	22.49	22.33	−36.51	−1.9	28.1
4.2 Private Creditors	28.11	31.97	76.93	559.8	215.8
a. Net Short-Term Debt Flows	*7.31*	*16.45*	*63.21*	*244.5*	*−12.7*
b. Net Medium- and Long-Term Debt Flows	*20.80*	*15.52*	*13.72*	*315.3*	*228.5*
Memorandum Items					
Official Grants[c]	**13.25**	**28.81**	**61.47**	**76.0**	**86.2**
Workers' Remittances	**20.36**	**53.29**	**164.56**	**281.8**	**326.7**

Notes: [a]Debt to private creditors + net FDI and portfolio equity investment; [b]official grants + debt to official creditors; [c]official grants include those from official sources, and a smaller proportion channeled through NGOs and vertical funds.

Source: World Bank (2009b). *Global Development Finance 2010*, CD-ROM.

GDP (World Bank, 2009a).[1] Although the effect on long-term investment flows (foreign direct investment [FDI] and commercial lending) has not been as strong as on short-term flows (investment in securities and short-term credit lines), the latter effect should not be underestimated: short-term credit lines provide liquidity for the corporate sector and foreign trade operations and allow for the refinancing of debts. This situation is similar for the public sector, which issues short-term securities to obtain liquidity and meet its obligations. The risk of an end to payments in the first few months of the crisis was the result of movements in these short-term flows, which significantly reduced liquidity.

First, between January and September 2008, developing countries issued an average monthly US$4.5 billion in bonds, of which 80 percent was corporate issuance. There were no additional issues from September through the end of 2008, and although they recovered modestly in 2009, their size and composition changed. Between January and July 2009, the average monthly issuance was only US$2.1 billion, but 70 percent were sovereign bond issues. Although the corporate sector increased the rate of issuance in 2010, this is the most risky area of finance in the medium term.[2] Between 2003 and 2007 the corporate sector based in developing countries issued close to US$1.2 billion via syndicated loans and bond issues (World Bank, 2009b:39). This debt has to be constantly refinanced, although not in such favorable conditions as those that the private companies had in 2007.[3]

Second, long-term investment flows and workers' remittances were more resilient, but their rate of growth has varied. FDI has fallen at a slower rate than short-term flows and corporate debt issuance, but it recuperated in 2010. However, net transfers to countries where parent companies are resident have increased, although this process can be expected as the investments made in past decades reach maturity. In addition, remittances have slowed their growth rate and may fall if unemployment continues to increase in developed countries.[4] Remittances fell by between 7.3 and 10.1 percent in 2009, while they grew at an annual rate of 15 percent in the period 2000–2008 (World Bank, 2009c).

Third, with the aim of mitigating the effects of the international crisis, net official flows have become positive again, particularly for low-income countries. However, most developing countries are using domestic resources to deal with the crisis.[5] Middle-income countries made use of temporary credit lines to mitigate the fall in private flows (multilateral banks and the International Monetary Fund [IMF]), but a major part of the resources used to strengthen their internal markets came from domestic savings, such as international reserves, public budgets and, in some emerging countries, sovereign wealth funds.

In general, official sources have shown limitations when it comes to tackling a financial crisis of this magnitude. For example, the IMF intervened relatively swiftly—its net flows became positive from negative US$2.1 billion in 2007 to US$10.8 billion in 2008—but it lacks the resources to meet all demand should more countries require finance (Eswar, 2009). Similarly, multilateral banks have responded swiftly, but they are reaching the limits imposed by their capital allowances, thus they have opted in some cases to request capital increases from their member countries (which we discuss later).

The reversal of private flows will not be fully compensated by public finance flows. To reduce the financing gaps in developing countries over the coming years will require a combination of higher domestic resource mobilization (higher domestic savings and better access to credit and capital markets) and enhanced mechanisms for accessing external resources, both private and official.

CHANGES IN THE INSTITUTIONAL COOPERATION CONTEXT

The international crisis came at a time when the international development finance system was undergoing a series of reforms. The recent emphasis on results and development effectiveness has its origin in criticisms regarding the effectiveness of aid, and also in the interest of some emerging countries to promote reforms of the development cooperation system. This has led to a number of initiatives being launched to improve the effectiveness of international cooperation. These include the Paris Declaration and the Accra Agenda for Action, the Millennium Development Goals, the Monterrey Conference, and the Doha Round, as well as other initiatives at both the regional and subregional levels.

However, these agreements are partial in nature, in the sense that they have not included the growing diversity of actors who participate in the international development cooperation system. In addition, some of these agreements confront the challenge of adapting to the changes in the institutional development architecture, such as the G-20's participation as a mediator in the reform of financial institutions, and the rise of urgent issues, including the war against terrorism, global warming, the fight against drug traffic, and the monitoring of capital flows to counter corruption and crime, among others. These new challenges are in addition to a number of aspects that have reduced the effectiveness of international cooperation, including the following:

• *Volatility of cooperation flows.* Flows of ODA have, on average, been five times more volatile than GDP growth, and three times that of exports for each aid recipient, generating negative shocks in some poor countries. Using an analysis that measures the cost of the volatility of the aid on the basis of the capital assets pricing model (CAPM), the deadweight loss may be 15–20 percent of the total of the aid and between 7 and 28 cents per dollar of ODA, depending on the donor (Kharas, 2008).

• *Fragmentation of cooperation and proliferation of donors.* In the 1960s only 8 percent of recipient countries received cooperation funds from twenty or more donor countries, while 40 percent of these had the support of fewer than ten OECD/Development Assistance Committee (DAC) funds. By 1990 some 80 percent of recipient countries received cooperation from twenty or more donors, and the situation has not differed since 2000 (Bourguignon, 2007). Currently the system has twenty-two OECD donors, eight from the European Union that are not members of the DAC (non-DAC), eight OECD non-DAC, and eighteen non-DAC. There are also 236 cooperation institutions, including international organizations, regional and subregional multilateral banks, multidonor programs, public-private associations, and global nongovernmental organizations (NGOs) (World Bank, 2008).

• *Low predictability of cooperation flows.* The OECD carried out a study to estimate the percentage of country programmable aid with a horizon of more than three years. It showed that only 51 percent of aid was programmed, ranging from 30 percent in France to 75 percent in the European Union (OECD, 2007).

The Paris Declaration and the Accra Agenda are core agreements in this context because they emphasize *the effectiveness of cooperation.* But the assessments made have concluded that progress is still limited (Wood et al., 2008). Because of this, Birdsall and Vyborny (2008) have proposed a six-point agenda, emphasizing measures that may be implemented quickly and that depend on a political decision (rather than changes in larger administrative budget processes), making them highly cost-effective.[6]

The renewed importance of public sources of international cooperation flows makes institutional reforms of bilateral and multilateral institutions increasingly urgent. Multilateral institutions have responded more swiftly, but their financial contributions would not be sufficient without the support of bilateral agencies and agreements to increase their resources and especially their concessional windows. In this context a new approach to the reform of cooperation has become increasingly critical. A systemic vision is now required to take into account the presence of new actors, the changing emphasis in motivations for development cooperation, and the new financial instruments that are available.

NEW ACTORS AND MODALITIES IN DEVELOPMENT COOPERATION

The institutional reforms to increase the effectiveness of international cooperation have emphasized changes in the financial architecture largely due to the growing influence of "emerging donors" or "new donors." The concept of "new donors" is generally diffuse, as it includes a variety of institutions and actors whose previous contribution tended to be marginal within the framework of the international system for development cooperation. However, in the last decade, some new donors have increased their influence in the design of development policies, and they are also altering the structure of financial and technical cooperation.

These new actors and modalities of cooperation include large private foundations, sovereign wealth funds, international NGOs, private corporate donors, schemes for mobilizing resources from individuals and consumers, arrangements for South-South and triangular cooperation, and initiatives of emerging countries. Although several of these have been operating for some time, their resource mobilization capacities and their interest in exercising greater influence in global and regional issues have now become increasingly visible. The dynamism of these actors brings about competition and innovation, together with new perspectives, methodologies, instruments, and forms of intervention, as well as additional sources for financing development. At the same time it poses challenges with regard to the coordination of efforts and the need to avoid greater fragmentation, conflicts of interest, increased administrative costs, and, in general, a reduction in aid effectiveness.

In general, the new actors are taking up an increasingly important role on the development financing and international cooperation stage. This is because of the presence of new bilateral donors such as China and Venezuela (whose role in South-South cooperation is analyzed later); growing direct investments from emerging countries (from China, India, Brazil, South Africa, Mexico, and Chile, among others) in other developing countries, associated with the growth of their capital markets (Saxena and Villar, 2008); the more active role played by subregional multilateral banks (Sagasti and Prada, 2006); the activation of agreements on regional monetary issues (Ocampo, 2006); and the mobilization of resources provided by individuals (Hudson Institute, 2009).

From the point of view of developing countries, a more diverse environment provides greater sources of finance and more options for strategic management of international cooperation, something we will discuss later. In a situation of financial crisis, this means that some countries benefit from a greater diversity of options and financial instruments that they can make use of, according to the conditions, approaches, or facilities offered by each (see CEPAL, 2009a, for the case of Latin America). However, this diversity also implies that the new donors could erode the efforts of the international community to exercise pressure on policies and questions of human rights, environmental protection, and the sustainability of foreign debt.[7] In addition, this multiplicity of actors and their additional resources could generate problems for some of the poorest economies, which will not be capable of absorbing greater flows of official aid without a probable deterioration of their macroeconomic and competitiveness indicators (Gupta et al., 2006).

China has been replacing Western countries as the main trading partner and donor in sub-Saharan Africa (Van Dijk, 2009; Reality of Aid, 2010), and India is also taking its position as an important actor (Feigenbaum, 2010) in this region, which has been a priority for traditional donors during the last two decades. These examples represent a new trend in the growth of quantities mobilized, and in levels of influence by the new regional powers. Although there are significant difficulties in calculating the payments made by these new bilateral actors, in 2008 South-South transfers had reached US$13.9 billion, or nearly 15 percent of the ODA of OECD-DAC countries (Reality of Aid, 2010). To this amount we must add around US$800 million from Russia (not normally considered part of the South or developing world) in 2009, compared to only US$220 million in 2008 (Anishyuk, 2010). In some cases there is a significant amount of aid from countries that are not emerging economies or members of the OECD-DAC. This is true for Arab oil countries, such as Saudi Arabia, Kuwait, and the United Arab Emirates, whose payments amounted to US$5.9 billion in 2008; in addition, amounts from Venezuela were estimated at between US$1.1 and US$2.5 billion for the same year (Reality of Aid, 2010).

New actors within the group are emerging donors whose motivations have become global in scope and that exercise significant influence, meanwhile maintaining high levels of financial independence due to their capacity to mobilize domestic resources. For example, the sovereign wealth funds of emerging economies such as China, South Korea, and the Arab countries, which have ample resources, were key in providing liquidity to commercial banks during the start of the financial crisis, acting as stabilizing agents in the global economy. Thus the China Investment Corporation acquired assets from Morgan Stanley for US$5.3 billion, the Korean Investment Corporation, together with the Korean Investment Corporation, invested US$5.4 billion in Merrill Lynch, and the Abu Dhabi Investment Authority acquired US$5.7 billion of stock in Citigroup (Singh, 2008).[8]

Nongovernmental actors are also gaining ground within the international system of development finance, moving significant resources and developing links with traditional bilateral and multilateral actors. For example, the total amount of aid from all private U.S. funds, including religious organizations, private foundations, and individual donations, was estimated at US$33.5 billion in 2005. Private foundations allocate around 30 percent of their grants to programs outside the United States (Sulla,

2006); if this percentage is applied to total private donations in America, they could be mobilizing US$10 billion—compared to US$27.8 billion of American bilateral ODA in 2005. Nevertheless, this US$10 billion figure would not necessarily correspond to development projects and could be considered the upper limit of private grants to international development projects (Reality of Aid Management Committee, 2008; OECD, 2010).

The relationship between these new actors and traditional actors, particularly bilateral and multilateral agents, is rather complex. Private philanthropic foundations play an increasingly important role in development finance. This is the case with the Bill and Melinda Gates Foundation, which mobilizes greater resources for health than most bilateral actors. Even foundations with a longer history, such as the Ford or Kellogg Foundation, contribute hundreds of millions of dollars per year (US$530 million in 2006 for the Ford Foundation), while CARE and Catholic Relief Services mobilize around US$500 million per year, on average. Although the influence of new actors is growing in some of these areas, their activities are not subject to the same scrutiny and assessment as traditional actors, since they are not conditioned by politics or alignments that govern the OECD donors, nor are their sector support strategies determined significantly by global agendas such as the Millennium Development Goals, for example (Chervalier and Zimet, 2006).

It is also important to highlight the significant amount of ODA channeled through NGOs and complemented with the resources that NGOs collect from civil society, individual donations, and other sources. Between 2005 and 2008, total ODA resources channeled through NGOs by OECD countries reached an unprecedented level of nearly US$15 billion a year (more than 10 percent of total ODA). This size varied widely between countries: in Japan it was 1.7 percent in 2007, but some European countries distribute up to 60 percent of their ODA through these organizations. The World Bank has also provided a great deal of funds for NGOs since the 1980s. However, there are opinions both for and against the growth of non-governmental actors and their effectiveness in supporting development. On the one hand, as these actors are closer to the beneficiaries and have greater autonomy, they can be more effective when it comes to implementing projects. However, Nunnenkamp and Öhler (2009) did not find evidence of greater effectiveness, and Nunnenkamp et al. (2008) found no indications of greater capacity for focusing on poorer countries. In fact, Fruttero and Gauri (2005) found evidence of strategic use and the presence of private interests with regard to assigning the aid provided through NGOs.

Two of these new actors and modalities of aid are worthy of particular attention because of their potential impact on the mobilization of financial resources, transfer of knowledge, and influence to initiate reforms that improve the effectiveness of development cooperation. First, South-South cooperation can help create a more horizontal relationship between donor countries and recipients on the basis of common interests[10] and solidarity, respect for sovereignty in domestic affairs, and, in many cases, efficiency, due to lower cooperation costs between developing countries. Second, corporate social responsibility initiatives could enable activities, programs, and resources financed by the private sector to be integrated into development cooperation programs and projects (which we discuss later in this chapter).

DEVELOPMENT FINANCING AND COOPERATION: THE SPACE FOR NEW ACTORS

In order to recognize and integrate the new actors within the larger group of activities related to development financing, this section examines three aspects: (1) the motivations of actors participating in the system of international development cooperation, whether as donors, recipients, or both; (2) the array of financial instruments and cooperation modalities available to developing countries; and (3) the capacity of different types of developing countries to mobilize external and domestic resources, and how this capacity relates to the use of instruments and cooperation modalities.

MOTIVATIONS OF THE ACTORS INVOLVED IN THE INTERNATIONAL DEVELOPMENT COOPERATION SYSTEM

"Developing finance" responds to the needs of financial resources of developing countries. However, decisions to both provide and access finance go beyond strictly financial considerations, taking other factors into account.[9] Donor motivations include strengthening diplomatic links, expanding areas of economic influence, guaranteeing access to natural resources, and increasing trade, as well as matters related to ideological compatibility, cultural and linguistic affinities, and historical relations. For their part, recipient countries have a variety of motivations for making use of international financing and cooperation, such as compensating for the scarcity of resources and low tax revenues, employing resources with greater flexibility than is allowed by domestic budget regulations,[10] using more effective and transparent management processes, acquiring knowledge, securing access to productive and management technologies, and complementing local initiatives with experience and knowledge available in other countries.

The core question is whether the range of conventional motivations, which have been studied mainly for cases of official aid and OECD/DAC donors, corresponds to the broadest set of current actors operating in international development cooperation. Table 6.2 lists donor motivations and how they relate to schools of thought in international relations.

Table 6.2   Motivations for Engaging in Development Cooperation Initiatives

General Orientation of Motivations	Tend More toward Altruism (concern for recipient's interests and objectives)	Shared or Mixed Interests (at the bilateral, regional, or global level)	Tend More toward Self-Interest (strategic donor interests and objectives)
Specific Donor Motivations	• Attention to recipient development objectives (subnational, national, or international plans)	• Strengthen economic interdependence	• Promote strategic and security interests
	• Reward institutional, political, social, and economic performance	• Promote processes of integration (economic, commercial, political)	• Obtain support for political agendas
	• Provide humanitarian aid and respond to emergencies	• Respond to problems of a global nature	• Promote donor economic and commercial interests
		• Promote the stability of international systems	• Religious proselytizing
Outlook for International Relations Explaining This Orientation	• *Political idealism* (essentially altruistic and pacific nature of the actors and of their relations)	• *Liberalism* (possibility of working together and shared values, importance of institutions)/ *complex interdependence* (takes into account non-state actors)	• *Realism* (emphasis on managing conflict, drive to increase power and security)/ *neorealism* (pays attention to actors beyond the system of states)

However, some considerations that guide the analysis of donor and recipient motivations need to be reexamined in light of recent changes in the context of development cooperation.[11] In particular:

• The dichotomy between altruism and self-interest, which has helped simplify the analysis of motivations of official aid (considering primarily the point of view of donor countries), fails to encapsulate the diversity of current motivations, for at least two reasons. First, this dichotomy has functioned within the framework of bilateral relations between sovereign states. However, it loses precision when extended to other actors. For example, an increasingly large proportion of bilateral aid is channeled through NGOs, which have their own agendas that are not necessarily in line with those of the donor agencies. Second, examples exist where altruistic objectives and self-interest motivations combine, converge, and crisscross. This is the case of CSR and socially responsible investment, which combine commercial and economic interests with altruistic and social benefit criteria. Strategic motivations of donor countries in a "global world" may even contain positive externalities that could be considered altruistic, as with the provision of certain global and regional public goods (financial stability, mitigation of climate change, and regional integration processes, among others).

• It is becoming more evident that strategy and self-interest considerations also exist in the motivations of aid recipients. For example, Argentina and Ecuador prepaid their debts to the IMF[12] to avoid the associated conditionalities and to strengthen their internal political discourse against multilateral financial institutions, even at the cost of more expensive sources of funding, such as issuing bonds in their domestic capital markets, or with a high opportunity cost, as in resorting to the use of international reserves. Middle-income countries now have access to a broad range of donors and financial instruments, allowing them to act more strategically in managing their international cooperation relations. However, countries with lower levels of development, such as least-developed countries, fragile states, or those in a situation of humanitarian disaster or post-conflict, experience greater restrictions in terms of the range of options available (UNCTAD, 2009).

• Countries in transition from recipient to donor status present conceptual challenges for categorizing their motivations. Brazil, Russia, India, and China (the BRIC countries) aspire to a varying extent to act as global powers, and their cooperation programs as donors reflect this attitude. But this is also the case with countries with regional influences, such as Indonesia, Turkey, South Africa, Mexico, and Venezuela that, together with the BRIC countries, aim for greater participation in the system of international cooperation, both through South-South cooperation and through multilateral initiatives (subregional development banks and regional integration mechanisms).

• Some private-sector actors are channeling more resources to development programs, and their experience is growing in areas that once were exclusively funded by official resources. Therefore, it is likely that motivations of private-sector actors will start to gain more weight in shaping the development agenda. For example, the U.S. government is an influential actor through its bilateral programs in the health sector. But the Gates Foundation, based in the United States and with annual donations of US$1.22 billion for health programs in 2007, is possibly more influential than the U.S. government in some fields related to health and international cooperation. It has its own agenda, which does not necessarily coincide with that of the U.S. government. In particular, some private foundations and CSR programs have found it difficult to align themselves with, or to complement, their countries' official aid programs.

As a result of the financial crisis, it is possible to anticipate three kinds of effects that could configure new trends in the motivations of the growing variety of actors in the system. First, the emerging economies have been able to show their growing influence on development cooperation issues, as well as their capacity to mobilize resources to help relatively less developed countries and to consolidate South-South cooperation.[13] Second, the crisis has challenged the paradigm that private financing might be capable of replacing official aid. As a result, it is possible that solidarity and altruistic motivations will be reinforced, particularly in the most vulnerable countries that have suffered a triple impact from the financial crisis, the effects of climate change, and the increase in food prices. Third, pressure on public budgets in developed countries will make it difficult for them to increase resources for official development assistance, especially when some of the temporary flows that contributed to increased aid in the 2000s are likely to dwindle in the medium term (including support for the reconstruction of Iraq and Afghanistan, and debt relief with bilateral creditors).

RECIPIENT COUNTRIES AND THEIR CAPACITY TO MOBILIZE DOMESTIC AND EXTERNAL RESOURCES

Bilateral aid agencies and multilateral development banks generally use average national income per capita as the main criterion for allocating their different types of financial resources to recipient countries. For example, grants and concessional loans are targeted at low-income countries; middle-income countries have access to a variety of combinations of grants, soft loans, and regular loans; and regular loans and private investment guarantees are channeled to middle-income countries.

However, this classification does not take into account the actual diversity of countries that have similar per capita incomes. In particular, developing countries are becoming increasingly differentiated according to their capacities to mobilize domestic and external resources. This can be seen, for example, by comparing the situation of some lower-middle-income countries according to World Bank criteria, that is, those whose gross national income (GNI) per capita was between US$986 and US$3,855 in 2008. This group includes the following: China, with a GNI per capita of US$2,980, which received US$147 billion in FDI and has a level of domestic savings close to 56 percent of GDP; Jordan, with a GNI per capita of US$3,130, which received FDI of US$1.9 billion and has levels of domestic savings of −13 percent of GDP; and Côte d'Ivoire, with a GNI per capita of US$980, which received US$430 million in FDI and has a rate of domestic savings of 14 percent of GDP. In other words, countries with similar incomes present very different features in terms of their capacity for domestic saving and investment, export levels, FDI, and net international reserves, among other indicators of resource mobilization.

This suggests the need to develop indicators based on the capacity to mobilize domestic and external resources, with the aim of better adapting the range of financial instruments used in aid and international financing to the needs of the different recipient countries. This section presents an updated and extended version of the "index of resource mobilization capacity," based on the work of Sagasti et al. (2005). This index helps identify various categories of recipient countries according to their ability to access external resources and generate domestic resources (see Appendix 2). To do this, we have used the statistical method of principal components, which allows information from a variety of indicators to be integrated in order to identify the factors that best explain their combined variation. In this way it is possible to "compact" the information from various indicators into only a few components (ideally a single factor) that represent the main characteristics of the population studied, in this case the capacity to mobilize the resources of developing countries. A number of indicators were initially identified for this purpose. In the case of *mobilization of internal resources*, a country has greater capacity when it has more domestic savings, tax revenues, capital investment, domestic lending for the private sector, and a lower fiscal deficit. In the case of *mobilization of external resources*, a country has greater capacity when it can attract more foreign direct investment, when there is a greater level of exports and imports, more international reserves, and lower levels of foreign debt, and when it receives a greater flow of official development aid.

For reasons of availability of information,[14] particularly for those countries with weaker statistical systems, the following indicators were chosen for calculating the two indexes: (1) gross fixed capital formation, domestic credit to the private sector, and domestic savings (as a proportion of GDP) for the *index of internal resource mobilization*; and (2) levels of foreign direct investment, volume of exports of goods and services, and net international reserves, all expressed in logarithms to reduce dispersion, for the *index of external resource mobilization*. The figures used for each indicator correspond to the average for the period 2006–2008.[15]

The principal component analysis allowed identification of four main groups of countries according to their resource mobilization capacities (Figure 6.1). The scale has been normalized (to a [0,1] scale), and China is the upper limit due to its relatively high capacity to mobilize external and domestic resources. In addition, the combination of a 0.5 cutoff point in each index defines four quadrants for illustrative purposes. This division allows us to identify four categories of countries:

• Type A countries, with a *high capacity for domestic and external resource mobilization* (both indexes with values greater than 0.5).[16] These are economies that are integrated in the international markets and receive high levels of FDI. In addition, they have well-developed domestic capital markets to finance the private sector and enough public resources to cover the majority of their current expenditures and investment needs. Emerging economies such as China, South Africa, Russia, Brazil, Mexico, and Chile belong to this category.

• Type B countries, with a *high capacity for external resource mobilization and a lower capacity for internal resource mobilization*. In general, these are countries at the intermediate level of development, with small domestic

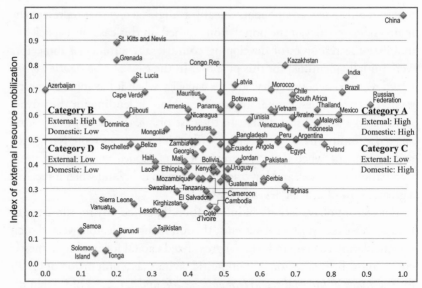

Figure 6.1   Developing Countries Classified by Their Capacity to Mobilize Domestic and External Resources (2006–2008)

economies that are open to international trade and foreign investment. Among them are exporters of commodities that can attract external financing, but whose capacity for domestic mobilization is constrained by their relatively low levels of savings and investment. This category includes Peru, Angola, Indonesia, Pakistan, and India.

• Type C countries, with a *low capacity for external resource mobilization and a greater capacity for internal resource mobilization*. This is generally the case of small economies in which the public sector is an important actor and where the small economies have high levels of domestic savings but have not been capable of attracting external investment or trade flows to the extent that emerging economies have. This is the case for countries such as Nicaragua and Armenia and for smaller economies such as Grenada and Dominica.

• Type D countries with a *low capacity for internal and external resource mobilization* (both indexes with values lower than 0.5). These are poorer countries with a relatively low level of development, whose links with international markets have not yet been developed and are dependent on bilateral and multilateral cooperation flows. This category includes the countries of sub-Saharan Africa and Paraguay, Bolivia, Ecuador, Haiti, and Cameroon, among others.

The financial crisis may have changed some countries' positions in the classification scheme according to their resource mobilization capacities, but no consolidated data for 2009 are yet available. However, even so, it is possible to appreciate some of the risks associated with the effects of the crisis. First, economies with a high capacity for external resource mobilization that depend on external flows to finance the private sector, through securities in international capital markets or credit lines from commercial banks, may have difficulties if the international economic conditions deteriorate in the medium term. The corporate sector in these economies has financed its investments by issuing debt and has to refinance its loans as they mature. It is estimated that the corporate sector of the emerging economies had to refinance debt for over US$1 trillion in 2010 (World Bank, 2009b). This could lead to serious financial problems if interest rates rise sharply, international capital markets reduce their levels of intermediation, or the liquidity of international commercial banks is restricted.

In addition, the impact of the financial crisis on poorer countries has led to the expansion of concessional windows of multilateral banks, including regional and subregional institutions (UNCTAD, 2009). Even though most international cooperation institutions committed their support to low-income economies, in practice these countries did not receive resources according to their financing needs. In contrast, middle-income countries had available several financial options to cope with the financial crisis (Ocampo et al., 2010).

The classification based on the capacity for resource mobilization allows for establishing a link between the use of certain kinds of financial instruments and modalities of cooperation and the country categories. This information allows for identification of some of the following trends:

• The supply and use of financial instruments tend to diversify over time, responding to changes in the environment, economic progress, and the introduction of financial innovations. This trend can be clearly appreciated in the group of new actors providing international cooperation (emerging countries, private firms, foundations, public-private associations) and in the different types of recipient countries. Initially some new donors focused on providing grants and technical cooperation to those recipient countries with the lowest capacity to mobilize resources, whether external, internal, or both. However, over time, it is possible to appreciate the use of a broader range of financing and cooperation instruments, both by providers and recipients. For example, some emerging donors are using instruments to finance trade exchanges, guarantees for private investments, concessional loans, and turnkey projects, among others, to finance initiatives in countries with a lower resource mobilization capacity, and particularly from external sources. Other donors are exploring instruments that combine the power of innovation of capital markets, such as securitization of future aid flows, to channel resources toward countries with a lower capacity for domestic and external resource mobilization. Meanwhile, donors in the private sector are using new mechanisms to mobilize additional resources, including guarantees, risk mitigation insurance, corporate social responsibility initiatives, support of government social projects, support for reconstruction and assistance in humanitarian disasters, and "public works for taxes" schemes, particularly in countries with a higher capacity for external resource mobilization.

• As capacity to mobilize resources increases, access to sources of financing diversifies and expands. For example, emerging economies have strengthened their domestic capital markets, issued bonds on international markets, increased their FDI inflows, and obtained access to instruments that mitigate investment risks. At the same time, they can access resources provided by the trust funds of international cooperation institutions for specific purposes, such as those designed to address the impact of and adaptation to climate change, and the financing of health programs. In contrast, economies with a reduced capacity for mobilizing external and internal resources are more dependent on ODA and have access mainly to concessional resources, budget support, and donations from public and private sources.

• Various countries with a greater capacity for financial resource mobilization are making the transition from recipients to donors and becoming increasingly involved in South-South cooperation initiatives. This is the case of the BRIC countries and other emerging economies, which have begun to expand their influence at the regional and subregional levels. These countries have "graduated" from some modalities of financing such as concessional resources and donations from multilateral bodies and the United Nations. However, it is more a case of *gradation* than graduation, as these countries continue to use resources from bilateral and multilateral sources with strategic aims, in accordance with their interests, although to a more limited extent. For example, some have strengthened their capital markets with the support of multilateral banks and by making use of instruments to reduce the costs of issuing local-currency-denominated securities. This has allowed them to increase their domestic credit, develop microfinance, and extend banking penetration. Similarly, some instruments of bilateral and multilateral sources are used flexibly to finance pilot projects and pre-investment studies, and also to cover additional costs that companies incur, for example, to make progress in the use of clean technologies and environmental conservation.

• The external and domestic resource mobilization capacity indexes better describe the diversity of development financing patterns than does the use of average per capita income. Here the case of middle-income countries is illustrative. Despite falling within the same category, these show major differences in their resource mobilization capacities and thus their capacity to access different sources of finance and modalities of cooperation. Many of these countries have a high level of inequality in the distribution of income, and a significant percentage of their population in poverty, but at the same time some of their economic sectors are very integrated in the international markets and able to mobilize resources from a diversity of financial sources. This is true for various countries in Latin America and Southeast Asia, which resort to regular loans from multilateral and bilateral sources and even have access to international capital markets. Other lower-middle-income countries also make use of grants from the United Nations agencies, the private non-profit sector, and even concessional sources. This diversity is not expressed when countries are classified using an indicator such as average income per capita.

• The categorization of developing countries based on their capacity to mobilize resources allows the identification of more adequate instruments and modalities of cooperation, taking their specific situations into account. As well as using instruments to mitigate investment risks (both the private domestic sector and foreign companies), countries with a greater capacity for mobilizing internal and external resources are able to access various combinations of instruments and sources of finance. For example, CSR and private foundation resources can be assigned to small-scale experiments with new approaches, procedures, and initiatives. Those that are most successful can then be repeated or extended in scale by using resources from bilateral or multilateral loans, or by issuing securities on the international capital markets. In countries with a low domestic resource mobilization capacity and a high external mobilization capacity, it is essential to promote the mobilization of additional domestic resources.

South-South cooperation initiatives, exchange of experience and technical assistance programs, and triangular cooperation schemes can all play a
key role in the creation of the capacity to mobilize domestic resources in
these countries.[17] In countries with a high domestic resource mobilization
capacity and a low external resource mobilization capacity, the main challenge is how to increase direct private investment flows. Risk mitigation
instruments for foreign investment are key in this case, and the experience
of multilateral banks and other developing countries can contribute significantly in this respect. Finally, countries with low external and domestic resource mobilization capacities require a combination of instruments
that channel financing at low cost (loans at concessional conditions and
donations) but at the same time contribute to the creation of internal resource mobilization capacity.[18]

The classification of developing countries according to the income base
per capita does not allow a focus on the types of instruments and modalities of cooperation that countries could use and have access to. It also con-
ceals profound differences among countries within similar income categories. Thus we should explore the possibility of transcending the use of
income per capita as a criterion for classifying countries receiving international financing and cooperation and move toward indicators that better
reflect their capacity to mobilize resources.

FINANCIAL INSTRUMENTS AND MECHANISMS FOR
CHANNELING INTERNATIONAL COOPERATION
TO DEVELOPING COUNTRIES

A variety of financial mechanisms and modalities provide the means that
give form to cooperation initiatives between donors and recipients. Each
of these instruments has explicit or implicit rules of application, such as
criteria for eligibility and access, conditionality, payment modalities, governance mechanisms, thematic areas, availability of resources, capacity to
mobilize additional funds (leveraging), and the complexity and requirements of administrative capacities. Table 6.3 lists these instruments grouped
according to the type of instrument and actors employing them. An overview of these instruments allows the identification of some of the trends
worth highlighting.

First, although the size of the resources mobilized is different, the
modalities of cooperation between DAC countries and bilateral emerging

Table 6.3 Types of Financial Instruments for International Cooperation[a]

| | Bilateral | | Multilateral | | | | Private Sector | | | |
Type	DAC	Other Donors	United Nations	World Bank, RDBs	IMF/ Regional	SRDBs	For- Profit	Non-Profit/ Individual	Capital Markets	Global
Loans	X	X		X	X	X	X	X	X	
Grants	X	X	X	X	X	X	X	X	X	
Bonds		X		X		X	X		X	
Foreign Direct Investment							X			
Remittances								X		
Market Creation/Support	X	X	X	X		X	X	X	X	
Specific Purpose Funds/ Facilities	X	X	X	X		X	X	X	X	
Taxes and Fees	X						X			
Payments for Services		X					X			X
Combined Value Instruments							X	X	X	
Public-Private Partnerships	X	X		X			X	X	X	
Risk Mitigation/Management	X	X		X		X	X		X	
Management/Reduction of Debt	X	X		X	X	X				
Provision of International Liquidity	X	X			X					

Notes: [a]Bilateral DAC donors represent the traditional official aid donors, in contrast to emerging donors in the category "Other Donors," which also include South-South cooperation activities. In the case of multilateral actors, a division has been made between the MDBs (the World Bank and regional development banks, or RDBs) and the subregional development banks (SRDBs), as the latter are examples of South-South cooperation. Finally, the global category implies a broad set of actors of various categories, such as multidonor programs in the case of specific-purpose funds or facilities, and consumers in the global market in the case of international taxes.

donors are very similar. For example, China and Venezuela have established concessional loan programs through their development agencies and public companies.[19] At the same time, following the financial crisis, some emerging donors have established contingency credit lines to support the finance of foreign trade, and others have supported South-South investments through guarantee and finance schemes similar to those of the Overseas Private Investment Corporation of the U.S. government or the export credit facilities of the United Kingdom. In addition, countries such as Brazil have expressed their support for instruments to reduce carbon emissions and deforestation. However, the new bilateral donors and those that participate in South-South cooperation have continued to use mainly the channels of technical cooperation, transfer of experts, and provision of study and training fellowships.

Second, multilateral institutions have been more dynamic in terms of innovation in financial mechanisms (Girishankar, 2009). To a large extent this is a result of their privileged position in the international system of development financing, where they function as a mediator between private-sector initiatives, capital markets, official donors, and governments in developing countries (Sagasti and Prada, 2004). For example, their contribution to the range of instruments for mitigating and managing private investment risk in developing countries, above all for the provision of infrastructure, has been quite important. Public-private associations have mobilized the resources of private investors through concessions, structured finance, and the use of derivatives and risk mitigation guarantees (political, foreign exchange, interest rate, and systemic). In addition, the support of these institutions has been key in strengthening domestic capital markets, for example, through the issue of local-currency bonds and the provision of technical assistance to regulatory bodies.[20]

Third, the entry of new actors, particularly from the non-profit private sector (comprising mostly foundations and organizations that channel individual donations), has benefited some sectors and thematic areas. For example, the Bill and Melinda Gates Foundation has helped mobilize additional resources from multilateral banks, United Nations organizations, bilateral institutions, and other donors to establish specific-purpose funds in the health sector (Lane and Glassman, 2009). Over a decade and a half, this has led to a quadrupling of resources targeted for this sector, which approached US$22 billion in 2007 (OECD, 2009a). At the same time, financial innovation has been fostered through the design of mechanisms such as the purchase of medicines and patents to create or strengthen markets that have problems of asymmetrical information (for example, the AccessRH, PG4Health, NetGuarantee, and Affordable Medicines Facility for Malaria programs). Something similar occurs with other foundations, such as the Moore Foundation and the World Wildlife Fund, which are providing financial resources to ensure a sustainable flow of resources for environmental conservation programs.

Two other sectors in which it is possible to detect the presence of new financial mechanisms for mobilizing additional sources are the mitigation of and adaptation to climate change and humanitarian assistance for relief from natural events. In the first case, and within the framework of the Kyoto Protocol, the Copenhagen Accord, and the Cancun Accord, the objective of these mechanisms has been to internalize the negative externalities associated with carbon emissions and to establish limits for these emissions, primarily by creating markets that facilitate trading in emission permits and help determine their price, as well as by strengthening the market for emission reduction certificates that provide incentives for private investment in clean technologies. In addition, various bodies have established trust funds with the specific aim of channeling funds for adaptation and mitigation activities (UN-DESA, 2009; Prada, 2009). In the case of aid for relief from natural events that turn into disasters, the response to recent tragedies such as the tsunami in Southeast Asia and the earthquakes in Haiti and Chile has allowed the channeling and consolidation of donations from various sources—official, private, and individual[21]—by using information technologies, social networks, and volunteer contributions to common funds, among other mechanisms.

Fourth, there is a trend toward using financial market innovations (and private-sector innovations in general) to fund and implement international cooperation programs. In addition to the instruments for creating and supporting markets, and for mitigating and managing risks, there are those that combine both economic and social returns. For example, CSR initiatives are frequently complemented with schemes for socially responsible investment, which encompass the activities of investment funds that support firms that comply with environmental and social standards, that provide start-up funds and equity investments for social investment projects, and that securitize future financial flows to guarantee liquidity in cooperation projects.

Some of these instruments could channel resources to the beneficiaries of cooperation programs and projects at a lower cost. For example, conditional transfer programs, grants and donations, microfinance operations, and remittances benefit from the deepening of financial markets and banking penetration in developing countries. The presence of bank branches in remote locations means that beneficiaries can be reached directly, for example, through the issue of credit and debit cards that do not generate additional costs of providing aid in kind and that also help consolidate local financial markets.[22] Some innovations also allow donors to channel resources directly for certain purposes, as happens with "green" credit cards that set aside a small percentage of each transaction to support the development of clean technologies, and with Product Red, where the associated companies channel a percentage of sales to the Global Fund to Fight AIDS, Tuberculosis, and Malaria.

The financial crisis has affected these trends in the use of cooperation instruments and modalities in various ways. The first impact has been through the reduction in available resources from donors in both the private and public sectors. The pressure to reduce public spending, the opportunity cost for private companies, and the restrictions facing individual donors will particularly affect those instruments that depend on voluntary contributions, which will see a drop in the resources channeled in the immediate future. Second, during the financial crisis, various contingency credit lines and implicit and explicit public guarantees were made available for developing countries to sustain trading operations and the capital markets. In addition, there have been negotiations to increase the capital of multilateral institutions[23] and to increase resources for trust funds with specific objectives. Although in the short and medium term this is important for mitigating the effects of the crisis, returning to a path of economic growth, and consolidating achievements in social issues, the experience of recent years indicates that public sources are important and more effective to the extent that they can act as catalysts for resources from a variety of sources, without relying solely or largely on public-sector sources. It is therefore important to maintain the capacity to innovate in the design and implementation of financial instruments, particularly those that involve private entities in development initiatives.

SOUTH-SOUTH COOPERATION

Since the Buenos Aires Action Plan was approved at the end of the 1970s, establishing the main lines for technical cooperation between developing countries, SSC has been defined by its capacity to transfer experiences and knowledge between countries in a "horizontal" fashion, in contrast to the "vertical" technical cooperation between developing and developed countries.[24] SSC covers various dimensions, from political commitments, joint negotiations, and trade integration treaties to collaboration agreements in specific areas (transport, education, monetary policy, working conditions, pension systems, science, and technology). It is executed through various modalities (financing, exchange of experts, technical assistance, information on best practices, and increased capacity for joint negotiation). Box 6.1 sums up a recent report that compiles 110 case studies and demonstrates that SSC involves a broad range of motivations, instruments, and sectors (TT-SSC, 2010).

A group of countries in Africa and Latin America promoted a consensus to include the SSC mechanism as part of the agreements within the framework of the Accra Agenda for Action (AAA). Three areas of work were established (paragraph 19 of the AAA): (1) adaptation of the principles of effectiveness of aid to SSC; (2) enrichment of the debate on effectiveness with a systematization of the experiences; and (3) identification of the areas where North-South cooperation is complemented with SSC. This has led to the activation of a variety of regional mechanisms that should converge to avoid duplication of efforts. For example, organizations such as the Economic Commission for Latin America and the Caribbean, the Ibero-American General Secretariat, the Organization of American States (OAS), the United Nations Development Programme, and various multilateral banks have established programs and facilities to promote triangular coordination and SSC. From this point of view it would appear that SSC could become a core idea in the international development cooperation system.

SSC has a broader range of motivations than traditional aid schemes. In addition to strategic, political, commercial, and solidarity concerns, it also covers ideological and cultural affinity, as well as pragmatic considerations referring to specific shared interests at the regional level, such as shared river basins and natural cross-border resources, among others. In particular, an important motivation for SSC consists of increasing the negotiating powers of developing countries in different international forums and in relation with developed countries.

Despite the obvious benefits of cooperation between developing countries, *it is necessary to move toward a more balanced vision of SSC*. This type of cooperation has often been seen from a rather idealistic perspective, but at first sight it would appear to suffer from the same limitations and to confront the same challenges as other forms of development cooperation. SSC has often been defined in ideological terms and in contrast with traditional bilateral North-South cooperation, whereas in fact it is an

BOX 6.1. A Broad Range of Experiences in SSC and Triangular Cooperation

In March 2009 the Colombian government, under the framework Working Group on Aid Effectiveness, proposed the creation of an initiative to reduce the information gap in SSC experiences. The response to the call to document experiences was launched in November 2009 and had a significant impact, as 110 case studies were presented in the High-Level Meeting for South-South Cooperation and Capacity Development (Bogota, March 24–25, 2010). The report points to various trends based on an analysis of the case studies:

The principles of cooperation effectiveness are broadly shared in the experiences registered. Most cases explicitly refer to the principles of the Paris Declaration on aid effectiveness, as there is the idea that SSC is an instrument that has advantages over other forms of development cooperation. For example, the report says SSC is characterized by greater confidence between peers, respect for countries' internal processes, the design of projects generated by common interests and specific demands, the use of regional cooperation mechanisms that help scaling, and by relatively lower technical cooperation costs compared to other forms of cooperation.

Importance of making the experiences known. There are still no specific definitions on what constitutes SSC, nor are there standard ways of quantifying financial contributions or contributions in kind. However, the number of cases compiled in only the six months following the call suggests that there are many more SSC experiences that should be registered and made known.

The range of subjects, experiences, and modalities is very broad. SSC is characterized by the use of a broad range of instruments such as triangular cooperation, establishment of financial facilities for the exchange of experiences (mainly through the offers of bilateral and multilateral donors), exchange of experts, establishment of missions for technical cooperation, etc.

Regional platforms are very important. SSC is characterized by having a strong regional emphasis; subregional and regional banks, regional cooperation bodies, and framework agreements play a key role in cooperation between developing countries.

Source: Task-Team on South-South Cooperation (2010), Boosting South-South cooperation in the context of aid effectiveness: Telling the story of partners involved in more than 110 cases of South-South and triangular cooperation, preliminary draft. The experiences are posted on: www.south-south.info

additional mechanism for solving specific problems that countries can use according to their specific interests.

RESOURCE MOBILIZATION FOR

SOUTH-SOUTH COOPERATION

Developing countries are increasing the level of resources they allocate to SSC. Although no precise and consistent data are available, estimates from ECOSOC (2009) and The Reality of Aid (2010) suggest that ODA between countries in the South has increased from a range of US$9.5–12.1 billion in 2006 to US$12.0–13.9 billion in 2008. This is equivalent to between 9.9 and 11.4 percent of the contribution in ODA of the members of OECD/DAC in 2008. The financial resources assigned to SSC show a high level of concentration: the three main donors (Saudi Arabia, Venezuela, and China) provide about 72 percent of SSC funds, and more than 90 percent corresponds to the seven main contributors, which in addition to those already mentioned include Turkey, South Korea, India, and Taiwan (see Table 6.4). Nevertheless, a recent study seeking to integrate a variety of sources of information about international cooperation flows similar to ODA from developing countries, including SSC flows, concluded that most of these figures are biased regarding their definitions and scope. Therefore, it is necessary that these new donors become more transparent, and that

Table 6.4 Selected South-South ODA Flows (US$ Million, 2008)

Country	Amount	% GDP	% Total SSC
Saudi Arabia[c]	5,564	1.5[a]	40.0
Venezuela[a]	1,166–>2,500	0.71–1.52	18.0
China[a]	1,500–2,000	0.06–0.08	14.0
South Korea[c]	802	0.09	5.8
Turkey[c]	780	0.11	5.6
India[b]	568.6	0.05	4.1
Taiwan[c]	435	0.11	3.1
Brazil[a]	356	0.04	2.6
Other Countries	900–910	—	6.4
Total	**12,076–13,915.9**		

Notes: GDP data used are those for 2007; [a]ECOSOC, Background Study for the Development Cooperation Forum: Trends in South-South and Triangular Development Cooperation, April 2008—table 2; [b]Indian Ministry of External Affairs Annual Report 2008–2009—appendix VII; [c]OECD/DAC (2009), table 33 (Statistical Annex of the 2010 Development Cooperation Report).

Source: The Reality of Aid (2010: 6).

their cooperation programs harmonize their definitions to allow for comparisons and identification of the modalities offered (Prada et al., 2010).

One set of cooperation mechanisms is used within the type A countries, those with high domestic and external resource mobilization capacity, as we described previously. They cooperate in a "horizontal" way for three main aims: (1) to learn and exchange experiences; (2) to increase their negotiating capacity at the international and global levels; and (3) to join efforts to cooperate with less developed countries. For example, the group of BASIC countries (Brazil, South Africa, India, and China)[25] is committed to fostering two-way negotiation mechanisms within the United Nations Framework Convention on Climate Change. Another example is the IBSA (India, Brazil, and South Africa) group of countries, which work through a trilateral cooperation alliance established in June 2003 via the Brasilia Declaration, and which aim to make their voices heard on global issues and to create links in various cooperation areas with less developed countries.[26]

A second set of cooperation mechanisms is between type A countries and those of the other three categories, whose capacities for external and domestic resource mobilization are lower. China has increased its cooperation as it has grown economically. Until 2008, China had provided aid to more than 160 countries around the world in various sectors and modalities, including the following: (1) projects in infrastructure, industry, agriculture, transport, telecommunications, education, health, and other areas; (2) exchange of experts for technical assistance, as has been the case with the health sector, where more than 20,000 doctors were sent to sixty-five countries; (3) financing through donations, credit lines, and concessional loans, such as the US$19 billion granted by Eximbank of China to restore and construct infrastructure networks in various African countries; (4) debt relief, for example, through the unilateral cancellation of US$10 billion in debt with African countries in 2003; (5) special tariff reductions, as in the case of imports from at least twenty-nine of the least-developed African countries; (6) development funds to promote Chinese investment in other countries, for example, the fund approved in 2007 by the Chinese State Council, being US$5 billion, to be administered by the China Development Bank and aimed at providing capital for Chinese companies committed to development, investment, and economic and commercial activities in Africa; and (7) foreign direct investment, particularly in the hydrocarbon and mineral sectors, which has, in recent years, focused on Latin America.[27] Moreover, China may have surpassed the World Bank as a provider of loans to developing countries in 2009 and 2010: the Chinese

Development Bank and the Eximbank alone lent more than US$110 billion, compared to US$100.3 billion from the World Bank (Dyer et al., 2011).

Until 2008, Brazil operated more than 240 SSC projects in areas where it has developed capacities, such as agriculture, biofuels, education, health (mainly in the fight against HIV/AIDS), support for elections (e-voting), urban development, information technologies (e-government), trade negotiations, and sports. Brazilian aid is characterized mainly by adapting its successful experiences to other zones with similar social conditions, usually by providing experts, technical cooperation grants and internships, and equipment (Federated Republic of Brazil, 2008). Some of the main motivations for Brazilian cooperation are to strengthen or open new markets for its products, services, and investments; to preserve national interests in countries where they could be threatened; and to consolidate Brazil's international prestige and thus achieve greater power in negotiations on international issues.[28] Nevertheless, figures on the actual size of its international cooperation program differ between sources, but could reach US$4 billion, including its contributions to United Nations programs (US$300 million to the World Food Program), its bilateral grant to Haiti (US$350 million), and its programs and bilateral loans through its national development agency and bilateral loans through the Brazilian Development Bank.[29]

India has established a broad network of support for African countries. The Pan-Africa E-Network Project for Medical Services, in which India has planned to finance US$125 million, helps fifty-three countries in the African Union. This electronic network allows India to connect via satellite with African countries and transfer knowledge through medical teleconferences and teleconsultations.

A third set of SSC initiatives takes place between countries with relatively lower capacities to mobilize external and domestic resources (categories B, C, and D). These exchanges focus on mutual learning and training, technological transfer to reduce gaps, progressing toward joint objectives, and achieving minimum conditions for development, particularly in compliance with the Millennium Development Goals. An example is the project between Cuba and Egypt for the joint manufacture of vaccines, which involves about US$1.8 million and consists of technical cooperation between specialist vaccine producers Finlay and Heber Biotec in Cuba and the Egyptian national vaccine producer, Vacsera.[30] Another example is a joint project between the Republic of Niger and the Argentine Republic to develop capacities in the remote provision of health services, learning to train human resources and to organize mutual health societies.[31]

THE ROLE OF SOUTH-SOUTH COOPERATION IN
REGIONAL INTEGRATION PROCESSES

Regional and subregional integration initiatives between developing countries in Africa, Latin America, and Asia have multiplied in recent years. These alliances between neighboring countries (or those belonging to the same region) have gained importance, largely through intensified trade and monetary exchanges. Despite not having fully complied with their broadest goals for integration, they have become platforms for SSC and triangular cooperation, for political and strategic reasons, and also due to the need to provide regional public goods.

In Africa the main areas of progress in regional cooperation and integration have been through monetary and exchange rate policies. It is considered that with the two monetary unions, the Central African Economic and Monetary Community and the West African Economic and Monetary Union, stabilization of the exchange rate within the Common Monetary Area, and the future monetary union of the Southern Africa Development Community and the West African Monetary Zone, Africa has taken the lead in the developed world in terms of regional monetary integration (Metzger 2008:26).

In parallel, other cooperation programs are being developed, such as the Pan-African Infrastructure Development Fund, initially between Ghana, South Africa, and Tunisia (to Kenya and, in the future, to all African countries). The mechanism consists in mobilizing resources from private investors and pension funds in member countries. The program was launched in 2007 with an investment horizon of fifteen years and aims to mobilize US$1 billion, of which US$625 million has already been raised.[32]

Starting in 1960 there have been various attempts to create subregional areas for economic, social, and institutional integration in Latin America. The most important have been the Andean Community, Mercosur, the Central American Common Market, and the Latin American Integration Association. To these were later added organizations such as the Bolivarian Alliance for the Peoples of Our America (ALBA), Petrocaribe, the Union of South American Nations, and, finally, the Community of Latin American and Caribbean States.

ALBA and Petrocaribe, two Venezuelan initiatives, have attained particular importance in the region. ALBA has launched joint initiatives through projects called "grandnational" in finance, education, health, infrastructure, science and technology, food, minerals, telecommunications, infrastructure, culture, and fair trade, among others. In addition, there are plans for creating a common monetary zone with ALBA member countries, through the establishment of a common account unit called the SUCRE and a regional clearinghouse system. Petrocaribe was created as a "body to facilitate energy policies and plans, aimed at integrating the Caribbean peoples through the sovereign use of natural energy resources for the direct benefit of its peoples."[33] Since its creation on June 29, 2005, eighteen countries have joined the organization.[34] According to the agreement, the amount corresponding to the difference between the cost of concessional finance and market rates will be used to implement development projects, set up joint companies between Petróleos de Venezuela and state oil companies with eight of the member countries, and develop an infrastructure for fuel refining, storage, and delivery.[35]

Regional integration and cooperation initiatives in Asia have precedents that go back more than two or three decades, but they have gained ground since the 1997–1998 financial crisis. Among them are free trade and economic integration agreements such as the Association of Southeast Asian Nations (ASEAN), the South Asian Association for Regional Cooperation, and the Bay of Bengal initiative for Multisectoral Technical and Economic Cooperation. Kumar (2007) identified the following priorities for regional integration and cooperation in Asia: (1) financial and monetary cooperation, to take advantage of the bulk of international reserves in the region for development and mutual benefit (notable is the recent signing of the agreement establishing the Asian Monetary Fund within the ASEAN); (2) cooperation on energy security, to ensure sustainability and energy security in the region and to demand energy management, taking environmental issues into account; (3) cooperation in key technologies to close the digital gap and to address health and nutrition problems through the use of biotechnologies; and (4) cooperation in order to improve global governance, promote peace and security, and achieve greater participation and influence in international institutions.

TRIANGULAR COOPERATION

Triangular cooperation refers to the set of instruments linking South-South cooperation with other actors such as donor countries in the North, international bodies, and private for-profit or non-profit institutions in developed countries. There are many different possibilities for association, so the concept is fairly diffuse. Originally, triangular cooperation consisted of support given by a cooperating source, generally from a developed country (although it extended to international organizations as well), so that two countries with similar levels of development could carry out technical cooperation and knowledge transfer activities. However, the diversity of developing countries, along with new cooperation sources, has allowed the combinations of association for triangular cooperation to increase considerably.

A major example is the *program for the exchange of experience on development between China and Africa*. This initiative is financed by the Chinese government with the support of the World Bank and the International Poverty Reduction Centre in China, whose aim is to transfer the Chinese experience in poverty reduction to African countries. Other examples of triangular cooperation include the association between Chile and OECD donors to support the creation of capacities in forest management in Nicaragua; Brazil and its program to support and provide aid to Portuguese-speaking Africa, financed by several multilateral institutions; and the South African program to train police forces in Rwanda and the Congo Republic, supported by Sweden and Japan, respectively (ECOSOC, 2009).

Another modality is the support for the development of regional public goods (RPGs), which links triangular cooperation with processes of regional integration. Since 2004 the Inter-American Development Bank (IDB), through its program to promote regional public goods, has boosted more than sixty projects to supply RPGs in Latin America and the Caribbean. The program offers non-reimbursable resources of up to US$10 million per year so that groups of at least three countries can generate RPGs in a sustainable fashion.[36] The premise behind the IDB to support RPGs is that many shared opportunities or problems between the countries in the region may be used or resolved more effectively within the regional sphere through international cooperation. However, the generation of RPGs is usually not paid sufficient attention, primarily due to the limitations and difficulties in obtaining financial and institutional support for joint regional efforts. The IDB acts as a supplier for seed capital, assuming the fixed costs of creating institutions, establishing coordination mechanisms, and designing implementation strategies that will lead to the production of these goods.

Another experience of triangular cooperation in knowledge transfer is the program for promoting social protection between Chile and the Caribbean with the support of the OAS. The Puente en el Caribe program aims to strengthen the social protection strategies in CARICOM countries through activities for capacity building, the transfer of knowledge, and lessons learned in the Puente de Chile program.[37] An interesting case of participation by the private sector in the triangulation of cooperation is the one of the investment of US$10 billion over the next ten years granted by the Bill and Melinda Gates Foundation to help the research, development, and distribution of vaccines in the poorest countries. It involves research institutions in developed and developing countries in various parts of the world.[38] In another example of participation by private foundations in triangular cooperation, but to a much lesser extent, the Rockefeller Foundation provides financial and logistical support for representatives of developing countries to meet within the scope of their own projects in any of their facilities around the world.

SOME PENDING ISSUES IN SOUTH-SOUTH COOPERATION

The main challenge when dealing with the policies and challenges for SSC is knowing what type of financial flows, modalities, and instruments are involved. Estimations of the volume of financial resources associated with SSC have focused on quantifying the direct flows between countries. However, there is a set of financial flows that could be considered in a broader view of SSC. These include (1) contributions to multilateral institutions, particularly subregional development banks, which can be seen as SSC mechanisms, as their partners are mainly developing countries; (2) interest payments made by developing countries to multilateral institutions, as these are a component of their net income and thus serve to finance items such as concessional windows to support the poorest countries; (3) financial support for capital increases in financial institutions (as has been the case of contributions by emerging and developing countries to the International Development Association) and to increase the capital of the IDB, among others; (4) the regional mechanisms designed to support the balance of payments, as in the case of the Latin American Reserve Fund and the recently created Asian Monetary Fund; (5) mechanisms supporting trade, such as export credits or financial facilities for foreign-exchange swaps for intraregional trade (CEPAL, 2009b:122); (6) the acquisition of sovereign bonds and securities from other developing countries through international capital markets, as in the case of the purchase by Venezuela of bonds from Ecuador and Argentina in 2006; and (7) the quantification of the contributions in kind for technical cooperation, which includes the time of experts, volunteers, missions, and the value of counterparties for investment projects, among other aspects.

Despite the fact that the amounts are growing in importance within the context of international cooperation, it has been pointed out (SEGIB, 2008; TT-SSC, 2010) that the value of SSC resides in its intrinsic characteristics and not in the amount of financial resources mobilized. First, SSC helps solve specific problems, for which it can use the knowledge and experience acquired in resolving similar problems in analogous situations. For example, with a modest investment (seed capital) and by promoting collective action, the IDB's non-reimbursable cooperation program for regional public goods has helped Latin American countries mobilize additional resources for specific South-South cooperation projects (Bocalandro and Villa, 2009).

Second, SSC can be a complement for other sources of cooperation and extend the range of options for financing, although it is not a panacea. The financial crisis has made the potential of emerging donor countries and South-South cooperation to channel resources and cooperation a subject of keen debate, particularly given the greater selectivity of the ODA provided by traditional donors and its probable reduction in the future. However, it is important to stress that South-South cooperation faces the same problems that have reduced the effectiveness of other methods of cooperation. For example, China requires 70 percent of its cooperation to be channeled through the country's own companies (Burgess, 2009). In addition, in some cases there are conditionalities, lack of transparency in selection criteria, an emphasis on concessional loans rather than on donations (e.g., Petrocaribe in Venezuela and China's concessional aid), little emphasis on evaluation and monitoring, and a reluctance to work with other donors (Reality of Aid, 2010; Ellis, 2009; Lederman et al., 2009).

Third, despite the obvious benefits in terms of pertinence and applicability in similar contexts, the possibility of replicating or extending the scale of South-South cooperation is limited by administrative capacity and aid management constraints. Unlike the case of official aid from OECD countries (which have standards for operations, information systems, mechanisms for evaluation and monitoring, and offices in recipient countries, among other features of an institutionalized system), SSC programs in general do not yet have the administrative resources to emulate these forms of cooperation. Only some countries with a high capacity to mobilize resources, such as China, India, Brazil, South Africa, and Venezuela, have established special administrative structures, usually associated with their ministries for foreign affairs and of trade, to support cooperation programs. For this reason, establishing regional cooperation mechanisms could be important for replicating, extending, and consolidating SSC programs and experiences.

In this context, triangular cooperation is a mechanism that could promote SSC and is one of the main means for extending its impact. For example, the work through networks of institutions of developing countries, supported by donations from developed countries, is a very effective mechanism for joint cooperation and learning. One instance is that of the Canadian International Development Research Centre, which has forty years of experience in financing networks of researchers in developing countries, often with the involvement of other donors, and is a classic example of triangular cooperation and SSC.[39] In addition, numerous experiences suggest that it is possible to make progress toward more effective cooperation through knowledge transfer and joint work with multiple donors, in partnership with international agencies that have the capacity to channel resources and implement projects. As South-South relations become more firmly established on the basis of the countries' specific interests, it is most likely that triangular cooperation initiatives will multiply (TT-SSC, 2010; Betancourt and Schulz, 2009).

In addition, considering that in the medium term ODA flows from developed countries to developing countries may decline, and that it is highly probable that they will continue to focus increasingly on low-income countries, flows toward middle-income countries will diminish. In order to maintain the relevance and effectiveness of development cooperation for a broader range of developing countries, it will be necessary to link other sources of finance, such as FDI, capital markets, philanthropic donations, remittances, and the creation of markets with official development cooperation flows (Sagasti, 2006). Some lines of action to respond to the challenges pending for South-South cooperation include the following:

- Strengthen the institutional framework for South-South development cooperation and finance, primarily through improvements in the capacity for designing, implementing, and monitoring cooperation programs and projects; through the systematization of instruments and mechanisms to ensure the control, recording, and transparency of information; and through establishing targets and common visions for the evolution of SSC initiatives. In addition, an international forum should be set up to exchange experiences and coordinate the activities of organizations involved in financing SSC at a subregional level.

• Promote synergies between the different types of countries by taking into account that, apart from strengthening South-South relations and taking advantage of the opportunities provided by the horizontal links in equal conditions, triangulation has to be strengthened with international organizations and with developed country agencies. Moreover, the diversity of developing countries has to be taken into account in promoting practices of solidarity and narrowing the gap between these countries, particularly between middle-income and less developed nations.

• Continue accumulating and sharing experiences between countries in the South by systematizing activities, transferring and developing joint capacities, training human resources, systematizing cooperation, financing instruments that have proved successful, carrying out independent evaluations that can be shared by the different actors, and strengthening the systems for recording compliance with quantitative and qualitative targets for SSC.

CORPORATE SOCIAL RESPONSIBILITY

The corporate sector, or private for-profit sector, has various ways of supporting development apart from its strictly business activities and the use of economic return criteria for the investment projects in which it engages. First, private corporations and foreign investors contribute to development by acting in accordance with the legal frameworks of the countries in which they operate (paying taxes, respecting labor and environmental regulations, acting in a transparent way, etc.), investing in productive and service activities, and generating wealth.[40] The amount of resources not contributed by companies that do not behave properly could be highly significant. For example, Hollingshead (2010) calculated that the tax losses in developing countries resulting from price manipulation in legal global trade documents (reporting higher prices in imports or lower prices in exports) may have reached between US$98 and US$106 billion a year, or 4.4 percent of the total tax revenues for the period 2002–2006. This figure is comparable to the total of ODA.

In addition, private companies frequently self-impose rules of behavior as part of their efforts to project a favorable corporate image, thus allowing them to better manage the impact of their activities. There are numerous reasons for this type of behavior: adherence to international regulations, tacit pressure from shareholders and investors in the countries of origin, access to finance from socially responsible mutual funds, or adherence to codes of conduct promoted by unions and national and international associations.[41] A special case among the reasons for self-imposed rules is to obtain a local "social license," required in some cases by national laws and regulations but sometimes voluntarily sought as a way to minimize the possible negative social impacts of investments and to generate a less conflictive environment in the company's relations with local communities. This is particularly important in the case of investment in the exploitation of natural resources when local communities, especially indigenous peoples and non-integrated populations, are present. The social license gives populations the "right to veto" the outcome of the investment. In principle, this increases their capacity to negotiate and obtain benefits from private investments.

Third, private companies are becoming increasingly involved in activities that are directly aimed at improving the living conditions of the populations in their areas of influence. This is done through actions that include the provision of technical assistance and management, provision of company staff time, and donations in kind and in cash. Through these activities the companies aim to improve their image, create a favorable environment for their operations, and increase the welfare of communities in areas where they operate. One example, controversial in many aspects, is that of multinational corporations involved in resource extraction in Peru (Box 6.2). The Peruvian government has also launched a "tax for public works" program by which some companies can obtain tax exemptions in exchange for building infrastructure in their zones of influence. The idea is to boost local economies, generate employment, and strengthen the economic links between the company and people in the areas in which it operates.

CSR practices transcend the traditional concept of public relations and involve more complex and sophisticated motivations that are linked to the role and projection of private business activities. In addition, they are giving rise to new alliances between the private sector, national and local governments, and bilateral cooperation agencies in joint interventions in areas where the companies operate, particularly in the case of natural resources and energy. This is giving rise to the possibility of linking CSR

Box 6.2. The Mining Program for Solidarity with the People

The Mining Program for Solidarity with the People has been in operation for four years in Peru, where mineral metal exports account for 6
percent of national GDP, 56 percent of foreign currency from exports,
and 15 percent of foreign direct investment. In August 2006 a group
of companies in the mining industry agreed with the Peruvian government to contribute 3.7 percent of their profits on a voluntary basis
to local development programs over a period of five years. Although
it is subject to changes in the international prices of minerals such as
copper, gold, silver, and zinc, this agreement is estimated to contribute an annual average of US$150 to US$200 million, around 0.1 percent
of GDP and about 0.5 percent of the government's national budget. This was largely done to prevent the government from implementing a windfall profits tax that was being discussed by Parliament as a result of the major increase in mineral prices between 2004
and 2007.

The government indicated the precise proportions to be invested
in strategic programs such as nutrition, health, and education, and
provided counterpart funds to align these resources to the existing
strategic and territorial plans, establishing objectives, milestones, targets, indicators, and baselines to ensure a quick and effective management of resources. According to the Ministry of Energy and Mining of the fund payments, as of December 2009, 37 percent of the
programmed resources had been executed, which is more than was
initially anticipated. However, the ministry itself indicates that since
there are no data on the beneficiaries of the nutrition or literacy programs, it has not been possible to measure the real impact of this
voluntary contribution, and still less to register the specific achievements expressed as improvements in the quality of life of the populations. Another limitation has been that the regions benefiting are
limited to the scope of action of the companies that exploit mining
resources, and are not necessarily located in the poorest regions:
eighteen of the twenty-six regions in the country benefit from this
fund, but only nine of them concentrate 90 percent of the resources
available.

Source: Chávez Granadino (2010).

initiatives with efforts by the public sector and bilateral and multilateral cooperation agencies. In this way, CSR opens up the possibility of mobilizing additional resources (technical, financial, materials, and equipment, among others) for development projects and programs, also making it possible to experiment and innovate with new institutional arrangements.

The acceptance and the voluntary implementation of CSR policies by corporations involve an explicit or implicit cost-benefit calculation. The CSR option may respond to an ethical perspective of economic activity or to practical considerations of business profit. Nevertheless, the gradual articulation of international and global initiatives for monitoring the activities of transnational companies, particularly with natural resources, generates incentives that tend to focus companies toward increasingly responsible behavior (see Box 6.3 for an example in Indonesia).

Many of the CSR initiatives are implemented as associations or agreements with public or private non-profit organizations and involve the exchange of intangible goods or services or contributions in kind.[42] This makes it difficult to clearly distinguish the amount of time, money, or human resources invested by the companies and their partners in executing CSR programs and projects. For example, information available for Costa Rica based on the global CSR survey of executive chairmen of 1,000 companies in 2003 indicates that the main forms of CSR investment are carried out in the following ways (in decreasing order of investment amount): support in kind for social projects; donations to educational institutions; increasing the skills of staff in CSR subjects; support for environmental projects; sponsorship of CSR activities; contributions to community associations; the development of community projects; and, finally, donations to NGOs. Most of these activities involve amounts under US$10,000, and only 3–15 percent of the contributions in these categories represent more than US$40,000, on average.[43]

As indicated earlier, one way of involving the private sector in development programs is through accepting standards of behavior for the implementation of CSR programs. Once again, multilateral banks have facilitated this process. For example, the Performance Standards of the World Bank International Finance Corporation (IFC) condition loans to the private sector into compliance with social and environmental standards prior to the evaluation of an investment. Some major investment projects have established amounts that must be destined for CSR programs. These average, and at times exceed, 1 percent of total investment, and some international corporations have established these ratios as the minimum acceptable

Box 6.3. The APRIL Operation in Indonesia

Indonesia's major economic development has been accompanied by significant processes of deforestation and soil deterioration. The country is considered one of the biggest emitters of greenhouse gases in the world. Population pressure, illegal logging, and slash-and-burn agriculture have devastated more than half of the forests in the country during recent decades. In this context, the presence of one of the biggest global pulp and wood products companies, Asia Pacific Resources International Limited (APRIL), may be considered high risk. Indeed, this company was harshly criticized by environmental organizations in recent years due to inappropriate practices of forest extraction.

However, in the last ten years APRIL has been implementing a strategy of sustainable forest management. As a result, it has gained the recognition and cooperation of many of its former critics, such as the World Wildlife Fund for Nature (WWFN). It is also the only company in Indonesia that forms part of the World Business Council for Sustainable Development (WBCSD). The zone of APRIL's concession in the Kampar peninsula sustains more than 100,000 people who live in hundreds of diverse villages in an area that until a few years ago was separated from the country's service and communications infrastructure.

Starting in 1999 APRIL began a strategy of empowering local capacities and capital to achieve sustainable forms of life, as well as constructing transport and service infrastructure to act as a catalyst for community development. From 2002 to the present day, the Integrated Crop Systems program has trained more than four thousand families, organized by village groups. They have improved their skills for horticulture, livestock farming, fish farming, composting, recycling of waste, and food processing, which enable subsistence activities with a low impact on the forest ecosystem. Since 2001 the company's training and skills-development initiatives began to boost the creation of small companies among those local people with the most skills, with various banks in the country giving advice and financial support. The company's most ambitious initiative, which has had a great impact on the control of local deforestation, is the community tree-pulp cultivation plan, under which the local communities associate with APRIL to develop their traditional lands with acacia plantations. The company

provides financial support, seeds, and fertilizers, and supports the local community to maintain their plantations. After six years, the wood
pulp is harvested and the people receive a 40 percent participation of
the income from the industrial processing of the forests under their
management. By converting these people into partners in the operation, the company takes advantage of the skills of traditional loggers,
who operate with licenses and permits and high profit levels and who
have abandoned illegal logging, which now represent a threat to them.

In coordination with the government, the company has helped
improve access roads, mobile health services, educational infrastructure, and access to electrical energy. This is leading to a quicker integration of the territory and the replacement of the subsistence economies in the area. Also in coordination with the government and
NGOs, the company is boosting a project to create a ring of acacia
forests as an environmental buffer zone that can help stabilize the
sustainable management of forests in the Kampar peninsula. As part
of its sustainable development plans for the coming years, the company expects that the funds resulting from the program of reducing
emissions from deforestation and degradation (REDD) may be focused
on local populations and thus complement the income generated by
the company's strategy of association.

Sources: Wootliff (2009); APRIL (2007); www.aprilasia.com.

for their social investment processes. Under the Equator Principles, signed
in 2003, ten banks from seven countries use the IFC social and environmental policies and guidelines to evaluate responsible investment in projects of more than US$50 million. Currently, twenty-six international
banks require this kind of evaluation. In all, they represent more than 60
percent of available finance for large private projects globally.

The lack of transparency and reporting standards makes it very difficult to ascertain the real size, impact, and effectiveness of CSR considered
within a broader framework of development cooperation initiatives. Many
private companies are reticent when it comes to providing information on
their CSR activities and coordinating their activities with public institutions or civil society (Porter and Kramer, 2008). In addition, it is not possible to estimate the real capacity of CSR to mobilize additional development resources. For example, companies in the United States have reported

that they contribute US$6.8 billion for aid programs, while other OECD countries generated US$12.2 billion in 2008, although the latter figure also includes private donations from individuals (Hudson Institute, 2009).

FINAL COMMENTS

The group of institutions that form part of what can be denominated the "international system of development finance and cooperation" is being transformed rapidly, particularly through the entry of new actors and through innovations in the modalities of cooperation and financial instruments. This makes it necessary to reexamine the justifications supporting the system, the motivations of the actors involved in it, the modalities and instruments used, and the ways in which the use of financing and international cooperation is conducted in recipient countries. The change and turbulence present at the start of the twenty-first century offer a window of opportunity for making progress toward an international system for financing and cooperation that leads to fairer, more equitable, more efficient, and more effective development.

The new actors in development financing and cooperation can help mobilize additional resources, allow a diversification of sources of finance, generate additional capacities, and increase pressure for the innovation and implementation of institutional reforms.

Even as such new actors enter the scene, new issues are appearing, many of them linked to the provision of regional and global public goods, which require joint action in the international field and which exercise pressure on the sources of official finance. Among them are mitigation of and adaptation to climate change, prevention and control of pandemics, preservation of financial stability, conservation of biodiversity, prevention of violent conflicts, response to humanitarian disasters, financial regulation, and the struggles against drug trafficking, money laundering, and international terrorism. Although the multiplication of actors, sources of finance, and modalities may generate instability and uncertainty in the development financing and cooperation system, it may also help in the joint efforts to confront the challenges that arise in these areas in the medium and long term.

It is thus necessary to adopt an integrated vision for the reform of the system, to establish new spaces for coordination between new and traditional actors, to jointly adopt new rules for the system, to create mechanisms for collective action, and to gradually advance toward a comprehensive development finance and cooperation system. Although framework agreements have been adopted to improve the effectiveness of aid, such as the principles of the Paris Declaration and the Accra Agenda for Action, these involve only a small portion of the wide range of institutions that actively participate in development finance and cooperation.

All this makes necessary a reexamination of the motivations behind international cooperation, reviewing the range of financial instruments for channeling flows to developing countries and explicitly taking into account the capacity of the various groups of developing countries for the mobilization of domestic and external resources.

However, it is important to stress that, despite the influence acquired by new actors in the changing context of the international development finance system, newcomers to the field of international cooperation, including private-sector and SSC donors, are not yet in a position to replace the traditional donors in financial terms. Their main contribution is linked to their capacity to innovate, to the synergies that they can create in conjunction with traditional donors, to their capacity to generate additional cooperation resources and instruments, and to their capacity to exercise pressure to generate institutional changes that can increase the effectiveness of the international system of development cooperation.

The financial crisis has significantly affected the capacity of new private-sector donors to mobilize development resources. Both the assets of the main foundations and corporate resources available for CSR activities have suffered significantly in recent years; still, there is no evidence that these effects will be permanent, as the major corporations had already begun to recover their sales and improve their financial situations by the first quarter of 2010. In addition, the capacity of individual donors and consumers to mobilize resources does not appear to have been significantly affected, as the results of recent humanitarian aid campaigns attest.

Based on these considerations, we identify some of the following initiatives that can reinforce the positive impact of new actors in the international cooperation scene:

• Some of the issues dealt with in this chapter are backed up by fragmentary information, not yet standardized, and efforts to gather and process data are only just beginning to transition from the academic world to the field of public policy. Thus it is necessary to support efforts for the

systematic monitoring of the changing context of international cooperation through specialized studies, the compilation of data and statistics on
new actors and financial instruments, and the preparation of case studies
that provide a more detailed understanding of actual conditions in the
field.[44]

• The institutions of the international system for development cooperation suffer various limitations to the effective incorporation of the approaches and activities of new actors. For this reason it would be useful
to establish a broad forum, with the participation of diverse actors, to exchange experiences and knowledge on new trends and features in the
system of development finance and cooperation, as well as to share the
responses currently being organized by the various providers and recipients of finance and cooperation. For example, the Accra Agenda for Action, which mentions the importance and potential of SSC, includes some
issues that should be on the agenda of a new financial architecture. Moreover, various countries linked to SSC activities have expressed doubts about
the OECD/DAC as the best forum for coordinating public policies for
these new subjects and actors in the structure of development finance.

• In order to realize the potential contribution of new private-sector
actors, it is necessary to design and employ a broader set of instruments and
policies. Many of these would combine public, private, and international
initiatives, such as guarantees for investment, the creation and strengthening of domestic markets, trust funds administered by multilateral bodies, public-private associations, and the issuance of bonds in domestic
capital markets. There should be no contradiction or substitution in the
mobilization of private and public resources: the two should complement
and reinforce each other, both at the domestic and international levels.

• Before the financial crisis, a trend already existed to guide ODA toward the poorest countries, as emerging and middle-income countries
gradually gained access to private sources of finance and international
capital markets. Among the latter, there are various successful cases of
"gradation," in the sense of gradual progress toward forms of finance
that depend less on ODA and international bodies, but without abandoning these sources altogether (China, the Korean Republic, Vietnam,
and Peru, among others). The challenge consists in learning from experience and designing mechanisms that allow developing economies to
move freely toward the use of a more extensive and varied range of financial instruments and modalities of cooperation.

• SSC is becoming the new fashionable subject in discussions around reform of the international development cooperation system.[45] However, SSC has a long way to go before becoming an effective instrument to significantly extend flows of international development aid without incurring North-South cooperation practices that have been widely criticized by recipient countries. Therefore, SSC should be expanded and strengthened through the exchange of experiences, through the creation of funds to cover the incremental costs of cooperation, and through the involvement of developed countries in SSC via triangular cooperation.

APPENDICES

APPENDIX 1

Table 6.A1 List of Financial Instruments by Functional Categories and Actors Offering Them

		Financial Instruments
Type	Subtype	Specific Instruments (examples)
Loans	Projects/programs	
	Mixed with donation to reduce interest	IBRD-IDA: blended loan
	Microfinance	Facility: Apex Fund
	Contingent credit lines	Disaster: CAT-DDO (*Catastrophe deferred drawdown option*)
		Liquidity: IMF ESF, FLAR
		General: Countercyclical DDO
		Sovereign lending
	Concessional loans	
	Trade financing/export credits	US OPIC, UK Export Credit Department
	Multidonors: Rescue programs	
Donations	Result based	Cash on delivery, output-based aid, result-based aid
		Millennium Challenge Corporation
	Conditioned transfers	
	Budget support	EU MDG Contract
		Global Fund, IDA Performance based
	Private donations	Philanthropy, CSR, individuals, pro bono
	Project/programs/preinvestments	
	Technical cooperation	
Bonds	Sovereign, MDB, corporate	
	Bonds indexed against various risks	Carbon, GDP, commodity prices, inflation
		For catastrophes
	Other	Diaspora bonds
	Social criterion	Green bonds
Foreign Direct Investment (FDI)	Includes incentives, as well as modalities (acquisitions, additional investment, investment in company securities)	
Remittances	For consumption, social investment	
Market Creation/ Support	Purchase agreement by contract	AccessRH, PG4Health
		Combat malaria
	Buyout	Patent purchase
	Auction/sale of emission permits	CERs, limits for carbon emission
	Bonds for the domestic capital market	

Actors									
Bilateral		Multilateral				Private Sector			
DAC	Other	United Nations	World Bank, RDBs	IMF/Regional	SRDBs	For-Profit	Non-Profit	Capital Markets	Global
X	X		X	X	X	X		X	
X	X		X	X	X		X		
X	X		X		X	X	X		
			X						
				X					
X	X		X						
X	X		X		X				
X	X		X	X	X				
X	X				X				
X	X		X	X	X				
X		X	X						
X									
X	X		X		X				
X									
X	X		X		X				
						X	X		
X	X	X	X	X	X	X	X		
X	X	X	X	X	X	X	X		
	X		X		X	X			
						X		X	
			X		X			X	
								X	
			X						
						X			
							X		
		X					X		
		X					X		
		X					X		
X	X					X		X	
			X		X	X		X	

(*continued*)

Table 6.A1 (continued)

	Financial Instruments	
Type	Subtype	Specific Instruments (examples)
Specific-Purpose Funds/Facilities	Via 2% sales of CERs	Adaptation fund
	Via 1% sales of companies	Digital solidarity tax
	Various contributions	Carbon fund
	Securitization of aid flows	Global FFI, FFI for immunization-FFIm
	Funds/programs/investment	
	Countercyclical funds	
Taxes and Fees	Global taxes	Arms, air tickets, transactions
Payments for Services	User fees, contributions	Environment services
		REDD
Combined Value Instruments	With social criterion	Sustainable invest
	Via consumption	(PRODUCT) RED, Visa green card
	Corporate social responsibility (CSR)	
	Global lotteries for charity	
	Person-to-person donation/loans	Kiva.org, MyC4, Babyloan, Wokai
	Securitization	Microfinance bonds mutual funds
Risk Mitigation/ Management	Provision of insurance	Disasters: Index-based insurance
		Micro-insurance
	Derivatives	CAT swap
		Cool Bonds
	Loans	In local currency
	Securitization	Aid flows
	Guarantees (partial, credit, based on policies, politics, regulatory, among others)	
	Risk investment	Venture funds and securities
	For default	CACs
Cancellation of Debt	Repurchase of debt	Debt Reduction Facility-IDA
		Multilateral Debt Relief Facility
	Debt exchange	Debt-for-nature, Debt2Health
	HIPC initiative	
	Unilateral cancellation of debt	
	Consultative groups	Brady, Paris Club
International Liquidity	FED credit lines—Central Banks	
	Special drawing rights (SDRs)	
	Monetary funds (Asian Monetary Fund)	

			Actors						
Bilateral		Multilateral				Private Sector			
DAC	Other	United Nations	World Bank, RDBs	IMF/Regional	SRDBs	For-Profit	Non-Profit	Capital Markets	Global
								X	
						X			
			X			X		X	
X		X						X	
	X							X	
									X
X	X					X			
X	X					X			
						X		X	
							X		
						X	X		
									X
							X		
			X			X	X		
X			X		X	X		X	
X	X		X		X	X			
			X		X			X	
			X						
X			X		X				
X			X			X		X	
X			X		X	X			
X	X		X		X				
								X	
X			X						
			X	X	X				
X	X		X		X				
X			X	X	X				
X	X		X		X				
X									
X									
				X					
	X			X					

APPENDIX 2

METHODOLOGY FOR ESTIMATING THE INDEX OF DOMESTIC AND EXTERNAL RESOURCE MOBILIZATION

A principal component analysis and factor analysis have been used to calculate the two indexes of resource mobilization (domestic and external).[46] Briefly, the econometric method of the main components allows information from a group of diverse indicators to be integrated through the extraction of their elements in common or *principal components*. These common elements are those that best explain the combined variation of the group of indicators. Thus this method allows the information of various indicators to be "compacted" into a few factors, ideally only one *factor*, that can be used as an index to establish a ranking among a group of countries, in the specific case of this work. This research has used the STATA statistical program to estimate the principal components.

The database used for the analysis has been constructed according to the indicators of internal and external resource mobilization available in the World Bank's *World Development Indicators* and *Global Development Finance* (World Bank, 2009b). The analysis has been carried out with developing countries according to the classification provided by the World Bank.[47] The index was calculated with information for 130 developing countries, but twenty did not have information in any of the indicators, so they were excluded. Of the remaining 110 countries, nearly 80 percent had information for all the indicators in both the internal and external mobilization index; the remaining 20 percent had at least information for one of the indicators in each index. With at least one indicator per index, it is possible to calculate its value. Although this is less precise, it does describe the relative position of these countries.[48]

For reasons of availability of information, particularly for those countries with lower relative levels of development in their statistics, the following indicators were chosen for calculating the two indexes: (1) gross fixed capital formation, domestic credit to the private sector, and gross domestic savings (as a proportion of GDP) for the *index of internal resource mobilization*; and (2) levels of foreign direct investment, volume of exports of goods and services, and net international reserves, all expressed in logarithms to reduce dispersion, for the *index of external resource mobilization*. The figures used for each indicator correspond to the average for the period 2006–2008.[49]

The analysis of principal components is calculated on the basis of the total variance of the series, which is distributed proportionally among its components. This proportion is calculated through the accumulation of the characteristic roots, or *eigenvalues*. This analysis is used to calculate the factors that each of the indexes will represent and to calculate each of the countries in the sample.

Tables 6.A2 and 6.A3 show the criteria for selecting the factors that arise after the analysis of the principal components for each of the groups of indicators of external and domestic mobilization. In the mobilization of external resources (Table 6.A2), it can be observed that only one of two factors presents a characteristic root greater than one, so that a unique index can be calculated for each period. In addition, the accumulated proportion explained for each of the factors indicates that the explanation of the combined variance is fairly high: in the period 2006–2008, it explains 60 percent.

In domestic resource mobilization (Table 6.A3), it can also be seen that only one of the factors presents a characteristic root greater than one. In this case, the accumulated proportion explains 55 percent of the combined variance in the period 2000–2002 and 44 percent in the period 2006–2008.

The next step consists of rotating the results to linearize them and to allow a greater correlation between the factors, so that the values of the factors

Table 6.A2   Extraction of the External Resource Mobilization Factor *(Period 2006–2008)*

Factor Analysis/Correlation			Number of Obs	= 110
Method: Principal-Component Factors			Retained Factors	= 1
Rotation: (Unrotated)			Number of Params	= 3

Factor	Eigenvalue	Difference	Proportion	Cumulative
Factor1	1.78829	0.81305	0.5961	0.5961
Factor2	0.97524	0.73878	0.3251	0.9212
Factor3	0.23647		0.0788	1.0000
LR Test: Independent vs. Saturated: chi2(3) = 95.81			Prob>chi2 = 0.0000	

Table 6.A3   Extraction of the Domestic Resource Mobilization Factor *(Period 2006–2008)*

Factor Analysis/Correlation			Number of Obs	= 108
Method: Principal-Component Factors			Retained Factors	= 1
Rotation: (Unrotated)			Number of Params	= 3

Factor	Eigenvalue	Difference	Proportion	Cumulative
Factor1	1.32577	0.35038	0.4419	0.4419
Factor2	0.97538	0.30996	0.3251	0.7671
Factor3	0.69885	0.0000	0.2329	1.0000
LR Test: Independent vs. Saturated: chi2(3) = 10.85			Prob>chi2 = 0.0126	

Table 6.A4 Values of the Indexes of Resource Mobilization

Country	Index of External Resource Mobilization	Index of Domestic Resource Mobilization
Albania	0.44	0.46
Angola	0.60	0.49
Argentina	0.70	0.50
Armenia	0.40	0.62
Azerbaijan	-	0.70
Bangladesh	0.53	0.50
Belarus	0.54	0.63
Belize	0.26	0.47
Bolivia	0.49	0.40
Bosnia and Herzegovina	0.49	0.33
Botswana	0.52	0.64
Brazil	0.83	0.69
Bulgaria	0.63	0.62
Burundi	0.20	0.12
Cambodia	0.46	0.23
Cameroon	0.46	0.34
Cape Verde	0.28	0.69
Chile	0.69	0.68
China	1.00	1.00
Colombia	0.65	0.49
Congo, Rep.	0.49	0.69
Costa Rica	0.52	0.49
Cote d'Ivoire	0.48	0.22
Djibouti	0.23	0.60
Dominica	0.16	0.58
Dominican Republic	0.50	0.35
Ecuador	0.51	0.46
Egypt, Arab Rep.	0.68	0.47
El Salvador	0.46	0.27
Ethiopia	0.39	0.37
Georgia	0.42	0.44
Ghana	0.46	0.50
Grenada	0.20	0.82
Guatemala	0.51	0.34
Haiti	0.31	0.41
Honduras	0.47	0.53
India	0.84	0.75
Indonesia	0.73	0.56
Jordan	0.54	0.41
Kazakhstan	0.67	0.80
Kenya	0.48	0.37
Kyrgyz Republic	0.39	0.23
Lao PDR	0.31	0.39
Latvia	0.53	0.72
Lebanon	0.61	0.34
Lesotho	0.33	0.20
Macedonia, FYR	0.44	0.34
Malaysia	0.76	0.57
Mali	0.39	0.41

(*continued*)

Table 6.A4   (continued)

Country	Index of External Resource Mobilization	Index of Domestic Resource Mobilization
Mauritius	0.44	0.67
Mexico	0.82	0.60
Moldova	0.40	0.39
Mongolia	0.34	0.54
Morocco	0.63	0.70
Mozambique	0.41	0.35
Nicaragua	0.40	0.59
Pakistan	0.61	0.40
Panama	0.49	0.62
Paraguay	0.47	0.37
Peru	0.65	0.50
Philippines	0.67	0.31
Poland	0.78	0.48
Romania	0.70	0.50
Russian Federation	0.91	0.64
Samoa	0.17	0.05
Senegal	0.41	0.49
Serbia	0.61	0.33
Seychelles	0.24	0.48
Sierra Leone	0.25	0.24
Solomon Islands	0.14	0.04
South Africa	0.69	0.66
Sri Lanka	0.49	0.48
St. Kitts and Nevis	0.20	0.89
St. Lucia	0.25	0.74
Sudan	0.47	0.39
Swaziland	0.37	0.29
Tajikistan	0.31	0.13
Tanzania	0.45	0.29
Thailand	0.76	0.62
Tonga	0.10	0.13
Tunisia	0.57	0.58
Uganda	0.43	0.34
Ukraine	0.69	0.59
Uruguay	0.51	0.38
Vanuatu	0.19	0.21
Venezuela, RB	0.68	0.55
Vietnam	0.64	0.61
Zambia	0.42	0.49

are more consistent and comparable in other cases. By estimating the rotated factor, this factor can be applied to calculate the value of each country and obtain each of the indexes of resource mobilization for the period 2006–2008. The values are shown in Table 6.A4. It is necessary to clarify that in order to present the results in a more intuitive way, the scale has been reduced in the text for two reasons. First, the idea was to exclude those countries with extreme values, particularly those with relatively small values or those whose indicators present high variance in the period 2006–2008. Second, by reducing the scale to [0,1] the results are more easily interpreted and the categories can be better appreciated. China corresponds to the upper level of the scale (1,1) because it has the higher value in both indexes. Moreover, the 0.5 cutoff point to divide the categories is arbitrary and has only been used to allow comparisons between the categories of countries.

NOTES

1. The fall has had a varied effect on the different regions. For example, it has been acute in countries in Eastern Europe and Central Asia, at around 47 percent, or US$221 billion. In sub-Saharan Africa the fall was US$19.5 billion, equivalent to the sum received by the region in official grants for their public budgets.

2. This is the case for the group of emerging economies, which represent 90 percent of these flows. Many of them have been able to mitigate this fall by strengthening their domestic capital markets, but the possibility of greater refinancing problems cannot be ruled out as the effect of temporary stimulus packages implemented in these economies is gradually reduced.

3. The corporate sector had very favorable conditions before 2007, when the average rate for refinancing debt was 6.4 percent. Interest rates increased to 11.5 percent at the end of 2009, and although they had fallen at the end of the first quarter of 2010, conditions are still difficult.

4. There is also evidence that families in developing countries have had to send remittances to members in developed countries as a response to the weak labor market (Lacey, 2009).

5. The fiscal measures to finance stimulus programs in developing countries through debt issues cost 4.4 percent of GDP in 2009, compared to 3 percent in developed countries.

6. These points recommend the following: (1) untie aid, including technical assistance; (2) implement transparency standards on expenditure; (3) publish and disseminate the results of evaluations, including the methodologies, data, and results, and report when these evaluations are not made; (4) progress toward results-oriented programs, for example, "$100 per student who graduates from school," and give national authorities leeway to implement them; (5) create a platform that lets recipient countries hire technical assistance and access evaluations of suppliers; and (6) make aid flows more predictable, probably by outsourcing the work of distributing aid, according to an agreed-upon time frame, to a third party such as a private investment bank.

7. There is an intense debate on the role of new donors that provide loans and donations without conditions, particularly when compounded by the concept of non-interference in the internal affairs of recipient countries (applied by countries

such as Cuba, Venezuela, and China when providing cooperation). In practical terms this kind of intervention could undermine other initiatives such as those encouraging debt sustainability, as has been suggested around the case of concessional loans by China to African countries (Reisen, 2008).

8. However, their assets suffered a significant impact: by September 2009 they were calculated to have incurred losses on the order of US$57 billion in their US$127 billion equity portfolio. In 2007 sovereign wealth funds were estimated to have managed assets of around US$9.7 trillion (Hagan and Johanns, 2009).

9. McGillivray and White (1993) review the various criteria that official donors have used to distribute aid to developing countries, analyzing geopolitical, cultural affinity, and linguistic criteria, among others. Sagasti and Alcalde (1999) extended the analysis of motivations of official actors in providing official development aid. A recent review of these motivations through official aid flows can be found in Hoeffler and Outram (2008).

10. Sagasti et al. (2006) present evidence of this kind of motivation for the Peruvian case.

11. See Alesina and Dollar (2000); Collier and Dollar (2002); Roemer and Llavador (1999).

12. *The Economist*, 2009b.

13. For example, four countries (China, South Korea, Egypt, and Turkey) recently graduated as recipients of concessional loans from the International Development Association (IDA), participated actively in the replenishment of resources in 2007 (IDA-15). A total of forty-five donors pledged to IDA-15; and, with more developing countries becoming contributors, the number of donors pledging to IDA-16—whose replenishment process ended in December 2010—increased to fifty-one. Total available resources increased 18 percent to US$49.3 billion for the period 2011–2014 (World Bank, 2010).

14. The index is calculated for the 110 countries that have sufficient information. About 80 percent of these countries have data for all the indicators, and the remaining 20 percent have less information for some of the indicators in each index. It is possible to calculate the relative position of these countries with at least one indicator for each index, although less precisely.

15. To avoid the effect of atypical years or large variations that could distort the calculation of the index and to give greater stability (lower year-on-year variance), a three-year average was used for each indicator. Using main components allows for estimating numeric values, which are used to rank countries in relation to their capacity for mobilizing resources, and to monitor the indexes over time.

16. The index shows a graduation between countries of high and low domestic and external resource mobilization, and the value 0.5 differentiates two main categories for each index.

17. For example, the Inter-American Development Bank (IDB) program to implement the external pillar of the medium-term action plan for development effectiveness invests in enhancing the capacity of the public sector in areas such as government procurement, national systems of public investment, e-government, and macroeconomic and international cooperation management, among others. The core

idea of this support is that after the intervention, these countries can access other sources, such as regular IDB sources in this case, to complement the implementation of the development effectiveness program.

18. The United Nations Development Programme provided support for a group of countries in sub-Saharan Africa so that risk-rating agencies could draw up a profile and classify these countries, thus enabling them to issue sovereign bonds on the capital markets that could also be traded on secondary markets. These kinds of low-cost interventions create the conditions for these countries to access additional sources of finance.

19. In the meeting between China and Africa in November 2009, China undertook to grant loans at low interest rates worth US$10 billion over the next three years. This came in addition to a commitment for half that amount in 2006. Similarly, Venezuela supports various Caribbean countries with the PetroCaribe program, which provides concessional loans and energy at subsidized prices.

20. The value of the instruments in circulation from domestic bond issues in twenty emerging economies increased from US$2.9 to US$5.5 billion between 2005 and 2009. In 2008 eight countries (Brazil, China, India, Malaysia, Mexico, South Africa, Thailand, and Turkey) represented 90 percent of the total domestic-currency issues (World Bank, 2009a:77).

21. In the case of individual donations for development purposes, information technologies have allowed resources to be channeled through innovative mechanisms such as Kiva.org, MyC4.com, Babyloan, and Wokai. There are also person-to-person mechanisms, where organizations allow individuals to channel their resources to people in developing countries (whose projects are presented on a website so that potential donors can choose them) through direct donations to specific programs (breakfasts, meals, payment for education). However, these programs may be controversial, as it is argued that rather than an innovative mechanism, these are marketing strategies to collect development funds (Roodman, 2009).

22. *The Economist* (2009a).

23. The IMF increased its available capital through the issue of special drawing rights by more than $250 billion; at the end of March 2010 an increase of 70 percent, to $170 billion, was approved in the capital of the Inter-American Development Bank. This will allow annual loans to the region of US$12–15 billion on average, compared with an average of US$7–9 billion in previous years. The replenishment of IDA-16 is in the process of negotiation. An increase of not less than 30 percent is expected in available resources. At the same time, discussions are under way to increase the capital of the World Bank, the Asian Development Bank (the G-20 has initially undertaken to increase the capital by 200 percent), and the African Development Bank. At the subregional level, the Andean Development Corporation, whose operations are no longer limited to the Andean region, increased its capital by US$2.5 billion in 2009 and carried out a share conversion to incorporate Argentina, Brazil, Paraguay, and Uruguay as full members (US$1.5 billion extra). In addition, negotiations have concluded to establish a regional fund in Asia, to operate in a similar way to the IMF to provide liquidity for the temporary balance of payments problems, as well as to manage reserves and swaps between local and international currencies. This

fund has been established for countries of the Association of South-East Asian Nations, China, Japan, and South Korea. It has resources of more than US$120 billion and was approved in mid-March 2010, as part of the Chiang Mai Initiative Multilateralization Agreement.

24. For a review of the history and motivations of this kind of cooperation, see Sagasti (2006).

25. The BASIC countries jointly represent almost 50 percent of the population of developing countries and just over 40 percent of world population. In 2005 they generated 43.1 percent of GDP in developing countries. This accounts for less than 25 percent of global GDP in international dollars using purchasing-power parity (Nayyar, 2008:3).

26. IBSA cooperates through specific projects and alliances with less developed countries. An example is its project in Guinea Bissau, where the program is oriented toward the improvement of techniques for self-sufficient food supply and assisting local farmers to learn good skills. The program lasted a year and had a budget of US$500,000. See http://www.ibsa-trilateral.org//index.php; http://www.impactalliance.org/ev_en .php?ID=49219_201&ID2=DO_TOPIC.

27. See Lan (2010); AFRODAD (2010).

28. For example, Ayllon (2010:2) highlights the interest of the president of Brazil in garnering support for Brazil's candidature for a permanent seat on the UN Security Council. Similar interests motivate other countries to continue improving their relations with countries that can support such ends.

29. *The Economist* (2010a).

30. See http://www.impactalliance.org/ev_es.php?ID=49069_201&ID2=DO _TOPIC.

31. See http://www.impactalliance.org/ev_en.php?ID=49123_201&ID2=DO _TOPIC.

32. See http://www.impactalliance.org/ev_en.php?ID=49371_201&ID2=DO _TOPIC.

33. See the Petrocaribe energy cooperation agreement at http://www.pdvsa.com/ index.php?tpl=interface.sp/design/biblioteca/readdoc.tpl.html&newsid_obj_ id=1349&newsid_temas=111 (revised in February 2010).

34. The member countries are Antigua and Barbuda, the Bahamas, Belize, Cuba, Dominica, Granada, Guatemala, Guyana, Haiti, Honduras, Jamaica, Nicaragua, the Dominican Republic, Saint Kitts and Nevis, Saint Vincent and the Grenadines, Saint Lucia, Suriname, and Venezuela.

35. These are some of the projects: the liquefied petroleum gas-filling plant, operating since February 2007 in Saint Vincent and the Grenadines; the fuel storage and distribution plant, which opened in Dominica in June 2009; and the Camilo Cienfuegos refinery, reactivated in Cuba and operating since December 2007, with a production capacity of 67,000 barrels a day. Electricity generation projects have also been developed in Nicaragua, Haiti, Antigua and Barbuda, Dominica, and Saint Kitts and Nevis. See http://www.petrocaribe.org/.

36. A list of the projects approved can be found at http://www.iadb.org/en /projects/projects,1229.html.

37. See http://www.impactalliance.org/ev_es.php?ID=49331_201&ID2=DO_TOPIC.

38. See http://www.gatesfoundation.org/press-releases/Pages/decade-of-vaccines-wec-announcement-100129.aspx.

39. See http://www.idrc.ca/en/ev-1–201–1-DO_TOPIC.html.

40. The academic literature has studied the role of FDI in developing countries, as well as the incentives and motivations for investment. Among these are geographical proximity, the possibility of saving labor and supply costs, the abundance of natural resources, the lack of strict regulations (as may exist in the home countries of the parent companies), and the growth in emerging economies that ensures the possibility of corporate finance at comparable levels to those in the countries of origin, as well as the presence of tax incentives for starting operations in various developing countries (as in the case of exploiting natural resources). However, various studies have pointed to the negative side of such incentives. In the 1990s many countries at a similar level of development competed by relaxing national regulations and creating ad hoc mechanisms to attract resources for their economies, using what became known as "race to the bottom" policies. This led to FDI presenting a balance sheet that combined positive and negative aspects, since the power and influence of some transnational companies have allowed them to generate swift returns, but at the cost of negative externalities, such as environmental damage, scant connection with local economies, tax exemptions, extraordinary earnings, repatriation of earnings, and, finally, the opposition of the population and the generation of social conflicts in the zones in which they operate.

41. The Institutional Investors Group on Climate Change (IIGCC, 2009), which includes 181 investors with US$13 billion in financial assets under management, has agreed to promote more ambitious targets than Copenhagen (a reduction of between 50 and 85 percent in emissions by 2050).

42. For example, the Canada Investment Fund for Africa is a public-private fund with more than US$200 million, designed to stimulate growth in Africa through investment focused on financial services, natural resources, logistics, and agro-industry. The fund is managed privately, but the government, through its development agency, CIDA, ensured that its limited partnership agreement stipulated social, environmental, and health and safety objectives as a basis for managing the fund. See http://www.international.gc.ca/trade-agreements-accords-commerciaux/ds/csr-strategy-rse-stategie.aspx.

43. See Price Waterhouse Coopers (n.d.).

44. For example, in SSC, various institutions, such as the Organization of American States, the Ibero-American Secretariat General, the Development Effectiveness Working Group, the Economic Commission for Latin America and the Caribbean, and the United Nations Economic and Social Council, are compiling statistics and case studies for good practices worldwide. This diversity of institutions is not found in CSR, where the main sources of information are still reports from the corporate sector itself.

45. Countries such as Venezuela and Saudi Arabia claim they have exceeded the target of 0.7 percent of GNI in their international aid budgets. Currently the most optimistic estimates put it within the range of 10 percent of official aid (ECOSOC,

2009), but some countries with a high capacity for mobilizing resources are trying to increase these budgets, even at a time of financial crisis.

46. With the collaboration of Néstor Aquiño.

47. See "Groups of Countries by Type of Economy" (World Bank).

48. Some of the countries presenting limited information from the period 2000–2002 for the construction of the index include the following: American Samoa; Kiratibi; Marshall Islands; Montenegro; Palao; Saint Kitts and Nevis; Saint Lucia; Saint Vincent and the Grenadines; Sao Tome and Principe; and Somalia. For the period 2006–2008 the data were limited in the following countries: American Samoa; Saint Kitts and Nevis; Saint Lucia; Saint Vincent and the Grenadines; Somalia; Turkmenistan; and Zimbabwe. In general, it should be taken into account that the poorest countries do not have good statistical information.

49. Averages were taken for three years to avoid the effect of atypical years or large variations that could distort the calculation of the index and to give greater stability (lower year-on-year variation). The calculation of the index through the main components allows the absolute values to be determined and ordered for countries in accordance with the capacity for resource mobilization, and to monitor the process over time.

REFERENCES

African Forum and Network on Debt and Development (AFRODAD). 2010. "Evaluando el creciente papel e impacto de China en el desarrollo como 'superpotencia' y donante en África." In *Cooperación Sur-Sur: ¿un desafío al sistema de la ayuda?*, edited by The Reality of Aid, 67–80. Medellín: Asociación Latinoamericana de Organizaciones de Promoción al Desarrollo A.C. (ALOP).

Alesina, A., and D. Dollar. 2000. "Who Gives Foreign Aid to Whom and Why?" *Journal of Economic Growth* 5 (1): 33–63.

Alexander, N. 2010. *Fostering Impunity or Accountability? Sweeping Changes at the World Bank-IDA*. Berlin: Heinrich Böll Foundation.

Anishyuk, T. 2010. "Government Raises Foreign Aid 4-fold." *St. Petersburg Times*, February 19.

APRIL. 2007. "APRIL Fact Sheet: Managing Kampar Peatlands for Sustainable Development." Singapore: APRIL. http://www.forestlandscaperestoration.org/media/uploads/File/kampar/managing_kampar_factsheet.pdf.

AT Kearney. 2008. *New Concerns in an Uncertain World: The 2007 AT Kearney Foreign Direct Investment Confidence Index*. Chicago: AT Kearney.

Ayllon, B. 2010. (March 25). "El eje Sur-Sur en la política exterior del gobierno de Lula: Cooperación e intereses." *INFOLATAM*. www.infolatam.com.

Bera, S., and S. Gupta. 2009. (July). "South-South FDI vs. North-South FDI: A Comparative Analysis in the Context of India." Working Paper No. 238. New Delhi: Indian Council for Research on International Economic Relations.

Betancourt, M. C., and N. Schulz. 2009. *La cooperación Sur-Sur a partir de Accra: América Latina y el Caribe*. London: FRIDE.

Bill and Melinda Gates Foundation. 2010. "Bill and Melinda Gates Pledge $10 Billion in Call for Decade of Vaccines." Press release, January 29. Seattle: Gates Foundation. http://www.gatesfoundation.org/press-releases/Pages/decade-of-vaccines-wec -announcement-100129.aspx.

Birdsall, N., and K. Vyborny. 2008. (August). "A Little Less Talk: Six Steps to Get Some Action from the Accra Agenda." *Centre for Global Development Notes.*

Bocalandro, L., and R. Villa. 2009. *Regional Public Goods: Promoting Innovative Solutions for Latin America and the Caribbean.* Washington, D.C.: IADB.

Boston Consulting Group (BCG). 2006. *The New Global Challengers: How 100 Top Companies from Rapidly Developing Economies Are Changing the World.* Boston: Boston Consulting Group.

————. 2009. *The 2009 BCG 100 New Global Challengers: How Companies from Rapidly Developing Economies Are Contending for Global Leadership.* Boston: Boston Consulting Group.

Bourguignon, F. 2007. (April 15). "Sustaining and Broadening Progress toward the MDGs." Presentation to the 2007 Development Committee Meeting, Washington, D.C.

Brautigam, D. 2008. "China's Foreign Aid in Africa: What Do We Know?" In *China into Africa: Trade, Aid and Influence,* edited by R. I. Rotberg, 197–216. Washington, D.C.: Brookings Institution Press.

Burgess, K. 2009. "Pension Funds Turn to Low-Risk Microfinance." *Financial Times,* October 8.

CEPAL. 2009a. *La reacción de los gobiernos de las Américas frente a la crisis internacional: Una presentación sintética de las medidas de política anunciadas hasta el 31 de julio de 2009.* Santiago de Chile: CEPAL.

————. 2009b. *Panorama de la inserción internacional de América Latina y el Caribe: Crisis y espacios de cooperación regional.* Santiago de Chile: CEPAL.

Chávez Granadino, J. 2010. *Responsabilidad social empresarial, crecimiento económico inclusivo y el rol de la cooperación internacional.* Documento de Trabajo, Foro Nacional Internacional.

Cheng, L., and Z. Ma. 2007. "China's Outward FDI: Past and Future." Working Paper No. 200706001E. Beijing: Renmin University of China.

Chervalier, B., and J. Zimet. 2006. "American Philanthropic Foundations: Emerging Actors of Globalization and Pillars of the Transatlantic Dialogue." German Marshall Fund of the United States, GMF, Washington. http://www.gmfus.org /galleries/ct_news_article_attachments/ABCDE_foundations_policy_paper.pdf;j sessionid=asPJRjRMMkKavkdA8d.

Collier, P., and D. Dollar. 2002. "Aid Allocation and Poverty Reduction." *European Economic Review* 46 (8).

Dang, H., S. Knack, and H. Rogers. 2009. "International Aid and Financial Crises in Donor Countries." Policy Research Working Paper No. 5162. Washington, D.C.: World Bank.

Dyer, G., J. Anderlini, and H. Sender. 2011. "China's Lending Hits New Heights." *Financial Times,* January 17. http://www.ft.com/cms/s/0/488c60f4–2281–11e0 -b6a2–00144feab49a.html#axzz1RGzyTwyz.

The Economist. 2009a. "Payment Cards and the Poor: A Plastic Prop." August 20.

———. 2009b. "Ecuador, Argentina and the IMF: The Price of Pride," September 10.

———. 2010a. "Brazil's Foreign-Aid Program: Speak Softly and Carry a Blank Cheque." July 15.

———. 2010b. "The World Turned Upside Down." April 15. http://www.economist.com/specialreports/PrinterFriendly.cfm?story_id=15879369.

ECOSOC. 2009. *South-South and Triangular Cooperation: Improving Information and Data.* New York: United Nations Economic and Social Council.

Eichengreen, B., and K. O'Rourke. 2009. "A Tale of Two Depressions." www.voxeu.org.

Ellis, E. 2009. *China in Latin America: The Whats and Wherefores.* Boulder, Colo.: Lynne Rienner.

Eswar, Pr. 2009. "IMF Bonds: Details and Implications." Report. Washington, D.C.: Brookings Institution. http://www.brookings.edu/articles/2009/0504_IMF_bonds_prasad.aspx?p=1.

Federated Republic of Brazil. 2008. (January 19–20). "Trends in Development Cooperation: South-South and Triangular Cooperation and Aid Effectiveness: The Brazilian Experience." High-Level Symposium, Cairo.

Feigenbaum, E. 2010. "India's Rise, America's Interest: The Fate of the U.S.-Indian Partnership." *Foreign Affairs* (March/April).

Foreign Affairs and International Trade Canada. 2009. (March). "Building the Canadian Advantage: A Corporate Social Responsibility (CSR) Strategy for the Canadian International Extractive Sector." Ottawa: FAITC. http://www.international.gc.ca/trade-agreements-accords-commerciaux/ds/csr-strategy-rse-stategie.aspx.

Fruttero, A., and V. Gauri. 2005. "The Strategic Choices of NGOs: Location Decisions in Rural Bangladesh." *Journal of Development Studies* 41 (5).

Gammeltoft, P. 2008. "Emerging Multinationals: Outward FDI from BRICS Countries." *International Journal of Technology and Globalization* 4 (1). http://ir.lib.cbs.dk/download/ISBN/X075239.pdf.

Girishankar, N. 2009. "Innovating Development Finance: From Financing Sources to Financial Solutions." CFP Working Paper Series 1. Washington, D.C.: World Bank—Concessional Finance and Global Partnership (CFP) Vice Presidency.

Gupta, S., R. Powell, and Y. Yang. 2006. *Macroeconomic Challenges of Scaling Up Aid to Africa: A Checklist for Practitioners.* Washington, D.C.: International Monetary Fund.

Hagan, M., and H. Johanns. 2009. *The Investment Dealers' Digest: IDD* 75 (33) (September). New York: IDD.

Hall, H., and S. Kean. 2009. "Bracing for Tough Times." *Chronicle of Philanthropy* 7 (February).

Hoeffler A., and V. Outram. 2008. "Need, Merit or Self-Interest: What Determines the Allocation of Aid?" CSAE Working Paper 2008–19. Oxford: Centre for the Study of African Economies Department of Economics, University of Oxford.

Hollingshead, A. 2010. (February). *The Implied Tax Revenue Loss from Trade Mispricing.* Washington, D.C.: Global Financial Integrity.

Hudson Institute. 2009. *The Index of Global Philanthropy and Remittances.* Chicago: Hudson Institute and the Centre of Global Philanthropy.

IBSA. 2010. http://www.ibsa-trilateral.org//index.php.

IIGCC. 2009. *Investor Statement on the Urgent Need for a Global Agreement on Climate Change.* London: IIGCC.

IMF. 2009. *World Economic Outlook: October 2009.* Washington, D.C.: International Monetary Fund.

Inter-American Development Bank. n.d. "Projects." Washington, D.C.: IADB. http://www.iadb.org/en/projects/projects,1229.html.

International Organization for Migration (IOM). 2005. *World Migration Report 2005.* Geneva: IOM.

Kharas, H. 2008. "Measuring the Cost of Aid Volatility." Wolfensohn Centre for Development Working Paper No. 3. Washington, D.C.: Brookings Institution.

Knack, S., and A. Rahman. 2007. "Donor Fragmentation and Bureaucratic Quality in Aid Recipients." *Journal of Development Economics* 83.

Kumar, N. 2007. "Toward Broader Regional Cooperation in Asia." UNDP/RCC and RIS Discussion Paper. Colombo: UNDP/RCC.

Lacey, M. 2009. "Money Trickles North as Mexicans Help Relatives." *New York Times,* November 16.

Lan, X. 2010. (March 22). "China's Aid to Africa: Challenges or Opportunities? To Whom?" Lecture at IDRC, Ottawa.

Lane, C., and A. Glassman. 2009. *Smooth and Predictable Aid for Health: A Role for Innovative Financing.* Washington, D.C.: Brookings Institution.

Lederman, D., M. Olarreaga, and G. Perry. 2009. *China and India's Challenge to Latin America: Opportunity or Threat?* Washington, D.C.: World Bank.

Leo, B. 2009. (November). *Will World Bank and IMF Lending Lead to HIPC IV? Debt Déjà-vu All Over Again.* Washington, D.C.: Centre for Global Development.

Maxwell, S. 2009. "Eliminating World Poverty: Building Our Common Future." *Development Policy Review* 27 (6).

McGillivray, M., and H. White. 1993. "Explanatory Studies of Aid Allocation Among Developing Countries: A Critical Survey." Working Paper No. 148. The Hague: Institute of Social Studies.

Metzger, M. 2008. "Regional Cooperation and Integration in Sub-Saharan Africa." Discussion Paper No. 189. Geneva: United Nations Conference on Trade and Development.

Monge, R., O. Céspedes, and J. Vargas. 2009. "Remesas Sur-Sur: Importancia del corredor Costa Rica-Nicaragua." San José: Academia de Centroamérica.

Nayyar, D. 2008. "China, India, Brazil and South Africa in the World Economy: Engines of Growth?" Discussion Paper No. 2008/05. New Delhi: UNU-WIDER.

Nunnenkamp, P., and H. Öhler. 2009. (July). "Aid Allocation through Various Official and Private Channels: Need, Merit and Self-Interest as Motives of German Donors." Kiel Working Paper No. 1536. Bonn: Instituto de Economía Mundial de Kiel. http://www.ifw-members.ifw-kiel.de/publications/aid-allocation-through-various-official-and-private-channels-need-merit-and-self-interest-as-motives-of-german-donors/kwp_1536.

Nunnenkamp, P., J. Weingarth, and J. Weisser. 2008. (March). "Is NGO Aid Not So Different After All? Comparing the Allocation of Swiss Aid by Private and

Official Donors." Kiel Working Paper No. 1405. Bonn: Kiel Institute for the World Economy.

Ocampo, J. A. 2006. *Regional Financial Cooperation*. Washington, D.C., and Santiago de Chile: Brookings Institution Press and the Economic Commission for Latin America and the Caribbean (ECLAC).

Ocampo, J. A., S. Griffith-Jones, A. Noman, A. Ortiz, and J. Vallejo. 2010. (June 9–10). "La gran recesión y el mundo en desarrollo." Draft for the Conference on Development Cooperation in Times of Crisis and the Achievement of MDGs, Madrid.

OECD. 2007. (December 11). "Donor Practices on Forward Planning of Aid Expenditures, Global Forum on Development—Policy Workshop on the Challenges of Scaling Up at Country Level: Predictable Aid Linked to Results." Paris: OECD.

————. 2009a. *Aid for Better Health: What Are We Learning about What Works and What We Still Have to Do?* An interim report from the Task Team on Health as a Tracer Sector. DCD/DAC/EFF (2009): 14: Working Party on Aid Effectiveness.

————. 2009b. "Aid Targets Slipping Out of Reach." Paris: OECD. http://www.oecd.org/dataoecd/47/25/41724314.pdf (last accessed February 20, 2009).

————. 2010. "Portal OECD Stat Extracts." http://stats.oecd.org/.

Petróleos de Venezuela (PDVSA) and Venezuelan Ministry of Energy and Oil. 2005. "14 Countries Endorse the Petrocaribe Energy Cooperation Agreement." In *The New PDVSA Contact N°1,* Caracas: PDVSA and Bolivarian Republic of Venezuela, p. 2. http://www.pdv.com/interface.en/database/fichero/publicacion/935/21.PDF.

Porter, M., and M. Kramer. 2008. "Strategy and Society: The Link Between Competitive Advantage and Corporate Social Responsibility." *Harvard Business Review* (December).

Prada, F. 2009. "Climate Change Financing: Developing Countries' Options and Challenges for Mitigation and Adaptation." Background report for the World Economic and Social Survey (WESS). http://www.un.org/esa/policy/publications/wess_background_papers.htm.

Prada, F., U. Casabonne, and K. Bezanson. 2010. *Development Resources beyond the Current Reach of the Paris Declaration*. Lima: FORO Nacional/Internacional. http://www.oecd.org/dataoecd/1/14/46486829.pdf.

Price Waterhouse Coopers. n.d. "Responsabilidad Social Corporativa." http://pwc-interamerica.com/RSC/Informe%20resultados%20RSC-CR.pdf .

Qasim, M. n.d. "Foreign Direct Investment among South Asian Countries: Concerns and Opportunities." Islamabad: Asian Institute of Trade and Development. http://aitd.com.pk/publications/FDI%20FINAL.pdf.

The Reality of Aid. 2010. *Cooperación Sur-Sur: ¿un desafío al sistema de la ayuda?* Manila: Reality of Aid.

The Reality of Aid Management Committee. 2008. *The Reality of Aid 2008. An Independent Review of Poverty Reduction and Development Assistance. Aid Effectiveness: Democratic Ownership and Human Rights*. Quezon: IBON Books.

Reisen, H. 2008. "Is China Actually Helping Improve Debt Sustainability in Africa?" G24 Policy Brief 9. Paris: OECD Development Centre.

Roemer, J. E., and H. G. Llavador. 1999. "An Equal-Opportunity Approach to the Allocation of International Aid." Working Paper 9910. Davis: University of California, Department of Economics.

Roodman, D. 2009. (October 2). "Kiva Is Not Quite What It Seems." *David Roodman's Microfinance Open Book Blog.* http://blogs.cgdev.org/open_book/2009/10/kiva-is-not-quite-what-it-seems.php.

Sagasti, F. 2006. *Rethinking Technical Cooperation among Developing Countries (TCDC) and South-South Cooperation (SSC): An Issues Paper.* Lima: FORO Nacional/Internacional.

Sagasti, F., and G. Alcalde. 1999. *Development Cooperation in a Fractured Global Order: An Arduous Transition.* Ottawa: IDRC.

Sagasti, F., K. Bezanson, and F. Prada. 2005. *The Future of the Financing for Development System: Challenges, Scenarios and Strategic Choices.* Oxford: Palgrave.

Sagasti, F., and F. Prada. 2004. "La banca multilateral de desarrollo en America Latina." In *Gobernabilidad e integración financiera: Ambito global y regional,* edited by J. A. Ocampo and A. Uthoff. Washington, D.C.: ECLAC.

———. 2006. "Regional Development Banks: A Comparative Perspective." In *Regional Financial Cooperation,* edited by J. A. Ocampo. Washington, D.C.: Brookings Institution Press and the Economic Commission for Latin America and the Caribbean (ECLAC).

Sagasti, F., F. Prada, and A. Espinoza. 2006. "Public Finance in a Globalizing World: Peruvian Case Study." In *The New Public Finance: Responding to Global Challenges,* edited by I. Kaul and P. Conceição. New York and Oxford: Oxford University Press. http://www.thenewpublicfinance.org/casestudies/ccs_peru.pdf.

Sahoo, P., D. Kumar Rai, and R. Kumar. 2009. (December). "India-Korea Trade Investment Relations." Working Paper No. 242. New Delhi: Indian Council for Research on International Economic Relations.

Santiso, J. 2008. "The Emergence of Latina Multinationals." *Cepal Review* 95 (August).

Saxena, S., and A. Villar. 2008. "Hedging Instruments in Emerging Market Economies." BIS Papers, 41. Basilea: Bank of International Settlements.

SEGIB. 2008. "Segundo informe de cooperación Sur-Sur en Iberoamérica." *Estudios SEGIB* 3. Madrid: Secretaría General Iberoamericana (SEGIB).

Singh, K. 2008. (October). *Frequently Asked Questions about Sovereign Wealth Funds.* New Delhi: Public Interest Research Centre.

The South-South Opportunity Case Stories. 2010. http://www.impactalliance.org/ev_en.php?ID=48720_201&ID2=DO_TOPIC.

Sulla, O. 2006. (December). "Philanthropic Foundations Actual Versus Potential Role in International Development Assistance." Draft note prepared for Global Development Finance Report.

Task-Team on South-South Cooperation (TT-SSC). (2010). *Boosting South-South Cooperation in the Context of Aid Effectiveness: Telling the Story of Partners Involved in More than 110 Cases of South-South and Triangular Cooperation.* Preliminary draft.

UN-DESA. (2009). *World Economic and Social Survey 2009: Climate Change and Development (WESS 2009).* New York: United Nations.

UNCTAD. (2009). *The Least Developed Countries Report 2008: Growth, Poverty and the Terms of Development Partnership.* Geneva: UNCTAD.

Van Dijk, M. (2009). *The New Presence of China in Africa.* Amsterdam: Amsterdam University Press.

Wood, B., D. Kabell, F. Sagasti, and N. Muwanga, 2008. (July). "Synthesis Report on the First Phase of the Evaluation of the Implementation of the Paris Declaration." Copenhagen: Ministry of Foreign Affairs of Denmark.

Wootliff, J. 2009. (December 19). "Business Has Role to Play in REDD in Indonesian Peatlands." *AlertNet,* http://www.alertnet.org/db/blogs/62079/2009/11/18–105257–1.htm.

World Bank. (2010). "World Bank's Fund for the Poorest Receives Almost $50 Billion in Record Funding." Press release No:2011/248/EXT, http://web.worldbank.org/WBSITE/EXTERNAL/NEWS/0,,contentMDK:22790700~pagePK:64257043~piPK:437376~theSitePK:4607,00.html.

CHAPTER 7

Governance of the Aid System and the Role of the European Union

Owen Barder, Mikaela Gavas, Simon Maxwell, and Deborah Johnson

This chapter is about governance of the aid system, with a case study of the European Union (EU). The EU makes a good case study, because the global questions about governance of international aid also apply at the level of the EU. Is this a coherent and planned system or one that is more random and chaotic in nature? Is it capable of being governed and planned? Should it be governed and planned in its entirety? And assuming governance or architectural interventions are possible, should the aim be consolidation into fewer entities or cooperation among many?

Within the world of official aid, two views currently dominate the debate. The first celebrates diversity and concentrates on the coordination of collaborative networks. It focuses attention on shared goals, harmonization of approaches, and better coordination regarding who does what. It finds its highest expression in the United Nations' work on the Millennium Development Goals (MDGs), and in the aid effectiveness initiatives of the Development Assistance Committee (DAC) of the Organization for Economic Cooperation and Development (OECD). In the EU the key instruments are the European Consensus on Development of 2005[1] and the Code of Conduct on Division of Labour,[2] agreed upon in 2007.

The second view seeks reform of the aid "architecture" in order to reduce the number of actors and to rationalize the supply of aid. It focuses on the allocation of aid between institutions, transactions costs, multilateral effectiveness, and issues such as governance reform of the Bretton Woods Institutions. Its ideal is captured in the phrase "Don't just harmonise, multilateralise." In the EU a key issue is the share of EU aid channeled through the European Commission (EC), currently only just over 20 percent.[3]

Outside the official world, some have taken the idea of collaboration further, advocating market or network approaches, within a largely self-organizing framework.

We begin by reviewing different concepts of governance and "good governance" and by providing a framework within which to assess the governance of the aid system as it currently stands. We focus on five criteria of good governance: effectiveness, efficiency, legitimacy, accountability, and adaptability.

In the third section we describe the aid system as it currently exists: growing and diversifying, variously governed, and often described as an aid "non-system."

In the following section we assess the governance of aid. We examine options connected to the DAC, the UN Development Cooperation Forum (UNDCF), high-level forums, ad hoc country-level coordination, and multilateralism. We find that none achieve full marks on our scorecard (though multilateralism comes close and will score higher as a result of the recent reform of Bretton Woods governance).

Next we turn to the EU. We summarize the role of the EU in the global context and assess the current governance of EU aid, with special reference to the European Consensus on Development and the Code of Conduct on Division of Labour. The EC scores reasonably well on governance, not least because of the accountability mechanisms built into the Cotonou Convention with countries in Africa, the Caribbean, and the Pacific.

Finally, we suggest two paradoxes. The first is that although the system as a whole would work better if most aid were given through multilateral institutions, there are coordination failures that leave many countries preferring a large bilateral program. The second is that there is a familiar trade-off between effectiveness and accountability with regard to some aspects of aid governance: the DAC, for example, scores highly for its work on statistics and reporting but remains essentially a rich country club. We conclude that the multilateral space is competitive. Good governance is one of the criteria that ministers will use in allocating resources.

WHAT IS MEANT BY "GOVERNANCE"?

In the case of nation-states, there are different views of what constitutes good governance, but a number of common themes emerge—and these can be applied to the governance of aid.[4] A typical summary is given by Hyden et al. (2004: 6):

The *Making Sense of Governance* book identifies six core principles that are widely accepted by researchers and governance stakeholders in developing and transitional societies around the world:

Participation: the degree of involvement by affected stakeholders;
Fairness: the degree to which rules apply equally to everyone in society;
Decency: the degree to which the formation and stewardship of the rules is undertaken without humiliating or harming people;
Accountability: the extent to which political actors are responsible to society for what they say and do;
Transparency: the degree of clarity and openness with which decisions are made in a clear and open manner; and
Efficiency: the extent to which limited human and financial resources are applied without unnecessary waste, delay or corruption.[5]

Governance of the international aid system is not exactly the same as governance of a nation, but many of these principles translate well into desirable characteristics of a governance system for international aid. Drawing from the governance literature, we suggest the following five dimensions against which a governance system should be assessed:

1. *Effective:* The governance of the aid system should improve the effectiveness of the aid system as a whole. This means it has to address issues in order to improve collective outcomes, while leaving to the discretion of developing countries and their development partners those questions that are best resolved individually.

2. *Efficient:* The governance arrangements should be efficient as well as effective, avoiding unnecessary costs for donors or recipients.

3. *Legitimate, fair, and decent:* The governance system must be legitimate, representing all affected stakeholders, setting rules that apply equally to everyone, and treating every stakeholder with respect. It should respect the rights of nation-states, both as recipients and donors, while achieving better collective outcomes than could be achieved without governance.

4. *Transparent and accountable:* Good governance must be transparent and accountable to stakeholders. These qualities underpin effectiveness and legitimacy, as well as the ability of the system to adapt.

5. *Adaptive:* Finally, the governance of aid must not only address the world as it finds it today but also ensure that it is fit for purpose in the future. As the environment continues to change, so the aid system should

evolve. The aid system has been handicapped by institutional arrangements that have been hard to change. The response to rapid changes in context—most notably the arrival of new kinds of donors—has been to add complexity rather than to simplify and evolve. The aid system must be organized in a way that allows, and indeed forces, it to adapt more quickly as circumstances change.

These qualities correspond closely to commonly used frameworks for government—for example, the UK Department for International Development refers to governments that are "capable, accountable, and responsive."[6]

AID—WHERE HAVE WE COME FROM, WHERE ARE WE, AND WHERE ARE WE LIKELY TO GO?

The system of development assistance originated at the end of the Second World War, with the establishment of the Bretton Woods Institutions. These institutional structures have remained largely unaltered despite very substantial changes in the context in which they operate. Since the Second World War, the political environment for foreign assistance has changed considerably.

The Marshall Plan, in which the United States contributed to the rebuilding of post-war Europe, gave respectability to the idea that rich nations could, in the interests of peace and trade, contribute to economic development. The perceived success of the Marshall Plan became a major impetus behind the emergence of aid programs to developing countries.

Decolonization was accompanied in Western countries by a growing sense of obligation to their former colonies, and so conventional foreign assistance programs began in the 1960s, partly modeled on the Marshall Plan.

The Cold War played out in the developing world, as well as in Europe, with the great powers using development assistance in pursuit of their global strategic interests. Huge amounts of aid were given to regimes such as those of Mobuto in Zaire and Mengistu in Ethiopia, with the aim of shoring up allies and with little regard to its effects on poverty.

The first oil shock in the 1970s led to the recycling of surpluses to developing countries, many of which needed additional funds to cope with rising oil prices; this recycling of surpluses laid the foundation for the subsequent debt crises, and eventually large-scale debt relief in the 1990s.

From the collapse of the Berlin Wall to the fall of the Twin Towers, donors were able to move away from using aid for geopolitical purposes; at the same time, the shift in industrialized countries to floating exchange rates reduced their obsession with the balance of payments, allowing development policy makers to focus on longer-term and broader objectives of reducing poverty and global inequality. It is not a coincidence that this was the period when the International Development Targets, later the MDGs, were established.

Since 9/11, and the subsequent wars in Afghanistan and Iraq, donors have used more of their development assistance in support of shorter-term political and security objectives and post-conflict reconstruction, not only on acute poverty. The threat of terrorism has both created a heightened sense of global interdependency and focused attention on the need to create the conditions in which violent extremism is less likely to be perpetuated.

Increasing environmental insecurity is becoming a new driver of a changing development relationship. Developing countries face the greatest costs of global warming, despite having contributed little to the problem. In the short term, the challenge is to reach an agreement on addressing global warming that does not slow down development and that compensates developing countries for the damage caused to them by industrialized nations; in the longer run, developing countries may benefit from changes in economic systems that put a higher value on natural resources, so reflecting part of the wealth of developing nations that is undervalued in today's markets.

THE CHANGING ROLE OF FOREIGN ASSISTANCE

Against the backdrop of broad geopolitical change, perceptions about the role of foreign assistance have also evolved. Following the Second World War, it was argued that long-run welfare depended on capital investment, and that helping countries raise savings through a "Big Push"[7] would launch them into self-sustaining growth or takeoff. As a result, donors funded infrastructure, such as dams and roads. However, by the 1980s, the development community had concluded that capital accumulation and technological progress depended not only on the level of investment but also on a better economic policy environment. The combination of policies that were thought desirable was subsequently dubbed the "Washington Consensus." By the 1990s, this approach too was in doubt, and it was argued that these policies could only have the impact intended if they were accompanied by more fundamental institutional reforms. A decade later, attention has shifted to even more fundamental causes of poverty, such as conflict, rivalry between different social and economic groups, competition for scarce natural resources, and lack of political accountability.

We can characterize this evolution as a search for the underlying causes of poverty. In part this has been motivated by an insistence that aid must be purely temporary, creating the imperative to find a way to catalyze permanent changes in developing countries. This evolution in thinking about the role of aid has inevitably changed the nature of the aid relationship, as it has placed the politics and institutions of developing countries center stage. As the objective of aid has increasingly been redefined as nothing short of social and political transformation, so it has been increasingly difficult to relate aid to the ambitions held for it.

AID VOLUMES

The target for rich countries of contributing aid of 0.7 percent of national income was first formulated by the Pearson Commission in its report of 1969, although it had its origins in the first meeting of the United Nations Conference on Trade and Development (UNCTAD) in 1964. Reflecting its time, the target was based on an estimate of the amount of capital from abroad that would be needed to increase investment and so accelerate growth in developing countries, though subsequent estimates of the amount of money needed to meet the MDGs have arrived at broadly the same orders of magnitude.

Until 2005, each industrialized country was committed to "exert its best efforts to reach"[8] the target of 0.7 percent of gross national income (GNI). Five nations met it: Denmark, Luxembourg, the Netherlands, Norway, and Sweden; two other countries (Belgium and France) were committed to doing so. In 2005 all EU-15 countries committed themselves to reaching the 0.7 percent of GNI target by 2015.[9]

Since the pledges in 2005 to increase it, aid has increased sharply, by 35 percent in real terms from 2004 to 2009. While substantial, this increase falls considerably short of what was promised in 2005. Over 60 percent of the increase from the period 2004–2009 has been from EU countries (Figure 7.1).

Figure 7.1   Aid as a Percentage of GNI

Source: OECD-DAC data, 1960–2008.

NEW ACTORS IN THE AID SYSTEM

Despite these significant changes over time in the purposes and ideology of development assistance, there was, until the 1990s, very little change in the organization of the development system. About 70 percent of aid is given bilaterally and 30 percent through multilateral channels; this has remained broadly constant (Figure 7.2).

Over time the EU has become a more important donor, rising from a third of official aid in the 1960s to 56 percent in 2009.[10] Although a growing proportion of official aid is given by European donors, they are not becoming dominant actors in the development system. Instead, they are faced with a rapidly proliferating environment of new donors and new agencies. The main characteristics of these changes include the following:

• The number of government donors, and donor agencies, has increased. The DAC now includes twenty-three nations plus the EC, which have between them more than 120 bilateral agencies providing aid to developing countries.

• There are now more countries that give official aid outside the DAC than within it, including China, Turkey, Russia, Brazil, India, Venezuela, and South Africa. These countries mainly operate in their spheres of

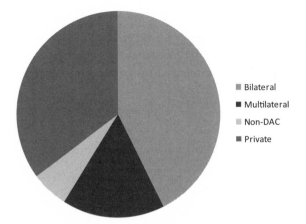

Figure 7.2   Proportion of Aid through Different Channels

Source: OECD-DAC data 2009.

influence. The oil-producing states also give large amounts of aid, mainly to Islamic states. These donors typically do not attach much value to the standards and norms set by the DAC, and because they do not report to the DAC, we do not know exactly how much aid is being given. Estimates suggest that China is giving perhaps US$5 billion a year,[11] a little less than the Gates Foundation, and about as much again is given by the other non-DAC government donors.

• There are more than 260 multilateral aid organizations, ranging in size from the World Bank to the Schistosomiasis Control Initiative. Although the overall share of aid going through the multilateral system has remained constant, at about 30 percent of ODA, for the last thirty years, within that the share going through the UN system has fallen, and multilateral spending now occurs through a much larger number of smaller multilateral agencies.

• International philanthropy has taken off over the last decade. This is a predominantly American phenomenon. The Gates Foundation is in a class of its own in terms of size, but the most spectacular growth is among large numbers of smaller foundations.

• International NGOs, such as World Vision, Oxfam, and CARE, have also grown rapidly and are increasingly funded by private individuals rather than governments. International NGOs raise more money for development assistance than the entire UN system.

• Total private development assistance—including foundations, NGOs, educational organizations, churches, and private companies—comes to about US$60 billion a year, about half of official development assistance.[12] This exceeds aid through the multilateral system, and may soon overtake bilateral aid.

• The private sector is increasingly involved in development, not only through (relatively modest) giving under the banner of corporate social responsibility but more fundamentally by changing business models to take into account their customers' growing preference for more ethical and sustainable behavior.

Total aid to developing countries was about US$200 billion in 2009 (this is an estimate with a wide margin of error, given the difficulty of establishing precise numbers for private giving and giving by non-DAC donors).

COMPETITION AND DIVERSITY: GOOD NEWS OR BAD?

The growing array of development actors, and the diversity of their approaches, represents both a challenge and an opportunity. New actors bring new money and ways of working that could make a substantial contribution to development.

New philanthropic donors bring more money to development, but, more importantly, they bring new attitudes and ways of working. Large foundations are less dependent on public support for future funding, so they may be willing to support unpopular or unphotogenic causes (e.g., supporting statistical systems in developing countries). Foundations are frequently founded by successful entrepreneurs, so they may be more inclined to operate along business principles, such as making decisions based on evidence, tightly controlling overhead, adopting new technologies, and focusing more sharply on results. They may be willing to take more risks and accept more failures in return for bigger success. They tend to select projects according to the characteristics of the project rather than the country. Foundations may be more able and inclined to work closely with the private sector, which plays a key role in development but with which official agencies have not found it easy to work.

The rise of new official donors, in particular, China, has caused concern among traditional donors, which worry that their implicit cartel is undermined by donors that are less concerned about governance and human rights, and that are prepared to be more open about their desires for access to raw materials and minerals. China has not been stuck with the DAC development model, and in many ways developing countries prefer China's approach. They rarely poach skilled staff; they provide turnkey infrastructure projects that do not overstretch developing country governments with meetings, reports, and workshops. They appear more genuine in respecting local ownership, they operate very differently in different countries, and they seem to be sincerely interested in learning about what works. They are willing to invest in infrastructure, irrigation, and university scholarships—all sectors that DAC donors have moved away from. They avoid embezzlement and corruption by rarely using cash: there is almost no budget support or policy loans, as aid is disbursed to Chinese companies that carry out the projects.

Private aid through charities tends to focus on supporting communities and individuals rather than developing countries. It tends to be more opportunistic and closer to the ground. People who give money this way value the sense that they can work with local civil society organizations rather than governments, which can bring about results more directly, although it is harder to bring about systemic change this way.

Specialized multilateral global organizations are growing in number. They can bring skills and expertise, they can learn more systematically and spread knowledge more quickly, they can bring together a number of different donors—the public and the private sector to work in a more joined-up way on a particular issue—and they can raise money from the public because they can be more specific about what they do.

On the one hand, this diversity of development actors could be a growing strength of international aid. Foundations could act like venture capitalists, taking bigger risks but leaving long-term financing of scaled-up successes to official aid donors. Private aid could focus on achieving community- and individual-level results. Specialized global organizations could provide particular expertise not available through generalist support. The diversity of official donors could provide innovation rather than a monoculture of ideas. Official aid agencies could focus on long-term funding and resource transfer, and support for institutional change. If these actors could all focus on their strengths, and if the aid system enables them to work together well, the changing development landscape might substantially improve the effectiveness of development assistance.

On the other hand, this proliferation can present huge challenges for everyone involved. Developing countries are forced to deal with a vast, growing number of partners, each with separate agendas, priorities, and requirements. Meetings, reports, milestones, and systems multiply. Skilled staff are hired away to serve in local agency offices or NGOs. Funding is fragmented and unpredictable, with developing countries unable to bring together the scale of long-term, predictable finance needed to undertake significant institutional reform and service delivery. Donors lose leverage and influence because they undermine each other; yet developing countries are not able to keep track of, let alone exercise sufficient ownership and control over, an increasingly fragmented system of aid delivery. Public accountability is impossible, since nobody has a clear view of which resources are being used by whom or for what purpose. Long-term strategy has to be sacrificed to short-term, measurable outputs to meet the immediate needs of individual stakeholders. Donors face rising costs, as administrative costs multiply when agencies proliferate, and the costs of coordination and harmonization rise exponentially with the number of aid agencies. Donor missions, offices, and staff proliferate and duplicate.

According to the 2008 survey monitoring the Paris Indicators, "More than 14,000 donor missions were fielded to the 54 countries that took part in this survey (Indicator 10a). In Vietnam alone, this amounted to 752 donor missions in 2007—more than three missions per working day! Of these missions, less than one in five was co-ordinated with another donor."[13]

The effects of this proliferation and lack of coordination substantially reduce the value of aid. A recent study by the EC[14] finds that

• EU Member States have designated a total of 400–500 priority country partners. Increased consolidation of programs and projects, use of joint financing arrangements, an agreed-upon division of labor, and delegated cooperation would save €200–500 million a year.
• EU Member States accounted for 40,000–50,000 entries in the OECD Creditor Reporting System database, an increase from 30,000 in 2003. About 22,000 new commitments were made in 2007 by EU countries alone, with an average budget of €0.7–1 million. The total costs of preparing these projects are estimated at between €2–3 billion a year.
• increased predictability of EU bilateral aid commitments could increase the value of country programmable aid by between €2 and €4 billion a year.

In Vietnam it took eighteen months and the involvement of 150 government workers to purchase five vehicles for a donor-funded project because of differences in procurement policies among aid agencies.

It is not only official aid agencies that have to be better coordinated. In the aftermath of the tsunami disaster a local doctor in Banda Aceh, one of the most affected areas, wrote: "In February, in Riga (close to Calang), we had a case of measles, a little girl. Immediately, all epidemiologists of Banda Aceh came in, because they were afraid of a propagation of measles among displaced people, but the little girl recovered very fast. Then we realized that this was not a normal case of measles and we discovered that this girl has received the same vaccine three times, from three different organizations. The measles symptoms were a result of the three vaccines she received."[15]

Although the costs of proliferation are well known, and donors have committed themselves to coordinate, harmonize, and make more use of country systems, in fact the number of projects is continuing to rise (Figure 7.3), and the average project size is continuing to fall (Figure 7.4).

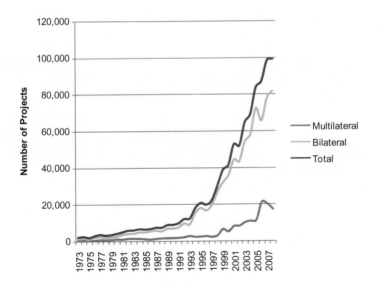

Figure 7.3   The Proliferation of Aid Projects

Source: AidData. http://www.aiddata.org/home/index.

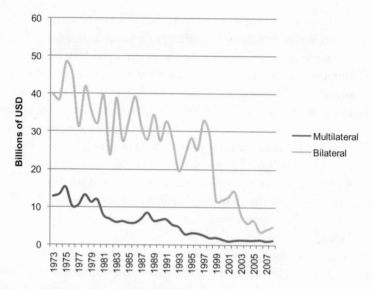

Figure 7.4   The Decreasing Size of Aid Projects

Source: AidData. http://www.aiddata.org/home/index.

THE GOVERNANCE OF AID

WHY DO WE NEED ANY SORT OF INTERNATIONAL GOVERNANCE OF AID?

What determines whether the benefits of diversity are secured and the challenges of proliferation avoided? Success and failure are divided by a knife-edge. If diverse actors can all play their parts, and the parts link together well, then this diverse, competitive, noisy development system can be a coherent whole, greater than the sum of its parts. This requires different actors to pursue their interests within shared rules of the game, with appropriate mechanisms to limit negative spillovers and to ensure the collective provision of public goods within the system. But if the governance of the system fails, the result will be that developing countries bear many of the costs of proliferation, but with many fewer benefits.

Sometimes the lightest governance is all that is needed. One of the most transformative social changes of our generation has been the spread of the Internet and the enormous range of uses to which it has been put. This revolution has occurred in the presence of very light governance arrangements. The Internet is largely self-governing and self-correcting. Where problems have arisen—such as e-mail spam—it has also provided the means to work around those problems. (Interestingly, the philosophy of working around problems is so much a part of the Internet culture that it is built in a fundamental way into the technical specifications of the Internet: if the shortest possible path for data to move is blocked, the system automatically looks for another path.) The thought leaders of the Internet have generally taken the view that the Internet is better off without government interference: it can solve its own problems, while retaining the freedom and individualism that enables it to innovate, adapt, and grow.[16]

Analogously, it is reasonable to ask why the international aid system needs any sort of governance. As with the Internet, there is a danger that any sort of governance arrangements will slow innovation, stifle change, and add to costs. Given that aid consists of arrangements freely entered into between sovereign nation-states, and among consenting adults, what is the case for any kind of governance arrangements?

Aid needs governance arrangements for the same reasons that intervention is warranted in other sectors: some results can only be achieved collectively, and individuals will tend to underinvest in these public goods; the actions of some individuals can have negative impacts on others, which need to be either regulated or at least priced. Suitable governance arrangements can, in these circumstances, make the aid system more effective. For the money that is spent on development, better outcomes can be achieved if these public goods are provided and spillover effects are properly managed.

Working from the principles of good governance laid out in the previous section, we imagine ten ways in which a system of collective governance could make the aid system more effective. These are described and summarized in Box 7.1 that follows.

Box 7.1

(1) ENCOURAGING POSITIVE SPILLOVERS

There is strong evidence of positive synergies between aid activities: one donor's investment in agriculture is more productive as a result of another donor's investment in feeder roads. Millennium villages are an example of efforts to bring about many different changes at the same time. Some development assistance is inherently collective—such as designing and implementing a reform program or filling a financing gap—and requires donors to work toward a shared goal.

(2) REDUCING NEGATIVE SPILLOVERS

The activities of an aid agency can adversely affect the impact of another. An aid agency that recruits a specialist from a government department undermines the efforts of another agency to build capacity. Aid agencies that require meetings with ministers or monitoring and review meetings with officials slow down broader progress (this is analogous to a form of "aid pollution"). The prices of scarce resources needed by aid agencies—offices, houses, and vehicles—can be driven up by the presence of multiple aid agencies. Incentives created by one aid agency can dull the carefully constructed incentives created by another.

(3) COORDINATION

The optimal behavior for one agency may depend on the behavior of others. A clear example is aid allocation, in which the optimal choice by one donor of where to work, and on what, depends directly on the choices being made by other donors. This is necessary in order to avoid some countries becoming "aid orphans" or "donor darlings," for example. Optimal decisions about the allocation of research funding similarly depend on what other donors are doing. Complex institutional change programs requiring sequenced reforms will work best if donors are making their contribution to a coordinated overall program.

(4) PREVENTING FREE RIDING

Everyone benefits from a more just, safer world, with prosperous trading partners. But some countries may be tempted to "free ride" on the generosity of others. For example, a country could give relatively little aid, in the expectation that others will give more, so benefiting from economic development without paying for it. A country may benefit from the fact that other donors "untie" their aid, so its firms can compete for other donors' contracts, while choosing not to untie their own aid. One of the original motivations for establishing the OECD-DAC was to monitor volumes of aid given by each donor. Countries that have provided debt relief are concerned by the possibility that this has opened the way for other countries to take advantage of this by making new loans to those countries in return for mineral concessions. If these fears are realized, it will reduce their willingness to give debt relief in the future.

(5) INFORMATION SHARING AND LEARNING

Aid agencies increasingly see themselves as organizations whose value is not *administration* but *knowledge*. Project administration is important, but it is also fairly straightforward; more complicated is learning what works, adapting it to different circumstances, influencing policies, sharing ideas, building capacity, and sharing commitments. This learning and knowledge sharing is needed across aid agencies as well as within them. The DAC networks (e.g., GovNet) and the peer-review mechanism are examples of this kind of role. Aid agencies also need a way to share basic aid information, which they do through in-country aid management systems, the two DAC databases, and the financial tracking service of the Office for the Coordination of Humanitarian Affairs. All of this contributes to reduced information asymmetries and a lower risk of principal-agent problems in administering aid.

(6) DIVISION OF LABOR

The overall effectiveness of the aid system is increased if organizations focus on the activities in which they have a comparative advantage. In market-based systems, concentration of comparative advantage is a result of profit-maximizing behavior, rather than a mechanism for making choices. Firms are driven toward the activities in which they can make the most profit: the forces of price, supply, and demand help ensure an optimal use of resources. In the absence of a market mechanism, some kind of mechanism is needed to push aid agencies into concentrating on the countries and activities where their opportunity cost is lowest, sometimes in the face of countervailing political pressures to spread themselves more thinly.

(7) INVESTING IN PUBLIC GOODS

Public goods tend to attract too little investment because, by definition, the benefits are widespread, so individual countries and agencies do not have a strong incentive to spend money on them. For example, the knowledge created by research and development is a public good, with benefits that spread far beyond the country that paid for it. There is significant global underinvestment in developing public goods, such as reducing climate change, financial stability,

(continued)

norms and standards, evaluation, and knowledge. Nation-states address the need for investment in public goods by a combination of government spending and regulation; there is no equivalent to either in the development system.

(8) KEEP INCENTIVES ALIGNED TO DEVELOPMENT OBJECTIVES (PRISONERS' DILEMMA)

Donors invest in foreign assistance for a variety of reasons. Some of these are shared global objectives: for example, reducing absolute poverty is a shared moral endeavor. All nations benefit when the world is less unequal, when world trade increases, and the risks of conflict, organized crime, drugs, and disease are reduced by economic advancement. But donors are also willing to invest in foreign assistance in pursuit of their own national interests to the disadvantage of other countries, for example, to win commercial contracts, gain geopolitical strategic advantage over rivals, or stake a claim to oil or mineral resources. The aid system is more effective at reducing poverty when shared goals are pursued in preference to the competitive interests of donors. This is a prisoners' dilemma problem—everyone is better off when aid is untied from commercial interests, for example, but each agency has an incentive to tie its own aid. A system of coordination among donors is needed to ensure that their actions are aligned with their collective interest in poverty reduction, and that this is not undermined by pursuit of individual national interests.

(9) PROTECTING LONG-TERM GOALS FROM SHORT-TERM PRESSURES

Most democracies have evolved governance institutions to protect the nation's long-term interests from immediate political pressures. Examples include written constitutions, an independent judiciary, and independent central banks. In development, long-term interests are frequently sacrificed to short-term expediency. For example, imported food aid may reduce hunger immediately, but at the expense of undermining domestic agriculture production in the long run. Donor-managed projects may provide services to the poor with lower risk of corruption and theft, but at the expense of undermining the capacity of the country's institutions to manage their own services. A good system of governance ensures that long-term needs are not ignored in the interests of short-term pressures.

(10) VOICE AND ACCOUNTABILITY
Finally, governance mechanisms are required to ensure voice and accountability for all stakeholders in aid, including, especially, developing countries themselves.

These themes constitute a compelling case for effective governance of the aid system. They demonstrate why it is not sufficient simply for each donor to pursue its own immediate interests; the result will be a lack of investment in public goods, failures of coordination, and behaviors that have negative spillover effects on others. There are examples in the aid system of all the reasons nation-states establish their own governance arrangements.

WHAT KINDS OF GOVERNANCE DO WE ALREADY HAVE?

The aid system already has some types of governance in place. The main components follow:

The DAC of the OECD: A "donor club" of twenty-four donors,[17] the DAC collects comparable information from donors, shares information and ideas through regular meetings of officials, sets implicit standards, and peer-reviews them. The Working Party on Aid Effectiveness, technically a committee of the DAC, has broader representation than the DAC but fewer instruments at its disposal.

The UNDCF: A multistakeholder forum hosted by the United Nations, including donors, recipient governments, and civil society, and so far mainly a talk shop, but with aspirations to do more.

In-Country Cooperation: Many of the issues of coordination are addressed in developing countries through donor cooperation forums, with the recipient government sometimes playing a leading role. So far these have tended to focus on information sharing and some harmonization of donor efforts.

High-Level Forums (Rome Paris, Accra, and Seoul): These meetings, held every two to three years, have brought together developing countries and donors, together with largely token representation by civil society, in an effort to set and enforce new rules of the game.

MULTILATERAL ORGANIZATIONS

Multilateralism can be viewed as an effort to overcome some of the challenges described earlier: by giving aid through international organizations, aid can be put more at arm's length from the political pressures of the donor, and aid from many donors can be coordinated into a single operation. Multilateral organizations have also played an important role in improving lesson learning and information sharing.

HOW WELL GOVERNED IS THE AID SYSTEM TODAY?

The aid industry stands accused of being ineffective and wasteful. The problems are serious and real: unnecessary proliferation of aid agencies without adequate division of labor, rising transactions and administration costs, short-termism and unpredictability, risk aversion, undermining of local systems of service delivery and accountability, inability to stop failing projects or organizations, ineffective provision of technical assistance, lack of mechanisms to take success to scale, underinvestment in public goods, lack of evidence of impact and results, inadequate learning, distortion of aid for national interests, and poor aid allocation.

Arguably all these challenges are the direct consequence of failures of collective governance. This failure of governance is encapsulated nicely by the process of agreeing to the MDGs. The declaration by world leaders was a historic event, setting a clear agenda for development for the following fifteen years. But there was no organization to translate strategic objectives into specific milestones and to monitor progress; no allocation of responsibilities; and no accountability of donors or developing countries for their contribution to the agreed-upon goals. In short, the Millennium Summit willed the ends but not the means.

This does not imply that the aid system necessarily needs a single governance mechanism, such as an overarching council or committee. But, as we have set out here, there are real issues of collective action that have to be addressed if the aid system is to be effective—which are currently not being addressed in a sufficiently effective way.

Table 7.1 sets out our subjective judgments of existing governance mechanisms in international development against the five dimensions of our governance model: effective, efficient, legitimate and fair, transparent and accountable, and adaptive. We find that not one scores the highest

Table 7.1 Assessment of Existing Governance Mechanisms against Criteria of Good Government

	Effective	Efficient	Legitimate and Fair	Transparent and Accountable	Adaptive
OECD-DAC	Effective at information sharing among donors; some lesson learning. Not good at preventing spillovers, investing in public goods, improving division of labor, aligning incentives, or promoting long-term development interests.	Very high transactions costs for donors and recipient countries	The DAC is a committee of 23 rich countries.	The DAC collects and publishes statistics about aid outflows from its members and publishes peer reviews. But decision making by consensus limits its ability to criticize members, and accountability is weak.	The DAC has almost completely failed to respond to a changing context. DAC donors lack transparency.
UN DCF	So far the UN DCF has been a talking shop and has little to show for its meetings.	Expensive for few results	Under the auspices of the UN, the DCF is representative.	The DCF is a fairly transparent and participative process.	Early days, but the process seems unlikely to be responsive to changing circumstances.
In-Country Cooperation	Some country-led processes have made progress toward harmonization. But many of the challenges cannot be solved at the country level—e.g., investment in global public goods, division of labor. In practice it is difficult for recipient countries to change donor incentives to pursue their national interests. In-country processes have not engaged new actors such as foundations.	Coordination processes can be labor intensive, with few results.	Developing countries can, in principle, exercise leadership over development activities in their country.	In-country cooperation happens behind closed doors, with very little involvement of either local or international civil society. Taxpayers from donor nations have no access to these forums.	Decision making close to the ground is most likely to be informed by the effects of those choices. The process lacks local transparency.

Table 7.1 (continued)

	Effective	Efficient	Legitimate and Fair	Transparent and Accountable	Adaptive
High-Level Forums	Declarations have been modest in ambition, reflecting lowest-common-denominator agreements, and poorly implemented or enforced. Many issues have not been addressed at all.	Very expensive processes leading up to summits; very expensive implementation and monitoring	Led by the DAC and World Bank, with rather token representation of hand-picked developing countries and little place for civil society	The HLF declaration is negotiated in a smoke-filled room from which civil society is excluded. The microphones were removed from the desks of civil society delegates in the plenary sessions at Accra.	These processes feel as if they were designed in the 1970s, with little recognition of the changing landscape.
Multilaterals	Providing money through multilaterals is easier and more effective than harmonizing. Multilaterals have been less susceptible to political second guessing. But they continue to underinvest in public goods, and multilateral proliferation is becoming a problem.	Some multilaterals—especially UN agencies—have high overheads. Proliferation adds to costs.	Many stakeholders are underrepresented in decision making—e.g., on the World Bank board. But UN bodies are legitimate.	Multilaterals are generally more transparent than bilateral aid. The World Bank, in particular, has advanced hugely in this regard.	Multilaterals seem to adapt more quickly to changing needs, partly because of the need to raise money from donors.

marks available on the scorecard. Multilateral options score relatively well, however.

REFORM PROPOSALS AND TIMETABLES

There are currently a number of proposals for reforming the aid system and individual institutions within it. In aggregate, these should improve performance across the indicators on the scorecard.

Following the recommendation of the OECD Council's In-Depth Evaluation in 2007, the DAC has recently undertaken a strategic reflection exercise in order to review its role, structure, functioning, and composition. The outcomes of the exercise are to form the basis for the reform of the DAC mandate, expected to be renewed by the council in 2011 for five years. The report concluded that the DAC needed to adapt its core activities—sharpening its principal tools and working methods and taking an active role in the process of reforming the global governance framework. Among other recommendations, the report outlined the need for the DAC to rearticulate its role in a changing development landscape in its mandate; to extend and deepen the inclusion of key development stakeholders in all areas of its work; to help the wider process of reforming and strengthening the multilateral development system; and, to adapt its internal structures and processes.[18] Presently the DAC is working on the details of implementing the recommendations and is expected to submit a draft revised mandate to the council in mid-2010.

In light of both the Paris Declaration and the Accra Agenda for Action, the DAC's Working Party on Aid Effectiveness recently underwent structural changes (principally by expanding its membership) and formulated a revised work plan to establish itself as the international partnership on aid effectiveness.

The biennial Development Cooperation Forum (DCF), hosted by the United Nation's Economic and Social Council, was launched in 2007, with the first forum meeting taking place in 2008. The second forum meeting took place in June 2010. Structured around three themes—mutual accountability and aid transparency, South-South and triangular cooperation, and aid policy coherence, in order to move to more long-term sources of development financing—the focus of the 2010 DCF was on priority issues for action that are based on practical outcomes.

The reform of the governance of the World Bank and the International Monetary Fund (IMF) has been the subject of debate for many years.

While both donors and recipients are member states and shareholders in the two institutions, voting power on the governing boards is determined primarily by financial contribution. In April 2010 the Development Committee approved a proposed voting reform for the World Bank. In summary, these changes instigate the following:

- an increase in the voting power of developing and transition countries (DTCs) at the International Bank for Reconstruction and Development (IBRD), bringing them to 47.19 percent;
- an increase in the voting power of DTCs at the International Finance Corporation (IFC) to 39.48 percent; and
- an agreement to review IBRD and IFC shareholdings every five years with a commitment to equitable voting power between developed countries and DTCs over time.

Proposals to increase aid effectiveness, such as the declarations made in Paris (2005) and Accra (2008), have worked to mitigate the problems of the aid system in ways that add layers of complexity. Harmonization and alignment have, in practice, been translated on the ground into donor coordination committees, with lead donors and sectoral plans. At their best, these have helped reduce transaction costs and harmonize donor approaches; at their worst, they have led to very little real change in behavior. At its most positive, the agreement of clear standards—particularly in the Paris Declaration (2005)—has emboldened some recipient countries to be clear about their expectations of donors. But addressing the symptoms without addressing the underlying causes results in new problems: to the extent that the expectations of recipient countries conflict with the underlying political and strategic interests of the donors, the long-term consequence is sometimes donors' reluctance to give aid to those countries. Aid effectiveness declarations describe a better way of giving development assistance, but they do not address the underlying reasons donors have given aid in less effective ways for the last forty years. If barriers to good aid are political, not technical, then technocratic agreements cannot overcome them.

THE EU IN THE GLOBAL AID CONTEXT

The EU should be in a good position to tackle not only the technical constraints to good governance of aid but also the political. As a model of multilateral cooperation itself, the EU claims to be a front-runner in the pursuit of value-based multilateralism. Formally, its commitment to effective multilateralism in all fields is a defining principle of its external policy. As noted in the European Commission (2003) communication on "The European Union and the United Nations: The Choice of Multilateralism": "Taking international co-operation as a precondition for meeting numerous global challenges, the EU has a clear interest in supporting the continuous evolution and improvement of the tools of global governance."[19]

As already noted, the EU, collectively, is the world's largest donor to developing countries, providing 56 percent of global development aid flows (around €50 billion of the €90 billion total given in aid).[20] At present, the share of EU aid channeled through the EC is currently around 20 percent.[21]

HOW DOES THE GOVERNANCE OF THE EU COMPARE?

Effective

Is the governance of EU aid effective? A decade ago, the UK Secretary of State for International Development at the time, Clare Short, characterized the EC as the "worst development agency in the world."[22] At the time, the EC suffered from a variety of ailments: the distinctive added value of EC aid was unclear; it largely failed to adopt a coherent approach to managing its external assistance; its policies were guided by individual instruments rather than by clearly defined development objectives per country, region, or sector; its aid system was fragmented in terms of small, ad hoc instruments, too many procedures, and opaque institutional mechanisms; and its organizational setup was outdated and incoherent. As a result, long delays built up in different parts of the system, and bureaucratization and centralization were rampant.

Since 2000 there have been substantial improvements to the effectiveness of EU external assistance, designed to restore the credibility, effectiveness, and legitimacy of EC aid, and also to articulate common values and principles.

Adopted in 2005 by the EC, the European Council, and the European Parliament, the European Consensus on Development[23] states the common vision of values, objectives, principles, and means to development shared by all Member States and the EC. It emphasizes poverty reduction as the central goal and asserts the priority of assistance to low-income countries (LICs). It sounds like a model of good governance for effective aid coordination.

In practice, the European Consensus was hard-won and has not been adopted as the visionary policy statement beyond its founders, the

Development Commissioner and DG Development, let alone by the EU Member States. The reasons for this are related to governance. In spite of the fact that the European Consensus calls for concentration of aid in LICs, EC aid retains the ambition of almost universal coverage. It is present in 120 developing countries. In 2007, 44 percent of EC aid was allocated to LICs. The DAC average for all donors was 63 percent, and the average for the EU was 65 percent. In 2008 EC aid to least-developed countries fell to 42 percent. The 2007 OECD DAC Peer Review of EC Aid[24] attributes this to the EC's limited ability to influence the European Development Fund (EDF; determined by Member States) and the community budget (determined by the Council of Ministers and the European Parliament). The DAC also points out that the EU attaches particular importance to its neighboring states, particularly in the context of their prospective membership in the EU. Turkey's status as the main recipient of EC aid during recent years is a case in point. Furthermore, while the European Consensus emphasizes the need for the EC to concentrate upon its areas of comparative advantage, these are broadly defined, with the number of priority areas for EC action increasing from six in the original Development Policy Statement to nine in the European Consensus—water and energy provision and social cohesion and development have been added to trade and regional integration, the environment, infrastructure and transport, rural development, governance, conflict prevention and fragile states, and human development.

The Consensus also proposes to enhance EU coordination through a greater emphasis upon a division of labor, exploiting individual partners' comparative advantage. In particular, it emphasizes the potential for cofinancing, either with Member States providing additional funding for EC-led programs or the EC supplementing Member State-led programs. In May 2007 the General Affairs and External Relations Council approved the EU Code of Conduct on Complementarity and Division of Labour in Development Policy.[25] This specifies, for example, that all donors should restrict themselves to a maximum of three sectors per country and either redeploy out of other sectors or work as a silent partner, allowing another EU donor to take the lead. A further constraint is that there should be only three to five donors per sector. But it remains voluntary and wills ends rather than means. National interests mean that implementation is patchy.

To date, coordination between Member States has proved to be an uphill task. Dilemmas about the current and future roles of the EC in driving division of labor continue to persist:

• European codes versus global decision making, with the EU Code of Conduct focused on EU donor sectoral specialization and the Accra Agenda for Action focused on global aid effectiveness, involving partner countries in the discussions on division of labor;

• European versus country-led comparative advantages, with the EU Code of Conduct defining the EC's comparative advantage based on "amount of money," "experience," "staff/expertise," "history of engagement," and so on, whereas most of the country-led criteria relate to alignment and harmonization, as well as dialogue skills, risk-taking, innovation, and credibility; and

• Brussels leadership versus stagnation on the ground, with the EU Code of Conduct lacking leadership both at the headquarters and country levels and the need for clarity as to the mandate of the EC in promoting the division of labor.

Efficient

Similar considerations apply in relation to efficiency. According to the EC study, "Aid Effectiveness Agenda: Benefits of a European Approach,"[26] the financial costs of donors failing to ensure aid effectiveness could be between €25 and €30 billion from now until 2015, or €5 to €7 billion per year. This amounts to around 10 percent of total aid spending. It is worth noting that throughout the study, the authors seemed to struggle to obtain the accurate data needed to calculate the real-cost savings of implementing the current aid effectiveness agenda. Even the most basic data on office costs or staff time were either unavailable or undisclosed by Member States. For the EC, while input and output of EC aid are documented quite well, efforts to analyze outcomes and impact are rare.

Table 7.2 gives the EU's performance on some of the key targets in the Paris Declaration and the Accra Agenda for Action (AAA). Progress on aid effectiveness has been slow.

The lack of progress on the division of labor has been due to, among other things, Member States' desire to remain engaged in politically attractive sectors, the lack of visibility when cooperation is delegated, the perception that coordination is time-consuming and not cost-effective for some interventions, the lack of overview on what different donors are doing in a given country or region, and, in some cases, hesitation by recipient countries that fear losing aid for particular sectors. Only 33 percent of EU donors' and the EC's missions are coordinated.[27] The EU target is 66 percent.

Table 7.2   Monitoring the Paris Declaration: EU State on Some Key Targets

Paris Indicators	EU (Member States and EC)	EC	2010 Target
Aid flows are recorded in countries' budgets.	44%	57%	85%
Technical assistance is aligned and coordinated.	53%	43%	EU target: 100% (Paris target is 50%.)
Donors use country systems for public financial management.	47%	35%	50%–80% (EU, and now Accra global target is 50%. Targets for each partner country depend on performance.)
Donors use country procurement systems.	54%	34%	50%–80% (EU, and now Accra global target is 50%. Targets for each partner country depend on performance.)
Aid is more predictable.	43%	53%	71%
Aid is untied.	94%	NA	Indicative: 100%
Donors use coordinated mechanisms for aid delivery (through program-based approaches).	46%	44%	66%
Donors coordinate their missions.	33%	33%	EU target: 66% (Paris target is 40%.)
Donors coordinate their (country) studies and analytical work.	62%	72%	66%

Source: EC Staff Working Paper: 'Aid Effectiveness after Accra: Where does the EU stand and what more do we need to do?, COM (2009) 160 final.

The lack of progress on the use of country systems has been a result of distrust in recipient country systems and legal impediments in the Member States. Another major impediment is the mode in which aid is delivered. Only five EU Member States now say budget support is their preferred way to scale up aid to Africa and to promote ownership, compared to ten in 2008. Budget support, granted for a three-year period, is the EC's "preferred aid modality where conditions allow."[28]

On conditionality, most Member States claim that it is irrelevant, possibly as a result of conditionality imposed by intermediaries such as the World Bank and the IMF, or because recipients accept conditions just to receive aid. Only five Member States told the Commission that they are actively reducing the number of conditionalities, while thirteen are not, and no result is recorded for the remaining nine. Fourteen Member States still do not make their conditions public, although this was one of the commitments in the AAA that was supposed to take instant effect.

On aid predictability, the lack of progress has been due to legal constraints in Member States and annual budget cycles. The consequences of short-term aid include conservative budgeting practices by recipient governments, poor resource allocation, investments in capital expenditure to the detriment of recurrent costs, and even macro-economic instability. In 2008 the EC launched the "MDG Contract," an innovative spin-off of budget support. It provides general budget support (GBS) for six years instead of three, including one mid-term review rather than annual assessments and a minimum guaranteed aid level (70 percent of total commitment). MDG contracts, which are subject to the provisions of the Cotonou Partnership Agreement, have been rolled out in eight African countries (Burkina Faso, Ghana, Mali, Mozambique, Rwanda, Tanzania, Uganda, and Zambia). Collectively, these account for €1.8 billion, or 50 percent, of all GBS commitments in EDF 10 national programs, and some 14 percent of all EDF 10 national programs. There has, however, been little forthcoming support from Member States to cofinance these contracts; only Belgium has, contributing €12 million to the MDG Contract with Mozambique.

And, finally, the lack of progress on untying aid has been largely due to inadequate procurement regulations and capacities in developing countries or risk aversion at the donor headquarters level. At present, around 10 percent of EU aid is still tied. While most DAC members have made commitments to untie aid in the future, this is the one Paris Declaration commitment to which a quantitative target has not been attached.

Legitimate and Fair

The EU does not consistently "speak with one voice" as a global actor, but its representation varies from the EC, to the rotating EU presidency, to the national positions of the Member States. For instance, the EC represents the EU on trade issues in the World Trade Organization; the rotating EU presidency negotiates on behalf of the EU (for example, in the climate change negotiations); and the Member States are dispersed over several voting groups that also include third countries in the complicated structures of the Bretton Woods Institutions. Since the early 1990s there have been increasing calls for a strengthening of the EU's external representation in international forums and for the EU to speak more with a single voice. This continuing fragmentation impairs the coherence and effectiveness of the EU's policies and undermines its commitment to multilateralism and global governance. As Coeuré and Pisani-Ferry (2003:19) argue, "The current arrangements involve significant deficiencies that weaken the European position in international negotiations and thus involve welfare costs."[29]

A combination of legal competences, institutional factors, and the EU Member States' constellation of interests and collective identity (or lack of it) prevents the EU from having its voice heard. From a legal perspective, development cooperation is a shared competence between the EU and the Member States. Its governance model is a mix of supervised delegation to the EC and coordination. Externally, EU development cooperation is represented both by the EC and the Member States. In the World Bank, for example, European representatives (plus the EC as an observer) meet at least once a week to exchange information and to reach coordinated or joint statements that are prepared by the EU presidency. At the biannual meetings of the Joint IMF/World Bank Development Committee, where the EC holds observer status, the Commissioner for Development submits a speech on behalf of the EU. However, the EC and the Member States may have different donor interests. In addition, several ministries may be responsible for World Bank matters at the national level, and coordination may be difficult both between and within ministries. The creation of an EU-level committee for World Bank issues has therefore lacked consensus so far. Finally, the lack of a collective EU identity may also prevent a joint external representation. A shared belief would have to be constructed about the appropriateness of a single EU seat or EU membership.

The Lisbon Treaty provides the EU with a full-time president of the European Council and a de facto foreign minister (the high representative for Foreign Affairs and Security Policy), assisted by a European External Action Service. However, it has not put an end to this patchwork of international representation. The EU now has four important players dealing with external policy and representation—the president of the European Council, the rotating presidency, the president of the EC, and the high representative. The question, however, remains as to how the high representative's role will be balanced with the other presidencies. A declaration to the Final Act of the Lisbon Treaty calls for the choice of the three positions (high representative and the respective presidents of the European

Council and the Commission) to "respect the geographical and demographic diversity of the Union and its Member States,"[30] which could give rise to the familiar jockeying between the Member States. This may, in turn, influence relations among the three positions.

Transparent and Accountable

The EC is not accountable in the way that bilateral donors are. On the one hand, this peculiar status insulates it from the direct political pressures experienced by bilateral programs, reflected in practices such as tied aid. On the other, this potentially reduces scrutiny and responsiveness. Although not explicitly mentioned in the European Consensus on Development, the EC is accountable to a variety of stakeholders: the Council of Ministers and the European Parliament; European taxpayers; legislative and executive powers in recipient countries; and citizens of the recipient countries.

Accountability at Home

Institutional rigidity has been commonly used to describe the EC. Part of the problem, however, lies in its accountability framework determined by the treaties, the basic and financial regulations, including college collective responsibility, Member States comitology, and European Parliament scrutiny. For example, the EC's multiannual/strategic programming phase, including approval and barring the occurrence of any unforeseen events, takes forty-two weeks. Although the time span is comparable with other donors, the EC has the longest approval period (twenty weeks) in order to accommodate the comitology[31] and parliamentary scrutiny procedures. Furthermore, approval of programs happens at the political level in the EC as opposed to the administrative or field levels. Finally, EU delegations do not have the authority to modify financing agreements.

Accountability Abroad

The European Consensus on Development recognizes the role of the EU in a "share(d) responsibility and accountability for their joint efforts in partnerships"[32] with developing countries whose ownership over development policies is to be respected and fostered. The EU's Cotonou Agreement is the most advanced form of partnership based on a contractual framework of political, trade, and development cooperation with the seventy-nine countries gathered under the umbrella of the African, Caribbean, and Pacific (ACP) region. It includes mutual accountability provisions as well as joint institutions and arbitration procedures.

In 2006 the EC issued a Communication on Governance, reaffirming its commitment to basic principles set out in the European Consensus on Development. It asserted that governance should be a homegrown process, as it cannot be imposed from the outside; that the EC and the Member States should work together to provide complementary and harmonized support to developing countries' governance efforts; and that responsibility lies both with donors and recipients to improve governance, emphasizing the notion of mutual accountability. The EC also introduced an incentive-based approach to programming within EDF 10. When preparing new strategies with the ACP, the EC grants additional financial support—an incentive tranche—to encourage ambitious, credible measures and reforms in governance. Access to these incentives is based on the outcome of an enhanced dialogue between the EC and the recipient country, facilitated by governance profiles. Action plans are then put forward by the government of the recipient country. No mention has been made of any methodology for monitoring the implementation of the action plans or the precise way performance in implementation will affect the country allocations.

Adaptive

The financial crisis provides an interesting lens through which to look at the adaptability of the EU in response to changing global situations. Following the meeting of the G-20 in April 2009, the EU came out with a support package for helping developing countries cope with the crisis. In its communication "Supporting Developing Countries in Coping with the Crisis," the EC proposed actions that would frontload €8.8 billion.[33] How this has affected the medium- and long-term predictability of funding remains to be seen. It set up two new finance mechanisms: the Vulnerability FLEX (V-FLEX) and the Food Facility.

The V-FLEX is an ad hoc and rapid countercyclical financing instrument to mitigate the social consequences of the economic downturn in the worst-hit countries. It is limited to the ACP. The fund dispensed €500 million in 2009 and 2010, and the money was set aside from the reserves of the national and regional indicative programs under the EDF 10. Given that the Member States decided against increasing the contribution ceilings, front-loading was managed by shifting payment priorities for programs in less vulnerable countries to the most vulnerable countries. Some have criticized the V-FLEX on the basis that donors need to allocate new resources to mitigate the effects of the financial crisis rather than just bring forward available funds. The problem is that most of the funding (almost 99 percent) comes from preexisting commitments. Furthermore, its responsiveness has also been questioned: the proposal was launched in April 2009, the country application deadline was the end of July, and the EC approved the package in December, for a total of €215 million. However, when the Democratic Republic of Congo's reserves fell to two days' worth of imports, the V-FLEX was not fast enough, and the IMF came to the rescue.

The Food Facility provides grants of €1 billion in unused European farm subsidies to farmers in the twenty-three developing countries most impacted by the crisis over seeds, fertilizer, and other agricultural projects. Following difficult negotiations among finance ministers of Member States, members of the European Parliament, and the EC, an agreement was finally reached on where the money would come from. Although the initial proposal recommended the use of €1 billion of surplus funds, only €760 million was agreed upon as additional funding. Furthermore, although the Food Facility was intended to be programmed over three years (2008 to 2010), by the end of 2009, over €800 million was disbursed. Criticism of the Food Facility has rested on the fact that the EC transferred the funds to other multilateral institutions to disburse instead of primarily using existing European bilateral modalities.

The EDF 10 regulation provides for additional voluntary contributions (AVCs). However, these AVCs are very restrictive in terms of their use and focus. In the past, AVCs have been used to cofinance the Africa Peace Facility (around €40 million from Member States, together with the €400 million from the EDF 9). Generally, most Member States are reluctant to provide AVCs.

In summary (see Table 7.3), governance of aid is more problematic than its "model" status might suggest. This is partly for technical reasons but also because the political constraints identified globally also apply in an EU context. Member States have been reluctant to cede real authority to EC institutions and have their own work coordinated from the center.

Table 7.3 Assessment of EU Good Governance

	Effective	Efficient	Legitimate and Fair	Transparent and Accountable	Adaptive
EU	Strong policy statements based on values and principles, but not adopted by Member States at national level; provides a forum for information sharing among Member States; good coordination of studies and analytical work with some lesson learning; slow progress in division of labor, aligning incentives, or promoting long-term development interests	High transaction costs spread over 120 countries; only 33% of missions coordinated; budget support not widely used	Legitimate, although not able to "speak with one voice" in international forums	Transparent and accountable to the Member States, the European Parliament, and partner countries through "mutual accountability" clauses in partnership agreement	Attempts to adapt more quickly to changing needs but constrained by accountability and decision-making procedures

CONCLUSION

Two paradoxes begin to emerge from the analysis.

First, good governance of the aid system obviously matters: it cuts transaction costs, reduces market failure, and ensures accountability. Multilateral channels offer a fast track to good governance, especially when the channels in question are characterized by high levels of accountability to recipients, as is the case for the United Nations, to a significant degree for the EU (at least for ACP countries), and increasingly for the Bretton Woods Institutions. At least, the multilaterals outperform the other governance mechanisms. Yet—and here is the first paradox—donors (and sometimes recipients) seem reluctant to follow the logic. In the EU only 20 percent or so of all official development assistance is channeled through the EC. This is a classic case of prisoners' dilemma: every country is better off if the multilateral channels are strengthened, but each country has a strong incentive to use bilateral channels itself.

Indeed, donors have multiple objectives in distributing aid, related to foreign policy, commercial interests, and domestic politics, as well as the purely humanitarian. Some also believe strongly in the value of a multiplicity of channels to encourage innovation and provide a degree of contestability. In this case they need the non-multilateral aspects of governance to perform more effectively than they do.

In this endeavor the DAC of the OECD is the obvious market leader, with a long history, an institutional depth, and a range of services that make it an indispensable tool for keeping score. It does, however, have restricted membership. As a rich country club, it has been ineffective in driving substantial change, and it has a deficit in terms of accountability to recipient countries. This remains true, however many new donors, developing country governments, and civil society representatives are invited to Paris. The United Nations-led process of the DCF does not suffer from these handicaps. However, it is new and underresourced and should not replicate the technical functions of the DAC. No doubt, also, decision making in the DAC is likely to be more efficient than in the DCF, at least if general United Nations cultures prevail. This, then, is the second paradox, and one familiar in other aspects of development cooperation: the most effective (or least ineffective) organization (in this case, the DAC) can never be the most legitimate and accountable.

It is not surprising that all stakeholders are struggling with these paradoxes. The reform agenda is full, whichever way one turns. Perhaps this is also a sign of good governance of the system as a whole. In an ideal world a kind of race might be under way: whoever improves governance fastest wins the prize.

If the DCF manages to improve effectiveness quickly, it could take a larger role and begin to assume some of the functions of the DAC. Conversely, if the DAC's Working Party on Aid Effectiveness can rapidly demonstrate that it provides a mechanism by which developing countries can hold donors to account, then the DCF might lose its appeal.

In terms of funding, if the governance reform can be completed, then the World Bank might win funds that would otherwise have gone to the EC. Or, if the United Nations can improve its effectiveness, then it might see its funding increased.

Of course, it is fanciful to think that the players of the aid game will be quite so instrumental in their decision making. Nevertheless, ministers do make choices in multilateral space, and good governance is one of the criteria they will use. Institutions and agencies would be well advised not to be left behind.

NOTES

1. See http://ec.europa.eu/development/policies/consensus_en.cfm.

2. See http://europa.eu/legislation_summaries/development/general_development_framework/r13003_en.htm.

3. OECD-DAC (2009b) data.

4. These are helpfully summarized in table 1 on page 14 in Grindle (2005). Also see http://www.odi.org.uk/events/states_ 06/29thMar/Grindle%20Paper%20gegredux2005.pdf.

5. Hyden et al. (2004).

6. See, for example, http://www.dfid.gov.uk/Global-Issues/Research-and-evidence/Poverty-Themes1/Politics-of-Poverty/.

7. The idea of the "Big Push" first came to prominence in Paul Rosenstein-Rodan's (1943) article "Problems of Industrialization of Eastern and South-Eastern Europe." The concept of "takeoff" was popularized by Walt Rostow (1960) in *The Stages of Economic Growth*. See http://www.unmillenniumproject.org/reports/costs_benefits2.htm; http://www.entwicklung.at/uploads/media/European_Consensus_01.pdf.

8. OECD-DAC (2009b) data.

9. Kharas (2009).

10. Ibid.

11. Ibid.

12. Ibid.

13. OECD (2008:15).

14. European Commission (2010).

15. El Pais (2005:217–29).

16. See, for example, Barlow (1996).

17. The EU-15 and the European Commission, plus Australia, Canada, Japan, South Korea, New Zealand, Norway, Switzerland, and the United States.

18. OECD (2009b:4).

19. European Commission (2003:3).

20. OECD-DAC (2009b) data.

21. Ibid.

22. See http://www.publications.parliament.uk/pa/cm199900/cmselect/cmintdev /669/66904.htm.

23. See http://ec.europa.eu/development/policies/consensus_en.cfm.

24. See http://www.oecd.org/document/0/0,3343,en_2649_34603_38897408_1_1 _1_1,00.html.

25. See http://europa.eu/legislation_summaries/development/general_development _framework/r13003_en.htm.

26. European Commission. (2008). "Aid Effectiveness Agenda: Benefits of a European Approach." See http://ec.europa.eu/development/icenter/repository/AE_Full _Final_Report_20091023.pdf.

27. European Commission (2009a).

28. Official Journal of the European Union (2006:para. 113).

29. Coeuré and Pisani-Ferry (2003:19).

30. Official Journal of the European Union (2007). A. Declarations concerning provisions of the treaties, para. 6.

31. The committee system that oversees the delegated acts implemented by the EC.

32. European Commission (2006).

33. European Commission (2009b:6–12).

REFERENCES

Barlow, J. P. 1996. (February 8). "A Declaration of the Independence of Cyberspace." Online essay. http://w2.eff.org/Censorship/Internet_censorship_bills/barlow _0296.declaration.

Coeuré, B., and J. Pisani-Ferry. 2003. (October 10–11). "One Market, One Voice? European Arrangements in International Economic Relations." Paper prepared for the conference on New Institutions for a New Europe, Vienna.

Department for International Development. 2010. "The Politics of Poverty: Elites, Citizens and States." Department for International Development. http://www .dfid.gov.uk/Global-Issues/Research-and-evidence/Poverty-Themes1/Politics-of -Poverty/.

European Commission. 2001. (July 25). "European Governance: A White Paper." COM (2001) 428 final. Brussels: European Commission.

———. 2003. (September 10). "The European Union and the United Nations: The Choice of Multilateralism." Communication from the Commission to the Council and the European Parliament. COM (2003) 526 final. Brussels: European Commission.

———. 2005. "The European Consensus on Development." Joint Statement by the Council and the Representatives of the Governments of the Member States Meeting within the Council, the European Parliament, and the Commission. Brussels: European Commission. http://ec.europa.eu/development/policies/consensus _en.cfmIssue Paper May 2008 29.

———. 2006. "Governance in the European Consensus on Development: Towards a Harmonised Approach within the European Union." Communication from the Commission to the Council, the European Parliament, the European Economic and Social Committee, and the Committee of Regions. COM (2006) 421. Brussels: European Commission.

———. 2007a. "DAC Peer Review: Main Findings and Recommendations." Review of the Development Cooperation Policies and Programmes of the European Community. Paris: OECD.

———. 2007b. "EU Code of Conduct on Division of Labour in Development Policy." Communication from the Commission to the Council and the European Parliament of 28 February 2007. COM (2007) 72 final. Brussels: European Commission. http://europa.eu/legislation_summaries/development/general _development _framework/r13003_en.htm.

———. 2008. "Aid Effectiveness Agenda: Benefits of a European Approach." Project No. 2008/170204 - Version 1. HTPSE.

———. 2009a. "Aid Effectiveness after Accra: Where Does the EU Stand and What More Do We Need to Do?" Staff Working Paper. COM (2009) 160 final.

———. 2009b. (April 8). "Supporting Developing Countries in Coping with the Crisis." EC Communication. COM (2009) 160/4.

———. 2010. "Aid Effectiveness Agenda: Benefits of a European Approach." Project No. 2008/170204—Version 1. Hemel Hempstead: HTSPE Limited. http://ec.europa.eu/development/icenter/repository/AE_Full_   Final_Report _20091023.pdf.

Grindle, M. 2005. "Good Enough Governance: Poverty Reduction and Reform in Developing Countries." *Governance: An International Journal of Policy, Administration and Institutions* 17.

Hyden, G., J. Court, and K. Mease. 2004. *Making Sense of Governance: Empirical Evidence from 16 Developing Countries*. London: Lynne Rienner.

International Development Committee. 2000. (August 8). "Select Committee on International Development Ninth Report." London: UK Parliament. http://www .publications.parliament.uk/pa/cm199900/cmselect/cmintdev/669/66904.htm.

Kharas, H. 2009. "Development Assistance in the 21st Century." Washington, D.C.: Brookings. http://www.brookings.edu/papers/2009/11_development_ aid_kharas .aspx.

Official Journal of the European Union. 2006. "Joint Statement between European Parliament, Council and Commission on European Union Development Policy: 'The European Consensus'" (2006/C 46/01). http://eurlex.europa.eu/LexUriServ /site/en/oj/2006/c_046/c_04620060224en00010019.pdf.

————. 2007. "Treaty of Lisbon Amending the Treaty on European Union and the Treaty Establishing the European Community" (2007/C 306/01).

Organization for Economic Cooperation and Development (OECD). 2008. "Better Aid: 2008 Survey on Monitoring the Paris Declaration: Making Aid More Effective by 2015." Paris: OECD. http://www.oecd.org/dataoecd/58/41/41202121.pdf.

————. 2009a. "Aid Statistics." Statistics Portal. http://www.oecd.org/topicstatsportal / 0,3398,en_2825_495602_1_1_1_1_1,00.html#497153.

———— (2009b). "Investing in Development: A Common Cause in a Changing World." DAC Reflection Exercise. Paris: OECD. www.oecd.org/dataoecd/14/1/43854787 .pdf.

El Pais. 2005. Quoted in S. Djankov, J. García Montalvo, and M. Reynal Querol. 2009. "Aid with Multiple Personalities." *Journal of Comparative Economics* 37 (2) (April 13): 217–29.

Rosenstein-Rodan, P. 1943. "Problems of Industrialization of Eastern and South-Eastern Europe." *Economic Journal* 53.

Rostow, W. 1960. *The Stages of Economic Growth*. Cambridge: Cambridge University Press.

United Nations Millennium Project. 2006. "Expanding the Financial Envelope to Achieve the Goals." Report. http://www.unmillenniumproject .org/reports/costs _benefits2.htm.

José Antonio Alonso is director of the Complutense Institute for International Studies and professor of applied economics at the Universidad Complutense of Madrid. He is a member of the Committee for Development Policy at the United Nations Economic and Social Council, and his main research areas focus on growth and the external sector, trade specialization and company internationalization, and development aid policies. He is the editor of *Principios: Estudios de Economía Política*. His most recent books are *Acción Colectiva y Desarrollo: El Papel de las Instituciones*, coauthored with Carlos Garcimartín, and *Corrupción, Cohesión Social y Desarrollo*, coedited with Carlos Mulas-Granados.

Owen Barder is a Visiting Fellow at the Center for Global Development. He is an economist and director of aidinfo at Development Initiatives, a program that aims to make information about aid more accessible. Before working on international development, he was the Economic Affairs private secretary to the British prime minister. He has also worked in the Treasury of the government of South Africa and began his career as an economist at the UK Treasury, where, among other roles, he served as private secretary to two chancellors of the Exchequer.

Carlos Garcimartín is professor of economics at Universidad Rey Juan Carlos, Madrid, Spain, and researcher at the Complutense Institute for International Studies. He has been affiliated with the Universities of Salamanca, Complutense de Madrid, and Rey Juan Carlos. He was researcher at the Istituto Affari Internazionali in Rome. His main research topics include public economics, international economics, and development economics. He has been involved in national and international research projects and has published articles in prestigious international journals.

Mikaela Gavas specializes in European Union (EU) development co-operation. She has worked in the EU institutions—Commission and Parliament—as well as for an EU Member State, the UK's Department for International Development, where she led the drafting of the department's EU Institutional Strategy Paper and analysis of the implications of the Lisbon Treaty for EU development cooperation. She managed BOND's (UK NGO network) EU program from 2002 to 2006 and chaired CONCORD's (European Confederation of NGOs) Policy Forum.

Stephany Griffith-Jones is financial markets director at the Initiative for Policy Dialogue at Columbia University and was Professorial Fellow at the Institute of Development Studies. She is a member of the Warwick Commission on Financial Regulation. Her research interests include global capital flows, with special reference to flows to emerging markets; macroeconomic management of capital flows in Latin America, Eastern Europe, and sub-Saharan Africa; proposals for international measures to diminish volatility of capital flows and reduce the likelihood of currency crises; analysis of national and international capital markets; and proposals for international financial reform. She has published widely on the international financial system and its reform.

Deborah Johnson is a research officer at the Overseas Development Institute (ODI), focusing primarily on a major CAPE initiative, the European Development Cooperation Support Programme. She joined ODI after eight years as a management consultant in the private sector. She previously worked for an NGO in southern India and as a research assistant in the European Parliament. She has an MA in modern and medieval languages from the University of Cambridge and an MSc in development studies from the University of London (SOAS).

Víctor Martín is an adjunct professor in the Department of Applied Economics at the Universidad Rey Juan Carlos. He has been a researcher in the Department on International Economic Analysis of Complutense Institute for International Studies since 2001 and at the Center for Studies

"Economía de Madrid" at the Universidad Rey Juan Carlos. He has a PhD in economics from the Universidad Rey Juan Carlos.

Simon Maxwell was the former director of the Overseas Development Institute. He is an economist who worked overseas for ten years, in Kenya and India for the United Nations Development Programme and in Bolivia for UKODA, and then for sixteen years at the Institute of Development Studies at the University of Sussex, latterly as programme manager for Poverty, Food Security, and the Environment. He has written widely on poverty, food security, agricultural development, and aid. His current research interests include development policy, aid, poverty, food security, linking relief and development, global governance, and bridging research and policy.

Andrew Mold joined the Organization for Economic Cooperation and Development Development Centre in February 2008, having previously worked for the United Nations in Ethiopia, Chile, and Costa Rica. From 2000 to 2004 he was the codirector of a master's program in development studies at the Complutense Institute for International Studies and was also the vice secretary general of the International University of Mendenez Pelayo. Since 2003 he has been an editor of the *European Journal of Development Research*. He has a master's degree from Cambridge University and a PhD in economics from the Complutense University Madrid.

Akbar Noman is an economist with a wide range of experience in policy analysis and formulation in a variety of developing and transition economies, having worked extensively for the World Bank as well as other international organizations and at senior levels of government. He combines teaching at Columbia University's School of International and Public Affairs with being a Senior Fellow at the Initiative for Policy Dialogue, where his tasks continue to include policy work with governments. His other academic appointments have been at Oxford University (where he was also a student) and the Institute of Development Studies at the University of Sussex.

José Antonio Ocampo is professor in the School of International and Public Affairs and fellow of the Committee on Global Thought at Columbia University. He has been a member of the United Nations Commission of Experts on Reforms of the International Monetary and Financial System and has served as undersecretary-general of the United Nations for Economic and Social Affairs, executive secretary of the United Nations Economic Commission for Latin America and the Caribbean, and minister of Finance, Agriculture, and Planning for Colombia. His most recent books are *Handbook of Latin American Economics*, coedited with Jaime Ros, and *Time for a Visible Hand: Lessons from the 2008 World Financial Crisis*, coedited with Stephany Griffith-Jones and Joseph E. Stiglitz.

Ariane Ortiz holds a master of public administration degree from Columbia University's School of International and Public Affairs and has worked at the Initiative for Policy Dialogue. She previously worked for Citigroup's Corporate and Investment Bank in Monterrey, Mexico.

Fernando Prada is associate researcher at the National/International Forum of Peru. He has carried out research projects at the University of Sussex and has published, along with Francisco Sagasti and Keith Bezanson, studies on financing development.

Annalisa Prizzon is a Research Officer at the Overseas Development Institute working particularly on development finance issues. She has been an economist at the OECD Development Centre and a consultant with the World Bank. She holds a PhD in Economics and Public Finance from the University of Pavia (Italy) with a focus on external debt sustainability in low-income countries.

Francisco Sagasti chairs the board of the Science and Technology Program (FINCyT) at the Office of the Prime Minister in Peru, is a member of the board of governors of the Canadian International Development Research Centre, a member of the international advisory board of the Lemelson Foundation, and advisor to private corporations, international organizations, foundations, and public-sector agencies. He is director emeritus of FORO Nacional/Internacional, a civil society independent organization created to promote democratic governance and to foster dialogue and consensus on critical development issues.

Judith Tyson is a PhD candidate at the School of African and Oriental Studies at the University of London. Her thesis focuses on the systemic risks of expanding financial access in developing countries, including through microfinance and the impact of financialization. She has worked as an investment banker, specializing in risk management and financial control.

Juliana Vallejo is an economist from Universidad de los Andes (Bogotá, Colombia) and completed her master in business administration degree at the Instituto Tecnológico de Estudios Superiores de Monterrey, Mexico. She has worked for Columbia University's Initiative for Policy Dialogue.